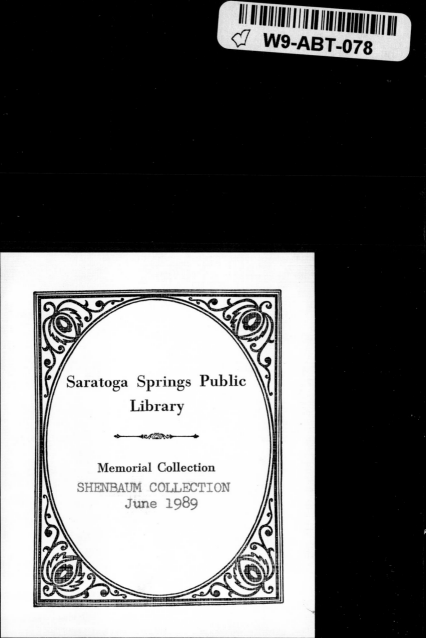

A Cup of Tears

A Diary of the Warsaw Ghetto

by
ABRAHAM LEWIN

Edited by
ANTONY POLONSKY

Translation of the Diary by Christopher Hutton

Basil Blackwell
in association with the Institute for
Polish-Jewish Studies, Oxford

First published 1988
First published in USA 1989

Basil Blackwell Ltd
108 Cowley Road, Oxford, OX4 1JF, UK

Basil Blackwell Inc.
432 Park Avenue South, Suite 1503
New York, NY 10016, USA

British Library Cataloguing in Publication Data
Lewin, Abraham
    A cup of tears: a diary of the Warsaw Ghetto.
    1. Poland. Warsaw. Jewish ghettos : Warsaw
    Ghetto, 1939–1945 – Personal observations
    I. Title
    940.53´15´03924
    ISBN 0-631-16215-1

Library of Congress Cataloging in Publication Data
Lewin, Abraham, 1893–1943.
    A cup of tears.
    Includes Index.
    1. Jews – Poland – Warsaw – Persecutions.
2. Holocaust, Jewish (1939–1946) – Poland – Warsaw
– Personal narratives.   3. Lewin, Abraham, 1893–1943.
4. Warsaw (Poland) – Ethnic relations.   I. Title.
II. Polonsky, Antony.
DS135.P62W314   1988   940.53´15´0392404384   88-16762
ISBN 0-631-16215-1

Typeset in 11½ on 13½ pt Garamond
by Joshua Associates Ltd, Oxford
Printed in Great Britain by
T. J. Press Ltd, Padstow.

Contents

Foreword v

Maps vii

Introduction 1

A Note on the Text 55

A Cup of Tears 59

 Part I From the Notebooks 61

 Part II Diary of the Great Deportation 135

Appendix 243

Notes 246

Index 301

'All the tears of the children of Israel from the period of the abductions should be caught up in a single cup and it given its place among the many such cups full of tears and blood. Let the people not forget its youngest martyrs!'

Abraham Lewin, *Kantanisten* (1934)

Foreword

The Jews in Nazi-occupied Europe were determined to record all aspects of the tragic ordeal they were undergoing. According to Emanuel Ringelblum, creator of the underground archive in the Warsaw ghetto, 'Everyone wrote – journalists, authors, teachers, social activists, young people, even children.' They wrote for posterity. According to another of the members of the underground archive, Menahem Kon:

I consider it a sacred duty for everyone, scholarly or not, to write down everything that he has seen or heard from those who witnessed the murderous actions committed by the barbarians in every Jewish settlement, so that, when the time comes – as it surely will – the world will read and learn what they have done. This will be the richest material for the lamenter who will write the elegy of our times; it will be the most potent inspiration for those who will avenge our sufferings.

The last words recorded in the diary of Chaim Kaplan before he was deported to his death in Treblinka were, 'If I die – what will become of my diary?'

One of the memoirs miraculously preserved in the material hidden by the underground archive and found after the war was the diary of Abraham Lewin. It is one of the most impressive and moving literary records of the *Shoah* to come down to us, and it has been a great privilege to prepare this first English-language edition of it. Many people have aided me in this work: Robert Lewin, who first brought the diary to my notice; Rafael Scharf, whose encouragement and wise counsel have been unfailing; Professor Yisrael Gutman and Martin Gilbert, who have read and criticized the manuscript; the staffs of the Jewish Historical Institute in Warsaw and of *Yad Vashem* and *Beit Lohamei Hagetaot*; the translators, Christopher Hutton and

Connie Wilsack; and Nathan Snyder, Judaica Librarian at the University of Texas at Austin. I am grateful to those who have kindly given permission to reproduce photographs: Kibbutz Lohamei Hagetadt (for plates 1, 2 and 3); the Jewish Historical Institute, Warsaw (for plates 4 and 5); the Bundesarchiv, Koblenz (for plates 6, 7, 8, 9, 10 and 11).

Emanuel Ringelblum wrote of Lewin's diary that it was 'an important literary document which must be published as soon as possible after the War'. This first English edition appears on the forty-fifth anniversary of the uprising in the Warsaw ghetto. It is a tribute to the 'Martyrs and Fighters' of the Jewish people who died in Warsaw and the death camps.

The publication of this diary was made possible by the generosity of Robert and Michael Lewin, in memory of their cousin Abraham Lewin and the many members of their family who perished in the *Shoah*.

Maps

Map 1 Administrative divisions in occupied Poland, 6 November 1940

Map 2 Administrative divisions in occupied Poland, 1 September 1942

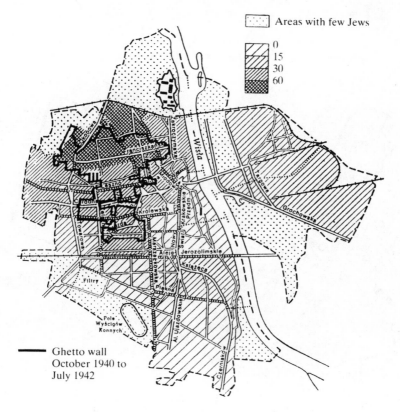

% of Jewish population in 1939

Areas with few Jews

0
15
30
60

Ghetto wall
October 1940 to
July 1942

Map 3 The location of the ghetto in Warsaw

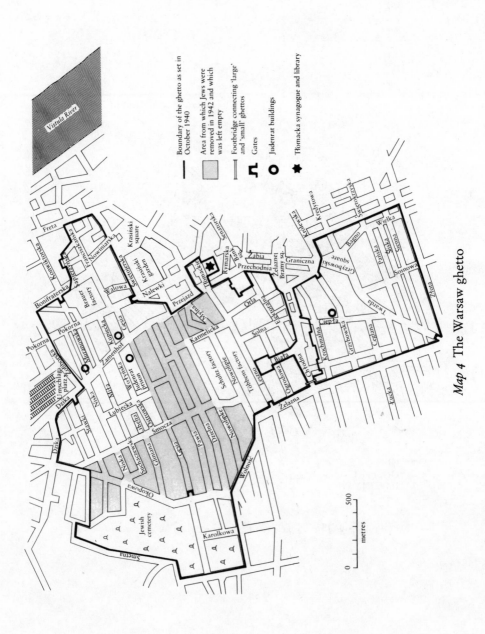

Vistula River

Boundary of the ghetto as set in
October 1940

Area from which Jews were
removed in 1942 and which
was left empty

Footbridge connecting 'large'
and 'small' ghettos

Gates

Judenrat buildings

Tłomacka synagogue and library

Freta
Krasiński square
Nowiniarska
Krasiński garden
Bonifraterska
Brauer factory
Walowa
Nalewki
Pokorna
Pokorna
Gesia
Konecka
Zamenhof
Przejazd
Tłomacka
Kymarska
Bank
Żabia
Przechodnia
Zelaznej
Bramy sq.
Graniczna
Orla
Solna
Karmelicka
Schultz factory
Nowolipie
Toebens factory
Leszno
Biala
Ogrodowa
Chłodna
Krochmalna
Ciepla
Krochmalna
Grzybowska
Ceglana
Wielka
Ciepla
Elektoralna
Czysmąąsizdo
square
Bagno
Panska
Sliska
Sienna
Złota
Twarda
Sosnowa
Kredytowa
Zlaw
Suzgo-krzynska
Mila
Wolynska
Judenrat prison
Lubiecka
Smocza
Dzielna
Nowolipie
Pawia
Zelazna
Gesia
Niska
Suchaczew
Gliniana
Wolność
Okopowa
Jewish
cemetery
Karolkowa
Smetina
Dzika
Stawki
Dzka plac 'U'
Niska

500
metres
0

Map 4 The Warsaw ghetto

Introduction

In these tragic times, whenever several Jews gather together and each recounts just a part of what he has heard and seen, it becomes a mountain or a swollen sea of misfortune and Jewish blood. Jewish blood pure and simple. We gather every Sabbath, a group of activists in the Jewish community, to discuss our diaries and writings. We want our sufferings, these 'birth-pangs of the Messiah', to be impressed upon the memories of future generations and on the memory of the whole world.

Diary entry for 6 June 1942

Those who are far away cannot imagine our bitter situation. They will not understand and will not believe that day after day thousands of men, women and children, innocent of any crime, were taken to their death. And the handful of those remaining after nine weeks is in mortal danger and, it seems, can expect the same fate. Almighty God! Why did this happen? And why is the whole world deaf to our screams?

Earth, earth, do not cover our blood, and let no place be free from our cries!

Diary entry for Yom Kippur, 21 September 1942

On 16 November 1940, the Nazis sealed off a large section of central Warsaw where they had compelled all the Jews of the Polish capital to concentrate. It included the districts with a substantial Jewish population but in order to ensure that all the Jews in Warsaw resided in this area and that non-Jews were excluded, the occupiers forced 113,000 Poles and 138,000 Jews to change their dwelling places. In this way was established what has come to be known as the Warsaw 'ghetto'. This was a term not to the liking of the Nazis. They forbade its use in the government-controlled Polish and Jewish press in occupied Poland, insisting that the area be referred to rather as the Jewish residential district (*Wohnbezirk*).

An official German document from 1941 stated:

The Jewish residential district covers an area of 403 hectares (995 acres). The *Judenrat* [Jewish Council] which claims to have conducted a census, estimates the population of this area to be approximately 410,000 Jews, while our own observations and calculations point to between around 470,000 and 590,000 Jews. Adopting the statistical figures of the *Judenrat* and subtracting empty lots and cemeteries, the population density equals 1,108 persons per hectare of built-up territory, or 110,800 per sq. km (247 acres). The corresponding figures for the city of Warsaw as a whole are 14,000 persons per square km of the total metropolitan district and 38,000 persons per square km of built-up and habitable space. The Jewish residential district comprises around 27,000 apartments with an average of two and a half rooms each. Consequently, the average occupancy can be put at 15 persons per apartment and six to seven persons per room. The Jewish quarter is separated from the rest of the walled-in streets, windows, doors and empty lots, fire and partition walls having been incorporated. The walls are 3 metres high; another metre is added by a parapet of barbed wire. In addition, surveillance is provided by police patrols on horseback and in motor vehicles.[1]

This chilling description is largely accurate, except that it under-estimates the overcrowding which characterized the 'ghetto'. In fact, according to post-war calculations, population density was 128,000 per sq. km and the number of people concentrated in each room was 9.2. The area was thus neither 'Jewish residential district' nor a 'ghetto' but a combination of the largest Jewish 'prison city' in Europe and a forced labour camp. This was clearly understood by its inhabitants. According to Emanuel Ringelblum, one of the most important diarists of the ghetto and the main organizer of under-ground historical activity there: 'Any comparison with the ghetto of the past is inappropriate because the ghetto then was the product of historical processes and corresponded to the general significance of such developments. But the ghetto today is a concentration camp whose inmates must support themselves.'[2]

The feeling of being incarcerated is well articulated by the baptized Jewish scientist Professor Ludwik Hirszfeld, who was forced to move into the ghetto:

The sensation of being locked in prison is reinforced by the fact that you can come up against walls and barbed wire at every turn. This is the way the authorities claim that they will isolate the carriers of deadly germs. This claim has been supported by people calling themselves doctors. Yet science long ago abolished medieval quarantines, not only because they were in-humane but because they were inefficient. Inefficient? Why, their intention is not to wipe out an epidemic but to eradicate the Jews.[3]

Certainly, the establishment of the ghetto was an important step forward in what Lucy Dawidowicz has rightly called Hitler's 'war against the Jews'. There is no need here to stress that anti-Semitism had always been central to the *Weltanschauung* of the inner core of the Nazi leadership. To Hitler and his closest adherents, the myth of the Jewish conspiracy to destroy the German people provided a central motive which could unite the disparate elements making up Nazi doctrine. Though the new Germany had been relatively slow to put the more extreme aspects of Nazi anti-Semitism into practice, by 1938 the regime was set in its deep-seated hatred of the Jews and its determination to root out Jewish influence wherever it could achieve this. That year had seen the unleashing in November of a ferocious pogrom over the whole of Germany in response to the assassination in Paris of a German diplomat by a desperate Jewish youth. Shortly after this *Kristallnacht*, on 24 November, Hitler had told the pro-German foreign minister of South Africa, Oswald Pirow, that 'one of these days the Jews will disappear from Europe', and that he had succeeded in exporting one idea 'not National Socialism – but anti-Semitism'.[4] On 21 January 1939, he had told the Czechoslovak foreign minister, Frantisek Chvalkovsky, that 'the Jews would be annihilated here' ('die Juden würden bei uns vernichtet').[5] He repeated this threat in public in the Reichstag on 30 January, assert-ing: 'If the international Jewish money power in Europe and beyond again succeeds in enmeshing the peoples in a world war, the result will not be the Bolshevization of the world and a victory for Jewry, but the annihilation of the Jewish race in Europe.'[6]

In Nazi-occupied Poland, the new regime did not immediately implement these threats of genocide, although in sporadic anti-Jewish violence during and after the September campaign about 5,000 Jews lost their lives at Nazi hands. Many synagogues and Jewish libraries were burnt, most notably the famous library of the

Khakhmey Lublin Yeshiva.[7] The Nazis divided the areas they occupied in two. One area was annexed directly to the Reich (Upper Silesia, the Warthegau and the area around Danzig). The remainder of German-occupied Poland was called the General-Government (referred to by Lewin as the *gubernia*) and had a population of 11,800,000, of which in September 1939, 1,500,000 were Jews. (After the outbreak of the German–Soviet war, Eastern Galicia, the southeastern part of Poland, was added to the General-Government, increasing the size of its population to 16.8 million.) After brief discussions with the Soviets, who had occupied eastern Poland, it was decided not to leave any vestiges of Polish statehood, although the Polish police force and some lower-level bureaucrats were left in place. The General-Government was ruled from Kraków and was to be treated as a colony, subject to ruthless repression. In relation to the Poles, the aim was to destroy the Polish intelligentsia and political elite, reducing the rest of the population to the status of rightless slaves of the Third Reich.[8]

Nazi policy for the Jews in occupied Poland had been laid down as early as 21 September by Reinhard Heydrich, head of the Reich Main Security Office (RHSA) which had in that month created a central body under the control of the SS to unite the state and party police. According to Heydrich's directives, Jews were to be expelled from the area directly incorporated into Germany with the exception of Łódź and concentrated in what was to become the General-Government. In order to control them more easily they were to be concentrated in ghettos. The various Jewish communities would be administered by Jewish councils (*Judenräte*) which would be 'fully responsible in the literal sense of the word for the exact and punctual execution of all directives issued or yet to be issued.'[9] At this stage, the Nazis did not seem yet to have adopted the goal of mass-murder of the Jews. Rather their aim was to impoverish and plunder them, exploiting their labour and being prepared even to consider the possibility of emigration, which was only stopped in practice from the General-Government in the summer of 1940, and prohibited from the Third Reich in November 1941. Jewish conditions were deliberately kept as harsh as possible. By 1941, for instance, the daily food ration for a Jew in Warsaw was 184 calories, compared to 669 for a Pole and 2,613 for a German.[10] Hans Frank, the Governor of the

General-Government, made clear his bitter hatred of the Jews. On 19 December 1939, he wrote in his diary: 'The Jews represent for us extraordinarily malignant gluttons. We have now approximately 2.5 million of them in the General-Government, and, counting half-Jews, perhaps 3.5 million. We cannot shoot 2.5 million Jews, neither can we poison them. We shall have to take steps, however, to extirpate them in some way – and this will be done.'[11]

One of these steps was the imposition of brutal forced labour. In October 1939, all Jewish men between 14 and 60 were compelled to register and could then be conscripted for work in labour camps. A further decree of 11 December made them liable to forced labour for two years with the possibility of extension if its educational purpose was not considered fulfilled. By the end of 1939, there were already 28 of these labour camps in the Lublin district, 21 in that of Kielce, 14 in the Warsaw district, 12 in the Kraków region and 10 in that of Rzeszów.[12]

The first ghetto was established on 8 October 1939 in Piotrków. In February 1940, a ghetto was established in Łódź (now renamed Litzmannstadt, after a victorious German General from World War I), which before the war had contained the second largest Jewish community in Poland. Here more than 165,000 Jews were forced into an area of under 4 sq. km, which was sealed off from the rest of the city in May 1940.[13]

The first efforts by the SS to establish a ghetto in Warsaw in October 1939 had been prevented by the *Judenrat*'s successful appeal to the military commander of Warsaw, General von Neumann-Neurode. This success was only temporary and gave the Jewish leadership an exaggerated view of the extent to which they could exploit the divisions of opinion within the occupying authority. By January 1940, a German attorney, Waldemar Schön, had been entrusted with organizing a 'property relocation programme' in Warsaw. In May, the Jewish district was declared to be a 'plague-infested zone'. The *Judenrat* was, as a result, required to build a wall around the infected area. By early June, 20 sections of the wall were already in place, although its completion would only be accomplished after the establishment of the ghetto. In August came the announcement that the city was to be divided into three quarters, German, Polish and Jewish. No Jew could live in the German quarter, although Jews in the Polish district could remain there for the time being. On 2 October, the German occupying authorities issued an order establishing the ghetto and ten days later the Jews were informed of this decision.[14] The Jews continued to hope that the Warsaw ghetto would not be closed, as was that in Łódź. Chaim Kaplan wrote in his diary on 24 October: 'An additional doubt is gnawing at us: Will it be a closed ghetto? There are signs in both directions and we hope for a miracle – which doesn't always happen in time of need. A closed ghetto means gradual death. An open ghetto is only a half-way catastrophe.'[15]

The transfer of a quarter of a million people in the city was accompanied by heart-rending scenes of terrible hardship. In the words of an eyewitness, Toshia Bialer:

Try to picture one-third of a large city's population moving through the streets in an endless stream, pushing, wheeling, dragging all their belongings from every part of the city to one small section, crowding one another more and more as they converged. No cars, no horses, no help of any sort were available to us by order of the occupying authorities. Pushcarts were about the only method of conveyance we had, and these were piled high with household goods, furnishing much amusement to the German onlookers who delighted in overturning the carts and seeing us scrambling for our effects. Many of the goods were confiscated arbitrarily without any explanation . . .

In the ghetto, as some of us had begun to call it, half-ironically and in jest, there was appalling chaos. Thousands of people were rushing around at the last minute trying to find a place to stay. Everything was already filled up, but still they kept on coming and somehow more room was found.

The narrow, crooked streets of the most dilapidated parts of Warsaw were crowded with pushcarts, their owners going from house to house asking the inevitable question. Have you room? The sidewalks were covered with their belongings. Children wandered, lost and crying, parents ran hither and yon seeking them, their cries drowned in the tremendous hubbub of half a million uprooted people.[16]

On 15 November came the fateful news. The ghetto was to be closed off from the outside world. Among the over 400,000 people sealed off in this way was a 47-year-old secondary school teacher, Abraham Lewin. Born in 1893 in Warsaw, he came from a strictly Orthodox Hasidic family. His father Shabtai was a scholar and rabbi and his grandfather a *shokhet* (ritual slaughterer). As a child, he went to *heder*, the traditional Jewish school, from where he proceeded to a *yeshiva* (rabbinical academy). In his youth, he often accompanied his grandfather on his pilgrimages to the Gerer rabbi, Rabbi Abraham Mordekhai Alter, head of one of the largest Hasidic dynasties in Poland, whose court was at Gora Kalwarja (*Ger* in Yiddish) about 40 kilometres from Warsaw. Though Lewin was gradually to distance himself from Hasidism, memories of his religious upbringing were to remain with him all his life. At the age of 20, he finally gave up the *kapote* and *shtreimel*, the traditional dress worn by orthodox Hasidim. His father had died while Lewin was in his teens and, as the only son, the obligation fell on him of supporting his mother and sisters. He had always shown a pronounced scholarly bent and at the beginning of the academic year 1916–17, although he did not possess any formal qualifications, he was appointed to teach Hebrew, Biblical Studies and Jewish Studies at a private Jewish secondary school for girls, the Yehudia School.[17]

Founded shortly before World War I, this school was a product of the increasing strength of Zionist ideas among Warsaw Jewry and also of the growing desire of sections of the town's Jewish population to give their daughters access to an education which would combine both traditional and Zionist values with a more general curriculum. The school was given its character, above all, by its headmistress, an outstanding teacher and administrator, Stefania (Bat-Sheva) Hertzberg-Schweiger. Mrs Schweiger came from an assimilated Warsaw family, receiving 'a secular education in which the spirit of Judaism had played no part',[18] and had completed her studies at the Sorbonne. She illustrates well the often made observation that in the trilingual world of Polish Jewry, Polish speakers with a Jewish consciousness often felt more affinity with the reviving Hebrew language than with Yiddish. According to Mrs Marmińska, who preceded Stefania Schweiger as headmistress: 'The emphasis was on Hebrew studies. Classes were conducted mostly in Hebrew and Polish, although the official language was Russian . . . The school was suffused with a Jewish atmosphere and the spirit of Zionism. Special emphasis was placed on religious festivals and other events in the Jewish calendar.'[19]

Lewin was very close to Mrs Schweiger and, under her influence, grew both intellectually and in administrative skills. He became secretary and treasurer of the school, important functions, since it was run 'as a sort of teachers' co-operative'.[20] The school became more firmly established in the post-war world of independent Poland and in 1926 was given accreditation by the Ministry of Education to administer matriculation examinations. In order to raise its standards, it employed a number of 'the best Polish teachers in Warsaw to teach Polish, history and Latin in the higher classes'.[21] It also had on its staff several outstanding Jewish scholars, including Alexander Hertz, who was subsequently to pursue a successful scholarly career in the United States, Emanuel Ringelblum, later the archivist and chronicler of the Warsaw ghetto and the principal expert on the history of Jewish Warsaw, and Yakov Shatsky, another leading Polish-Jewish historian.

In 1920, the school hired, as an additional teacher of Hebrew, the 20-year-old Luba Hotner. She came from a distinguished rabbinical family – her father was a Warsaw rabbi, Rabbi Yehuda Leib Hotner, while her mother Bat-Sheva was the daughter of Reb Yehuda Segal, a well-known figure in Orthodox circles in Warsaw. Lewin clearly fell deeply in love with Luba, who, according to a friend of her family, 'had a special love of learning and research. She was of noble bearing, had a warm heart, compassion for her fellow man and sought truth and honesty at all times.'[22] They did not marry immediately, because Luba, a deeply convinced Zionist, emigrated to Palestine in 1921, working as a teacher at Ein Harod until 1923. She succumbed to malaria there, and, after a brief spell at an educational establishment for workers' children, felt compelled, for health reasons, to return to Poland. Here she again returned to the staff of Yehudia and also married Lewin, bearing him a daughter, Ora, in 1928.

His marriage to Luba intensified Lewin's already strong Zionist convictions. In 1911 he had been one of the founders of the Halutsey Tsion group in Warsaw, a number of whose members soon emigrated to Palestine. He made his own first visit to Palestine in 1925, and on his return introduced a fundamental change in the teaching of Hebrew at Yehudia: the Ashkenazi pronunciation which had up till then been used was replaced by the Sephardi (*Ivrit*) pronunciation used in Palestine. Lewin often reflected on the question of whether he should go on Aliya. He wrote, in January 1933, to one of his pupils who had settled on a kibbutz in Palestine:

I often ask myself if I could put the diaspora life, with all the doubts and soul-searching that characterize those around me, behind me and start an entirely new life there, of the sort that you live? The question arises of its own accord and cuts deeply, but I admit without shame that I find it difficult to give a positive answer. It seems that within me there is a terrible fear of 'there', a fear that cannot be quieted solely by logic and reason. Yes, I think that this is a weakness that has its origins in man's too great love for himself . . . I do not have the internal resources to throw off the chains of the past and to involve myself in the new life I have dreamt about, even if the fetters constraining me to my present circumstances were to be removed.[23]

The following year, he returned to Palestine with his wife and daughter, spending some time on the Kibbutz Heftsibah. Again Luba's poor health, as well as that of Ora, who proved a rather sickly child, led them to return to Poland. Throughout this period, Lewin continued his pedagogic career at Yehudia. He was by all accounts an outstanding teacher. According to one of his pupils:

Avraham Lewin was a wonderful teacher and a great educator. His image is before me as if he were still alive – there he is standing by his table in the classroom, explaining a chapter of the Bible or analysing a poem by Bialik or Tchernihowsky. Mr Lewin taught us to love the Book of Books, to see Hebrew as our own language. He was of noble spirit yet had an easy way with his fellow man and was sensitive to all human suffering.[24]

Another wrote:

In reading and analysing the Bible in Lewin's classes, we absorbed and became enthralled by the landscape of the Holy Land; it was no longer remote for us . . . it was not two thousand years ago that we had been forced to leave our country but now, in our own childhood. No one else had his ability to enthuse us with the teachings of the prophets; who among us did not take a vow to fight for social justice, equality, and honesty on earth? It is no wonder that many of the girls from Yehudia found their way to kibbutzim and made their homes there. Avraham Lewin was an honest person through and through; he was frank and never tried to conceal his weaknesses. The values preached by our prophets were the keystone of his world-view. He was a pacifist to the innermost recesses of his soul. When he was called up to serve for a short while in the Polish army we his pupils feared that he might rebel against the state.[25]

His influence extended beyond the classroom. Nina Danzig-Weltser, who knew him not only as a pupil but also as a colleague, wrote:

He was not only a teacher; to us he was a rich personality and a thinker of some depth. His appearance reinforced this impression. He was tall and thin, with fair hair and a pale complexion. He spoke softly and in a restrained manner, although in interpreting the prophets he was enthusiastic to the point of ecstacy. Lewin was blessed with a deep appreciation of the beauties of nature. In class outings he used to talk with a small group of the girls about the beauty of the landscape. He spoke not as a teacher but as a friend talking to equals. The outings to Góra, Wilno and Troki are etched particularly deep in my memory.[26]

Another student wrote:

His house was always open to us, and more than once I went to visit him there on Shabbat. I felt that I was wanted. He would welcome me with a smile and engage me in long conversations. In these conversations Lewin showed himself to be a lover of his fellow human beings and a man of absolute morality. We always felt he had great affection for us and a fatherly concern for our future.[27]

Yehudit Garbitsky-Shechter described a meeting with Lewin:

It was getting dark in his flat where we had gone as usual to talk after school. It was quiet in the room, we were watching the miracle of the sunset and our hearts were full of an awesome silence. 'You must listen to the silence within,' he used to say, 'and then the great understanding will come, you will understand yourself in the world, and your heart will yearn to the end of the universe, to the bounds of eternity, for that which is beautiful.' And thus I was to carry with me for years the magical skill of contemplation, the ability to sense the message in the fragile silence that goes beyond words; beyond the words I shall always see the man who through my identification with him gave my life, then and in the future, a special flavour, an everlasting flame.[28]

Although heavily burdened with teaching and administrative responsibilities, he worked hard to make good the limitations of his formal education and in 1930 he passed the government teacher training examinations with distinction. In that same year, he gave a series of lectures at the academic seminar organized in Warsaw by the Zionist movement Hehalutz. Among the topics he dealt with were the role of learning in Hebrew literature, the works of Haim Luzatto, above all his *Migdal Oz (Tower of Strength)*, Hebrew literature in Germany, and Hebrew prose in Galicia and Russia. In 1934 he wrote a monograph in Yiddish, *Kantanisten (The Cantonists)* on the forced conscription of Jewish boys into the Russian army in the first half of the reign of Tsar Nicholas I (1825–56). It was a subject which moved him profoundly. He wrote his study under the pseudonym Kantono-wicz (which could be taken as meaning 'son of a Cantonist') and remarked, with an awful prescience, in the Introduction: 'All the tears of the children of Israel from the period of the abductions should be caught up in a single cup and it given its place among the many such cups full of tears and blood. Let the people not forget its youngest martyrs!'[29]

The teachers at Yehudia attempted to carry on the work of the school after the Polish defeat of September 1939 and the German occupation, in spite of an official ban on Jewish education. We have a vivid recollection of this clandestine schooling from Nehama Eckheizer-Fahn:

I was destined to be at Yehudia during World War II. Almost the entire staff, with Stefania Schweiger at their head, continued to teach. Lewin and his wife taught Hebrew and Bible Studies, Rachel Brotmacher taught German, Dr Cecilia Weinberger and Gustava Złotowska taught Polish, and Leonora Moronovitch taught physics. Yitshak Berman taught at the Laor school and from his salary was able to support two pupils, but after reading the description of the 'action' in Hrubieszow [i.e. the deportation of the Jews from there to a death camp] he had a stroke. Dr Emanuel Ringelblum stopped teaching at the beginning of the war to become the manager of the Joint Self-help Committee.

Lessons were conducted in a different place every day, in the houses of teachers or pupils. They were conducted clandestinely, in small groups, by the light of a single candle, each evening somewhere else. More than once, teachers or staff were ill or weak from hunger, but I don't think there was ever more enthusiastic studying or teaching. It was not an escape from the dreadful reality but an expression of opposition to the iniquity and the desecration of cherished values. Over and over again, the teachers empha-sized that even in times such as these we must not abandon human values. They hoped that their pupils would stay alive and tried to maintain their spiritual integrity. Relationships between teachers and pupils also changed; continual fear in the cold evenings in darkened rooms created strong ties

and great affection between us. We became one family. I remember particularly the last full assembly of the school, which took place in an institute
for abandoned children. We sang and we danced, even though the tension in
the ghetto had reached its height and we knew that the end was very near.
At the end of the party one of the teachers got up and said: 'If we stay alive
after this war, we shall try to live as human beings worthy of that exalted
title; and if it has been decreed that we are to die – we shall die proudly.
Whatever our fate is to be, there is no doubt in my heart that the world that
emerges after this war will be a better place.'[30]

As Lewin described movingly in his diary, most of these teachers
and pupils perished in the great deportation to Treblinka which
began on 22 July. On 20 September he records meeting Adina, the
daughter of Stefania Schweiger. He noted 'I receive the shattering
news that the whole of Yehudia has perished: her mother,
Brotmacher, Złotowska, Weinberger, and everyone, everyone. A
terrible scene.'

Lewin was also active on a wider plane. He continued to lecture
and teach to adult and youth groups on topics of Jewish history and
literature. Thus on 13 September 1941 he read an address at a meeting
to commemorate the second anniversary of the death of the Polish-
Jewish writer Yitshak Meir Weissenberg (1881–1939). This is
reprinted here as an Appendix. He was active in the Jewish Self-help
Organization (Żydowska Samopomoc Społeczna), a charitable body
set up during the siege of Warsaw in September 1939 and reorganized
in January 1940. Although nominally under the control of the
Judenrat, it retained a good deal of autonomy and acted as an im-
partial and disinterested body, dispensing what inadequate help it
could to the distressed inhabitants of the ghetto. It divided the ghetto
into five districts, in the second of which Lewin was active. There are
frequent references in the diary to his work in this body.[31]

His principal activity during the ghetto period was as a member of
the directorate of the underground archive, entitled *Oneg Shabbes*, set
up and directed by his former colleague at Yehudia, the historian
Emanuel Ringelblum. It included many leading communal activists,
among them Shmuel Winter, Eliyahu Gutkowski, Hirsch Wasser,
Menahem Kon and Rabbi Shimon Huberband. Conscious of the
momentous times in which they lived and of the deadly peril facing
the Jews of Europe, they determined to chronicle all aspects of life in

the ghetto to serve as a record for future generations. Its members were conscious of their terrible responsibility. Ringelblum described the organization as follows:

The members of *Oneg Shabbes* have constituted and still constitute a homogeneous body, ruled by a single spirit and pervaded by a single idea. *Oneg Shabbes* is not an association of scholars who compete and strive against each other. It is a single entity, a brotherhood where all help each other and strive to achieve a common goal . . .

Every member of *Oneg Shabbes* knows that his devoted labour and effort, the severe hardships he undergoes, the risks he takes 24 hours a day while engaged in the undercover work of carrying documents from place to place – all are undertaken for an exhalted ideal and that in the days of freedom to come, society will know how to evaluate his contribution and will reward it with the highest honours available in liberated Europe. *Oneg Shabbes* is a fellowship, a fraternal order on whose banner is inscribed its members' willingness to dedicate themselves completely to their cause and keep faith with each other in the service of the community.[32]

As its name implies (a reference to the Jewish custom of celebrating the end of the Sabbath) the *Oneg Shabbes* directorate met weekly on Saturday evening to exchange news and information. Its archives were buried in a number of milk churns and tin chests, some of which were found after the war, in September 1946 and December 1950. Among the material found then was a diary written by Abraham Lewin extending from 29 March 1942 to 16 January 1943. This is only a part of the whole because we learn from Ringelblum's essay on *Oneg Shabbes* written in late December 1942, that: 'The diary of A. L—n, the author of the book *The Cantonists* is a valuable document. The author has been keeping it now for a year and a half.'[33]

We do not therefore possess any diary entries dealing with the first 15 months of the ghetto's existence. This was a period when the Nazis had not yet decided on their 'final solution' of the 'Jewish problem' by mass-murder. As a result, the ghetto seemed to have achieved a modicum of stability. Its population, swollen by the influx of refugees from the rest of Poland, reached a high point of 445,000 in March 1941, making it the largest concentration of Jews under German rule.[34] The Germans continued to exercise tight control over these hapless individuals. In September 1941, Ludwig Fischer, governor of the Warsaw district, wrote chillingly in an official report: 'The creation of ghettos in the Warsaw district has considerably facilitated the registration of Jews on card indexes.' On 15 October of that year, Hans Frank issued a decree imposing the death penalty on Jews who left the ghetto, on those who helped them to do so and on those who sheltered them outside.[35]

Yet, at the same time, the institutions of the ghetto appeared to have acquired a degree of stability. The *Judenrat*, headed by the assimilated engineer Adam Czerniaków, an adherent of Piłsudski and an unsuccessful government nominee for the Senate in 1930, could hope by the sedulous implementation of the Germans' directives to protect the Jews of the ghetto from the worst consequences of Nazi rule until the dawn of better times. This was, of course, a policy as old as the diaspora. Persecution was a periodic fact of Jewish life, and if only one kept one's head down, one could hope that bad times would pass and that at the cost of sacrificing some of its members, the substance of the community could be preserved.[36]

The powers of the *Judenrat* were considerably wider than those of the Warsaw *Kehilla* (Jewish communal authority) from which it claimed to be derived. It was, in the first place, to carry out the orders given by the Nazi authorities to the ghetto. From May 1941, when a Berlin lawyer, Heinz Auerswald, was appointed 'Commissar of the Jewish Quarter', this meant negotiating with him on a day-to-day basis. The *Judenrat* was also responsible for distributing food, accommodation and work, as well as organizing public services and imposing taxes to pay for its activities. Its position was accurately described by the official *Gazeta Żydowska* on 24 December 1940:

The *Kehilla* has now taken on the character of an *Office for the Jews* [italics in original]; with the creation of the Jewish quarter, this character has been reinforced. The *Kehilla* must be careful to fulfil the obligations imposed on the Jewish population by the authorities, while simultaneously representing the needs of the public before these same authorities. Thus the *Kehilla* has become the *only representative and agency mediating between the Jewish public and the regime* [italics in original].

This intermediary role was even more emphatically underlined in an official announcement printed in *Gazeta Żydowska* on 14 March 1941, stating that 'in accordance with instructions from the authorities, Jews in Warsaw may make approaches to a representative of the regime only through the auspices of the *Judenrat*. Direct approaches in writing will be left unanswered.'

The *Judenrat* attempted to play this mediating role to the best of its ability and to mitigate the harsh nature of German rule. This was a thankless task and the organization was soon the target of bitter attacks from the Jewish population. In Kaplan's words: 'The *Kehilla* – or, as the conqueror calls it, the *Judenrat* – is a disgrace to the Warsaw community. Whenever the subject comes up, everyone's blood begins to boil.'[37]

The Germans well understood that by using the *Judenrat* to impose their will on the ghetto, they could deflect much of the Jewish hostility on to its members. As Commissar Auerswald himself observed with some satisfaction in a letter in November 1941, 'The disappointment of the Jewish population is directed against the Jewish ghetto apparatus rather than against the German authorities.'[38]

Many of the leading members of the *Judenrat* had previously held positions in the Jewish community and clearly regarded themselves as charged with a special responsibility made all the heavier by the flight from Warsaw (along with many members of the Polish elite) of many Jewish leaders. Czerniaków himself had been appointed head of the Warsaw *Kehilla* by Stefan Starzyński, the mayor of Warsaw before the capital had fallen to the Germans. Czerniaków replaced Maurycy Majzel, the former chairman, who had fled eastwards. His diary shows him to have been a somewhat unimaginative if benevolent individual, with little faith in the abilities of the average individual inhabitant of the ghetto, but it also shows his motives in assuming and exercising office to have been above reproach. He was well aware of his powerlessness. As he wrote in his diary, 'I have to suffer in a stuffy room which looks like a prison cell ... Besides all these Jewish complaints.'[39] His sense of responsibility was also shared by a number of the other leading members of the *Judenrat*, such as Abraham Gepner, who before the war had been chairman of the Union of Jewish Merchants and a member of the Warsaw City Council, Shmuel Winter, who had been active in Yivo, the Yidishe Visenshaftlikhe Organizatsye (Jewish Scientific Organization), a scholarly body established in Wilno in 1925, and who had many links in the ghetto with the underground opposition, and Józef Jaszuński, who had been head of ORT, the Jewish vocational retraining organization in Poland.

The *Judenrat* quickly developed a large civil service to carry out its functions. Whereas the pre-war *Kehilla* had employed barely 530 persons, the *Judenrat* staff soon grew to over 6,000, including special departments for Economic Affairs, the Budget, Labour, Health, Social Welfare and Burial. It organized a large vocational training network, sometimes without the knowledge of the German authorities. When in October 1941 the Germans gave official permission for the reopening of schools, it set up a school network based on the various ideological groupings (Zionist, Bundist (socialist) and Orthodox) into which the pre-war private Jewish school system had been divided. This provided school places for 7,000 of the 50,000 children in the ghetto. It was also responsible for the establishment and administration of a Supply Authority (Zakład Zaopatrzenia) which distributed ration cards and was responsible for the provision of the small amount of food which the ghetto authorities were legally allowed to purchase as well as for the obtaining of other essential goods, above all coal. The Authority, headed by Abraham Gepner, was well administered and, in spite of its sensitive functions, enjoyed greater confidence among the inhabitants of the ghetto than any other institution controlled by the *Judenrat*. The *Judenrat* even undertook from the beginning of 1941 to organize a postal service in the ghetto. According to its contract with the Post Office administration in Warsaw, the workers in this Jewish Post, with its headquarters at 19 Zamenhof Street, were to receive all post addressed to the Jewish population in bulk. This included not only letters but also food parcels both from occupied Poland and from neutral countries, of which, until June 1941, the most important was the Soviet Union.[40]

The essential fact, however, given the nature of German policy, was that the *Judenrat* was in an impossible situation. Its position was further undermined by the presence within it of many opportunists and people prepared to profit from the situation, not to speak of outright German agents like Dr Alfred Nossig, who was later shot on the order of the underground Jewish Fighting Organization (Żydowska Organizacja Bojowa – ZOB).[41] In addition, some of its policies reflected its socially conservative outlook and its willingness to sacrifice those it regarded as expendable in the interests of the higher good of ensuring the survival of at least some of those in the ghetto. Thus, for instance, its policy of using indirect taxation to finance its needs bore heavily on the poorest elements in the ghetto. Similarly, when required to supply men for forced labour, the *Judenrat* tended to take those who had least influence or position. These policies were maintained in spite of the establishment of public watchdog committees on which sat prominent social activists such as Ignacy Schipper and Shakhne Sagan. These were attached to agencies of the *Judenrat* and their task was to monitor their activities.

In order to maintain order, the Nazis instructed the *Judenrat* to establish a *Jüdischer Ordnungsdienst* (Jewish Service for the Maintenance of Order) which became known as the Jewish police or ghetto police. Headed by Józef Szeryński, a Jewish convert to Catholicism who before the war had been a colonel in the Polish police, it was first organized on a voluntary basis and numbered initially about 1,000 members. Its enrolment rose by December 1941 to about 1,600 and to nearly 2,200 in July 1942 on the eve of the great deportation from the ghetto to the Treblinka death camp. Within its ranks it contained a considerable number of educated people, above all men who had been officers in the Polish army as well as many lawyers. Nominally, it fell under the control of a *Judenrat* department, headed by the honest and well-intentioned Bernard Zundelewicz, but in practice his authority proved to be extremely limited. The force was also subject to the Polish police (*Policja granatowa* – navy blue police, so-named because of the colour of its uniform), the 30,000 strong pre-war force maintained in being by the German authorities after the Polish defeat. Since the Jewish police did not possess the power to deal with crimes, it was obliged in the case of such offences being committed to hand suspects over to the Polish police. In practice, there was a marked disinclination to resort to such drastic action and the Jewish police often acted as arbitrators in criminal disputes, meting out a rough-and-ready but usually accepted justice. Ultimately, the ghetto police was responsible to the German authorities, above all the *Sicherheitsdienst* (Secret Service) and Gestapo, by whom it was strictly controlled. The functions of the Jewish police included not only the maintenance of order and the prevention of crime and smuggling, but also the direction of traffic and the supervision of sanitation and garbage collection. From June

1941, in order to accommodate the growing number of Jewish prisoners held outside the ghetto, it was allowed to open a prison. By May 1942, this prison, located on Gęsia Street, held nearly 1,300 prisoners, most of them smugglers and many of them children.[42]

Alongside the Jewish police, characteristic of the multiplicity of competing authorities which was a feature of Nazi rule was the Office to Combat Usury and Profiteering established by the Gestapo shortly after the creation of the ghetto in November 1940. Called the 'Thirteen', because its offices were at 13 Leszno Street, it was headed by a gangster-like figure called Abraham Gancwajch. Its staff comprised about 300–400 men and it furnished information to the Germans while also providing a range of welfare services. In this way, it aimed to supplant both the Jewish police and even the *Judenrat* itself. By July 1941, the Germans had tired of the 'Thirteen' and Auerswald closed down its office. Nearly half of its 'supervisors' were incorporated into the Jewish police. For the moment, however, Gancwajch remained a force in the ghetto, his final downfall coming on 18 April 1942, as Lewin recorded in his diary entry for 24 May.[43]

Initially ghetto opinion was not unsympathetic to the Jewish police. Mary Berg recorded in her diary 'I experience a strange and utterly illogical feeling of satisfaction when I see a Jewish policeman at a crossing – such policemen were entirely unknown in pre-war Poland.'[44] Similarly Chaim Kaplan, who was usually very harsh in his judgements, wrote on 21 December 1940:

The residents of the ghetto are beginning to think they are in Tel Aviv. Strong bona fide policemen from among our brothers, to whom you can speak in Yiddish! First of all it comes as a godsend to the street vendors. The fear of the Gentile police is gone from their faces. A Jewish policeman, a man of human sensibilities – one of our brothers – would not turn over their baskets or trample their wares. The other citizens of the ghetto are relieved, too, because a Jewish shout is not the same as a Gentile one. The latter is coarse, crude, nasty; the former, while it may be threatening, contains a certain gentility, as if to say: 'Don't you understand?'[45]

These views were shared by Ringelblum, who wrote in mid-December 1940 that 'the Jewish police is composed of experienced and sympathetic men' and on 19 February 1941, 'The public stands behind the Jewish policeman: "would you obey a Pole and not a Jew?"

There are intelligent men among the police who prefer persuasion to giving orders.'[46] Yet even before the great deportation of July–September 1942, in which the Jewish police made itself notorious by its cooperation with the Nazis in rounding up Jews, the police had become a hated symbol of authority. To quote Ringelblum again in a report written in December 1942, 'The Jewish police had a bad reputation even before the deportation. Unlike the Polish police, which did not take part in the abduction for the labour camps, the Jewish police did engage in this dirty work. The police were also notorious for their shocking corruption and demoralization.'[47] Certainly it was the role of the Jewish police in the round-ups for labour camps from spring 1941 and its increasing susceptibility to bribery which had already undermined its reputation even before July 1942. Round-ups for labour camps were a feature of ghetto life from its establishment and are referred to by Lewin in his diary entry for 21 May 1942. One of the most brutal was that which took place between 19 and 21 April 1941 and which involved the sending of thousands of young men to labour camps. The horrific work regimes and living conditions here killed or crippled many of those deported in this way. On this occasion, as Ringelblum recorded, members of the community complained to the *Judenrat* that the people being sent to the labour camps were those too poor to buy themselves out.[48]

Although initially German policy had been concerned ruthlessly to exploit Jewish labour in this way while at the same time expropriating Jewish industry, the occupying authorities gradually came to the realization that they might be able to benefit from Jewish economic skills. Frank himself articulated the new attitude in his usual crude manner. Speaking at the University of Berlin in November 1941, he explained to his audience:

Not all these Jews are useless from our point of view. It is astonishing, but there are Jews who fall into a different category, something we discovered only on the spot. Difficult as it is to believe there really are Jews there who work and are employed as transport and building workers or as craftsmen, in tailoring, shoemaking etc.'[49]

The *Judenrat* was eager to respond to the new German mood, believing that if the Jews made themselves indispensable to the German war effort, they would have a better chance to survive. This was a widespread view in the ghetto. Ringelblum recorded in his diary in March 1942 that 'within the community, there are those who claim that the danger of deportation which hangs over us has now passed thanks to the workshops that are producing for the German army.'[50] The *Judenrat* tried to expand employment by attracting German-owned or supervised plants to the ghetto. In August 1941, it even sanctioned the establishment of an incorporated company which was to foster crafts, the ghetto authorities providing orders, finance and tools. Its efforts were not very successful. Since the Germans paid what were, in effect, starvation wages, there was a marked disinclination to take employment in the workshops they set up. As late as the beginning of 1942, only 4,000 people were employed in these shops, along with another 5,000–6,000 in factories (called *placówki* in Polish and *palatsovkes* in Yiddish) outside the ghetto. The shops only became more attractive as places to work during the great deportation when it became apparent that employment in them afforded a degree of security. Many Jews were, however, employed in semi-legal workshops, which supplied not only the Polish black market but even the German authorities and the *Wehrmacht*. According to one post-war memoir:

As a rule, Jewish industry operated clandestinely and therefore avoided any planning. It [also] totally ignored German plans and did not submit to them. Moreover, to its great good fortune, the large masses of German troops were in urgent need of various supplies and equipment. Thus with the support of the German authorities, there sprouted up plants to manufacture brushes, mattresses, beds, clothing, furs, shoes.[51]

The number of people involved in these activities has been variously estimated. According to the Jewish Self-help Organization, in December 1941, 65,000 people were employed in the ghetto (55,000 wage-earners and 10,000 self-employed). In July 1942, the Labour Department of the *Judenrat*, which was in fact directly supervised by the Germans, assessed the number of workers in the ghetto as 70,000 (60,000 men and 10,000 women).[52] This, of course, meant that there was a very large group (according to some estimates numbering, with dependants, as many as 200,000) which had no means, apart from the sale of their property and their savings of providing a livelihood for themselves. In these circumstances, widespread poverty was a feature of ghetto life. According to the post-war memoirs of Stefan Ernest, a senior official in the *Judenrat*:

Perhaps twenty, perhaps thirty thousand properly nourished people, members of the 'social elite'. In contrast are the masses of a quarter of a million beggars and totally destitute, who struggle just to postpone the hour of death from starvation . . . And in the middle, between these two ends of the spectrum, a mass of about 200,000 'average people' who make do, more or less, and are still considered 'personalities', still surviving, decently dressed, their bodies not swollen by hunger.[53]

Along with poverty went malnutrition. We have already seen how low Jewish rations were (184 calories per day), far below what was needed for survival. This was openly admitted by the occupying authorities. According to a report by Ludwig Fischer, governor of the Warsaw district, 'the amount of food supplied legally is inadequate effectively to counteract hunger in the Jewish district.' By 10 June 1941, he reported coolly, 'An official doctor has labelled the existing shortage of food in the Jewish district as a famine disaster.'[54] One consequence of this was the very high death rate in the ghetto, the result both of starvation and the susceptibility to disease induced by malnutrition. Between January 1941 and July 1942 nearly 61,000 people died in the ghetto, mostly from these causes.[55]

Another was smuggling. Even before the establishment of the ghetto, the introduction by the Germans of strict rationing as well as control over what farmers produced had created severe problems over food supply for both Poles and Jews in the towns. Under these conditions, food smuggling became widespread. The creation of the ghetto did not stop this illicit trade in food – on the contrary, given the desperate shortage of food there, it encouraged its further development. According to the diary of Symkhon Szymkowicz, one of the inhabitants of the ghetto, the official food ration was barely sufficient to provide nourishment for three days. The balance could only be met by smuggling – it was Czerniaków himself who estimated that 80 per cent of the food entering the ghetto was provided in this way.[56]

The attitude of the German authorities towards smuggling was not wholly consistent. In principle, it was strongly opposed and often ruthlessly repressed. One way of doing this was by cutting down the links between the ghetto and the outside world. In November 1940, when the ghetto was established there were 22 gates for entry and exit. When the mass deportations began in July 1942, the number had fallen to four. At the same time many within the administration, from the highest to the lowest echelons, were prepared to tolerate a degree of illicit trading in food, partly because of its lucrative by-products in the form of bribes and confiscations and partly because it alleviated somewhat the famine conditions in the ghetto and thus kept the ghetto work-force in better condition. It was Fischer himself who observed cynically in a report, 'The amount of food which is supplied to the Jewish district by illicit trade is, of course, considerable, but it can only be used by rich Jews due to its price.'[57] Similarly, smuggling was only possible because of the complaisance of many members of both the Polish and Jewish police, both of which were ultimately dependent on the occupying authorities.

Smuggling was undertaken partly by individuals who hoped, in this way, to provide for themselves and their families. Many of them were people who worked on the Aryan side. Children too, were frequently engaged in the clandestine transfer of food. It was also carried out in a more organized way by professional smugglers who, in fact, provided most of the food consumed in the ghetto. It was a profitable if risky operation and many of those who became active in it paid with their lives. According to the study of smuggling written in the ghetto by Mojzesz Passenstein for the *Oneg Shabbes* archive:

The lives of the smugglers were filled with danger. Not a day passed when one of them was not cut down by machine-gun fire from the gendarmes, but the smuggling did not stop. After the corpse was removed, it continued with the same intensity and the same temptation of the fates which placed the smugglers at the front line of the ghetto's struggle against Hitlerism.[58]

Many of the smugglers were people who before the war had performed tough labouring occupations like portering. Some were simply members of Warsaw's Jewish underworld. They became part of the new ghetto elite able to enjoy a relatively high standard of living on the proceeds of their operation. Yet they were generally respected. Szymkowicz wrote: 'These . . . vulgar figures are worthy of mercy. Without them the ghetto would simply have been sentenced to starvation.'[59] Similarly Passenstein, in his study of smuggling in the ghetto, comes to the conclusion that 'the role of the smugglers in the struggle against the evil plan of the authorities to starve the Jewish population was so great that they deserve to be placed in the first rank of those who fought the tyrant.'[60] Henryka Lazowert's poem in Polish, 'The Little Smuggler' was widely read at gatherings in the ghetto. Ringelblum described it as 'a song in praise of the thousands of children who endangered themselves countless numbers of times in order to sustain their families and the community as a whole'.[61] Its last verse reads:

> I shall not return to you again
> No more a voice from afar,
> The dust of the street is my grave
> An infant's fate is sealed
> And on my lips alone
> A single care is frozen
> Who, my soul's delight,
> Will bring you a crust tomorrow?[62]

Rachel Auerbach, in her diary, accords 'a place of honour to Jewish and Polish smugglers alike . . . for their persistence and bravery in the on-going battle between unequal parties . . . honour to the unknown smuggler, the grey soldier on the walls of the besieged city.'[63] Similarly, Leon Berensohn, the renowned Polish-Jewish lawyer and veteran defendant in political trials, advocated the erection after the war of a monument to the 'unknown smuggler'.[64]

During the second half of 1941, the Germans stepped up their activities against smuggling and Commissar Auerswald ordered the execution of all smugglers, including women and children. Even this did not stop smuggling, although the amount of food reaching the ghetto diminished and black market food prices soared. As Ringelblum wrote in his diary in May 1942, according to ghetto opinion, 'three things are invincible: the German army, the British Isles and Jewish smuggling.'[65]

There was one organization in the ghetto to which we have already referred which while loosely linked with the *Judenrat* retained a degree of both integrity and independence. This was the Jewish Self-help Organization, which after October 1940 changed its name to the Jewish Organization for Social Care (Żydowskie Towarzystwo

Opieki Społecznej – ŻTOS). It was the only Jewish organization whose activities covered the whole of the General-Government and until the entry of the United States into the war continued to receive funds from the Joint Distribution Committee. It attempted, above all, to use its resources to aid those sections of the population – refugees, starving children – who were neglected by the Social Welfare Department of the *Judenrat*, which, under German orders, was forced to favour 'active' and 'productive' sections of the population.

The Self-help Organization operated on two levels – legal and clandestine. Thus it used part of its funds to aid the underground and also held illegal classes and set up youth groups for children in the soup kitchens it organized. Similarly, through the Society for the Encouragement of Agriculture (Toporol), it sent Jewish youngsters, many of them youth movement activists, to do seasonal work on farms around Warsaw. Perhaps its most important activity was in the maintenance of soup kitchens, although its ability to do this diminished as its fund dried up. It also gave financial support to the underground archive.

Political life also began to revive in the ghetto, though it was inhibited by the conditions of Nazi terror, which had been particularly intense in relation to the Jews in Warsaw, as elsewhere in Poland in the first months of the occupation. Thus on 22 November 1939, 53 Jews, all of 9 Nalewki Street, were killed. This mass-execution was said to be a reprisal for the murder of one Polish policeman and the wounding of another, an incident which was in fact the result of a settling of underworld accounts. The Germans announced this publicly (in Warsaw and Kraków) in order to spread fear among the Jewish population. Similarly, in January 1940, some 100 Jewish intellectuals in Warsaw – doctors, lawyers and teachers – were arrested and executed. The pretext for this was the activities of one Andrzej Kott in one of the Polish underground organizations. It was claimed that Kott, who had been born a Christian, was of Jewish descent. When they were unable to arrest him, the Germans ordered the *Judenrat*, which of course had no power to do this, to hand him over or they would execute the Jews they had arrested.[66] After the creation of the ghetto, Nazi terror diminished somewhat, although the revival of political activity was also adversely affected by the departure of much of the established Jewish leadership. As Hirsch

Berlinski of the Poalei Tsion-Left commented, 'And the Jewish political parties? The best elements left for distant lands. Second and third echelon leaders remained and, to our regret, the war has also left its mark on them.'[67] Similarly Ringelblum commented in late 1941 that 'the departure of the leaders of institutions and enterprises who left during a difficult hour, and abandoned everything behind them, is often a subject of debate.'[68] An important consequence of the departure of the established political elite was that communication with Polish political groupings, with all its implications both for contact with the outside world and for obtaining arms, was made much more difficult.

Yet quite soon, around the Self-help Organization, political activity began to develop, partly under the stimulus of the historian Emanuel Ringelblum. Ringelblum himself has described the informal discussions which developed:

The war confronted the Jewish public circles with crucial questions. It was imperative to abandon the pre-war political relationships and forge a united front from right to left: Hitler's campaign against the Jewish population bore the stamp of annihilation. It was directed against all strata and classes of Jewish society. For Hitlerism, there was no difference between a Zionist and a Bundist; both were hated to the same degree. It wanted to destroy them both. Thus it was necessary to define the course of struggle for the Jewish public . . . The institution of consultation by all the parties across the political spectrum was not defined by name, but it became a permanent body whose opinion was solicited by the *Judenrat*, the Self-help Organization, and more than once by the community as well.[69]

Yet it did not prove an easy task to overcome the bitter divisions of pre-war years. In addition, disputes over whether the political objectives to be pursued should be relief, cultural development or political resistance soon surfaced and rapidly became more acute. Lewin, who was not particularly interested in party politics, about which he hardly ever expressed opinions, played an important role in the cultural sphere. As we have seen, he took an active part in the creation of the underground *Oneg Shabbes* archive and was a member of its directorate.

The features of ghetto life we have described were still dominant when the section of Lewin's diary which we possess begins. Yet by this time, an ominous change had already come over German policy. The invasion of the Soviet Union in June 1941 was accompanied by the notorious *Kommissarbefehl*, empowering German commanders to shoot out of hand any Soviet commissars who fell into their hands and by the creation of mobile killing squads (*Einsatzgruppen*). These followed the advancing German troops and were given the task of murdering Jews as well as communist officials. In the six months between June and December 1941, nearly half a million Jews perished at the hands of these squads. In January 1942, at the Wannsee conference, held near Berlin, the fateful decision was taken, in which Hitler was almost certainly personally involved, to 'solve' the Jewish problem by mass-murder.

The first part of Lewin's diary, from 26 March to 12 June, reflects the dual character of this period. It takes the form of long accounts, written in Yiddish, describing both the features of life in the ghetto which we have already outlined as well as recording the increasingly ominous echoes of the policies of mass-murder on which the Germans had embarked. Lewin was determined to record for posterity the almost incredible events he was forced to witness. After describing a poignant scene, typical of the subterfuges to which a Jewish husband had to resort to meet his Christian wife (entry of 3 June), he asked, 'Will future generations believe that this is how everyday life was in 1942?'

In the face of 'the greatest disaster which has ever befallen us', he feared that he would not find the words to express his feelings:

... perhaps because the disaster is so great, there is nothing to be gained by expressing in words everything that we feel. Only if we were capable of tearing out by the force of our pent-up anguish the greatest of all mountains, a Mount Everest, and with all our hatred and strength hurling it down on the heads of the German murderers of our young and old – this would be the only fitting reaction on our part. Words are beyond us now.

Our hearts are empty and made of stone. (25 May)

Yet he was determined to find the appropriate words. After talking to a simple meat-vendor from Tłuszcz, he recorded:

Speaking of the expulsion from Tłuszcz, she said: There is no way to put into words what happened to us. I thought over what the woman had said and concluded that she is right. There can be no words, no images, no embellishments – just cold hard facts. The day will come when these facts will shake the world and will be transformed into an impassioned appeal 'Remember!' against hatred and shame and against the degenerate murderers. As for us – tortured and murdered though we are innocent of any crime – the world will be duty bound to show love and compassion for our suffering. (12 June)

Lewin was certainly an acute and critical observer of the ghetto world. He was not impressed by the people who dominated the *Judenrat*, observing on 21 May:

In our parochial intimate little world there are certain individuals who have made their way up to the top, to pray at the Eastern Wall, individuals who are not fit or suitable to be at the head of a Jewish community and this the greatest in Europe, and at such an appalling time. This is one of the inevitable results of war, the calamity of 'the good are cast down and the lowly raised up', the curse of leaders who are not fit for their office.

Yet as late as 10 May 1942, he seems to have shared the belief of the *Judenrat* leadership and of many of the inhabitants of the ghetto that if only the ghetto could demonstrate its productivity to the Germans, it would be able to avoid large-scale deportations of Jews from Warsaw. On that day, he records in some detail a meeting at which the creation of a special boarding-school in Otwock or Falenica for beggar-children was proposed as well as the establishment of craft workshops to employ women in the ghetto. He also observed the brutal round-ups for labour camps which took place in spring 1942, commenting bitterly on the venality of the Jewish police and what he described as their 'sad complicity' (pp. 104–5, 106). He was fully aware of the hardship of life in the labour camps, commenting on 30 May, when he learnt of a large transport of labourers at Bobruisk, 'Nine hundred young lives are now as good as over, lost.' (p. 108). In addition, he gives a detailed account of conditions in the women's section of the ghetto prison on Gęsia Street, which he obtained from his former pupil, Hanka Tauber (pp. 91, 93–4).

Lewin devoted considerable space to the question of smuggling, providing many details about how it was carried out and noting the many deaths which it occasioned. On 18 May, he recorded, 'No matter how many are devoured by the smuggling trade, it still continues to flourish and develop. Even the shadow of death cannot wither it.' He observed on 18 May how, in exchange for food the Jews were forced to give up all their household possessions:

It all began with the Jews selling off clothes, furniture, then linen, covers, next pillows, and now it is the turn of the pot and the wash-tub. The poorest Jew or Jewess will have nothing to cook a meal and nothing to wash his last remaining shirt in. This is a sign of the extreme deprivation into which the broad mass of the people has fallen. Now we shall have to start saying that someone has sold the pot from the kitchen, instead of 'the shirt off their back'!

He gives an unforgettable picture of child smugglers:

Once again we can observe the scores of Jewish children from the age of ten to 12 or 13 stealing over the Aryan side to buy a few potatoes there. These they hide in their little coats, with hems swollen so that the children look like balloons. Whole hosts of them can be seen climbing over the walls, crawling through the gaps or so-called 'targets' and passing through the official entrances where gendarmes and Polish police stand guard. There are some Germans who show a little mercy for these unfortunate children and pretend not to see, turning away deliberately, and the children dart through with their little overcoats bulging, scampering along like birds. There are also vicious guards who hit the children with murderous blows, take away their potatoes, and often even use their weapons. More than one child has fallen victim to their bloodlust. These poor unfortunate Jewish children! What wonderful human potential is being lost to us. (22 May)

He noted, too, how smuggling necessitated co-operation between Poles and Jews. Of this, he wrote, 'Of course the main thing in business, in the eyes of the two sides, is profit. Nevertheless, when we consider how these ordinary Poles are capable of acts of humane generosity and great self-sacrifice towards the Jews – we can see that the matter requires further investigation and the reaching of certain conclusions.'

He was also fully aware of the service the smugglers performed for the ghetto. On 2 June he quoted the Rosh Hashanah prayer, 'Man earns his bread at the risk of his life', and commented 'each piece of bread that we buy on the open market is soaked with Jewish blood.'

Lewin noted the pervasive poverty and hunger which characterized ghetto life:

We live in a prison. We have been degraded to the level of homeless and uncared-for animals. When we look at the swollen, half-naked bodies of

Jews lying in the streets, we feel as if we found ourselves at some sub-human level. The half-dead, skeletal faces of Jews, especially those of dying little children, frighten us and recall pictures of India, or of the isolation-colonies for lepers which we used to see in films. Reality surpasses any fantasy; and possibly one thing only could still surprise us. This would be mass-murder in the place of the systematic extermination. (Speech on the second anniversary of the death of Yitshak Meir Weissenberg; see Appendix)

His puritanism comes out when he describes the desire of Jewish women, even in ghetto conditions, to adorn themselves:

The ghetto is most terrible to behold with its crowds of drawn faces with the colour drained out them. Some of them have the look of corpses that have been in the ground a few weeks. They are so horrifying that they cause us to shudder instinctively. Against the background of these literally skeletal figures and against the all-embracing gloom and despair that stares from every pair of eyes, from the packed mass of passers-by, a certain type of girl or young woman, few in number it must be said, shocks with her over-elegant attire. Their new outfits, their wavy peroxide hair, beautifully styled, their brightly powdered cheeks and their purple-red lips, stab at the eyes of the onlooker. Walking the streets, I observe this sickly elegance and am shamed in my own eyes. These women look as if their silk garments are pulled over shrouds. It seems that a hunger for jewellery and fine clothes is a national weakness of ours. It is not for nothing that we can find regulations and decrees against women's silk dresses and jewellery in the records of the Council of the Four Lands and in many other places. (21 May)

He also outlines the class divisions which had developed in the ghetto by analysing the various types of midday meal (the main meal of the day in Poland) available to its inhabitants (pp. 126–7). The depressed character of life on the 'Aryan' side is also set down:

Warsaw, the bustling, jostling Warsaw, is no more. It has become a dead, dreary, melancholy, deeply provincial town. I often sit on a balcony on Sienna Street from which you can clearly see the corner of Marszałkowska and Sienkiewicz Streets. It is quite astonishing: there are a few lone passers-by. Very occasionally a droshky or a tram. It is as quiet as at four in the morning. (27 May)

He movingly records tragedies which befell individual families he met in the course of his work for the Self-help Organization:

It is well known that whole families are being wiped out. Even a year, a year and a half ago, there were two- or three-room flats standing empty because the inhabitants had all died. Every official in the ghetto has a lot to tell on this subject. But it still happens that the loss of certain families chokes us with sadness, even though we have become hardened and insensitive to human tears and the shedding of blood.

These episodes, he observes, 'are only a small link in the chain of disaster that has befallen Polish Jewry. In fact, the whole of European Jewry. But the destruction of Polish Jewry will be the crowning glory of Hitler's crusade against the Jewish people.' Certainly a large part of the diary deals with the continuous series of acts of terror unleashed by the Germans against the ghetto. As Lewin asked on 9 June, 'Day after day, night after night, Jewish blood flows like water in the ghetto. When will we see the end of this lawlessness? When?' He carefully records these bestial acts, from what he refers to as the 'Bartholomew's Night' of 18 April 1942 when the Gestapo arrested 60 Jewish activists in the ghetto as well as some of its own agents and immediately murdered 48 of them in individual acts of random brutality.[70]

He clearly saw that these acts were intended to sow terror in the ghetto:

An unremitting insecurity, a never-ending fear, is the most terrible aspect of all our tragic and bitter experiences. If we ever live to see the end of this cruel war and are able as free people and citizens to look back on the war-years that we have lived through, then we will surely conclude that the most terrible and unholy, the most destructive aspect for our nervous system and our health was to live day and night in an atmosphere of unending fear and terror for our physical survival, in a continual wavering between life and death – a state where every passing minute brought with it the danger that our hearts would literally burst with fear and dread. (16 May)

German brutality stimulated him to reflect on the question of collective guilt. At first he attempted to distinguish between 'Germans and Germans', recording individual acts of kindness by German soldiers or by policemen. As the situation worsened, his views became, understandably, harder:

Is the whole German people responsible for the Nazis' crimes? Once again we find that we are in conflict with ourselves when we try to give an answer

to this question. We want to answer: yes, they are responsible, yet it is difficult to answer categorically. We are after all not crazed like the Nazis. But
for all that there will remain with us – and not only with us – an eternal
grudge, a grievance against the German people in its totality for having
hatched such a poisonous snake as Hitlerism and nurtured and raised it.
(17 May)

He began too, uncharacteristically for him, to think of vengeance:

It is impossible that so much innocent blood should be spilled without
retribution. The day of judgement, the day of reckoning, must and will
come.
    The level of Nazi brutality is beyond our power to comprehend. It is
inconceivable to us and will seem quite incredible to future generations, the
product of our imagination, over-excited by misery and anger. (20 May)

It was above all, the murder of children which aroused his wrath:

There is no greater crime, no greater savagery than the murder of young and
innocent children. The blood of our children will never be erased from the
mark of Cain of the German people. Only now in these days have I come to
appreciate and understand Bialik's song of anguish and rage: 'The
Slaughter'. I must confess that, though I am one of Bialik's most fervent
admirers, his 'In the Town of Murder' and 'The Slaughter', where there is
such fiery talk of blood, murder and revenge, have never been my favourites.[71] I have always been drawn to his transcendent lyrics and his superb,
brilliant epic poetry. But now I recall his cry from the heart: 'Accursed be he
who cries out "Avenge this!" Vengeance for this, for the blood of a small
child, the devil himself has not created'. Or 'If there is such a thing as justice,
let it show itself now! But if only after my destruction, justice appears under
the heavens, may its seat be destroyed for ever!' (25 May)

Other aspects of ghetto life also did not escape Lewin's attention.
He notes, as did other diarists, the Germans' pathological desire to
record in a falsified form the character of the ghetto before they
destroyed it (pp. 71–2, 75, 80, 91, 112). He records too, their prohibition in the ghetto of public performances of works by non-Jewish
composers. When German Jews are resettled in the ghetto, he
remarks:

In the last few days we have begun to see very many German Jews in the
ghetto. They are recognizable by a yellow Star of David with the legend

Jude. They go in procession to and from work. They also walk around singly. For the time being no contact has established itself between them and us. Between us and them there still stands a wall of many hundreds of years of prejudice and linguistic division. In the final analysis it is difficult for a Jew from Hanover to have a conversation with a Jew from Piaseczno or Gryca and vice versa. They simply are not able to communicate. Let us hope that time will bring about a rapprochement. They will mix in with us and assimilate with us. Similar things have happened more than once in our history: the exiles from Spain in Germany and Poland, and recently the Yemenite and German community in Palestine... We and the German Jews are... brothers who have been separated from each other for rather a long time. In fact we left Germany in the fourteenth and fifteenth century. Now we meet again under tragic circumstances. We still feel estranged from each other, but this estrangement will soon disappear and we will be at ease with one another like brothers once again. (21 May)

Similarly, when Gypsies are forced to move into the ghetto,[72] he writes:

This is a blow to the ghetto as the overcrowding will be even more unbearable and disease will spread even faster. Even so, I have only compassion for the unfortunate Gypsies. They are our companions in misery. In my eyes they have gained the stature of holy martyrs. They will undoubtedly awaken in us feelings of compassion and pity, though we will not be able to help them, just as we cannot help the thousands of our own refugees who are dying each day before our very eyes. The Gypsies' blood, like our blood, will cry out for ever from the earth and will cover with shame and contempt the faces of Hitler's blond beast. The 'voice of thy brother's blood that cries to me from the earth' will, I believe, never be stilled and will demand for ever: 'Revenge!' (28 May)

These words should be set alongside his rather unfortunate observation in his speech about Weissenberg (see Appendix, pp. 243–4) that 'we used to occupy a place higher than the Gypsies or any of the wild tribes of Africa.'

He also addresses himself to the question of Polish–Jewish relations, which was much discussed in the ghetto.[73] There were two views on this question, he asserted. Some believed that Nazi persecution had drawn the Jews and Poles closer together, others that the Poles had learnt an awful lesson in anti-Semitism from the Nazis:

I personally incline to the first view. I see Polish–Jewish relations in a bright light. I think that this war will wash this earth of ours clean of much filth and savagery. From East and West will blow towards us winds of freedom and love of humanity. Poland after the war will also adhere to ideals for which the Russians, the English, the Americans, the Free French and the Polish legions have been fighting. There will be no refuge here for anti-Semitism, at least not for public, aggressive anti-Semitism. They will be ashamed to deal in it. I believe that the Polish people too has been purified by the terrible fire that has swept the face of the earth. Let us not forget: the Poles are in second place in the table of tragic losses among the nations, just behind the Jews. They have given, after us, the greatest number of victims to the Gestapo, and this does not take into account the destruction of the country. All this will of necessity leave deep traces in the people and lead to a loathing of the hatred of other races and peoples which is the source of National Socialism and anti-Semitism. Thus I dream of the coming of a time when Jews and Poles will live together in harmony. (7 June)

The ghetto lived on hope. Lewin recounts:

One of the most remarkable incidental phenomena seen in the present war is the clinging to life, the almost complete cessation of suicides. People are dying in vast numbers of the typhus epidemic, are being tortured and murdered by the Germans in vast numbers, but people do not try to escape from life. In fact just the contrary: people are bound to life body and soul and want to survive the war at any price. The tension of this epoch-making conflict is so great that everybody, young and old, great and small, wants to live to see the outcome of this giant struggle, and the new world order. Old men have only one wish: to live to see the end and to survive Hitler.

I know an old Jew, grey with age, about 80 years old. This old man was hit by a terrible misfortune last winter: he had an only son aged 52 who died of typhus. He had no other children. The son is dead. He hadn't remarried and had lived together with his son. A few days ago I visited the old man. As I was saying goodbye to him (he is still in complete command of his faculties) he burst into tears and said to me: I want to live to see the end of the war and then live for just another half hour longer.

We may well ask: what has such an old man to live for? But he does have something: he too wants to live 'for just half an hour' after the last shot is fired and this is the passionate desire of all Jews. (5 June)

Lewin himself sedulously recorded many rumours of an impending German collapse. He was moderately sceptical about them. On 11 June 1942 he discussed the vital question of when the war would end:

This question, one of decisive import for us, which signifies for us to be or not to be, gnaws away at the mind of every one of us and impels us to concentrate all our intellectual and emotional strength to give an answer to it. It is clear to every Jew that if the war finishes soon, there is still a prospect and hope of remaining alive, but if the war drags on, then our hopes of surviving it are almost nil.

I tried posing this question to various Jews. Naturally the answers were all different. Many thought that the war would be over soon. But there are Jews who hope that the war will be finished by the end of July. They told me about a fortune-teller who foretold the disappearance of the ghetto walls from Warsaw in the course of June, that is, this month. There are those who put the end back to the later autumn months, but think that the whole nightmare will be over by winter. Set against these are those who hold more realistic opinions, since they are preparing themselves for the fact that the end is a long, long way off. They think that the earliest possible date for the end of the war is the summer or autumn of next year. This means that the war has to go on for at least another year.

I should record that the 'lengtheners' of the war are in a decisive majority. Even though Jews are in general optimists, when we come to consider the final conclusion of the war, the proportion of 'lengtheners' to 'shorteners' is of the order of one to five or it may be even one to ten.

If this poll had any influence at all on events, these would be fatal for the Jews. I personally think that the decisive point will fall before winter and the Germans, the German people, will not dare and will not have the strength to continue their campaign for a fourth winter. Their nerve will not hold. That is how I see it.

As we know, he was wrong. Throughout this period, well informed as he was through his membership of the *Oneg Shabbes* group and his many contacts, he records the melancholy toll of Jewish communities destroyed by the Nazi killing machine: Wąwolnica, Słonim, Nowogródek, Ostrowiec, Wilno, Kowno, Lwów, Lublin, Golub, Kraków, Włocławek, Gostynin, Aleksandrów-Kujawski, Kielce, Pabianice, Radzyń, Ciechanów, Tłuszcz, Zduńska, Wola. The destruction of all these communities is recorded in the diary, and they were only a small part of the victims.[74] Lewin was aware that it was only a matter of time before the blow fell on Warsaw. On 16 May, he wrote:

The abyss is getting ever closer to each one of us, the bestial visage of the Nazi apocalypse, with the words death, destruction, doom, death-agony written on its forehead . . . After the outbreak of the war between Germany and the Soviet Union, since the tidings of Job have begun to reach us, of mass-murders and the extermination of entire historic and illustrious Jewish communities such as Wilno, the Jerusalem of Lithuania, Kowno, Słonim, Lwów, Lublin and dozens of others – who can begin to comprehend it all? The burden on our souls and on our thoughts has become so heavy, oppressive, that it is almost unbearable. I am keenly aware that if our nightmare does not end soon, then many of us, the more sensitive and empathetic natures, will break down. I feel that we are standing on the threshold of the intolerable, between existence and annihilation.

On 3 June, he affirmed:

Reason and the heart tell us that humankind, embodied in the peoples of Soviet Russia, England and America, will be victorious and not the wild animals of Hitler and Mussolini-land.

The desire is so strong in us to see the day of redemption, the triumph of righteousness, but at the same time there is a worm of doubt and despair gnawing at the heart. Every day we receive such terrible news from the provinces. Every day a new misfortune, a new pogrom, a new expulsion that heralds a new mass-murder. Last week I was told that Kraków Jews are to be forcibly resettled. I didn't believe this tragic news and so didn't write it down. Today I was told that Dr W. rang from Kraków and gave the news that 2,000 Jews have already been deported and it is not even known where they are to be taken. From our bitter experience we must conclude that they are being secretly murdered. The circle around Warsaw is drawn ever tighter. Will they leave Warsaw alone and be content with smaller massacres and pogroms? It gives me a feeling of deep unease to ask such questions: what makes us better than the Jews of Wilno or Kraków? Why are they dying and we have hope of staying alive? Why? Why?

The blow was not long in falling. From early July rumours of the impending deportation circulated widely in the ghetto. On 20 July, when arrangements for its implementation had already been completed, the German authorities in order to lull the population into a false sense of security, assured Czerniaków, head of the *Judenrat*, that these were entirely without foundation. The following day, many hostages, including *Judenrat* members or their wives, were seized and a number of individuals were shot. On 22 July at first light, Polish police, augmented by Ukrainian, Latvian and Lithuanian troops, sealed the exits from the ghetto. At ten o'clock, SS Major Herman Höfle appeared at the *Judenrat*. According to the diary of Czerniaków, who killed himself the following day:

We were told that all the Jews, irrespective of sex and age, with certain exceptions, will be deported to the East. By 4 p.m. today a contingent of 6,000 people must be provided. And this (at a minimum) will be the daily quota.

... *Sturmbahnführer* Höfle (*Beauftragter* in charge of deportation) asked me to his office and informed me that for the time being my wife was free, but if the deportation were impeded in any way; she would be the first one to be shot as a hostage.[75]

For the next seven weeks, with a brief intermission between 28 August and 2 September, the Nazis deported daily between 2,000 and 10,000 people from the ghetto. They were first assembled at the *Umschlagplatz*, a square on the outskirts of the ghetto, and from there sent by train to Treblinka, where they were gassed with carbon monoxide from the exhausts of lorries. The deportation culminated in the comprehensive *Selektion* which lasted from 6 to 10 September, called the cauldron (Yiddish *kesl*, Polish *kocioł*) because it was carried out in so confined an area. During these days all Jews left in the ghetto were compelled to leave their homes and assemble in the streets adjacent to the *Umschlagplatz*. All those not part of the quota allocated to recognized workplaces were deported to Treblinka. The German plan was for 35,000 such slave labourers to remain in the ghetto. The final stages of this *Selektion* took place on the Day of Atonement, 21 September, when the Jewish policemen and their families were deported. The ghetto police was now reduced to 380 men. In all, according to German statistics, 235,741 people were deported to their deaths. In addition, more than 10,000 died or were shot in the violence accompanying the *Aktion*, another 12,000 were sent to labour camps and 8,000 sought refuge on the 'Aryan' side. As well as the slave-labourers left in the ghetto, another 20,000–25,000 Jews remained there in hiding.

The description of this appalling crime, 'with all its atrocities and animal savagery, the like of which human history has not seen' (diary entry, 16 August) forms the central and most valuable part of Lewin's diary. We possess very few first-hand accounts of this period, since many of the diarists of the ghetto, such as Chaim Kaplan, perished early in the deportation. Lewin was determined to record all he saw and heard. He seems to have realized almost immediately the momentous character of the events he was witnessing, noting on

21 July: 'The Day of Judgement' – whence will come our help? We are preparing ourselves for death. What will be our fate?'

He switches now from Yiddish to Hebrew, perhaps feeling that only a sacred language was fit to record a martyrology which made the massacres of Chmielnicki or of 1918–19 pale into insignificance. His Hebrew, although sometimes stilted and convoluted, with many Yiddishisms or Polonisms, is filled with the spirit of the Hebrew prophets he so loved. These biblical echoes give to his narrative an almost poetic quality. This is one of the great documents of the holocaust, to be set alongside Yitshak Katznelson's *Song of the Murdered Jewish People* or Anne Frank's *Diary*. From the first brief notes he made on 20 July, which gives the impression of a cine-camera swinging wildly, almost out of control, from scene to scene, to his account of the appalling episodes which accompanied the final selection between 6 and 10 September, there is not a single false note.

Lewin was well aware of the inadequacy of the means at his disposal. On 1 August, he noted 'the tragedies cannot be captured in words', repeating on 7 August, 'there are no words to describe the tragedies and disasters'. He was fully conscious of the scale of what was taking place. 'The whole of Jewish Warsaw has been laid waste', he wrote on 15 August. 'That which remains is a shadow of what was, a shadow that tells of death and ruin.' On 11 September he noted, 'Today is the 52nd day of the greatest and most terrible slaughter in history. We are the tiny remnants of the greatest Jewish community in the world.' At the end of December, three months after the deportation, he wrote:

Warsaw was in fact the backbone of Polish Jewry, its heart, one could say. The destruction of Warsaw would have meant the destruction of the whole of Polish Jewry, even if the provinces had been spared this evil. Now that the enemy's sword of destruction has run amok through the small towns and villages and is cutting them down with murderous blows – with the death-agony of the metropolis, the entire body is dying and plunging into hell. One can say that with the setting of the sun of Polish Jewry, the splendour and the glory of world Jewry has vanished. We, the Polish Jews, were after all the most vibrant nerve of our people.

In terms of the number of victims, Hitler has murdered an entire people. There are many peoples in Europe who number fewer than the number of our martyrs. The Danes and the Norwegians are no more than three million.

The Lithuanians, the Letts and the Estonians have far fewer. The Swedes – six million. The Slovaks fewer than two million, and so on. And Hitler has already killed five, six million Jews. Our language has no words with which to express the calamity and disaster that has struck us. (29 December)

Yet, although Lewin clearly feared the worst from the inception of the *Aktion*, referring on 29 July to rumours that the Germans intended to deport 250,000 Jews from the ghetto, he continued to hope that the deportation would be limited in scale. On 31 July he noted, 'At four o'clock they suddenly took those who had been rounded up out of the wagons and announced that the action was being suspended. The joy and hope that this brought forth. At six to half past six the blockades started again.' On 4 August he recorded, 'Again there is talk that the savage round-up will stop today. But we have heard this before and nothing came of it.' On 24 August, he wrote:

Rumours are going around that the Germans have allowed 120,000 food-cards to be prepared and distributed for September. This would seem to indicate that they are going to leave behind that number of Jews. But this is only a rumour and nothing more. On the other hand, there are other rumours, much more pessimistic. There is talk again that the 'action' will be extended for another week.

He also sedulously noted all rumours which suggested that deportation might not mean death. On 30 July, he writes of 'a letter from Białystok that a Polish policeman brought, from a woman to her husband. She and her sons are together with several other families and have to work hard in the fields, but they are receiving food.' On 4 August he refers to 'a letter from Baranowicze. The writer is working as a farm labourer. She asks for underwear. Life is cheap, 7 zloty for white bread, 1.80 for potatoes. It would be good if she could be sent underwear. The letter came by post.' Similarly on 16 August: 'Rumours have reached me again that letters have allegedly arrived from the deportees saying that they are working in the area of Siedlce and conditions are not bad. Lifschitz's son (my friend from elementary school) told me that his daughter had herself read one of these letters from an elderly couple.'

These letters were probably partly genuine messages from individuals who had escaped from trains to Treblinka, but feared to reveal this, partly the result of the conscious spreading of false rumours by the Germans and partly the creation of Poles who hoped in this way to persuade the inhabitants of the ghetto to send money and goods to dependants in the country, many of whom were probably no longer alive. Well-informed as he was, Lewin soon became aware that there was no substance to the false hopes they aroused. On 6 August, he records that deportees were being sent to Treblinka which was 'the place of execution?' The following day he refers to 'the crematorium near Malkinia and Sokołów', which was in all probability Treblinka, while on 9 August he observes grimly, 'It is clear that 99 per cent of those transported are being taken to their deaths.' He was soon in possession of much more detail. On 11 August, he writes:

Smolar rang Sokołów. He was told that those that are deported, or if they are deported to Tr., are going to their 'death'. The news that K. brought. In Warsaw there is a Jew by the name of Slawa who has brought reports of Treblinka. Fifteen kilometres before the station at Treblinka the Germans take over the train. When people get out of the train they are beaten viciously. They are then driven into huge barracks. For five minutes heart-rending screams are heard, then silence. The bodies that are taken out are swollen horribly. One person cannot get their arms round one of these bodies, so distended are they. Young men from among the prisoners are the gravediggers, the next day they too are killed. What horror!

Even more information was provided on 28 August by Dowid Nowodworski, a member of the left-wing Zionist youth movement Hashomer Hatsair, who managed to escape from the camp:

Today we had a long talk with Dowid Nowodworski, who returned from Treblinka. He gave us the complete story of the sufferings that he endured from the first moment that he was seized to the escape from the death camp and up to his return to Warsaw. His words confirm once again and leave no room for doubt that all the deportees, both those who have been seized and those who reported voluntarily, are taken to be killed and that no one is saved. This is the naked truth, and how terrible, when we remember that in the last weeks at least 300,000 Jews have been exterminated, from Warsaw and other towns: Radom, Siedlce, and many, many others. From his words we put together a testimony of such stark anguish, so shattering, that it cannot be grasped and put into words. This is without doubt the greatest crime ever committed in the whole of history . . .

God! Are we really to be exterminated down to the very last of us? Now it is certain that all those deported from Warsaw have been killed.

Subsequent reports brought clear confirmation. On 21 September, Lewin wrote:

A Jew has returned to our workshop who was taken away from here three weeks ago and worked as a gravedigger in Treblinka for nine or eleven days before escaping in a train-wagon in which the martyrs' belongings were being taken away. He tells horrific and shattering things. In any case we have another eyewitness to the fate of those who are deported. According to what he said, not only Jews from Warsaw and of the *gubernia* are being exterminated in Treblinka, but Jews from all over Europe – from France, Belgium, Holland, among others. Such a calamity has never before fallen us in all the bitter experiences of our history.

Confirmation about what had occurred became even more firm after the end of the *Aktion*. On 27 September,

I spent the evening with the Wassers. Rabinowicz was there, a relative of the Rabinowicz's, who escaped from Treblinka. For hours on end he recounted the horrors of Treblinka. His central observation: it has nearly reached the point that the Jews are more afraid of a German than of death. The facts that he recounted show that his observation was correct. 'Graves for the *Führer*'. The women go naked into the bath-house – to their death. The condition of the dead bodies. What are they killing them with? With simple vapour (steam).[76] Death comes after seven or eight minutes. On their arrival they take away the shoes of the unfortunates.

On 26 November Lewin wrote, giving figures whose accuracy has mostly been confirmed by subsequent research:

I have heard that the SS have passed on to the Jewish Council the numbers involved in the bloody 'action' that was carried out from 22 July onwards. It goes as follows: transported (read: annihilated in Treblinka) 254,000; murdered during the blockades – 5,000; and those sent to work in *Dulag* [*Durchgangslager*] – 11,000. In total therefore according to the Germans' figures 270,000 people have been taken from us. We must assume that these numbers are incomplete and do not reflect the true extent of our losses – the number of martyrs. And these are only the victims from Warsaw, and where are all the other towns, townlets and villages throughout Europe, on which – that is, on the Jews – Hitler's avenging sword of destruction has fallen? God! How is it possible?

Lewin provides considerable information on how the Germans were able to organize the deportation with relatively little difficulty. He stresses the shortage of food and the resulting hunger as the Germans stopped providing rations and smuggling almost ceased. This was a major factor in inducing Jews to give themselves up and allow themselves to be deported. He refers continually to the 'terrible hunger' which 'haunts us' and to the enormous increase in the price of food (27, 28 July, 9, 10 August). On 31 July, he notes 'In our courtyard a woman threw herself from the third floor – she was starving.' The commander of the ghetto police announced, shortly after the start of the deportation, that people presenting themselves at the *Umschlagplatz* of their own free will on 29, 30 and 31 July would receive 3 kg of bread and 1 kg of jam. This proclamation was re-issued on 1 August, when the offer was extended for another three days.[77]

Most witnesses have bitterly criticized the role of the Jewish police in the *Aktion*. Ringelblum wrote that 'The Jewish police were known for their terrible corruption, but they reached the apogee of depravity at the time of the deportation'.[78] Katznelson even went so far as to refer to them as 'the shame of creation, the decomposing rat floating on the surface of the swamp'.[79] These views were shared by Lewin. It is true that he records on 29 July that 'so far eight Jewish policemen have committed suicide', but this is an isolated positive reference. On 24 July, he comments on 'the savagery of the police during the round-up, their murderous brutality. They drag girls from rickshaws, empty out flats, and leave the property strewn everywhere. A pogrom and a killing the like of which has never been seen'. On 26 July he refers to 'the terrible corruption of our police and their assistants. An outrage, an outrage.' On 23 August, he writes: 'The savagery of the Jewish police against their unfortunate victims; they beat viciously, they steal, and they loot and pillage like bandits in the forest. What degeneracy; who has raised these bitter fruits among us?' On 23 September, he records, 'A large number from the ranks of the Jewish police have also been sent to the *Umschlagplatz*, together with their wives and children. The Jews who watched the scene felt a definite satisfaction. This is the reward for their brutal acts against the Jews of Warsaw.'

Generally speaking, he did not regard resistance to the Germans as a feasible, or even desirable, option. He does record some acts of individual courage. On 9 August, he wrote:

The 19th day of the 'action' of which human history has not seen the like . . . One hears only of isolated cases of resistance. One Jew took on a German and was shot on the spot. A second Jew fought with a Ukrainian and escaped after being wounded. And other cases of this kind. The Jews are going like lambs to the slaughter.

Yet when the Jewish Fighting Organization organized an unsuccessful attempt on the life of Józef Szeryński, he commented:

I have heard that there was an assassination attempt on the chief of police Szeryński. He was wounded in the cheek. According to rumours he was wounded by a Pole from the Polish Socialist Party (PPS) disguised as a Jewish policeman. Today leaflets were distributed against the Jewish police, who have helped to send 200,000 Jews to their deaths. The whole police force has been sentenced to death.

Thus, although he had links with the underground through *Oneg Shabbes* and was working in the Ostdeutsche Bautischlerei Werkstätte, the factory where many of the Jewish Fighting Organization's members were sheltering, Lewin never suspected they were involved in the attack on Szeryński.

There were other factors which made escape from the German killing machine difficult to achieve. In the first place, there was the paralysing effect of Nazi terror. As Lewin wrote, 'Sometimes I am quite calm about my life and sometimes a little indifferent, but suddenly I am gripped by fear of death that drives me insane' (29 July). The scale of the disaster also induced an inability to act. 'The numbness of everyone is staggering. Gorny loses his mother and sells meal tickets. Smolar has lost his wife and daughter. Tintpulver – widowed – goes around in despair, a broken man, and tries to "find" work, so as to be involved in something, not to be superfluous.' The Germans also exploited very successfully the desire to survive of those who had not yet been deported. On 27 August, he records:

The meeting of all the workers [at the Ostdeutsche Bautischlerei Werkstätte, the factory where Lewin worked] and the speech of commissar Hensel and his words of thanks from the Landau brothers [the Jewish owners of the factory]. He spoke of the benefits for us and of his efforts on behalf of the workers during the terrible 'action' which was now coming to an end for us. His efforts had met with partial success and partial failure, perhaps because of a lack of understanding on our part. In return for these benefits he appealed for dedication to the work and loyalty to the firm. He would hunt down saboteurs. The workers applauded and thanked him, as did the Landau brothers. This was a performance, prepared in every detail. Unfortunate slaves – when they hear an encouraging word – it goes to their heads and they get excited and enthusiastic.

Except for the small group of assimilated Jews who had links with Polish society, flight to the Aryan side was virtually impossible. Most Jews were clearly distinct in language and appearance from the majority of the population. Even those Poles who were willing to hide them were thus, for the most part, deterred by the danger (the Germans imposed the death penalty on all members of a family caught hiding Jews). Their reluctance was intensified by the presence of *smalcownicy* (blackmailers) willing to denounce Jews for financial gain or because of anti-Semitism. Concealment in the ghetto also offered no refuge. According to Lewin:

As things are developing, a handful of Jews will be left, those of a designated age. Apart from this there will be no way for a Jew to survive: there will be nowhere to live and no bread. The position of the old is especially tragic: they have no way out. They can either give themselves up into the hands of the butchers, or take their lives themselves, or hide out and live in dark corners and cellars, which is also very difficult because of the general expulsions from the buildings and the upheaval of the residents. In those buildings that have been taken over by new occupants, no strangers are let in. It is easier for an animal to find a hiding place and a refuge in the forest than for a Jew to hide in the ghetto. (16 August)

Under these circumstances, the situation was virtually hopeless. Among the most powerful pages in the diary are a series of vignettes illustrating the Dante-esque character of the unfolding tragedy: 'Someone saves his sister and her four-year-old child, passing her off as his wife. The child does not give the secret away. He cries out "Daddy!"'

Only the immediate dependants of the Jewish police were exempt from deportation. 'At the *Umschlagplatz*, a policeman is crying. He is struck. "Why are you crying?" "Meine Mutter, meine Frau!" "Frau, ja;

Mutter nicht" ["My mother, my wife". "Wife, yes; mother no"]'
(25 July).

The terror and violence which accompanied the deportation was
unremitting. 'Huge numbers of dead at 29 Ogrodowa Street. The
remaining occupants were taken out, no notice was taken of their
papers. The cause – a piece of glass fell on to the street when there
were Germans passing. Shooting all day. Dead on Pawia and other
streets' (27 July).

Lewin also records some of the attitudes of the surrounding
population: 'A Christian woman on Leszno Street, seeing the wagons
with those who have been rounded up, curses the Germans. She
presents her chest and is shot. On Nowy Świat a Christian woman
stands defiantly, kneels on the pavement and prays to God to turn his
sword against the executioners – she had seen how a gendarme killed
a Jewish boy' (29 July).

Children were not exempt from the terror: 'Yesterday the
Germans rounded up mainly women and children with rampant
viciousness and savagery. I was told that a prettily dressed 10-year-
old girl was seized. The girl screamed in anguish and cried out: "Mr
Policeman!" But her pleas were of no avail. He was deaf to her
screams and put her in a rickshaw to the *Umschlagplatz*' (23 August).

He observes the preoccupations of the Orthodox: 'I have heard
that Rabbi Kanal of Warsaw decided to die so as to be buried as a Jew.
When he was seized, he refused to enter the wagon. He was shot and
killed by a gendarme. His wish was fulfilled, he was given a Jewish
burial' (30 August).

At a *Selektion* round-up, an SS officer goes berserk:

A young officer hit out with murderous blows shouting wildly: 'Über euch,
verfluchte, verdammte, kräzige Juden habe ich 3 Jahren Lebens verloren, 3
Jahren schon plaget ihr uns, ihr Hunde ...' ['Because of you, accursed
damned, leprous Jews I have already lost three years of my life, for three
years we have been plagued, you dogs'] and so on. I have never before seen
such bestial hatred. There was also killing. (11 September)

Throughout these terrible days, Lewin is preoccupied with the fate
of his own family. He worries about his sisters, his mother, his grandmother. He seems almost relieved when his grandmother is killed on
2 August by a stray bullet while looking out of her window. On the

day the deportation began, he writes 'I am thinking about my aged mother – it would be better to put her to sleep than to hand her over to those murderers.' On 24 August he again records: 'the matter of my mother is causing me great anguish. What can be done with her? I have given permission to put her to sleep, eternal rest, rather than hand her over to the executioners. But J. [his brother-in-law, a doctor] refuses to carry it out. Even the devil would not have conceived of such a situation.'

Three weeks after the beginning of the deportation, on 12 August, tragedy strikes:

Eclipse of the sun, universal blackness. My Luba was taken away during a blockade on 30 Gęsia Street. There is still a glimmer of hope in front of me. Perhaps she will be saved. And if, God forbid, she is not? My journey to the *Umschlagplatz* – the appearance of the streets – fills me with dread. To my anguish there is no prospect of rescuing her. It looks like she was taken directly into the train. Her fate is to be a victim of the Nazi bestiality, along with hundreds of thousands of Jews. I have no words to describe my desolation. I ought to go after her, to die. But I have no strength to take such a step. Ora – her calamity. A child who was so tied to her mother, and how she loved her.

The following day he recorded:

Today is Ora's fifteenth birthday. What a black day in her life and in my life. I have never experienced such a day as this. Since yesterday I have not shed a single tear. In my pain I lay in the attic and could not sleep. Ora was talking in her sleep: 'mamo, mamusiu, nie odchódź beze mnie!' ['Mother, Mama, don't leave me'] . . . I will never be consoled as long as I live. If she had died a natural death, I would not have been so stricken, so broken. But to fall into the hands of such butchers! Have they already murdered her? She went out in a light dress, without stockings, with my leather briefcase. How tragic it is! A life together of over 21 years (I became close to her beginning in 1920) has met with such a tragic end.

As time passed, his grief grew:

The pain over the loss of L. is getting more and more intense. During the day I am often choked with tears. The fact there is no news about her suffering and torment, whether she is alive or dead, how she died – gives me no peace. If I knew that she was alive and that she was not suffering too much, I would be calm. And if I knew that she had died but did not suffer much at her death – then I would also be calm.' (16 August)

He is tormented by guilt. On 11 September he writes:

The Świeca family has perished. He gave himself up after seeing how his wife and two children were taken. Initially he went with us to Gęsia Street, later he went back, gave himself up and was sent away. I feel a great compassion and admiration for this straightforward person. Strong in mind as well as strong in body. I think that Luba would have done the same, but I didn't have enough strength to die together with her, with the one that I loved so much.

These feelings continue to torture him:

The pain for the loss of the person dearest to me grows from day to day. Only now do I understand the full meaning of the words of the Bible: 'Thus a man leaves his father and his mother and goes unto his wife and they become of one body.' I have lost a good sister whom I loved dearly, I have lost so many who were close to me. But their absence does not hurt me as much as that of my life's companion who shared my life with me for more than 22 years. And what makes the pain more intense – until I almost go insane – is the way in which she left this vale of tears. It is not easy to make peace with this thought and with the images that accompany it. How was this gentle and delicate woman killed, whom I used to call 'child'? And when I wake at night this thought drills into my head and my whole being cries out the cruel piercing sentence: 'My child is no longer with me. Wild animals have appeared and murdered her! Where are you, child of mine?' (30 October)

The end of the deportations led to the establishment of a degree of normality in the tiny remnant of the ghetto.[80] Yet the threat of annihilation was ever present. Both during the period of the *Aktion* and in the months that followed the killing process did not cease. Lewin records carefully the destruction of many ancient Jewish communities both large and small: Kielce, Wołomin, Skarzysko, Mława, Częstochowa, Jabłonna, Białystok, Płońsk, Kraków, Grodno, Nowy Dwór, Kałuszyn, Siedlce, Radomsko, Sobolew, Opoczno.

The ghetto was now little more than a ghost town:

The devastation in the streets of the reduced ghetto which now only extends over a few streets: Miła, Zamenhof, Franciszkańska and a few alleyways: Ostrowska, Wołyńska, Niska among others, are desolate. It is forbidden to be on the street. Not a single Jew to be seen. Every factory is a prison, locked and bolted. One can't go from Schultz's factory on Nowolipie Street to Többens' factories on Leszno Street. We are shut in the whole day at 30 Gęsia Street. We go in a group to and from work, before seven in the morning and at six in the evening. (1 October)

There was a pervasive atmosphere of gloom:

The days themselves are full of radiance and light, glorious, sun-filled days at the close of autumn, golden autumn days of which Poland used to be so proud. But for us, here in our cramped and gloomy little world, the days are black, desolate, with a tedium which is in itself almost deadly.

My life and that of all my companions is passed between the 'shop' and the 'block'. At seven o'clock in the morning we walk to 30 Gęsia Street and there we spend the day. Everyone does something, or gets out of work and idles the day away somehow. At five in the evening we return home to Miła Street to our block and kill time in the evening and spend the night there, only to get up at five or half past six, and so on continually. We have no holidays or rest-days. We work both Saturday and Sunday. There is only the concession that on Saturday we finish work at four in the afternoon and on Sunday at two.

When will our suffering end? When will our situation and that of the whole of Europe change? (30 October)

Fear that the deportations would resume was universal:

Days of turmoil and great fear have gone by at the workshop. A number of days ago a representative of the management of the German company, Kazparek, announced the sad news that the SS were reducing the number of workers in the OBW to 140 people. It became clear that they are to leave behind in the first instance only the carpenters and the family members, that is, the Landau family and their relatives. Then they spoke about efforts to raise the number of workers to 250. There was also talk the factory would be closed altogether.

The mood of the workers was one of deep despair. People are walking around like shadows. They ask each other: what will happen to us if the factory is closed, or if the work-force is reduced? Will we be allowed to go on living in the block? Or will they come and take us to the *Umschlagplatz*? And what will we do then? What protection is there for our lives in these circumstances? (20 October)

Yet hope that somehow the remaining Jews would survive began to surface. As early as 18 September, Lewin recorded:

New and extreme difficulties are besetting us. The ghetto-boundaries are being reduced further. The whole rectangle: Pawia, Lubiecka, Gęsia, Zamenhof Streets is being removed from the ghetto. My two remaining sisters are losing their flats. In any case they have no right to be alive, since they have not received a number from the community authorities. All my belongings are over there. If they lose the flats, what little clothing and bed-clothes I have left will be endangered and I will be naked and destitute. This disturbs me deeply, even though we are in mortal danger and there is no need to get upset at the prospect of having nothing to wear or no pillow for one's head, at a time when our very survival is in doubt. But perhaps a miracle will happen and our salvation will come suddenly?

Smuggling also began to revive:

Most of the Jews who have survived are still living by selling their possessions. The prices are incredibly low. A dress is sold for 50 zloty (a new, good quality dress), that is for two kilos of black bread or for one kilo of white bread. The smuggling is carried out by the groups who go to work outside the ghetto. The smugglers can sustain themselves: they eat and feed their families. The vast majority goes hungry. (1 October)

Many Jews, including Lewin's daughter, also found employment in the *Werterfassung*, the German department responsible for looting the property left behind by Jews in the ghetto.

By the beginning of November, the atmosphere in the ghetto had begun to improve. Lewin wrote on 1 November:

The weather in this period is unusually warm and bright. Not like autumn, like spring. The sun shines and warms. The air is so clear. A warm, caressing breeze. You can walk around in summer clothes. We are not used to being spoiled in this way by nature. As far as I can remember, this day, the Christian day of remembrance of the dead – *zaduszki* – has always been a rainy one, with cold winds and even snow. This year is such a pleasant surprise.

Among the Jews as well there was an air of relaxation. The streets were full of strollers. The few Jews who have remained alive came down from their cramped flats and went outside. Miła and Zamenhof Streets have filled up with these few Jews. True – they are gloomy, broken, emaciated, but they have dared to show themselves in the streets, something that has not been seen for weeks and months, since the intensification of the 'action'.

What has affected the Jews' spirits? First of all the release of the children from the *Umschlagplatz*. It actually came about: yesterday they decided to free children up to the ages of 14–16. Officially they were freeing 14-year-olds, but because they didn't require any kind of papers, 15- and 16-year olds were able to get released, if they were small. Two children of our neighbour Racimor's family (out of six boys and girls, only a 14-year-old girl remained), the daughter and a nephew, came home yesterday. Those who have no one to go to are being taken into the orphanages run by the Jewish community. The number of freed children was 118.

The release of adults has also become easier and cheaper. I have heard that one can buy one's freedom for 2,000 zloty instead of 6,000. It seems as they really have stopped sending people to Treblinka and the *Umschlagplatz* is on the point of being closed.

On 3 November, he recorded:

I have heard, and it seems that the report is true, that the SS commandant Brandt announced during his visit to the community offices that he would return the Torah scrolls that were found in the streets that Jews have moved out of and that he will permit the allocation of space for prayers, not a synagogue but *minyonim* (*kleine Gebethäuser* [small houses of prayer]).

There is also talk that a theatre and a cinema will soon be opening in the new, miniature ghetto. I have also heard it said that permission has been given for shops to open. The day before yesterday it was a surprise to see a barber-shop open at Miła in the miniature ghetto, in which Jews were sitting and having a shave. One gets the impression that the Germans want to create the illusion of life and movement in the ghetto. Why do they need it? The devil only knows. Perhaps a commission really will be coming from abroad? According to rumour there will soon be a cabaret opening on Wołyńska Street.

Yesterday I was told that Treblinka, which has been a place of execution for hundreds of thousands of Jews, no longer exists. Supposedly there is a huge work-camp there now. Perhaps this story is true as well?

Particular encouragement was taken from the German announcement that in the district of Warsaw ghettos would be established in Warsaw itself, Kałuszyn, Rembertów, Siedlce, Kosow and Sobolew. Lewin commented:

All Jews (that is, those who are still alive and hiding or are living with Christians) must choose one of the designated places by 1 December. After this deadline any Jew found outside a ghetto will be sentenced to death. Christians (Aryans) are forbidden to be in or to enter the ghettos, under penalty of a fine of 100,000 zloty. What is the purpose of this decree? Is it not a trick to get hold of those Jews who are hiding with Christians and shut them in a cage, so as to be in a better position to destroy them too one morning? Or perhaps they intend to allow the remainder to live and to shut them into these five holes. The coming days and months will show the intentions of the murderers and looters. (6 November)

Resistance still remained very alien to Lewin. On 16 October, he recorded the savage reprisals meted out by the Germans in response to Polish acts of sabotage. He still seems to have been unaware of the existence of the Jewish Fighting Organization which on 29 October assassinated the deputy-head of the ghetto police. He noted on 30 October:

At about five o'clock yesterday evening at 10 Gęsia Street, the deputy-head of the Jewish police, the lawyer Lejkin, was shot dead. His adjutant Czapliński was wounded in the leg. There is not much precise information about the killing. It is assumed that this is an act of revenge and retribution against those Jews whose hands are stained with Jewish blood, who have sent hundreds and thousands of Jews to the *Umschlagplatz* and to Treblinka.

Similarly, on 30 November, when the Jewish Fighting Organization struck again:

Yesterday a political assassination was carried out in the ghetto: Israel First, the head of the economic division of the Jewish community, and a close associate of the 'regime', one of the Jews whom the Germans prized greatly, was killed by two shots in Muranowska Street. This Jew was involved in large-scale dealings in partnership with and under the aegis of the German authorities. He had certainly become very wealthy. Who killed him? I can't give a definite answer to this question. There are two possibilities. Firstly, the Germans disposed of him as they have previously disposed of their assistants who have become superfluous ... But there is also a second possibility. He may have been cut down by either a Jew or a Pole, and killed as a traitor, because he had sold his soul to the Germans and assisted them during the 'action'. In fact I do not know if he took part in the terrible events of those days, but at any rate he continually associated with them and mixed in their circles. In the ghetto I have heard that the PPS [Polish Socialist Party] has issued a proclamation, announcing that it has sentenced to death 150 Jews for leading their brothers to their death. Among those who have been sentenced are Lejkin and First. Lejkin was shot dead a few weeks ago, now First's turn has arrived. According to this version he was shot by a Pole from the PPS or a Jew. This event has made a deep impression on the Jews and terrified those who do not have a clear conscience and whose hands are stained with the blood of our martyrs. For myself I incline more to the first possibility, that like the others, First fell victim to these new Huns, as the modern barbarians are called in England.

He did note, with considerable accuracy, Western expressions of concern for the fate of Polish Jews, but had little hope they would affect its fate. Indeed, fears of a new deportation soon surfaced. On 10 November he wrote:

There are further developments here that are intensifying the tension and increasing our terror and dread. Word has it that more gendarmes have arrived in Warsaw and that there is activity starting up at the *Umschlagplatz*: they are clearing out further large rooms there. We should bear in mind that the days of 10, 11 and 12 November are the holidays celebrating Polish independence, and that they are capable – especially during English and American attacks and at the beginning of a second front – of raising the level of disorientation and turmoil among us, in Warsaw in general and among the Jews in particular.

Terror had also returned to the streets:

Yesterday there was a renewed hunt in the streets. The SS were stopping people in the early morning and the afternoon. They were inspecting work-papers. Those detained they handed over to the control of the employment office of the Jewish community and to the *Werterfassung*. Two people were killed. There are two versions of how they died: one that they were ordered to stand on the spot and they didn't stand, but tried to run away; the second is that they were trading in the streets. Whatever the truth of the matter – after a short pause fresh victims have fallen in the ghetto and innocent Jewish blood has been spilled once again. (24 November)

The mood of the ghetto was further undermined by a series of murders on 25 November:

Yesterday was another day of blood-letting for our small community in Warsaw. Many victims fell in the streets. How many? From the community official G. we were given the number 26, but this does not reflect the true figure. It is possible that there were more deaths than this . . . These murders have hit the morale of the Jews hard and plunged them into a bitter, black despair. Are they starting on the survivors now? Were we not told, just a few days ago, through Git. [Giterman], that the Germans gave assurances to the *Judenrat* that no harm would come to the survivors, and life in the ghetto would take on a fixed pattern (stabilization) and so on? And now suddenly a new slaughter, in miniature.

On 6 December Lewin reported rumours of a new *Aktion*. On 4 January he wrote:

In the past few days we have been seized with anxiety and with a terrible dread. The cause of our disquiet is the arrival of Ukrainians in Warsaw. I have heard that a group of 600 men – Ukrainians – has arrived here. All kinds of theories have been put forward to explain their presence. The Jews have been walking around in gloom and despair. We were afraid that they had come for us, that we were on the brink of a new liquidation, this time a complete one.

A week later, he noted:

Someone who knows many people, including those at present at the head of the *Judenrat*, told me that there really was a very grave danger hanging over our heads these past days. There was a proposal, or a plan, for a new expulsion of the Jews of the ghetto or of the survivors. It was to have been carried out at night, when everyone is asleep in bed and it is impossible for them to take refuge anywhere. This time we escaped disaster because of the opposition of the military authorities, of the *Wehrmacht*. One of the generals opposed the planned expulsion on the grounds that the Jews were working and that their output was necessary at the moment. The opponents of a new slaughter came from the supply authorities, from the *Rüstungs-kommando* and not from the *Wehrmacht*, as I wrote above. But it is necessary that we recognize the bitter and terrible truth: *over our heads hangs the perpetual threat of total annihilation.* It seems they have decided to exterminate the whole of European Jewry. (11 January)

These rumours became more ominous. On January 15:

The Jews have been living in dread of this day. Many Jews did not go to sleep until very late last night. The fear of a new 'action' set them on edge and robbed them of sleep. In the past few days, rumour after rumour has been circulating among us, good and bad. As I have already mentioned, an 'action' had been predicted for the 15th of this month. Later it was said that the Germans denied these rumours and the community-leaders reassured the Jews. Do we not recall that on Sunday, three days before the beginning of the 'expulsion' – the slaughter, the commissar of the ghetto, Auerswald, reassured the leader of the Jewish community, Czerniaków, that no 'action' would be carried out in Warsaw and just three days later the action began?

We cannot believe the Germans, the servants of savage killers. We can be content that the night passed peacefully, and that today there is no news of incidents or tragic events. But one cannot but be afraid none the less, since we will be unable to help ourselves and to rescue the few remaining survivors when the day of destruction comes.

The new *Aktion* began on 18 January. We must assume that Lewin perished in it, along with his daughter. The last entry in his diary is in fact for 15 January. Lewin thus does not record this new act of German brutality. He also did not witness the development of the Jewish Fighting Organization, and its heroic resistance to the Nazis first in January and then in April–May 1943.[81] Of Lewin's diary, Emanuel Ringelblum wrote:

The diary of A. L—n, the author of the book *The Cantonists*, is a valuable document. The author has been keeping it for a year and a half and has poured all of his literary talent into it. Every sentence in it is measured. L. has packed the diary not only with everything he has managed to learn about Warsaw, but also with the terrible suffering of the provincial Jews. During the deportation, even as bitter misfortune struck him when his wife Luba was taken away, he continued to record in his diary under the most impossible conditions. The clean and compressed style of the diary, its accuracy and precision in relating facts, and its grave contents qualify it as an important literary document which must be published as soon as possible after the War.[82]

As the martyrdom of Warsaw Jewry reached its height, Lewin called out to God and to the world to avenge the victims:

Those who are far away cannot imagine our bitter situation. They will not understand and will not believe that day after day thousands of men, women and children, innocent of any crime, were taken to their death. And the handful of those remaining after nine weeks is in mortal danger and, it seems, can expect the same fate. Almighty God! Why did this happen? And why is the whole world deaf to our screams?

Earth, earth, do not cover our blood, and let no place be free from our cries! (Yom Kippur, 21 September)

How terrible it is that a whole generation – millions of Jews – has suddenly become a community of 'martyrs', who have had to die in such a cruel, degrading and painful manner and go through the torments of hell before going to the gallows. Earth, earth do not cover our blood and do not keep silent, so that our blood will cry out until the ends of time and demand revenge for this crime that has no parallel in our history and in the whole of human history. (11 November)

Avenging God! Take vengeance for our blood that has been shed, and whatever may be, let them never be forgiven the blood of our innocent children, of our mothers and of our parents. May they reap their just reward! (21 December)

His most profound message is, however, contained in his address on the second anniversary of the death of Yitshak Weissenberg (see Appendix):

Nowadays, death rules in all its majesty; while life hardly glows under a thick layer of ashes. Even this faint glow of life is feeble, miserable and weak, poor, devoid of any free breath, deprived of any spark of spiritual content. The very soul, both in the individual and in community, seems to have starved and perished, to have dulled and atrophied. There remains only the needs of the body; and it leads merely an organic-physiological existence . . .

Yet, we wish to live on, to continue as free and creative men. This shall be our test. If, under the thick layer of ashes our life is not extinguished, this will prove the triumph of the human over the inhuman and that our will to live is mightier than the will to destruction; that we are capable of overcoming all evil forces which attempt to engulf us.

Like the Jews of Warsaw, of which he was a part, Lewin did not outlive these forces. But his words have, miraculously, survived, to move us to compassion and anger, to give a human face to all the victims of the inhuman policies of the Nazi mass-murderers.

A Note on the Text

A large part of the archive of the *Oneg Shabbes* organization was buried in two hideouts, one at 68 Nowolipki Street and another at 34 Świętojerska Street. That at Świętojerska Street could not be found after the war, but the Nowolipki deposit was dug out in two stages. The first part was removed on 18 September 1946 and the second, after the clearing of a large mass of rubble, on 1 December 1950. The first part of Lewin's diary, 'From the Notebooks', was found in the first deposit, the concluding Hebrew section, 'Diary of the Great Deportation', in the second. What has come down to us is certainly not everything Lewin wrote. As we have seen, Ringelblum pointed out that in December 1942 Lewin had been keeping his diary for 18 months, whereas the first entry we possess is for 26 March 1942. The entries in the first half of the diary are not continuous and some may have been lost. In the documentary collection edited by B. Mark, *Tsum tsentn yartog fun oyfshtand in varshever geto* (*On the Tenth Anniversary of the Warsaw Ghetto Revolt*) (Warsaw, 1953), p. 17, there also appears a short list of articles attributed to Lewin and dated 1 May 1942. These are not in the manuscript in the Jewish Historical Institute in Warsaw nor in that possessed by the Kibbutz Lohamei Hagetaot, Israel.

The diary was first published in instalments in Yiddish in *Bleter far geshikhte* (Warsaw) – BFG – as A. Lewin, *Fonem geto togbukh* (*From the Ghetto Diary*). BFG, V, no. 3 (1952), pp. 22–68; VIII, no. 1 (1954), pp. 42–99; VII, nos 2–3 (1954), pp. 110–240. It was translated, not very satisfactorily, into Polish and appeared in *Biuletyn Żydowskiego Instytutu Historycznego*, 19–20 (1956), pp. 125–37; 21 (1957), pp. 171–205; 22 (1957), pp. 85–107; 23 (1957), pp. 71–9; 24 (1957), pp. 42–55; and 25 (1958), pp. 119–30. Both the Yiddish and Polish texts have some curious omissions, which may be the consequence of shortage of space or could result from censorship. I list the most important of them:

1 *8 April*: 'Germans and Germans' does not appear. This is also the only section that we were unable to locate in Warsaw in the Jewish Historical Institute.

2 *16 May*: One paragraph is omitted concerning radio broadcasts from London and Moscow, and a coming food shortage (p. 74 in the text).

3 *24 May*: The sentences wondering whether the conscience of the German had been awakened are omitted (p. 96 in the text).

4 The slogan: 'Lieber der König/Lieber der Kaiser von Gottesgnaden/Als der Lump von Berchtesgaden' is omitted from the entry for *28 May*.

5 *30 May*: The section describing the wealth of the Wilners and the fact that the barber was a member of the *Bund* is omitted (p. 107).

6 In the entry for *31 May* the sentences stating that the Rudas were well-off have been omitted (p. 110).

7 In the same entry, *31 May* (p. 111), the reference to Lewin's cousin being in the Jewish police is replaced by dots (indicating illegibility?) (Yiddish text, p. 60).

8 *2 June*: The paragraphs describing the 'English' counter-offensive in Africa and the air-raids on Lübeck and Rostock are omitted (p. 114).

9 *29 July*: The sentence stating that the *Oneg Shabbes* group discussed the transfer of the archive to Yivo in the US is omitted (p. 141).

10 *30 July*: Paragraph omitted describing a report in the *Deutsche Allgemeine Zeitung* of an SOS message being broadcast in London (p. 143).

11 *16 August*: The line 'If they [the Jewish police] do not fulfil their quotas they are liable to the death-penalty' is omitted (p. 157).

12 *21 August*: Mention of an air-raid is omitted (p. 162).

13 *24 August*: A sentence explaining Roosevelt's silence is omitted (pp. 165–6).

The Hebrew version, which has been of great value to us in preparing this edition, was published by *Beit Lohamei Hagetaot* and Kibbutz Hameuchad in 1969. It has a most useful introduction and notes by the late Tsvi Shner. A short extract from the diary, which was translated by Josef Kermish, appeared in *Yad Vashem Studies*, 6 (1967), pp. 315–30. The text in this edition was translated by Christopher Hutton of the University of Texas at Austin.

A Cup of Tears

A Diary of the Warsaw Ghetto

Part I
From the Notebooks

Thursday, 26 March 1942 – *In Just Half an Hour*

As a proof and illustration of the depths of the seas of misfortune in which we are drowning let me adduce the page of 'news' that I gathered whilst walking about the ghetto for just half an hour. Today I went out at one o'clock in the afternoon to go and visit someone who is ill who lives on what used to be called Kupiecka Street, later Meisels and today, under the German occupation, is called Koza Street. I met a girl there aged around 19 or 20 who arrived today from the small town of Wąwolnica in the district of Lublin. The girl gave me an appalling account of the slaughter carried out there by the Germans last Sunday, 22 March 1942.[1] A few days before a 'fresh-baked' *Volksdeutsche* had been killed in the town.[2] It was probably Poles who killed him. However, it was sufficient pretext for the Germans to attack and massacre a whole community of Jews. Last Sunday three lorry-loads of Germans arrived and led all the Jews who had been rounded up, including the *Judenrat*, to the market-place and shot them there. As many Jews had hidden in Christian homes, the Germans went to each Polish household and wherever they found Jews they took them outside and shot them on the doorstep. The number of Jews murdered in Wąwolnica was approximately 90. I failed to get a clear answer to my question as to the number of Jews living in the town. The girl just responded by saying that 'All, all the Jews in Wąwolnica were murdered.'

I returned by way of Nowolipki Street and met a Jew with whom I had been acquainted before the war and who arrived just two weeks ago from Słonim.[3] In the short conversation that I had with him he laid bare for me again the horrific wound of events there. 'Right in front of me, before my very eyes,' he told me, 'they seized mothers and children and slaughtered them. I escaped by a miracle. Out of the four families who lived in my building only myself and an old Jew survived. Come home with me and I'll tell you the whole story. All the Jews of Novaredok [Nowogródek] were massacred as well.'⁴ I arranged to visit him in a few days and walked on. Coming into the street where I live, Nowolipie Street, I ran into another acquaintance who told me several tragic pieces of news that had come to him by letter. They went as follows:

1 On Purim this year in Zduńska Wola, ten Jews were seized and other Jews forced to hang them on ten gallows in the market-place.⁵
2 This also happened in Łęczyca which is in the same district. (Apparently also in Biezuń.)⁶
3 All the Jews of Izbica, district of Lublin, numbering about 500, have been deported and 1,000 Czech Jews brought in in their place carrying their belongings in suitcases.⁷

As Yehuda Halevi puts it: 'Cup of sorrow may you now be slowly emptied a little, for my limbs and my soul have been filled with your bitterness.'

It was in truth all too much for just one half-hour.

8 April – *Germans and Germans*

A woman acquaintance of mine told me the true story of an incident that happened one day recently and that she was witness to. As is known, there is as yet no wall at Krochmalna Street, only a wire fence. Consequently the location serves as the main centre for smuggling in the ghetto. While my friend was standing at a window that looks out over the fence she saw that the wire was being raised and from the Aryan side a sack of rye or something or other rolled into the ghetto. This was happening in full view of the Polish police-man standing on guard.⁸ So far there is nothing remarkable in all this, for this is a regular occurrence. Except that the policeman failed to see that a German gendarme was slowly approaching. They were a little late in shouting the warning to him – that is, the shout '*Avrom-Peysekh*' was delayed slightly, the meaning of which at this location (or 'target' [*meta*] as such locations are known⁹) is 'Danger, gendarme approaching'. The gendarme arrived, but in the meantime the sack had disappeared. The Polish policeman stood there completely terrified and distraught. The gendarme had spotted the sack 'vanishing'. The gendarme said to the policeman: 'I will come back in 20 minutes and by then the sack must be back where it was.' The gendarme went off, and the policeman was left standing completely helpless. His position really was a difficult one. There was no way of getting the same sack back, as it was far out of his sight. The minutes were ticking away fast. What could he do? Just at that moment he saw a Jew passing by on the 'Semitic' side carrying a sack at his side. The policeman shouted out 'Halt! Bring that sack here!' The Jew protested: he had a permit and the goods were perfectly legal. But the policeman didn't give up: 'I put myself in danger for your sakes and turn a blind eye to your smuggling and you're giving me trouble over some sack. There is nothing to discuss: the sack stays here!' Other smugglers came up and tried to calm the Jew down. They promised to collect money and to compensate him for the sack and its contents. The Jew stood there confused, uncertain what to do. The 20 minutes passed and the gendarme returned exactly as the time was up. He asked the policeman whether the sack had been returned. The policeman pointed to the sack and said: 'There it is, in front of you!' The gendarme asked: 'Is this the same sack?', accompanying the question with a wink. The policeman replied that, yes, it really was the same sack.

The Jew, who the whole time had been standing to one side listening intently to the exchanges, did not stand idly by, but went up to the gendarme and returned to his refrain, that he had a permit, that the sack was his and the goods were perfectly legal. Hearing this, the gendarme ordered the Jew to take the sack and rebuked the policeman severely. 'What is the meaning of all this?' The policeman stood deathly pale, not knowing what to do or to answer. Finally he explained, stammering, that the sack in question had disappeared and he didn't know where. He had been unable to get it back. 'In that case,' said the gendarme, 'this will cost you 500 zloty.' Without much hesitation the policeman took out his wallet and paid the gendarme 500 zloty in cash. The gendarme took the money, stood looking round him, then, catching sight of an old Jew crossing the street, he called out to him: 'Come here!' The Jew, trembling with fear, came up to the gendarme. 'How old are you?' asked the gendarme. 'Seventy-two,' the old man managed to splutter. 'There you go,' said the gendarme, 'here's 72 zloty for you', and handed him the sum. Then he called over a girl from among those begging for a handout and put the same question to her. The Jews whispered in her ear that she should say '15'. The gendarme gave her 8 zloty. The gendarme went on like this until he had distributed all of the 500 zloty.

The Jews began to crowd round the strange gendarme. He smiled at them and said 'Ja, ein guter Deutcher, nicht wahr?' [Yes, I'm a good German, aren't I?][10]

The same woman told me about two other events that happened in the last few weeks on this well-known street.

In the first, a German gendarme chanced upon a Jewish girl, about ten years old, on the Aryan side. He ordered her to move some linens from one place to another. The girl refused to carry out the order and replied stubbornly: 'What will you do to me? Shoot me? Go ahead, shoot! I've got nothing to lose and I couldn't care less.' (Both the gendarme and the girl were speaking in Polish.) When the girl tried to get back into the ghetto through a hole in the wall the gendarme fired and killed her on the spot.

In the second incident, a gendarme came across a group of Jewish children, nearly 20 in number, in the corner of one of the courtyards on the Aryan side. Of course they were absolutely terrified. The German smiled at them from a distance and ordered them to come up to him. The children approached him and the gendarme called over a Jewish policeman and ordered him to lead the children back to the ghetto. One girl was sobbing bitterly. The gendarme asked why she was crying, and was told that she had left behind a few potatoes collected from the Christians. She had left them in the corner of the courtyard, where they were discovered. The gendarme went with the girl, took her back to the corner of the courtyard and told her to gather up the potatoes. He then accompanied her until she reached the Jewish side of the wall safely.

Yes, it seems that there are Germans and Germans.

9 May – *End of Shabbat, Heard and Seen*

In Ostrowiec, district of Kielce, which had the reputation of being a quiet town where Jews – including many driven out from other areas, mainly from Pomerania and Poznań and the so-called 'Warthegau'[11] – were able to make some kind of existence for themselves and where food was also cheap, terrible things have been happening lately. One day recently – I don't know the exact date – they were quite simply massacring Jews. Several hundred Jews were shot down in the street. But this wasn't enough for the German butchers. After the massacre in the street they drew up a list of the 250 Jews, those best known in the town, and shot them.[12] The news was brought by a woman who fled to Warsaw to the ghetto in the past few days. Her husband, a practising doctor in Ostrowiec, was on the list of the 250 Jews and was shot. (Heard from Dr Syrkin-Biernstein,[13] in the Jewish community (*Kehilla*) building.[14])

After seven and a half months' confinement in the Daniłowicz-owska and Gęsia Prisons,[15] Hanka Tauber, the daughter of Dr Majer Tauber,[16] has been released. Last autumn she was arrested at one of the gates to the ghetto trying to smuggle her way in. She had worked the whole summer labouring in the fields in the Hrubieszów area, near Lublin. She and her friend Rubinsztajn travelled together as Aryans with Aryan papers on them. They were both arrested jumping off an Aryan tram-car that at that time still traversed the ghetto. The young man took the whole responsibility on himself. In the last few days Miss Tauber was brought before a German court and sentenced to seven months' imprisonment. Since she had already been in prison for seven and a half months, she was released.

The young man decided not to wait for his trial, which would have had much graver consequences for him as the main defendant. A short while ago he escaped. He was afraid that he would be sent to a concentration camp, something which recently has been happening repeatedly to Jewish prisoners in the Gęsia Prison. He got over the prison wall at dawn with a ladder and disappeared. As a punishment the Gestapo arrested his entire family, that is, his father, mother, sister and brother. They are all in the Gęsia Prison.

My sister who lives at 17 Dzielna Street gave me the following authentic account of what happened to someone who lives on the same courtyard this week. A 38-year-old house-painter who had not been living in the building very long left for work at five o'clock in the morning. In the street he was stopped by a gendarme and asked what he was doing on the street so early. He replied that he was a painter and that he was going to work. In that case, said the gendarme, come and block up a hole in the ghetto wall. The Jew went with the gendarme to the hole, took a look at it, and began to get ready to fix it. In the meantime a second gendarme arrived from a different direction and saw from the distance the Jew busy at the hole. Suspecting him of trying to smuggle himself out to the Aryan side, he didn't stop to ask questions and opened fire. The Jew fell dead on the spot.

Today on Lesh [Leszno][17] Street, in the direction of Tłomackie or Karmelicka Streets, at about six o'clock in the evening I saw a police car drive by in which there were two Gestapo officers in the front and three or four bearded Jews in the back, with white faces and terrified, extinguished eyes. The sight of these Jews in this elegant limousine made me shudder, as it did no doubt many of the other Jews who saw them pass.

In the ghetto there are persistent rumours of disturbances or even of a revolution in Italy. There are several different versions. Version one: there is supposed to have been an uprising in Italy. Mussolini has been killed. Version two: Mussolini has been deposed from power and a great demonstration of women has taken place against the war. The army is said to have been ordered to open fire on the women, but refused to carry out the order. The German Gestapo has been dispatched to Italy to bring the situation under control.

Many Jews in the ghetto are quite certain in their belief that the war will end in the coming months. The most fervent optimists claim that the war will be at an end in the next two months, in June or July.

Sunday, 10 May

Two Jews told me today that the governor-general, Frank,[18] has published an order requiring that the anti-Jewish policies be softened slightly. It is for this reason that the expulsion of Warsaw Jews has not been carried out as planned. One of my informants added that this order is the result of the efforts of German millionaires in America. Apparently there were threats to do to the Germans in America what is being done to Jews here. American-German million-aires are supposed to have intervened in Berlin and as a consequence Frank's decree was issued.

Refugees from Aleksandrów Kujawski told me a few days ago that all the remaining Jews in the entire Nieszawa district[19] – about 70 in number – have been deported. From this same source I heard that Poles were deported as well, because fortifications were being constructed there, on what was the German–Russian border. Today this same refugee told me that the Nieszawa Jews and all other Jews left there were believed to have been deported to Romania. This rumour is most probably close to the truth, as another Jew happened to remark to me that reports had arrived from Bessarabia from Lublin Jews who had been transported there by the Germans. Someone else told me that news had also been received from Romania from Jews who had been deported from Łódź. The Jews were said to be being deployed in agricultural labour.[20]

One of my closest friends told me the following, which was recounted to him by someone who took part in the meeting I am about to describe: a meeting was held to discuss the removal of the Jews from Warsaw. At this meeting (exactly who the participants were I do not know) it was shown that Jews in the ghetto are produc-tive and contribute a lot to the German economy, and in the context of this meeting two plans emerged: (1) the removal from the ghetto of all the beggar-children, and (2) the introduction of home-work or small-scale production by women at home. For the first plan ten Jewish concerns were said to have committed themselves to give 5,000 zloty a month, making a total of 50,000 zloty a month, and with this money all the beggar-children would be collected up and sent out to a boarding-school which would be specially set up for them in Otwock or Falenica. For the second plan, Jewish women teachers of handicrafts from the former Jewish elementary and middle-schools would act as instructors to teach Jewish women how to make various handicraft articles which would also go to the Germans. Several Jewish businessmen would also take part in this initiative. As a result of this meeting it is said that the plan to remove all the Jews from Warsaw had been cancelled.[21]

Yesterday I heard that Polish policemen numbering several hundred – 200 to 600 – have received an order to report on Monday at six o'clock in the morning ready to travel. They must be being sent away from Warsaw. Where to – is not known. Perhaps to Lublin?

Word has it that all the Poles have been removed from the even-numbered side of Marzałkowska Street and from the Aleje Jerozolimskie. It is said that many women, especially pregnant women, have been brought to Warsaw from Germany.[22]

Someone called Manel, who works at the headquarters of the Jewish police,[23] told me an almost unbelievable yet true story about a Polish Jew who served for some time ... in the German army.

This is the story as I heard it. A young Jew, a farm-worker, who comes from the area of Nowy Dwór on the Vistula, a big, strong, well-built blond-haired man, set off eastwards at the outbreak of the war, when the Germans were approaching Modlin, and got as far as Estonia,[24] where he got work as a farm-worker with an Estonian peasant, a *Volksdeutsche*. The Jew worked for the German, who was very pleased with his work, until the German army occupied Estonia. Even then he continued to work. As everywhere else, the authorities raised the ethnic Germans to the status of first-class citizens and granted them certain privileges. The Germans accepted these with open arms. Then an order was issued requiring that every *Volksdeutsche* was to give up to the army's supply convoy a cart and two good horses and ... one of his sons as a driver. Our *Volksdeutsche*, who was probably a good patriot and a devoted follower of Hitler, was not enthusiastic about the idea of giving up a son, his own flesh and blood. So he turned to the Jew and offered him 200 marks in payment for presenting himself with the horses and the cart as his son. The Jew agreed to the suggestion. For a while he served in a supply-convoy and drove back and forth at the front, until the whole convoy was destroyed by the Russians. Then all the remaining personnel from the convoy were taken into active service in the army. Our Jew from Nowy Dwór became a German artilleryman. He has horrific stories about the front. Whole fields were blasted into the air. People and earth were hurled dozens of metres into the air and then down into a deep pit. Mines were everywhere. The Jew was also involved in burying the dead bodies, of which there were vast numbers. In the course of this work, the Jew – and he was not alone in this – filled up his two breast-pockets, one with around 75,000 marks, the second with a large number of gold rings, all this found on the bodies of the dead German soldiers.

The Jew continued to fight until he was wounded. He was brought into an army hospital. Firstly they emptied his two pockets, then they examined him and discovered that he was . . . a Jew. An inquiry was set in motion. The truth surfaced like oil on water and the 'criminal' impostor was handed over to a military court. The Jew said that he was well liked in his unit and his superiors didn't want him killed. To cut a long story short, a trial was held and our Jew was sentenced to just six months in a work-camp. The Jew spent the six months in a work-camp near Chełm. Later he returned to Nowy Dwór, which he was subsequently forced to leave. Today he lives in the Warsaw ghetto. However, his boss, the Estonian *Volksdeutsche*, and his son, were both sentenced to death. Nazi justice.

Lately cases of Jews being grabbed on the street and taken into the Pawiak Prison have been on the increase.[25] Inside, appalling things are done to them. I have heard the details of two such cases and wish to recount what happened. (a) Two Jews were seized; one of them was given a piece of wood and forced to hit the other. After being subjected to prolonged and brutal torture, one of the Jews was released at about nine o'clock that evening. He managed to run home in time. The second was not set free until eleven that night. The unfortunate Jew was shot dead by a German patrol.[26] (b) A respectably dressed Jew was brought into the Pawiak. First he was viciously beaten. Then a beggar was brought in. Both were told to strip off naked. The well-dressed Jew had to put on the rags of the beggar, who in turn had to put on the clothes of the better-off Jew.

These seizures are carried out in various ways. People are pulled off the street into cars, gendarmes on foot stop anyone they feel like. It seems that in the main they pick on Jews with beards. But they also grab clean-shaven Jews. One place that has become particularly dangerous is the alleyway by the prison between Dzielna and Pawia Streets, the so-called Więzienna. It is overlooked by a watch-tower with a guard, probably a *Volksdeutsche*, who looks down at the passing Jews. When the mood takes him he shouts out: 'Halt! Come here!' Down below there is a Polish policeman. When the German orders it he stops the Jew and leads him into the Pawiak. Lately Jews have been avoiding the alleyway past the prison.

The rumours about unrest in Italy still persist in the ghetto. The strangest stories are going round: Italy has surrendered, Ciano is said to have gone to London, the old King Emmanuel has abdicated, there are serious disturbances in northern Italy etc.[27] Today a Jew who generally has accurate information told me the following in connection with the situation in Italy. Living in the ghetto is a young Jewish woman who before the war worked in the Italian consulate in Warsaw. Recently a Polish woman, a friend of hers, came to see her. She had worked with her at the consulate and still works today in an official Italian institution. She told her that Italy was in chaos and in the process of disintegration. The top officials are leaving their posts and fleeing.

The same person, the Jew who told me all this, through his work as an official in the Jewish community, comes into contact almost every day with Polish official circles. According to him, there is a widespread belief prevailing among the Poles that ultimately it must come to war between England and Russia, since otherwise England will be unable to implement the restoration of the Polish state, that is, a victorious Soviet Union would not permit this. I can recall that the well-known revisionist Dr von Weisel many years ago predicted that war was imminent between England and Russia.[28] His prophecy was not fulfilled then; let us hope that it will not be this time.

Tuesday, 12 May

Scarcely a day goes by without Jewish blood being spilled on the streets and paving stones of the Warsaw ghetto. Yesterday a woman involved in smuggling was shot dead on Krochmalna Street. Last night there were two further victims of the continuation of the Bartholomew Night massacre carried out in the ghetto on the night of 17–18 April, that tragic Friday night. Then, as is well known, 52 Jews were shot down in the streets like dogs.[29]

The head of the community-kitchen at 2 Orla Street, Sklar, was taken from his home that night, but his body was not found among the dead in the streets.[30] No one knew where he was. He was thought

most likely to be in the Pawiak Prison. In fact he had spent a few
weeks in prison, in the Pawiak, and last night his body was found.
The Nazi murderers shot a second Jew at 19 Zamenhof Street at the
Jewish post office.[31] According to what I have heard he was a former
tram-worker, Bac.[32] Apparently he had also been in the Pawiak. This
morning I saw with my own eyes the large bloodstain on the pavement outside the post office. 'Woe to the eyes that must look upon
such things.' According to another source, the murdered man was a
currency-dealer, who had been held in the Pawiak.

Wednesday, 13 May

According to additional information that I have received today, not
two, but four bodies of executed Jews were found yesterday. As
follows: at 19 Zamenhof Street, at the post office, at 54 and 68a
Nowolipki Street, and at 64 Pawia Street. The Jewish tram-worker
was apparently called Bas [sic]. Who the other martyrs were I do not
know.[33]

Last Wednesday, 6 May 1942, almost all the Jews of Dęblin and
Ryki were deported. I was told that about 50 Jews remained in
Dęblin, those fit and strong, healthy and capable of manual work,
along with their families. The others were sent off to an unknown
destination.[34]

Something happened yesterday for which there is no name in our
impoverished tongue. I know of no word that could convey or do
justice to what happened. I will simply recount the facts as I heard
them from different people, as well as from someone who heard
about it from one of those involved . . . just after the devilish game
had ended.

Yesterday the Germans, with the help of the Jewish police,
rounded up young Jewish girls, and women both young and old, and
also men with and without beards on the streets and in particular
among the occupants of 38 Dzielna Street. Two lorry-loads of
Germans, airforce, SS and men from other units, as well as a smaller
vehicle with officers in it, drew up at the entrance to 38 Dzielna
Street. First of all they photographed all the young girls – incidentally, they had picked out girls and women who were particularly

respectable-looking and expensively dressed. They they pushed all the Jewish men and women into the bath-house that is in the corner of the courtyard of the above-mentioned building. Once inside they photographed all the women again. Then they forced the men and women to strip completely naked. German officers divided them into pairs made of one from each sex from among the Jews. They matched young girls to old men, and conversely, young boys with old women. Then they forced the two sexes to commit a sexual act. These scenes, that is, the sexual relations (we must assume that they were only apparent relations) were filmed with special apparatus that had been brought in for the purpose. The number of Nazis present is estimated at 200. These horrifically cruel and macabre barbarities took place in the Warsaw ghetto on Tuesday, between three and six o'clock in the afternoon.[35]

I have heard that large-scale round-ups took place yesterday on the Aryan side. Kercelak Square was surrounded, all goods were confiscated and all men and women detained.[36] Only the old people were allowed to leave. Everyone else was taken off directly to the railway-station. Most probably they were sent to Germany to work.

In connection with the deportation of Poles to Germany, Jewish workers, in the first instance mechanics and metal-workers, are being sent to work on the Aryan side in the German *placówki*, so-called.[37] These Jewish workers spend the whole week at their place of work where they are fed. On Saturday afternoon they are brought back inside the ghetto, where they remain until Monday morning. Then they have to go back to work on the other side of the ghetto wall.

Saturday night, 16 May

This Sabbath has been for me heavy with gloom and depression, although it may be that the first rays of light are glowing on the dark horizon, heralding a bright dawn. This depressed state of mind was brought on by the sad news heard from Rabbi H.,[38] of five murdered Jews whose bodies were taken by the Jewish police to 19 Zamenhof Street in the middle of the night. They lay there until five in the morning. Later there was talk of nine to eleven martyrs. Who these victims were and where they were murdered is for the time being unknown.

When I hear news of this kind my throat is choked and there is a terrible weight on my heart. I feel as if I am being throttled and suffocated by a black fear. The abyss is getting ever closer to each one of us, the bestial visage of the Nazi apocalypse, with the words death, destruction, doom, death-agony written on its forehead. An unremitting insecurity, a never-ending fear, is the most terrible aspect of all our tragic and bitter experiences. If we ever live to see the end of this cruel war and are able as free people and citizens to look back on the war-years that we have lived through, then we will surely conclude that the most terrible and unholy, the most destructive aspect for our nervous system and our health was to live day and night in an atmosphere of unending fear and terror for our physical survival, in a continual wavering between life and death – a state where every passing minute brought with it the danger that our hearts would literally burst with fear and dread.

It all began in mid-November 1939 with the murder of 53 innocent Jews from 9 Nalewki Street.[39] Soon after this there followed the Kott affair when a further 300 Jews were seized and killed.[40] They were for the most part from the free intelligentsia, doctors, lawyers, teachers etc. From that moment on there has been no respite. A never-ending series of round-ups on the streets for forced labour, searches and looting, continual insults and humiliations. After the outbreak of the war between Germany and the Soviet Union, since the tidings of Job have begun to reach us, of mass-murders and the extermination of entire historic and illustrious Jewish communities such as Wilno, the Jerusalem of Lithuania, Kowno, Słonim, Lwów, Lublin and dozens of others – who can begin to comprehend it all? The burden on our souls and on our thoughts has become so heavy, oppressive, that it is almost unbearable. I am keenly aware that if our nightmare does not end soon, then many of us, the more sensitive and empathetic natures, will break down. I feel that we are standing on the threshold of the intolerable, between existence and annihilation. I remember that before the war a woman who was living in Vienna at the time Hitler occupied Austria told me that the most terrible thing for the Viennese Jews was the fearful, sleepless nights, a continual pounding of the heart, a waiting for 'them' to come.[41] In Vienna as here Jews were dragged from their homes and taken to concentration camps.

In the afternoon the megaphone announced the sad news of the fall of Kerch.[42] The news hit me very hard. For the truth is, nowadays our hearts beat in time with the events taking place on Russian territory, where a life and death struggle is being waged between man and beast, between hope for a better tomorrow for a harried and bloodied humanity and fear of the victory of the most bloodthirsty Nero the world has ever seen. Every shift in the balance in Hitler's favour fills us with boundless misery and despair.

But I also heard something cheering towards evening. I know a Jewish electrician who works the whole week for the Germans, in the midst of the degeneracy, at 25 Aleje Sucha.[43] This Jew listens all week to radio announcements from London and Moscow, even from America. Among other things, he gave me the following two items of news today. The first was as follows: on Thursday in London a political broadcast was transmitted in Polish. Its basic message was that Hitler is no longer in sole command of the German army, and that the war can be won only by someone who has the army on his side. The announcer also added that it is no secret that von Papen is going round in Ankara telling everyone that the establishment of a Fourth Reich is imminent.[44] Could there be any basis to all this? The second item was the following. The Jewish workers receive a loaf of bread when they go home for half of Saturday and Sunday.[45] Yesterday they were given only half a loaf, with the explanation that there may be a shortage of bread. Bread has to be saved and stored for a time when no bread at all will be arriving. Instead of bread there will be soup. This goes to show that they are not exactly overflowing with supplies.

At this workplace, 25 Aleje Sucha, a worker by the name of Winokur was shot dead yesterday at half past one in the afternoon. It happened in the following way: it is forbidden for Jewish workers to return individually to the ghetto, even though each receives an individual pass. The murdered man had obtained his pass at half past seven in the morning, because he said he needed to go home early. But for some unknown reason he didn't go with the group of workers in the lorry which took part of the work-force back to the ghetto at eleven. At about one o'clock he set off for home alone. His boss, driving by on Nowy Świat Street, recognized him. The Jew also spotted his boss and tried to make a run for it. The boss set off after him and caught up with him, took him back in his car to 25 Aleje Sucha and shot him there twice, killing him on the spot.

As regards further cases of filming. I was told the following: at the corner of Żelazna and Chłodna Streets is a Jewish restaurant. Yesterday morning at nine the Germans took out all the waitresses, young girls, and made them line up on the street, instructing them to put on happy and appealing expressions. At the same time they got together a crowd of beggar-children and made them line up on the street and told them to parade past the elegant waitresses with outstretched hands, into which nothing was put. This was recorded on film, and is intended to show that Jews are living in luxury and do not share anything with the hungry. After this the waitresses were taken to chairman Czerniaków's flat at 20 Chłodna Street,[46] made to sit at a table and then orders were given that they be served with carafes of water, to simulate vodka, and other refreshments. The waitresses were again ordered to be cheerful and appear in high spirits. This scene was filmed as well. Later the Germans took pictures in private Jewish flats at 6 Chłodna Street and elsewhere. Only finely furnished flats were filmed. This is supposed to be proof to the 'world' that Jews have it good in the ghetto. And here it is for all to see.[47]

The Jew from 17 Dzielna Street, a house-painter, who was murdered at five o'clock on his way to work – I gave the story a few days ago – had the surname Dziedzic.

Sunday, 17 May

Yesterday a decree was issued forbidding non-Germans from moving to Warsaw. The decree applies in actual fact just to Poles, since Jews are in any case denied all freedom of movement. They are confined to the ghettos, and if they step outside the walls without special permission they are punished with death. In the Jewish prison on Gęsia Street alone, 25 Jews – men and women – have been shot for this sin. Nevertheless a dread has descended on the Jews of Warsaw. Everyone is terrified. For a while now rumours have been circulating of plans to deport the Jews from Warsaw. Exhausted by this continual fear and trembling, waiting for something terrible and unexpected to happen, people were gradually beginning to calm down, since the days were passing and nothing unexpected had happened. But this order has revived the dread of an expulsion once again, b people are making comparisons with the case of Lublin. A short time before the terrible expulsion of the Jews of Lublin a similar decree was issued, forbidding any movement to Lublin from elsewhere.[48]

The extent to which the terror of the Warsaw Jews is justified we do not know. One thing we do know is that it is hard, very hard, to live with permanent terror, and this we feel with body and soul, with every fibre of our being.

I can recall the German correspondent of *Reich* and of the *Deutsche Allgemeine Zeitung* writing about a year ago in *Reich* (Goebbels' weekly) that Roosevelt had published a declaration beginning with the words: 'We cannot accept a world of permanent terror and uncertainty.' This sentence was the substance, the essence of the president's declaration. And in truth Roosevelt captured in these words the tragedy of all the European peoples, and especially that of the Jews. What is important is security; a safe and certain existence must be fought for and won for Europe, one where people will be able to lift their eyes up to the sky, to the sun, and not flicker and tremble like a candle-flame in the wind.

I have heard talk that the Germans have used gas for the first time on the Russian front, beginning with the attack on Kerch. 30,000 Russian soldiers are said to have died as a result of the use of this horrific weapon. Someone told me that Churchill has spoken of this in the House of Commons and had 'sworn' that the whole of Germany would be covered with gas. Of course, the news of Churchill's 'oath' is not genuine and indeed it is questionable whether the Germans really did use gas. The rumours and stories that are born in the ghetto typify the moods and the feelings that govern us Jews. It is a human wish: 'I will see your revenge upon them.' A higher morality cannot accept such feelings and desires. However, these are human yearnings, thoroughly human, in _____ the inhuman and satanic acts of the Germans _____ peoples.

_____ man people responsible for the Nazis' crimes? _____ that we are in conflict with ourselves when we _____ to this question. We want an answer: yes, they _____ it is difficult to answer categorically. We are _____ ke the Nazis. But for all that there will remain with us – and not only with us – an eternal grudge, a grievance against the German people in its totality for having hatched such a poisonous snake as Hitlerism and nurtured and raised it.

Monday, 18 May, towards evening

Spring is late this year. It has been continually cold and wet. Not until today have we had a mild spring day. I am sitting at an open window and do not feel cold. But it is not possible to take pleasure in nature, in the beauty of God's world. We are rotting in a prison, the like of which has never been seen, for the ghetto the Germans have set up for us has no model or precursor in human history. I can remember a spring day, also 18 May, several years before the war, which has become engraved on my memory. I had to deal with some matter at the school administration in the office at 12 Bagatela Street. I set off there at nine in the morning. By ten I had finished dealing with the matter. I took the tram back to my school on Długa Street along the Aleje Ujazdowskie.[49] I was enthralled by the sea of green, the splendour of the tree-lined avenues and the wonderful radiance of the light, the tranquillity. This is why that morning is so deeply etched on my memory. Where can we find today a patch of green, a tree, a field and the chance to walk without terror over God's earth? When will the hour of our liberation strike? When will the sun rise for us, we who are tortured and spat upon?

Today Jewish Warsaw again mourns the loss of human life. Seven Jews have been shot at the corner of Waliców and Chłodna Streets. Among the dead are said to be two Jewish policemen. Also a Jewish woman, a sweet-vendor from 36 Leszno Street, was among the victims. She left home at six this morning with her box of sweets and it was only half past six when they brought back her body. No matter how many are devoured by the smuggling trade, it still continues to flourish and to develop. Even the shadow of death cannot wither it.

I live by the wall that divides the ghetto from Przejazd Street. A gap has appeared in the wall through which someone could quite easily crawl, or which is wide enough for a sack with 100 kg of potatoes or corn or other foodstuffs. The smuggling goes on without a break from dawn at half past five until nine in the evening. What they must go through, those who spend all day busy at the wall, these smugglers, both Jews and Christians (who crawl through the wall to settle their accounts) and the carriers. So often the Germans appear suddenly, or 'Junaks'[50] and civilian German agents, not to mention Polish policemen who for certain reasons will not allow themselves to be bought off. So many of the goods have been confiscated and so many people, Jews and Christians, have perished. A few weeks ago a 33-year-old Jew, Lewinski, was shot dead there; so was a young Christian. An hour ago three shots were fired through the gap into the ghetto, though luckily no one was hit. But five minutes later the crowd of smugglers was back swarming and bustling round the hole. Every few minutes there is complete turmoil, everyone makes a run for it, like mice to their holes. A minute later the smuggling starts up again at full throttle.

Flour, potatoes, milk, butter, meat and other produce are brought into the ghetto. And out of the ghetto still pours a continual stream of Jewish possessions to the Aryan side. Jews are selling up everything they own. Lately a certain distinct type of smuggler has come to my attention. These are Christian women, young and older, who arrive at around dusk loaded down with sacks full of kitchen utensils such as pots and pans, dishes, wash-tubs, frying-pans and other items that they have acquired in the ghetto and smuggle through the gap or over the wall to the Aryan side. It turns out that these Christian women have become specialists in this area: they are buying out the Jewish kitchen. This is a new development. It had all begun with the Jews selling off clothes, furniture, then linen, covers, next pillows, and now it is the turn of the pot and the wash-tub. The poorest Jew or Jewess will have nothing to cook a meal with and nothing to wash his last remaining shirt in. This is a sign of the extreme deprivation into which the broad mass of the people has fallen. Now we shall have to start saying that someone has sold the pot from the kitchen, instead of 'the shirt off their back'.

A telephone call was made this morning from Garbatko-Letnisko to Warsaw.[51] For the time being the Jews are staying where they are, but they are terrified of expulsion. As regards Radom, it was said that there is talk that all Jews without jobs will be deported.

The expulsion from Dęblin was apparently carried out in a particularly bestial fashion. It is said that all those being expelled from the town were divided into separate groups, children separately, women separately, men separately. If this is really what happened, then it is not difficult to imagine what became of the children.

Tuesday, 19 May

There are further stories of Jews being dragged off into the Pawiak Prison. Recently I was told about two such cases. Two bearded men were seized and pulled inside. Their beards were shaven off, with their faces being cut about in the process. They were beaten until they bled, their clothes ripped and their faces half smeared over with tar. In this state they were released. This happened a few days ago.

Yesterday two more Jews were grabbed on Smocza Street and dragged off to the Pawiak. One of them was released in the evening. The second was brought out dead early this morning.

This morning a Jewish woman with two small children came into the ghetto through the gap in the wall by our house. She had the appearance of a Christian. She told me the whole tragic story of what happened on her way to Warsaw. She is from Lublin. Early this morning she had taken the train from Lublin to Warsaw with her husband and children. They were travelling as Aryans. In Otwock the gendarmes recognized that her husband was Jewish. He was taken off the train and shot dead before her eyes. She managed to be strong-willed enough not to betray the fact that she belonged with him, continued her journey and got herself and her children through the gap in the wall into the ghetto. The Germans' crimes and the Jews' tragedies are such that there are no words adequate to describe them. A similar story was recounted to me by an acquaintance of mine named Bergson a few weeks ago. During the expulsion of the Jews from Lublin he had spoken with the wife and daughter of a Lublin barber-surgeon (whose name I can't now recall) who arrived in Warsaw by train travelling as Aryans. Their husband and father was shot down right in front of them. He had got down from the train to go to the toilet (the one in the carriage was closed). On the platform he was stopped by a gendarme, his identity was checked, he was told to run on and was shot from behind. The mother and daughter saw it happen through the train window and managed to hold on to themselves. Shortly afterwards the train moved off.

The filming that the Germans have been carrying out in the ghetto continues. Today they set up a film-session in Szulc's restaurant at the corner of Leszno and Nowolipki Streets. They brought in Jews they had rounded up, ordinary Jews and well-dressed Jews, and also women who were respectably dressed, sat them down at the tables and ordered that they be served with all kinds of food and drink at the expense of the Jewish community: meat, fish, liqueurs, white pastries and other delicacies. The Jews ate and the Germans filmed.[52] It is not hard to imagine the motivation behind this. Let the world see the kind of paradise the Jews are living in. They stuff themselves with fish and goose and drink liqueurs and wine. These despicable scenes went on for several hours.[53]

Today the Germans set up an original film-set at the corner of Nowolipie and Smocza Streets. It involved the finest funeral-wagon in the possession of the Jewish community. Around it were gathered all the cantors of Warsaw, ten in number, with Szerman at their head.[54] This had been arranged by the Germans for the purpose of the film. It seems that they want to show that Jews not only live a cheerful, decent existence, but they also die with dignity, and even get a luxury burial. No good will come for us out of this film lunacy.

This morning at quarter past nine my wife was stopped at the corner of Nowolipie and Karmelicka Streets and made to take part in a film. One German shouted out: 'Look, this one is dressed perfectly well, without jewellery!' She was kept in front of the camera lenses for half an hour. Of course she wasn't the only one. Many women of various ages and classes were held for the same purpose.

Wednesday, 20 May

Once again we have been shaken and dismayed by a new crime committed by these twentieth-century Huns. Yesterday afternoon, at half past two in the afternoon, two officers drove a 17-year-old Jewish girl out from the Pawiak Prison. They took her as far as 11 Pawia Street, led her into the entrance-way, let her walk a few steps in front and shot her several times from behind with a revolver. They had found out that the girl was living on the Aryan side. Yesterday morning she was arrested in her flat, not fully dressed, wearing slippers. She was taken away as she was and after several hours in the Pawiak she was executed without further ado.

It is impossible that so much innocent blood should be spilled without retribution. The day of judgement, the day of reckoning must and will come.

The level of Nazi brutality quite simply lies beyond our power to comprehend. It is inconceivable to us and will seem quite incredible to future generations, the product of our imagination, over-excited by misery and anger.

On Leszno Street, next to Zelazna Street, stand two Jewish boys aged about ten to twelve, quite well-dressed, and look into a shop-window. Two gendarmes come up, raise their right legs and kick the boys with all their strength in the behind. It should not be forgotten that the boots of the Teutonic soldiers are heavily shod. I'm not making this story up, God forbid. It happened today, Wednesday, at half past twelve.

There are a few fortunate Jews who in the coming days will have the privilege of leaving our vale of tears, the whole European valley of blood and weeping, and will depart for one of the free South American countries.

In the Warsaw ghetto there are up to about 20 Jews who hold a passport from Uruguay, Paraguay or some other South American republic. Some of the passport-holders are return immigrants who obtained this citizenship whilst in America, while others have been sent a passport from Switzerland since the outbreak of the war. It turns out that according to the laws of some of these South American countries one can also obtain citizenship from abroad, by buying a plot of land there. In the consulates of these countries in Switzerland it has been possible to buy a passport for a large sum of money.[55]

There is a family by the name of Wajngot in Warsaw that consists of the parents and children, two sons and one daughter. One of the sons lives in Switzerland and is rich. The second son was living in Lwów when the Russians were there. The brother in Switzerland sent two Uruguayan passports, one to the brother in Lwów and the other to the sister in Warsaw. The Germans, it seems, also viewed this sudden acquisition of a foreign nationality as legal. When the

Germans occupied Galicia,[56] the son was able to get to Warsaw without difficulty on the strength of the passport and for a long time was able to make daily visits to the Aryan side.

A few weeks ago the son Wajngot received an invitation to come on such and such a day at a given hour to the Pawiak Prison. The whole family was very frightened and went through several sleepless nights. The father is a Hasidic Jew and his rebbe lives in the ghetto. He went to the rebbe to seek his advice as to whether his son should keep the appointment. The rebbe examined the invitation closely and said that it was all right to go. This advice was justified by the rebbe by the fact that on the invitation – not instruction – was written 'Mr' and not 'The Jew'. This being the case, reasoned the rebbe correctly, there was no need to be afraid.

At the appointed hour – ten in the morning – Wajngot presented himself at the Pawiak. He was led into a large, heated room. There were 14 Jews gathered there, men and women. Several officers came in. One of them addressed the Jews in a dignified and respectful manner and informed them that relations with the states in South America were deteriorating and that it was possible that relations would be broken off. At present there existed a possibility of exchanging Germans in South America for Jews who held appropriate passports (for each Jew, three Germans would be sent over). He proposed to the Jews therefore that they should leave Warsaw, travel to Switzerland and then continue across the Atlantic. The Germans would afford them every assistance and whoever wished to marry, had no wife, could carry out the formalities quickly and take her as well.

All the Jews present immediately expressed their willingness to travel. There was just one old woman who explained that she was old and weak, lived with her children in Warsaw and couldn't set off alone into the wide world. The officer tried to persuade the old woman that she should, none the less, leave Warsaw, saying gently, she could see, couldn't she, how things looked in the ghetto, and that things would most likely get worse. It would be better for her if she left the ghetto.

After this strange conference, all those Jews who years ago returned from overseas have produced their American passports that they had not previously registered with the authorities. The Germans are searching high and low for Jews such as these and are not making any difficulties at all for them to leave. It's possible that some Jews have already left or are leaving in the next few days. These Jews are fortunate indeed.

Thursday, 21 May – *The Eve of Shavuot*

There is great sadness in our souls and a fearful weight on our heart. News arrives constantly of the slaughter of Jews. I have heard that six Jews were killed in the Pawiak Prison last night. People say that one of the victims was an official of the Łódź community, Nadel. Mr K.[57] told me today of the mass-slaughter of the Jews of Tomaszów Mazowiecki.[58] Last week they murdered all the members of the *Judenrat* with their families – 170 people in all.

I am amazed that I still see Jews bustling about and busy with 'important' matters. I have such an uncanny and terrible feeling when I hear bad news, and there is sadly no good news, that my heart begins to hurt, the pain nearly drives me insane. Is there any hope left for us? When will the dance of death come to an end? When will we glimpse the brilliance of the morning star?

Yesterday a Jew was killed in a manner that was exceptional for its refined cynicism and human degradation even by the standards of the Nazi murderers and barbarians. At ten in the evening the Germans rang the bell of 17 Dzielna Street. They brought in a poor and elderly Jew and said that he should be fed, since they had found him out late, when no one is allowed on the streets, and he had explained to them that he had nowhere to spend the night and that he hadn't eaten all day. On the same courtyard there is a bakery. The Jews in the air-defence who were standing guard at the entrance to the courtyard went in to see the baker, took a loaf of bread from him and gave the homeless and hungry Jew this to eat. An hour later the Germans called again. They wanted to know if their order had been carried out and the Jew had been fed properly. On receiving a positive answer they took the Jew and shot him on the spot. If I hadn't heard this from the mouth of my own sister who lives on the same courtyard, I wouldn't have believed that such barefaced savagery was possible.

People are saying that lists have already been prepared of

candidates for the work camps. This afternoon there were rumours
going around that the Jewish police has been mobilized for tonight in
order to carry out the round-up [in Polish, *łapanka*], well-known to
us from a year ago. This means that we are once again faced with the
prospect of orgies of violence like those in the summers of 1940 and
1941. Once again, hundreds and thousands of ordinary Jews, Jewish
workers and labourers, will pay with their health and their lives, and
Polish earth will be covered with the fresh graves of Jewish martyrs.[59]

I have learnt from a completely reliable source that the industrial
concerns that are being opened on the Aryan side are being obliged
by the German authorities to employ exclusively Jews. A certain
metal-works, Jewish property that is under the management of a
commissioner, has been closed up to now. Recently the commissioner made an approach to the authorities about opening the
factory. An inspection-committee concluded that the factory was
important for the war-effort and gave permission for it to open, but
on the condition that all skilled workers had to be Jews. Apparently
Poles with special skills have to be sent to Germany. The round-up
that the Jews are dreading is supposedly directed at the metal-
workers who registered for work in the factories on the Aryan side
but didn't present themselves for work. In Rudski's enormous
factory in Mińsk Mazowiecki all the workers are Belgian and French.

Hitlerism in this respect represents a throw-back to the dark days
of Babylonia and Assyria. For Hitler plans to uproot and drive entire
nations from one end of Europe to the other and even from one
continent to another.

The ghetto is most terrible to behold with its crowds of drawn
faces with the colour drained out them. Some of them have the look
of corpses that have been in the ground a few weeks. They are so
horrifying that they cause us to shudder instinctively. Against the
background of these literally skeletal figures and against the all-
embracing gloom and despair that stares from every pair of eyes,
from the packed mass of passers-by, a certain type of girl or young
woman, few in number it must be said, shocks with her over-elegant
attire. Their new outfits, their wavy peroxide hair, beautifully styled,
their brightly powdered cheeks and their purple-red lips, stab at the
eyes of the onlooker. Walking the streets I observe this sickly
elegance and am shamed in my own eyes. These women look as if

their silk garments are pulled over shrouds. It seems that a hunger for jewellery and fine clothes is a national weakness of ours. It is not for nothing that we can find regulations and decrees against women's silk dresses and jewellery in the records of the Council of the Four Lands and in many other places. These regulations and decrees were also issued as far as I remember in times of great upheaval and disaster for our people, for instance after the Chmielnicki massacres. It pains me that Jewish women have so little sense of modesty and moderation, so little of what in Polish is known as *umiar*.[60] But what might have been expected is that in terrible and tragic days such as these this weakness for clothes and external beauty would have been contained and set aside.

Even in peace-time the contrast between women's clothing in Berlin and here in Warsaw was very marked. There there was unadorned simplicity, the hair combed neatly under a hair-net, a clean, simple dress. Here, by contrast, we can recall the dazzling elegance of the Warsaw streets. It is understandable that certain Germans, even the better ones, gape in amazement at our decked-out ladies. The worst ones, the Nazis, hate us all the more for this. In either case this is in my opinion a very undesirable and unhealthy phenomenon. It would be a good idea if action was set in motion in our own little world against blatant female elegance. Of course, I am talking about an information-campaign only.

In the last few days we have begun to see very many German Jews in the ghetto. They are recognizable by a yellow Star of David with the legend *Jude*.[61] They go in procession to and from work. They also walk around singly. For the time being no contact has established itself between us and them. Between us and them there still stands a wall of many hundred years of prejudice and linguistic division. In the final analysis it is difficult for a Jew from Hanover to have a conversation with a Jew from Piaseczno or Gryca and vice versa. They simply are not able to communicate. Let us hope that time will bring about a rapprochement. They will mix in with us and assimilate with us. Similar things have happened more than once in our history: the exiles from Spain in Germany and Poland, and recently the Yemenite and German community in Palestine. Here I would just like to draw attention to the external appearance of the German Jews, to the anthropological side of the problem. I look closely into their faces and am amazed at the powerful similarity to us: they resemble us like two peas in a pod. If it wasn't for the yellow star on their chests we would have no way of telling that we have a German Jew in front of us of many generations. Thus hundreds of years of climatic (to some extent), linguistic and cultural differences have not been able to erase or blur our common origin and shared anthropological build. On the basis of this observation we can say that the concepts 'Western European' and 'Eastern European' Jews are merely superficial, without substance. For in reality we have been formed of the same dough, we are like two brothers, one of whom fate has dispatched to some far-off place, to America, whilst the second remains in his Polish or Lithuanian town. When the two meet after 15 or 20 years there is a certain feeling of estrangement or bashfulness between them. In the course of time the sense of brotherhood conquers all the feelings of alienation that time and differences of culture have given rise to. Thus Abe Kahan (the editor of *Forverts*) tells in his memoirs how, when his younger brother came to America, it was difficult for him to address his older brother as a member of the same family, with *du* for 'you'.[62] Kahan had to work very hard to break down the distance and timidity of his younger brother. We and the German Jews are also brothers who have been separated from each other for rather a long time. In fact we left Germany in the fourteenth or fifteenth century. Now we meet again under tragic circumstances. We still feel estranged from each other, but this estrangement will soon disappear and we will be at ease with one another like brothers once again.

In one of his stories (if I'm not mistaken in 'Rvatch' ['The Grabber']) Ehrenburg describes in an aesthetically successful way, full of seriousness and truth, the tragedy of a woman who had been the director of a *Gymnasium* [secondary school] before the revolution and who was transformed subsequently into a helpless and ridiculous creature, into a wet rag, as Ehrenburg puts it. This is the tragedy of the declassed, of people who have lost their property and position in society. They have to suffer not only material deprivation but moral humiliation and shame. The tragedies of this kind are no less grave, pitiful and dismaying than the tragedies that are caused to us by the German vandals.

In our parochial, intimate little world there are certain individuals who have made their way up to the top, to pray at the Eastern Wall, individuals who are not fit or suitable to be at the head of a Jewish community, and this the greatest in Europe, and at such an appalling time. This is one of the inevitable results of war, the calamity of 'the good are cast down and the lowly raised up', the curse of leaders who are not fit for their office.

It seems that no part or sector of our public life is free from this curse. Apparently this is how things have always been with us Jews. Of the period of seizures of children under Tsar Nicholas I the writer Josef Rabinowicz writes that at the head of the communities could be found either holy men, ready to sacrifice themselves for the good of the whole, or contemptible scoundrels. The righteous are moved aside, the contemptible remain, the dregs of our society. Today we find ourselves in this position again. These men are the cause of the tragedies that I recount in these lines.[63]

These thoughts came to me as I was standing in one of our societal organizations and I watched as Messrs K. and S. bustled about in the pose of leaders, directors. They don't see anyone around them, do not recognize anyone (except of course other important people), so their whole demeanour cries out: 'Nie troń mienia!' ['Keep your distance!'].

Let us hope that this cancer will be removed from our collective body along with Hitler.

Friday, 22 May – *First Day of Shavuot*

To put the record straight I will set down the exact details of the murder that happened on Wednesday at 17 Dzielna Street. The murdered man was a Jewish beggar aged about 30. A German patrol ran into him in the street at half past nine. One gendarme wanted to shoot him, but the other stopped him. They took him to the above-mentioned building and ordered that he be fed and given a place to sleep. He was fed without delay. The question of a place to sleep was more difficult. In the same set of buildings there is a public brothel. The 'tenants' live four to a room. The Germans went to the brothel and gave instructions that the beggar was to sleep there. The gendarmes then left. A row started between the girls, their boss and the beggar. They didn't want to let him sleep there with them as he was so dirty. They offered him money. The beggar stubbornly refused to leave; he wanted to sleep there, since that is what the Germans told him to do. When they tried to get him out by force he began to shout 'Police!' A second patrol arrived. The girls explained that they were too disgusted to sleep with the filthy beggar. The Germans told the Jew to go with them, took him to the church opposite the Pawiak and shot him.

Even though people said that nothing would happen there was a round-up last night carried out by the Jewish police. The Jewish police came to our building three times, looking for certain young people. Two of them were not sleeping at home and one has a chest illness so they did not take him. However, they took away a young man who had hidden in our building. The poor man fell into their hands by pure chance.

As yet I have no knowledge of the round-up or how it was carried out.

Today I received political news that sounds quite sensational. Goering has had a meeting with Laval.[64] As a result of their meeting Laval has approached Roosevelt as an intermediary with a peace proposal on behalf of Germany. Germany proposes the following conditions: Hitler and Himmler will leave power, a new government will be created with Goering, Hugenberg (the representative of manufacturing industry),[65] von Papen at its head. Roosevelt has informed the government in London of the peace proposal. Because of the importance of peace, a special sitting of parliament has been called. The parliament decided unanimously that no kind of negotiations would be entered into with this Germany, that is, that only capitulation can end the war. After the sitting Churchill made a speech and stated that if the German people does not come to its senses, peace will be concluded over the ruins of the German cities.

A degree of confirmation of this news can be seen in the denial published today in the German press. There it is stated that it is true that Goering has been in Paris, but he had no political discussions with Laval and also has no intention of having any such discussions in the future. And everything that the enemy press writes on this subject is untrue.

If something is denied, it is a sign that something did indeed happen: 'qui s'excuse, s'accuse' ['to excuse oneself is to accuse oneself']. The Pope also approached England on behalf of Germany and Italy with a favourable peace proposal. The Pope proposes a peace between the two Axis powers and England and America, without including Russia. This is the old German notion of dividing up the Russian bear. Hess probably flew to England on 10 May with a similar offer.[66] My informant knew no further details about the Pope's peace proposal. Let us hope that the Anglo-Saxon world will have sufficient decency not to accede to such an evil plan. The Spanish foreign minister, Serrano Suner,[67] is supposed to have made an attempt to act as an intermediary for peace. We have no further details. If it is true that the Germans have begun such an energetic peace campaign, it would be very cheering news indeed, proof that we are approaching the end of the greatest tragedy that the world has ever endured. In 1918 it all began (the beginning of the end) with the approach to Wilson and with changes in the German government. Ludendorff dismissed,[68] Max von Baden,[69] with liberal tendencies, Chancellor. All this with the proviso that the news is true.[70]

I have also been told about a typical letter that has reached Warsaw from Sweden. The correspondent writes that he is not planning to send any further parcels here given that the post is so slow and we are on the brink of important and decisive events, which will make the sending of parcels superfluous. He hopes that they will see each other soon.

Could it be that these are swallows heralding an imminent spring?

Once again we can observe scores of Jewish children from the age of ten to 12 or 13 stealing over to the Aryan side to buy a few potatoes there. These they hide in their little coats, with hems swollen so that the children look like balloons. Whole hosts of them can be seen climbing over the walls, crawling through the gaps or so-called 'targets' and passing through the official entrances where gendarmes and Polish police stand guard. There are some Germans who show a little mercy for these unfortunate children and pretend not to see, turning away deliberately, and the children dart with their little overcoats bulging, scampering along like birds. There are also vicious guards who hit the children with murderous blows, take away their potatoes, and often even use their weapons. More than one child has fallen victim to their bloodlust. These poor unfortunate Jewish children! What wonderful human potential is being lost to us. After the war we will have a serious problem with abandoned children and children without families, just as there was in Russia after the revolution: *bezprizornyje dieti* [deserted children].

It is high time that we gave some thought to this enormous and difficult problem.

Saturday, 23 May – *Second Day of Shavuot*

Five weeks ago took place the events of that terrible Friday, the Bartholomew Night put on for us by the Germans that unforgettable 18 April. Since then there has been a never-ending series of murders and violence in the ghetto. Not a day passes without word of a murder or of Jewish arrests, of people being dragged into the Pawiak and so on. This morning a woman came to us who works as a washerwoman and cleaner. She told us that a Jew was shot dead yesterday on Pawia Street next to the prison alleyway that has become so deadly (Więzienna). He was a flour-dealer named Hurwicz. A German Gestapo officer suddenly turned off Więzienna Street on to Pawia Street which is very crowded as Jews avoid going along the prison alleyway and take Pawia Street. All the Jews in the street threw themselves into the entrances of courtyards to escape the Angel of Death. Every German, and above all every Gestapo officer, is an Angel of Death in the eyes of every Jew. I can recall that my friend Henig[71] from Kraków made a confession to me in the first weeks of the war, saying: 'I was an officer in the Austrian army and served throughout the war at the front, but whenever I see a German in the distance my heart misses a beat.' The officer chased after the Jews, ran into an entrance and dragged out the Jew who was murdered, Hurwicz, killing him in a bestial fashion on the street. According to another version that I heard from Mr W.,[72] he didn't kill him but beat him up brutally in the street and then dragged him off to the Pawiak. Later he was let out.

In the last few days the level of anxiety has risen again among prominent political and social figures, especially from among the Bundists, because a great many of the victims have come from their ranks. They had started to breathe more easily and had begun sleeping at home again. Now they live in fear of acts of terror and as a precaution are not sleeping at home.

The frenzied filming continues unabated. I was told about one of these filming sessions that took place last Thursday morning at 22 Twarda Street at a bread-shop. A large crowd of Jews was rounded up, each given a 500 zloty note to hold, and made to press forward to buy a loaf, of course, a white loaf. A ragged young boy had to try and steal a loaf of bread, be seized by a Jewish policeman and beaten severely. Of course this last detail was also part of the scenario. The intention of the film is quite transparent. Rich Jews stuff themselves on white bread and pastries and are rolling in money whilst the poor have to steal their meagre daily crust and are beaten for it.

Viewed objectively, the position really is like that. Those who have money can get anything, from white pastries to the best fish, and the poor are dying on the streets from hunger. Who though is responsible for the indescribable misery and the vast and widening gulf of inequality in the ghetto, if not the Germans and their anti-Jewish policies?

Whether we can say with a clear conscience that 'our hands did not spill this blood' is a separate question which is well worth careful consideration. On another occasion I will try and give an answer to this question.

The 500 zloty notes were of course collected in again from the Jews. The boy who was beaten received 50 zloty as recompense for the blows he was handed out.

Today my former pupil Hanka T. visited me.[73] She spent seven and a half months in prison . . . for not wearing a Jewish armband and for travelling by train without permission. Her use of Aryan papers and illegal entry into the ghetto went unpunished.

I have already recounted that she worked in the fields last summer in the Lublin area, had wanted to see her parents and travelled home for Sukkot with the papers of a Christian woman. She entered the ghetto with the number 17 tram and tried to get out with her friend R. at Świętojerska Street. They were stopped by a gendarme who happened to be passing. She was held for two weeks at Daniło-wiczowska Street, together with prostitutes. She went hungry there. Later she was moved to a Jewish prison on Gęsia Street for a further seven months. Miss T. shared with me her impressions of the time working in the fields and of the prison on Gęsia Street. I will set down here many of the details that seem to me to be really interesting and that have stayed in my memory. The estate where she was working, which is situated in the Hrubieszów area, near Sokal and Belz, is very large. It is 600 *morgs* [approximately 800 acres][74] and has belonged for a long time to a Lwów Jew, Max Glazerman. He and his father before him have run the estate which is called Dluźniów. The local population is Ukrainian and hostile in its attitude to the Jews and even more so to the Poles. Production there is massive and is used in manufacturing industry. Corn and potato in the distilleries, beet in the sugar-factories, barley in the breweries, clover for perfume and . . . gases for military purposes (this means that for some time now the Germans have been preparing and producing gases). Wheat is also produced. Glazerman is perhaps the only Jew whom the Germans have allowed to continue managing his own property in the role of tenant, because he is known to be a good administrator and is by training an engineer. He has good relations with the authorities (the *Landrat*[75] in Hrubieszów), and to this day manages the estate, which has the character of an industrial farm. The greater part of the production he gives over as part of the so-called 'forced-quota'. But he has an agreement with the Germans that after the quota has been filled he has a free hand to sell a considerable amount of produce. This, it turns out, is how he makes a living.

The farm is worked by Ukrainian peasants, farm-workers, in very great numbers. The Betar movement [the revisionist youth movement] organized a large youth group from Warsaw, young men and women, school children from better-off families, which has been working there since early summer last year.[76] They are 30 in number. They live in two rooms, in a brewery, and have a communal life style, on the model of the kibbutzim in Palestine. Three of them stay behind each day and prepare food for the whole group. One of them, a cook, works in the kitchen each day, the other two change over each week. The working day lasts as a rule from sunrise to sunset, with a break at midday. Only during the very long summer days are they allowed to work at six in the morning, so that they will not have to work 15 or 16 hours a day. They receive full board from the owner in the following measure: half a kilo of bread, one and a half litres of milk, potatoes, grits, beans, peas, meat and bacon. Bread and milk are daily rations for each person. In addition they each receive one zloty a day. They work six days a week. Sunday is a rest day. They spend it at home, mend linen and clothing, and in the remaining free time they sing or read a book. The Jewish young men and women are all employed exclusively in the fields, doing the same work as labourers from generations of peasant stock. The work is hard, says the tall, slender Miss T., but they are able to keep up with the Ukrainians. The owner is satisfied with them, otherwise he wouldn't employ them. He is apparently a simple Jew, not a man of ideas. The group have work-cards and are under the protection of the office of employment. Relations between the group and Glazerman are in general quite cordial, although from time to time there are the tensions which are unavoidable between employees and employer. Thus he complains that they don't work hard enough and are rather lazy. The young people have complaints about the food, which deteriorates periodically. Then they have an argument and the air is clear again.

From where they are living to the former Russian–German border is no more than 12 kilometres. Large numbers of German troops assembled there, mostly Austrians. They took a friendly attitude to the group. They were – in the main – hostile to Hitler. They maintained that they would rather be Jews under Hitler's rule than Austrians. They had known in advance that war would break out with Russia and had predicted the day. (The whole thing is somewhat mystifying: something that every German soldier on the frontier knew as early as 15 June was still unknown to the Russian general staff on 21 June.)

Of life in prison Miss Tauber recounted the following. There were 11 girls held in a small cell, all of them in prison for leaving the ghetto illegally. One time they were visited by the doctors from the Swiss Red Cross. They asked each prisoner in turn why they had been locked up. On receiving the same answer each time they shook their heads: 'Is that a crime? Is it forbidden? And people are executed for this? Then this must be the only prison in the world where the inmates are not criminals.'

The rations in the prison are as follows: 200 g [7 oz] of bread a day with bitter coffee, soup twice a day, at midday and in the evening. Of course this is a starvation diet. Many prisoners receive parcels from home – these are shared with those who do not get them. In the prison there are 1,600 Jews, roughly half men and half women. Many die from hunger. There is no sick room or hospital in the prison.

Those who are ill lie in their cells until they die. Only then are they
carried out. Everyone is in prison for leaving the ghetto or for
smuggling. The female guards treat the prisoners humanely. Serving
as guards are intelligent Jewish women, some of them highly educated.[77] One of them has taken the exams to enter the judiciary. The
prisoners are let out four times a day to tend to their natural needs. In
an exceptional case one can be let out specially, or can use a container
in a cell. There are frequent cases of starvation-diarrhoea, which is a
sign that death is imminent. In such cases people are not let out of the
cell. They dirty themselves until they die. The prisoners spend the
whole day sitting locked up in the cells, so life is extremely mono-
tonous. The more intelligent read books sent in from outside. Every
now and then the prison goes through certain upheavals. On
9 January 1942, the *Judenrat* member Rosen came to the prison and
spoke to the assembled prisoners – men and women separately – and
solemnly announced an amnesty from the Germans, in recognition of
the large number of furs that had been handed over and the contribution the Jews had made. The release – also carried out with much
pomp and circumstance – took place on 11 March when the chairman, Czerniaków, and a representative of the German authorities,
among others were present. Czerniaków made a speech, bread and
sweets were distributed, and about 250 people were freed.[78] There is
also no shortage of tragedies to report from the Jewish prison. On
two occasions large groups of prisoners were sent to Treblinka, to the
notorious work and concentration camp, from which there is no
return, as with Oświęcim.[79] On the first occasion it was a group of
men and women who had broken the edict requiring furs to be given
up. The second group of deportees was made up of men who had
been arrested for smuggling. One of them was a tall, powerfully-built
man – a giant. He had gone to the aid of a poor Jewish woman from
whom a 'Junak' had tried to snatch some potatoes. He beat up the
Junak and disarmed him when he tried to fire his revolver. The prison
has also seen two horrific mornings of executions, when eight and
seventeen Jewish men and women were executed for the sin of leaving the ghetto. Women made up the vast majority of those executed.
Among these were also women of prominent families, for example,
the 27-year-old Mikanowska, the niece of Herman Czerwinski, who
was active in the community and died a few days ago.[80]

The R. family, who had been arrested because their son escaped from prison, has been released in the past few days.[81]

Here is a small illustration of the tragi-comedy of German justice. The Germans' special court sits on Długa Street. Last Friday (yesterday) this court, acting in the second instance, considered the appeal from a Jew in Łowicz who had been sentenced to a year in prison for ... slaughtering a goose in a ritual manner with *a normal kitchen knife*. He was seen by a German sergeant. The court on Długa Street gave the Jew an extra six months. Thus for the sin of cutting a goose's throat with a simple kitchen knife the Jew was sentenced to a year and a half hard labour. Perhaps he will be saved by the swift demise of these new Hamans?

Sunday, 24 May

Last night once again a number of Jews were shot. At the moment we know the names of four of them: Szymonowicz, Hurwicz, Mandel and Lewin. They are all said to have been closely connected with the 'Thirteen', the German agency at 13 Leszno Street, headed by Gancwajch.[82] Early this morning I went to see the spot where Szymonowicz was shot, at 9 Przejazd Street. I found his congealed blood still between the paving-stones, and there were bloodstains on the window of the shop next to where he was standing when he was shot. It is said of Szymonowicz that he had recently made a fortune dealing in brush production, almost four million zloty. Last week he married off a daughter. The wedding-dinner is supposed to have cost 25,000 zloty. It wasn't because of this wedding-dinner that his life was ended but because of his close relations with the Gestapo. The Nazis treat their assistants and servants, Jewish renegades and informers, according to an old German practice: the Moor has done his work, the Moor can go. This is how they dealt with the Jew Hanusel, whom they murdered as soon as they got into power, even though he had served them with all his heart and soul and worked so closely at their side. This is how they behave down to the present day. Word has it that they visited the homes of the two 'big men' Gancwajch and Szternfeld but they were not there. They are in hiding.

A certain engineer by the name of Sz., a reliable man, told me about a murder the Germans committed on a young girl at 11a Pawia Street last week. The man who murdered her was an older German officer, aged between 50 and 60. After the shooting he went out into the street. Just at that moment a woman was passing, an acquaintance of the above-named engineer. The street suddenly emptied. However, the woman didn't manage to take refuge anywhere. The officer was deathly pale. He took the woman by the arm, led her into the entrance, pointed to the dead body and told her to find the janitor and make arrangements to get the body moved to the side of the courtyard and the blood washed away. At the same time he explained to her that it wasn't his fault, he was just following orders. He showed her the order on a piece of paper. Is it possible that a German Gestapo officer should feel a twinge of conscience? Maybe he too has one or more daughters the same age as the murdered girl?

Monday, 25 May

From the groups of refugees from Łódź we hear that terrible reports are arriving from there, so terrible that if we did not know of other well-documented cases of equal bestiality we would not be able to believe them. A Jew from Łódź, an engineer called R., told me that children up to the age of ten are being slaughtered in the ghetto there.[83] It is hard for the tongue to utter such words, for the mind to comprehend their meaning, to write them down on paper. There is no greater crime, no greater savagery than the murder of young and innocent children.

The blood of our children will never be erased from the mark of Cain of the German people. Only now in these ways have I come to appreciate and understand Bialik's song of anguish and rage: 'The Slaughter'. I must confess that, though I am one of Bialik's most fervent admirers, his 'In the Town of Murder' and 'The Slaughter', where there is such fiery talk of blood, murder and revenge, have never been my favourites. I have always been drawn to his transcendent lyrics and his superb, brilliant epic poetry. But now I recall his cry from the heart: 'Accursed be he who cries out "Avenge this!" Vengeance for this, for the blood of a small child, the devil himself has not created.' Or 'If there is such a thing as justice, let it show itself now! But if only after my destruction, justice appears under the heavens, may its seat be destroyed for ever!' [See note 71 to Introduction.]

And if Kishenev was able to evoke such anguished echoes in a Jewish heart, what will there be in our hearts after the greatest disaster that has ever befallen us? But perhaps because the disaster is so great there is nothing to be gained by expressing in words everything that we feel. Only if we were capable of tearing out by the force of our pent-up anguish the greatest of all mountains, a Mount Everest, and with all our hatred and strength hurling it down on the heads of the German murderers of our young and old – this would be the only fitting reaction on our part. Words are beyond us now.

Our hearts are empty and made of stone.

My sister who lives at 17 Dzielna Street came to me deeply agitated and upset. She had witnessed two incidents. An officer had two Jews brought to him from Pawia Street, one young and one older. He took them into the Pawia Prison. Twenty minutes later the young man came out. He was covered in blood, it was literally pouring off him, from his head and face. She didn't see the older Jew come out. The second incident: on top of the watch-tower of the Pawiak Prison overlooking the infamous alleyway (Więzienna) were standing five Gestapo men. The alleyway was deserted. Jews avoid passing along it. An elderly Jew turned off Pawia Street. He was walking in the middle of the alleyway. The butchers above shouted out: *Komm her!* ['Come here']. The Jew became disorientated and terrified. He ran as fast as he could towards Dzielna Street. The five murderers took out their Brownings and took aim at the old man. They didn't shoot. When the old man had disappeared into Dzielna Street they all broke out into a devilish laughter.

The Jews of Pawia and Dzielna Streets are living through a life in Golgotha – more on this follows.

All flats overlooking Pawia and Dzielna Streets have for some time been obliged to have their windows completely covered and screened with black paper, just as for the regulation black-out at night, only 24 hours a day. It is extremely dark in these Jewish front rooms, and they can never be aired out. I hardly need describe what it means for the occupants' eyes and lungs, their state of mind, this continual dark existence without fresh air, even ghetto air. If there is electricity, then they can have electric light by day, but since the electricity is cut off in a lot of homes, and in those places where it isn't its use is severely restricted, people sit the whole day in the dark. The guard at the Pawiak watches to make sure that the unthinkable doesn't happen and a Jewish window is opened and the black paper or blankets removed to one side. A few weeks ago a Jew at 30 Pawia Street who shifted the window-covering to one side was shot dead.

The grabbing of Jews and the dragging of them into the Pawiak, the brutal beating of Jews by the Gestapo heroes as they pull up at the Pawiak or walk in or as they come out again also goes on in the neighbouring streets such as Karmelicka, Nowolipki, Dzielna and Pawia. The Germans often carry out raids on buildings – by day or by night. What the people go through who live in those buildings is not hard to imagine. All that is needed is for a ray of light to shine through the window and the Germans take all the men from the building into the Pawiak.

The lot of the inhabitants of the ghetto is hard and bitter, but the lot of those who have the misfortune to live opposite the prison is still harder and yet more bitter.

Tuesday, 26 May

The Germans have gone on the offensive on the Russian front. Their starting point was at Kerch, now they are reporting victories to the south of Kharkov. Strangely enough, these announcements didn't make a particularly deep impression. Somehow my heart is at peace and full of hope. Either consciously or unconsciously I am making comparisons between the present German attack and their last general offensive in March 1918. Just as then this was their last great push, which was followed six months later by their retreat and ultimately their collapse, so it will be this time, more or less. It may be that they will have some victories in Russia, but in at most six months, and perhaps a lot sooner, they will reach the end of the road. In the last few days I have become more and more certain that the war will end this year – 1942 – by the time winter comes. Is this just a mood or simple presentiment? Of course a mood can suddenly overtake us without rhyme or reason, quite irrationally, and this has a lot to do with it. It is possible that tomorrow, when our hearts may be overflowing with gloom and bitterness because of news of fresh disasters for Jews, I will see the political and strategic position differently, and will look into the future with less optimism. Today I'm in good spirits and think that my clairvoyance is based on a sober appraisal of the facts. I consider it a certainty that the Anglo-American invasion of Europe, or the creation of a second front, must and will come to fruition in the near future. I think that America is rapidly developing into the greatest military power in the world. According to an article in the latest edition of *Reich*, the American army will have grown by the autumn to 3,600,000 men. And England has an army a million strong. In the British Isles alone there are close to four million soldiers.

This huge army will hit the continent like an avalanche and strike a death-blow at the enemy of humanity, Nazism, which is bleeding profusely, but still winning occasional victories.[84]

In general, Jews are stubborn optimists. An uneducated Jew gave me the following interpretation of the stories in the newspapers which are very unfavourable to us. The Germans have surrounded the Russians, but the Russians have surrounded the Germans as well. The Russians control the territory 130 kilometres west of Kharkov, and in Kharkov itself are the Germans. Who will eventually surround whom and keep the upper hand we will have to wait and see. And here is another sensation: the Italian Crown Prince is said to have ordered the army to be ready . . . to lay down its weapons when the order is given. Hitler has convened the Reichstag on account of this.

This is how a people creates its own legends and dreams of a better tomorrow. And perhaps this old and new dream: 'If you want something, then it's no fairy-tale.'

This morning the exit from the court-house on Leszno Street,[85] where the ghetto tax offices are situated,[86] was blocked off and all the Jews who were in the hallway had their papers checked. All the cash that the Jews had on them was taken and they were issued with receipts. This is highway robbery, plain and simple, with the fig-leaf of a receipt. Only under Hitler would such lawlessness and thuggery be conceivable.

Today at four o'clock a German wagon loaded with carrots was driving along Smocza Street. A young Jewish boy ran up to the wagon and snatched a carrot. The German who was walking behind the wagon took out a revolver and with slow deliberation took a shot at him. With the same nonchalance he put the revolver back in its holster.

The boy was wounded in the leg and he was taken by rickshaw to hospital.[87]

Wednesday, 27 May

Today we have ended 1,000 days of war. What a terrible and tragic anniversary.

The action of the tax authorities against the Jews continues. During the day today they closed off the street markets in the ghetto, on Grybowska, Ciepła and Leszno streets. All the dealers and traders had their money confiscated, also their goods were confiscated and payment was demanded for their return. My next-door neighbour happened yesterday to be at the courts when the confiscations were being carried out. German gendarmes pushed all the Jews into a large hall and officials carried out the searches, taking everything the Jews had on them, from money to valuables. The Jews were beaten in the process.

Word has it that the special ghetto-trading has become completely stagnant, is at a complete standstill. As is well known, a large percentage of Jews in the ghetto live from selling off their belongings, from clothes to bed-linen to the kitchen pot. Everything passes over to the Aryan side. Lately the Poles have stopped buying on account of the repressive measures taken by the tyrants. A great many businesses and goods have been confiscated from them. Also vast numbers of them have been rounded up in the streets and sent to Germany to work. An atmosphere of great insecurity and anxiety reigns over there. The men stay inside at home, just as the Jews were doing. My brother-in-law, Dr T.,[88] who last Thursday had been in the German court-house on Długa Street, told me that the Polish streets are completely deserted. You see very few passers-by. Warsaw, the bustling, jostling Warsaw, is no more. It has become a dead, dreary, melancholy, deeply provincial town. I often sit on a balcony on Sienna Street from which you can see clearly the corner of

Marzałkowska and Sienkiewicz Streets. It is quite astonishing: there are a few lone passers-by. Very occasionally a droshky or a tram. It is as quiet as at four in the morning. No, even quieter. The streets used to be busy with droshkies and cars even in the middle of the night, never mind daytime or evening. You had to wait several minutes to be able to get across on one of the streets that insersects with Marszałkowska Street. This street was one of the liveliest in Warsaw's nervous system. So much life, movement, prosperity. Today it has become a graveyard.

If the Poles are not buying, then there is no one to sell to. The price of all valuables has fallen. Even at these lower prices it is difficult to find customers. (Prices are 30 or 40 per cent lower in comparison with two or three months ago.) But the price of foodstuffs has risen. The crisis in the ghetto is getting more acute. What is there for the Jews to live on?

Today a new decree was issued by the commissar of the ghetto, Auerswald,[89] concerning the armband that Jews wear on their right arm as an identifying mark. The decree states that Jews may only wear the regulation armband, and are forbidden to wear more than one and to alter it in any way, with the exception of the *Ordnungsdienst*,[90] who in addition to their normal Jewish armband wear a special armband designating their office. Up to now different kinds of officials, such as officials of the Jewish community, and others, and also certain professions such as doctors and dentists, have created special armbands designating their specialization, thus supposedly bestowing on themselves a certain degree of protection in the street against German thugs. These special armbands were intended to announce: we are not simple, ordinary Jews, we are carrying out important duties and therefore should have certain privileges. This decree puts an end to all that. There are no different categories of Jew. There is just one great mass of Jews, without rights, without status, hunted, tortured, spat upon, trodden on, raped and murdered. Hitler's thugs on the ghetto street will not have to stop and consider if they should also bash in the head of the Jew who is a doctor. From today we have become one great, undifferentiated and indistinguishable flock of sheep, without a shepherd and surrounded by wolves and tigers.

Thursday morning, 28 May

Yesterday at about nine o'clock in the evening a Jewish boy aged 13 to 14 was shot dead in front of my window. The murder was committed by a Polish policeman. He shot through the gap in the wall and hit the boy in the heart. The boy ran on another ten steps and then fell dead. A small pool of blood was left behind on the pavement. I was told that his mother was involved in smuggling. Now he has left this life, so young, and under such tragic circumstances.

The hole in the wall on Nowolipki and Przejazd Streets has been blocked up countless times. Each time the Polish and Jewish policemen on both sides of the wall are bought off and before the lime has a chance to dry the bricks are taken down and the smuggling continues. Yesterday the hole was blocked up for the umpteenth time. This happened at about six or seven in the evening. Immediately an operation was launched to take down the bricks. Apparently the policeman had not been settled with, or he had not wanted to agree to the smugglers' proposal. As soon as a small opening had appeared in the wall the size of a brick he put his gun in the gap and fired. The victim was not one of the rich, well-fed smugglers, but an impoverished young boy, an errand-boy of the smuggler-entrepreneurs.

Today there was an announcement in the only rag of a newspaper that appears under the occupation in Warsaw,[91] in Polish, declaring that all Gypsies who are detained in the administrative district of Warsaw will be deported and confined to the ghetto. In addition, certain 'humanitarian' warnings are given: the men 'may be' sent to work-camps and all their property 'may be' confiscated without compensation, meaning their meagre possessions such as the tools of their trade and their horses. In short, everything that a Gypsy family owns and travels around with. In practice this will mean that the Gypsy men will be transported to work in labour camps, and that they will die from overwork and undernourishment. The others will be sent naked and barefoot and without any means of earning a livelihood into the ghetto where they too will die of starvation and disease.[92]

This is a blow to the ghetto as the overcrowding will be even more unbearable and disease will spread even faster. Even so, I have only compassion for the unfortunate Gypsies. They are our companions in misery. In my eyes they have gained the stature of holy martyrs. They will undoubtedly awaken in us feelings of compassion and pity, though we will not be able to help them, just as we cannot help the thousands of our own refugees who are dying each day before our very eyes. The Gypsies' blood, like our blood, will cry out for ever from the earth and will cover with shame and contempt the faces of Hitler's blond beasts. The 'voice of thy brother's blood that cries to me from the earth' will, I believe, never be stilled and will demand for ever: 'Revenge!'

Last Sunday the Germans took Jewish musicians into the Pawiak Prison and had a really good celebration. The entertainment lasted from six to nine. Since then the streets around the Pawiak have been quiet. The Jews presume that the group of sadists who had preyed on the streets around the Pawiak has left Warsaw and taken its farewell from us to the accompaniment of Jewish music. This is the reason that everything has been quiet since that night. May everything that in our hearts we wish upon them happen to them.

A Jewish woman, one of the recent refugees from Germany (Berlin) told me that dissatisfaction and opposition to Hitler is growing in Germany. This woman believes that the war will not last long and that a revolution is only a matter of time. In Germany the number of anti-Hitler slogans appearing in public places is increasing. The popular propaganda that can be read on the streets is as follows:

Jews hold on!	(Juden haltet aus
The scum are almost done!	Mit den Lumpen ist bald aus!)
Better the King	(Lieber der König
Better the Kaiser by God's grace	Lieber der Kaiser von Gottesgnaden
Than the thug from Berchtesgaden.	Als der Lump von Berchtesgaden.)[93]

No great significance can be attached to the prophecies of a Jewish refugee, but it is a sign of a certain fermentation and unrest in Hitlerland, a *signum tempori*. The wall-slogans tell us to hope.[94]

A few days ago at exactly five past nine in the evening a Jew was shot dead by the wall at the corner of Grzybowska and Gnojna Streets. I heard this from a Jew, Mr. A., an occupant of 6 Grzybowska Street who was standing at the window that looks out on to the street and was an eyewitness to the terrible crime.

This morning there were more killings, several Jews were shot dead on Bagno Street for their involvement in smuggling. Among the murdered was also a Jewish policeman. As for the number of dead, I have heard different versions. The first gave the number of victims as two, the second as three and the third as five.

Literally not a day passes without the stones of the ghetto being stained with Jewish blood.

The taking of detainees into the Pawiak continues unabated. My sister, who lives opposite the prison, told me just today, Thursday, she has seen two lorry-loads of prisoners being taken in. In one she saw eight Poles, their heads hanging down, looking totally wretched. Those in the second lorry were not visible since four Germans were sitting at the back and they obscured any view of those sitting inside. The annihilation-machine never rests.

I heard the following details about the boy who was shot on Wednesday evening. He was being brought up by an aunt, Mrs Szparag, who is involved in smuggling things over to the Aryan side. That Wednesday she was arrested by the Polish police. They demanded 10,000 zloty for her release. Between them the smugglers raised 5,000 zloty and she was set free. The boy was waiting for her and had taken out the bricks from the wall so that his aunt could crawl through. It was then that he met his death.

Friday, 29 May

Yesterday I passed by the ghetto wall at the corner of Nalewki Street and Świętojerska Street and saw how a gendarme was mistreating a young Jew for wearing a dirty armband. He made him stand still (as if to attention) and his thundering voice could be heard far and wide. What the Jew went through is not difficult to imagine. But not only the Jew being mistreated endured several anguished moments. A cold shudder went through all the Jews that were witness to this barbaric scene.

From one o'clock onwards today the Jewish police were carrying out round-ups on the streets of the ghetto. Jews up to the age of 40 whose work-cards were not in order were seized, that is, those who are not registered with the labour ministry as being employed. The purpose of carrying out this round-up is not immediately clear to me. Be that as it may, it offers new possibilities for abuses by the Jewish police. Those who can pay a few zloty will manage to get themselves out of trouble. The poor will suffer again, just as they did last year and the year before. I have heard that in the course of the round-up last Friday night 350 Jews were detained.

Today rumours have been going round that Gancwajch has been caught in Otwock (others say it was in Radomsko or Częstochowa) and shot dead. As is well known, the following four are wanted by the Germans: Gancwajch, Szternfeld and the Zachariasz brothers. In every entrance-hall in the ghetto there hangs an announcement that whoever hides the wanted men or helps them in any way whatsoever will be shot along with their entire family. The same fate threatens all the occupants of the building where one of the fugitives is found. All of them worked together with the Germans and now they are being disposed of. I heard a maxim on this subject today: 'If you eat the Germans' meat you have to give them up your bones.' Very true and succinctly put. If you sell your soul to the devil you have to give him your body too.

In the last issue of *Reich* there was an announcement which is of great significance. In Germany they are putting 10 per cent of all banks into liquidation, that is, a tenth of all branches are being closed. This means that economic conditions in Nazi-land are getting tighter and tighter. How much longer will Germany be able to last out the deep crisis that is gnawing and digging at its foundations?

Eight in the evening. Something extraordinary has just happened. On Leszno Street opposite the court-house young Jewish men were rounded up to be deported to work-camps. They were put into a tram and were being taken to 19 Zamenhof Street where a collection-point had been set up for those destined for the work-camps. When the tram reached Karmelicka Street the young men broke open the tram and fled. Two of them came back to the building where I live. This feels like a foretaste, a prelude in miniature of what will happen when the hour of our liberation comes and we tear off the chains of our servitude.

Saturday night, 30 May

This day has been among the most difficult, the most nightmarish of all days that we are now living through. Firstly the round-up. Yesterday's round-up brought a rich harvest. I do not know the exact number of those seized, but by all accounts their numbers ran into the hundreds. This means that hundreds of Jewish lives are exposed to the gravest danger, the danger of destruction. This morning they were all taken away, in closed trains of course, in freight or cattle-trucks. Where they were being sent is not known for sure. I have heard from several sources that they were being sent as far away as Bobruisk to build fortifications. If this is so, it may be that their position will be even more tragic and bitter than that of those seized and sent to work-camps last year or the year before, because at that time the Warsaw Jewish community organization and also that of the town nearest to the camp tried to do something for the unfortunates. Their position was not greatly alleviated, but a certain protection and small-scale help did reach them, and it was of some slight consolation. Today? If those who have been rounded up are sent to the former Russian territories there will be no one to take care of them and help them in some way. In Russia proper there are no Jewish community organizations and the Jews have disappeared from all those areas occupied by the Germans: either they have retreated with the Russian army or they have been slaughtered by the Germans. Whole Jewish towns have vanished. It is horrific, quite horrific.

And once again we see the sad complicity of the Jewish police. With great regret they are 'obliged' to carry out their duties and round up people. They carry out these duties conscientiously. Thus both large numbers of Jews are seized and the pockets of the Jewish police are filled with ill-gotten gains. Apparently one could get released with no difficulty for 10 zloty.

Last night we had a repetition of the Bartholomew Night action on a smaller scale. It was another Friday night, like the infamous 18 April. The number of those brutally murdered is said to be 11, among them a woman. All the Jews living at 11 Mylna Street were killed, four men from one flat: an elderly Jew, his son and his son-in-law, Różycki, as well as his tenant. The elder Wilner was partly paralysed. In his terror he couldn't speak and was unable to move. The Germans put him on a chair and threw him out of the second-floor window. The old man was killed instantly. The other three men were taken down into the street and shot. There is also talk of a murdered barber from 50 Nowolipie Street, and a policeman, who six months ago had been on duty in the hospital on Stawki Street when two Jewish reserve officers in the Polish army escaped, Gomuliński and one other.[95]

Also a Mrs Judt was shot.[96] She had worked for the Germans and had managed to obtain permits for the Jewish theatres. Altogether, as mentioned above, 11 Jews.

The background to these murders in the night? Hard to say. One opinion I heard was that they were all racketeers. This is, however, not completely accurate. Thus I have heard that the Wilners owned a brick-factory in Grodzisk; the son-in-law is supposed to have been a teacher and a very respectable person. The barber from 50 Nowolipie Street is said to have been a member of the Bund [the Jewish socialist party]. In short, we do not have the key to these terrible murders and none of us has any idea what fate awaits us. All people more or less involved in the running of an organization lives each day in terror for their life.

This morning the gendarmerie drove up with Junaks on Przejazd Street and took away four Jews who were involved in smuggling. They were standing on the ruined wall at number 11, looking over to the Aryan side. I heard that Auerswald, the Nazi commissioner in charge of the ghetto, was present at the arrest and that on his orders the group was deported immediately, along with those Jews who had already been rounded up. The mother of one of those deported was sobbing pitifully outside my window.

Today a group of community officials were sitting together and for two hours a lawyer from Lwów recited to us the book of lamentations of Lwów and the whole of eastern Galicia. And what he said was so horrific and gruesome that words cannot convey what has happened. Lwów alone has lost 30,000 martyrs. The slaughter was carried out in three main stages. As soon as the Germans entered Lwów they carried out a large-scale round-up and thousands upon thousands of Jews were murdered in the prisons. The second stage took place later, when Jews had to move into the ghetto, next to the 'bridge of death' that became so tragically notorious, and the third took place in March during the great resettlement of the Lwów Jews, when up to 10,000 Jews died.[97] In the action to dispose of people over 60 several thousand Jews were killed. The details of these events are so devastating that they are not for the pages of a diary. This must all be told in full. I hope and believe that this will one day happen, that the world's conscience will be taken by storm and that vile beast that is at the throat of the peoples of Europe and choking them to death will be bound and shackled once and for all. The lawyer from Lwów estimates that the number of dead in eastern Galicia is in excess of 100,000.[98] All the Jewish communities along the Hungarian border have been obliterated from the face of the earth. Thus Jaremcze, which had a population of 1,000 Jews, has become *judenrein*. The same in Tatarów and so on.

When the lawyer had finished his account of these horrors and Mr G.[99] had thanked him, many of us had tears in our eyes.

Those two hours belong to the darkest of my life.

On my way home from this meeting I had the 'good fortune' to be stopped and made to work at loading bricks. The Germans were stopping only more respectably dressed Jews. The work lasted an hour. It wasn't so much hard work as humiliating. A soldier stood over us and yelled insults: 'Verfluchte Juden!' ['Damned Jews'] and struck one of us with the back of an iron rod. It is certainly no pleasure to taste German barbarity and Jewish servitude, even for just one hour, but I did none the less have a certain feeling of satisfaction. I have experienced at first hand, albeit in small measure, that which millions of Jews have been enduring for almost three years now. For this reason it was worthwhile.

Sunday, 31 May

I have heard that the number of those deported in the 'Todt-sections'[100] to work in Bobruisk was around 900. Nine hundred young lives are now as good as over, lost. There are said to be 150 prisoners from the Jewish prison on Gęsia Street among them. Several people also told me that 120 male children aged between 12 and 14 were also removed from the prison and deported. Where to and what for? To work or to be killed? Who can know? There is nothing of which they are not capable, no crime and no bestiality which they could not commit.

It is interesting to hear how some Jewish women reacted in one incident during the round-up and saved a young Jewish student, a person of great qualities, our friend Fl. He was seized on Komitetowa Street, bundled into a bus belonging to the firm Kohn–Heller,[101] and was on his way to the assembly-point. On Ciepła Street several of the young people jumped out through the small windows. Fl. also jumped and tried to get away. A Jewish policeman ran after him. He ran into an entrance-way. Women – ordinary women – began to argue with the policeman, who hit a woman in the face with his fist. He grabbed hold of Fl. and began to lead him out of the entrance. In the street the women – whose numbers had grown in the meantime – began to attack the policeman again. He started struggling with the women. Taking the chance offered by the scuffle Fl. ran off. So in this way he was rescued, we can be pretty sure, from death. Bless you, Jewish women, who have saved one of the children of Israel.

Whilst carrying out my duties in the second district,[102] I made a one-off payment of 25 zloty to a woman named Mrs Rywa Ruda. I got to talking with her and an old wound was opened up in front of me, the destruction of a historic Jewish community of 700 families or three to four thousand souls. This woman comes from (Golub-)Dobrzyń on the River Drwęca. She told me that the Germans entered the town as early as 3 September 1939, the third day after the outbreak of war. After no more than six days all the Jews without exception had been removed from the town. The Germans were so devilish in their execution of this plan that they announced that if the Jews were to give up their gold, money and diamonds, no expulsions would take place. The Jews brought to the town-hall baskets full of gold, silver and precious stones. This was all collected in and the expulsions were carried out without further delay. The Jews were given 10 minutes to leave town. Not a single cart was given to them. Old people, small children, pregnant women who were due to give birth that day, they were all ordered to leave their homes and were unable to take anything with them. Even those who set off with a pack on their back threw it away later because they had no more strength to carry it. The woman's husband, Josef Chaim Ruda, had taken a case of belongings with him. He dragged it for 10 kilometres, then threw it down by the side of the road, completely unable to carry it any further on his old man's shoulders. These are old people in their sixties. Mrs Ruda – a woman of great dignity – told me that on the way terrible things took place, things inconceivable to us. As she puts it, they walked into the 'forest of death'. Children were dying, women gave birth in the fields, old people were falling down dead. The first night the Ruda family of three stayed with a Polish peasant who showed a great deal of humanity. Sixty Jewish families found temporary refuge in his stable. He milked the cows at night – something which is very harmful for them – and warmed up milk for the refugees. At no point did he take any money. The homeless and dispossessed Jews distributed themselves over other towns like Płońsk, and also some reached as far as Warsaw. Mrs Ruda says that almost the entire Dobrzyner community lost their lives, that only a few individuals survived the hunger and the cold. The Rudas were one of the wealthier families in the town. They left behind a house, their own house, and three shops, also a garden. They had substantial wealth. They have three daughters in Palestine. Today they are dying of hunger: 25 zloty is a drop of joy in their sad lives. Now she will be able to buy her husband a piece of bread.

And Dobrzyń is only a small link in the enormous chain of disaster that has befallen Polish Jewry. In fact, the whole of European Jewry. But the destruction of Polish Jewry will be the crowning glory in Hitler's crusade against the Jewish people.

It is well known that whole families are being wiped out. Even a year, a year and a half ago, there were two- or three-room flats that were standing empty because the occupants had all died. Every official in the ghetto has a lot to tell on this subject. But it still happens that the loss of certain families chokes us with sadness, even though we have become so hardened and insensitive to human tears and the shedding of blood. I wish to recount here two cases where entire families were lost.

In Warsaw there was a family by the name of Erenberg. The family had four members: father, mother, one son and one daughter. Mrs Erenberg was a distant relative of the banker Szereszewski. Because of this, the husband worked in Szereszewski's bank as a messenger and was able to earn a living. Although himself without education, he had sent his children to middle-school and both graduated with their matura. The girl went to the Yehudia School and the son to Laor.

From the onset of the war the family began to go short of food. The father left Warsaw and died somewhere in a village of hunger and disease. Later, the mother died in Warsaw, also from hunger. The son and the daughter, the secondary school graduates, were reduced to begging. By chance I met them yesterday. The girl is already in the process of dying. Her days are numbered. Likewise her brother is existing at the lowest level of human survival. He too will not last much longer, unless the war ends.

I had a cousin, an athletically-built man. He had served in the artillery in the Russian army and went through the world war. He had an only son, who was 18 years old, also a giant. The boy got himself out of the ghetto and set off to look for work in the Lublin area. On the way he was recognized and sent to prison in Lublin. The father took his son's fate to heart so much that he fell ill and seven months ago he died. His son died three months ago in the prison, of dysentery. Two months ago his mother died as well.

These are just two examples. In this way thousands and thousands of Jewish families are cut down.

I have a cousin in the Jewish police and he told me about a murder that the Germans committed last Thursday, 28 May, at half past nine in the evening at 64 Pawia Street. That evening he was on his way home. As he went up to the entrance of 49a Pawia Street a car drew up, stopped in front of number 64 and three Germans and an older, grey-haired Jew got out. The Germans put three shots in the Jew's head, killing him instantly. They caught sight of my cousin some distance off, called him over and instructed him that the dead body should be removed. The car had driven out of the Pawiak. In the dead man's hat was found a slip of paper with 'Zwolniony z więziena' ['freed from prison'] written on it.

Along with the rumours that Gancwajch has been detained and shot, there are others that claim that he has already established himself far from here in Switzerland.[103]

The caretaker of 5 Mylna Street gave some details of the terrible murder that the Germans committed against the Wilner family last Friday night. Wilner, old and sick, was lying in bed. He was 69 years old. They stripped him naked, set him down in a chair and threw him from the second floor down on to the courtyard, then shot at him, finishing him off. They shot the son inside. The son-in-law they led down into the courtyard and shot him dead there. The tenant, a cousin of the Wilner's, was shot not far from the entrance-way.

All the occupants of 11 Mylna Street were left prostrated and broken on Saturday and Sunday after the tragic events that Friday night. The reason for the murders is not clear. People are saying that they gave over a business on Królewska Street to a *Volksdeutsche* and that he was paying them a certain amount of money. Recently he had stopped the payments. Because the Wilners were making insistent demands for the money he apparently took his revenge and set the Germans on them.

Following the round-up for the work-camps a very large queue has formed at the corner of Leszno and Żelazna Streets at the Kolegium building,[104] where the ministry of employment has its offices in the ghetto. Everyone is having their papers put in order. Yesterday, Sunday, scuffles broke out in the queue. A gendarme fired twice. One Jew was killed and a second wounded.

Tuesday, 2 June

The frenzied filming continues unabated. On Sunday afternoon the Germans filmed scenes in the street-market on Ciepła Street. While I was watching they paired up two Jews: one who was carrying a pack of old newspapers on his shoulders, and a second, an old man with a grey beard. The two Jews were trembling and were frightened to death.

Yesterday on Żelazna Street at the corner of Chłodna Street elegantly dressed women were seized and dragged into cars. Rumours went round that women were being seized to be put to work. It is more precise to say that they were taken off to be used in film-making.

Word has it that the Germans are planning to set up guard-posts of Jewish policemen along the ghetto walls, with a policeman every 50 metres. Further, that the Jewish police would be made responsible for dealing with smuggling and be liable to the death penalty. This is said to have persuaded a lot of Jewish policemen to request to be released from duty.

Lately letters have been arriving from Paris with a hidden political content of a clearly optimistic character. This raises our spirits, encourages us and is simply intoxicating.

A family of my acquaintance received a card from a brother in Paris, a medical doctor. The first few sentences of the card read in translation roughly as follows (the card was written in Polish): I cannot write any news to you about the war, because in this war, as in all wars, unexpected and miraculous things [niespodzianki i cuda] have been happening lately. X and Y [here are two names of Jewish doctors from Warsaw who had set up practice in Paris], who had not been able to work up to now, are able once again to practise their profession.

Dr Sz. told me that he had read a letter from Paris in which it was stated explicitly that very important things would soon be happening, and that we would shortly be receiving guests, that is, on Dr Sz.'s interpretation, the English and the Americans.

Today I was shown a card from Paris, dated 23 May, from which I have excerpted the following sentences that seem to me to be of some interest. The card is written in a Germanized Yiddish, of course, and in Latin letters. It reads as follows: 'Paris, 23 May 1942. Dear Josef, I received your card and was sad to read that you have been ill. As for me, I am in good health and feel very, very well. I am not suffering any more from my persistent complaint (this means that he had been afraid he would be sent to a work-camp, but he has no further worries on that score), but I have no resources and am powerless to help you. *However, I am in the best of moods, since the business with Pepi (means America) and Lea (that is, England) and also Rivke (that is, Russia) is getting very interesting. Mr Chazen (the cantor) - obviously this is a reference to the 'Führer' - has lost his beautiful tenor voice and doesn't sing at all any more.* Otherwise I don't have anything to tell you.'[105]

Could this be just coincidence and just the same old rumours? Or does it have a basis in fact? Our frequent and bitter disappointments notwithstanding, we hope and believe that the day of justice and of the triumph of the human being in his struggle with the Nazi beast must and soon will come. And perhaps it really will be soon?

The lawlessness of the tax officials against the Jews of the ghetto has become pure and unadulterated banditry. I heard that Jews are being dragged off the streets into the shops, searched, and all the money they have on then taken.

In my building there is a poor barber who lives on the floor above mine. He lost his barber-shop in the events of September 1939. Since then he has been working a little in his flat. Acquaintances, former customers, come up to have their hair cut. Sadly, he is extremely hard-up, and in great distress. Today a tax official arrived and demanded 60 zloty tax on the flat. As the barber had no money to pay him, the official began to search the flat and all those present at the time. One customer who happened to be there had 2,500 zloty in his pocket. The official took the whole 2,500. With great difficulty and much effort, shouting and pleading, he was eventually prevailed on to take just 200 zloty as a bribe and to give back the rest.

It transpires that the German and Italian offensive in Africa, which they were so triumphantly celebrating, was cut short at the outset. It began on 26 May. Today, 2 June, they are already writing about English counter-attacks while there is a deafening silence over their victories. It looks as though they have had a setback. That would be very cheering news. Also the latest air-attack on Cologne makes the pulse beat faster.[106] If the greatest of the German cities will have nights such as Lübeck, Rostock and Cologne have had – then the war will soon be over.

The English really are phlegmatics. Their hand is slow to strike back, but strike back it does. Their promise made in spring 1941 to reduce the German cities to rubble is being carried out slowly, but it is being carried out.

The Germans are already talking about the 'catastrophe' of Lübeck (in one of the recent issues of *Reich*) and Rostock. Now they will be talking of the catastrophe of Cologne, and let us hope that there will soon be talk of Germany's catastrophe.

Then we will see our deliverance and salvation.

Half past eight in the evening. Just now my neighbour R. came home and told me that at the corner of Pańska and Bagno Streets a gendarme had shot down – from the wall he was standing on – and killed two Jews, a young boy and an older man. They were involved in smuggling. Last week two Jews were killed on Bagno Street: 'Man earns his bread at the risk of his life.' Each piece of bread that we buy on the open market is soaked with Jewish blood.

Wednesday, 3 June

The letters that arrive from Germany, Austria and Czechoslovakia testify to a certain revolutionary ferment throughout the whole Reich. For instance from Berlin we hear that proclamations are pasted up in the street with the following content: 'We demand peace, we demand the return of our husbands and sons.' The letters from Czechoslovakia also have this strongly revolutionary character. Someone writes that the shooting of the greatest of all villains (Heydrich) marks the beginning of a Czech awakening.[107] All these letters pulsate with the belief in a swift end to this worldwide slaughter. Is it possible that the whole of oppressed Europe could be mistaken? The heart longs so deeply for salvation. We go to sleep with this dream; we wake with this dream. Is it possible that the most passionate yearning of 95 per cent of all inhabitants of the globe should go unfulfilled and the evil power of a band of degenerates and savage murderers should triumph? Reason and the heart tell us that humankind, embodied in the peoples of Soviet Russia, England and America, will be victorious and not the wild animals of Hitler and Mussolini-land.

The desire is so strong in us to see the day of redemption, the triumph of righteousness, but at the same time there is a worm of doubt and despair gnawing at the heart. Every day we receive such terrible news from the provinces. Every day a new misfortune, a new pogrom, a new expulsion that heralds a new mass-murder. Last week I was told that Kraków Jews are to be forcibly resettled. I didn't believe this tragic news and so didn't write it down. Today I was told that Dr W.[108] rang from Kraków and gave the news that 2,000 Jews have already been deported and it is not even known where they are to be taken. From our bitter experience we must conclude that they are being secretly murdered. The circle around Warsaw is drawn even tighter. Will they leave Warsaw alone and be content with smaller massacres and pogroms? It gives me a feeling of deep unease to ask such questions: what makes us better than the Jews of Wilno or Kraków? Why are they dying and we have hope of staying alive? Why? Why? We have also had the terrible news of massacres and expulsions from Hrubieszów, Tyszowce and a whole series of other communities in the area of Lublin.[109] A woman by the name of Wermus returned from Sosnowica, near Parczew. She said that very many Jews in these areas had been murdered by electrocution. She puts the number at 2,500. In the set of buildings in which I live there is a Mrs Raduszyńska. Her husband was in Tłuszcz during the final expulsion of Jews and was shot dead there. She says that 110 Jews died. Today two lorries arrived in the ghetto packed with Łódź Jews. They got here with Kohn–Heller's help or by virtue of coming from well-to-do families. To bring a Jew from Łódź costs 5,000–6,000 gilden. Their belongings were sent off to the customs authorities for the correct amount of duty to be charged since they are from – the other side of the border – from the kingdom of Łódź, doesn't that sound like a curiosity?[110]

Part of the trading between Jews and Christians takes place in the court-house on Leszno Street. The caretakers give over their private flats for this purpose. According to estimates I have been given they make hundreds of zloty a day. A few days ago all Jews found in the court-house were arrested and taken over to the Aryan side, where they were checked to see what grounds they had for being in the building. The court-house is also a meeting-place between Christian men and their Jewish wives who are in the ghetto, and also vice versa, between Christian women and their Jewish husbands who have stayed in the ghetto. Someone who has been witness to these reunions described them to me. There is in these meetings an over-flowing of human tragedy and suffering. A Christian woman arrives and kisses her Jewish husband. She brings him a small parcel of food. They talk for a few minutes, move away to one side, kiss again and separate. He back to the ghetto and she to the Aryan part of Warsaw.

Will future generations believe that this is how everyday life was in 1942?

Something is happening in this kingdom of darkness, this kingdom of the devil, something is stirring here. A young man who works for the Germans at a so-called *placówka* on the Aryan side told me recently that he had seen with his own eyes street slogans on Puławska Street saying the following: 'Mai 1942. Nieder mit dem Faschismus! Es lebe internationaler Solidarität! [May 1942. Down with Fascism! Long live international solidarity!] As clear as day!

In the course of the last few days the following strange incident took place. A Jew from Germany who is living in the synagogue building on Tłomackie Street,[111] was passing through the ghetto gate on Nalewki Street. In the last couple of days there has been an official there who searches everything and everybody who walks or drives through the gate. The official also searched the case of the German Jew and insulted him in some way and gave him a bit of a shove. The Jew – and perhaps he was only one-quarter Jewish, a Protestant – struck the official back without hesitation. The gendarme did not intervene. The Jews think that this is because he is angry at the official, who is disturbing him in his smuggling activities. The German Jew was led away by the Jewish police into the Jewish side.

Thursday, 4 June

A few days ago notices of regulations from our 'chairman' Czerniaków were posted in the ghetto concerning among other things the fact that Jews are not allowed to play, indeed not even to listen to, the musical works of non-Jewish musicians and composers. Jews are not allowed to perform dramas by non-Jewish authors and no foreign-language books are allowed in the libraries. Of course it is obvious that these decrees were issued on the orders of Germans.

The Saturday concerts that take place each week in the Femina Theatre have been forbidden for the next few months since the works of Beethoven, Mozart and others were performed there. That was the sin, and the punishment followed quickly.[112]

It is hard to know what is the more amazing: the patently philistine, numbskulled wrong that is done here or the bottomless depths of Nazi stupidity and Teutonic idiocy. Whatever the cause may be, a feeling of our superiority is awakened in us. If the struggle against us becomes so all-embracing then we must draw the conclusion that we are the salt of the earth, or as Yehuda Halevi has put it – the heart of all nations, the heart of the world. Whether one wants to or not, one falls into mystical, messianic, Towiánski-like thoughts.[113]

This morning brought fresh Jewish victims in connection with smuggling. At seven o'clock two gendarmes drove up outside my window and made a horrendous scene, giving warning that if the gap in the wall wasn't closed off by twelve o'clock they would shoot

30 Jews, 10 from each of the three nearest buildings. At the same time a Jew who had been shot and badly wounded was found at 32 Święto-jerska Street, a completely innocent occupant of the building who had happened to be going out of the gate. At the same time on Bagno Street – that fatal street – gendarmes shot four Jews and arrested 15.

A rich harvest for a single morning.

But for all this, the gap in the wall outside my window was not blocked up and the smuggling is still going on. 'The world goes on in its accustomed way.' And we live on and do not go insane.

Today I witnessed the following event. A Jew was passing along Nalewki Street next to the ghetto gate. The gendarme called him over. The Jew stood to attention. The gendarme told him to stretch out his right arm, took out his bayonet and cut off the Star of David armband, this because it was dirty. How much health and well-being must this Jew have lost while this drama was being played out.

Letters and news of any kind have ceased altogether to reach us from the towns and townlets of the Reich such as Włocławek, Gostynin, Aleksandrów-Kujawski and others. This means that all these places where there have been Jewish communities for 700 or 800 years are now *judenrein*.[114] What has been done with these Jews is not known. Once again we must make the appalling and most probably correct assumption that they have been murdered. We no longer have any strength to react as we should to the never-ending misfortunes.

The families of those taken in the last round-up for the work-camps are terribly distressed and anxious. They have no idea what has happened to their sons, brothers and fathers: on Tuesday sealed train wagons were still standing on the tracks in Warsaw. The relief agency of the Jewish community delivered bread and honey,[115] but can people survive week after week in closed freight cars? Do they have facilities to attend to their natural human needs? It is said that there were already deaths in the cars on Tuesday. But the cars were not opened to take out the bodies. What does the word 'terrible' mean in the face of this?

Friday, 5 June

Last night on the ghetto bridge the Nazis' murderous hands claimed a fresh victim. At half past twelve a Jew was driven to 18 Dzielna Street, probably from the Pawiak Prison, and shot there. On Szczęśliwa Street a Jew was shot dead yesterday morning. He was a smuggler.

The cup of Jewish blood is still not full.

One of the most remarkable incidental phenomena seen in the present war is the clinging to life, the almost complete cessation of suicides. People are dying in vast numbers of the typhus epidemic, are being tortured and murdered by the Germans in vast numbers, but people do not try to escape from life. In fact just the contrary: people are bound to life body and soul and want to survive the war at any price. The tension of this epoch-making conflict is so great that everybody, young and old, great and small, wants to live to see the outcome of this giant struggle, and the new world order. Old men have only one wish: to live to see the end and to survive Hitler.

I know an old Jew, grey with age, about 80 years old. This old man was hit by a terrible misfortune last winter: he had an only son aged 52 who died of typhus. He had no other children. The son is dead. He hadn't remarried and had lived together with his son. A few days ago I visited the old man. As I was saying goodbye to him (he is still in complete command of his faculties), he burst into tears and said to me: I want to live to see the end of the war and then live for just another half hour longer.

We may well ask: what has such an old man to live for? But he does have something: he too wants to live for 'just half an hour' after the last shot is fired and this is the passionate desire of all Jews.

Today's edition of the German newspaper in Warsaw cheered me up immensely. The chief executioner and Grand Inquisitor of Czechoslovakia – Heydrich – is dead. The shot fired by the two heroes was not in vain. It might be that the shooting of Heydrich and his death will be a signal and rallying cry for general European turmoil and an uprising against the German tyrant. If only! In fact the general tone of the German press in the last few days has been more modest, more restrained. It does not speak with such confidence of its own victory; on the contrary, indirectly, it talks of an Allied victory. Thus today the German newspaper in Warsaw has a story about important conferences between America, England and Russia on the future boundaries of Europe after their victory and on Germany's fate after its defeat. The motif of Germany's fall and the Allies' victory is finding a quiet but perceptible echo in the press. It seems that the latest air-strikes on Cologne, Duisberg, Essen, Bremen and elsewhere have opened the eyes of the Germans who are drunk with their own victories and they are beginning to see their own unavoidable and tragic demise. The game is getting very interesting. It will be even more interesting to see how November 1918 will be replayed. May we only live to see it with our own eyes.

6 June – *The End of Shabbat*

In these tragic times, whenever several Jews gather together and each recounts just a part of what he has heard and seen, it becomes a mountain or a swollen sea of misfortune and Jewish blood. Jewish blood pure and simple. We gather every Sabbath, a group of activists in the Jewish community, to discuss our diaries and writings.[116] We want our sufferings, these 'birth-pangs of the Messiah', to be impressed upon the memories of future generations and on the memory of the whole world. We meet every Sabbath, and we talk over our duties in this matter and in doing this we are unable to refrain from recounting to each other everything they are doing to us, these old–new Amalekites. These stories always fill me with deep gloom, and my head begins to ache, as if a heavy lead weight was pressing down on me. This is how it was today too. They talked and talked and I felt a chillness and utter despondency.

They recounted the following:

For the smallest of sins, literally for something completely trivial, the Jews of Lida are punished with what the Jews call the 'smallest' German punishment, that is, death. And the punishment on these occasions is collective. Firstly they shoot all the Jews of the house where the 'offender' lived. Recently they have become more 'liberal' and shoot only the sinner's family. Thus there was a case where a girl lost her Jewish armband and it was found next to her in the street: she was executed along with her whole family. This is just one tragedy, one of very many that happened in Lida. The elderly and distinguished surgeon Dr S.,[117] who arrived here from Lithuania and spent a month in Lida, was our informant.

In Pabianice the old people – those of 60 years and over – were shot, and before they were taken to be executed, the chief executioner, the officer, ordered the Jews to sing 'Hatikva' and then 'Tehezakna'. Then he taught them a nationalist Jewish song in German called 'Moses'. He sang the song over and over and only after they had managed to repeat and to sing it were they taken out to be killed.[118]

Some of the Jews of Ciechanów have been transferred to the nearby village of Nowe Miasto, where the Jews are living in appalling conditions, as if in a camp in strict solitary confinement.[119] The Germans warned that if anyone tries to return to the town they would shoot five Jews for every one who flees back. Two weeks ago a young girl ran away from Nowe Miasto, a relative of one of the *Judenrat*, its deputy-chairman. The girl was shot, along with the member of the *Judenrat* and three other Jews. This took place just two weeks ago.

Our tradition of martyrdom from the times of the Crusades, the Chmielnicki massacres and the period of the Middle Ages in general is being revived, times when Jews went to their deaths in a state of intense religious devotion and joy, as in the words of Bialik: 'Go out and meet your death with joy.' I have heard that in Zduńska Wola on the day before Shavuot 10 Jews were hanged, along with them the rabbi of the town. The rabbi turned to the Jews and appealed to them to rejoice, since they had been granted the privilege of representing the whole Jewish people and of dying a martyr's death for the Jewish faith.[120]

The Jewish community in Kraków is indeed being liquidated. Many of the Jews have already been deported. I have heard that the members of the *Judenrat* have been shot and the number of murdered has reached 57. The remaining ghetto has been turned into a giant work-camp.[121]

In Włodawa they killed the rebbe from Radzyń. One young man tried to save him and said that *he* was the rebbe. But the Germans saw through the 'deception', caught the rebbe and killed him and the young man as well.[122]

Telegrams and letters reach Warsaw from various small towns in the provinces with SOS messages: Save us! Help us! What can the Jews of Warsaw do for their relations, when they themselves are confined in the ghetto and their souls and their lives are hanging in the balance? Those who have financial resources at their disposal send

Christians to save the surviving members of their families or use other means. There is a Warsaw Jew from 18 Smocza Street who sent his family to a small town in the district of Lublin to make it easier for them to pass the war. The family consisted of the mother, daughter and son. The father stayed in Warsaw. The son was sent to a work-camp in Zamość and is thus still alive for the time being. The mother and daughter were sent 'to an unknown destination'. The father hired a Christian to look for his wife and daughter. The efforts were in vain, and no trace of them could be found. The despairing father is deter-mined to save his son. He set up a charge of theft against the son, who was then taken to Warsaw to stand trial. They will have him brought here in the next few days and in this way they hope to be able to hide him in the ghetto.

The two projects, the fictitious case and the sending of the Christian to find the mother and daughter cost 3,000 zloty each – in total therefore 6,000 zloty.

I have been told that there are Jews who have Aryan-like features who travel around the small towns where the Jewish communities have been destroyed and rescue the few remaining isolated small children who are found living with merciful Christians or elsewhere. My sister met one of these Jews and spoke with him. To judge by his looks and his Polish accent it would be hard to guess that he was a Jew. He goes on assignments on behalf of families of the locality and risks his life to save the life of isolated Jewish children. May these heroes be blessed who risk their lives to save these cherished, innocent Jewish children who are free of all wrong. (These Jews travel with Aryan papers on them of course.)

Is it any wonder that after listening to such stories for hours on end my head is heavy as lead and my eyes are dim. I feel the desire to bury my face in my pillow and to weep and weep endless tears for the tragic fate of my people, for the destruction of the frail Jewish sheep being choked and devoured by the wild and savage German leopard. Outcast lamb of Israel, who will give us a second Ezekiel who will sing words of comfort and summon up a second valley of bones?

Sunday, 7 June

Last night the German murderers in uniform claimed further victims, a Jewish man and a woman. At around one o'clock in the morning a car drew up at Karmelicka Street at the corner of Nowolipie Street, and a Jew aged about 35 and two German officers got out. They told the Jew to start walking and then gunned him down. The Jew didn't die immediately and they shot him again and then again until he was dead. Then they rang the bell of 22 Nowolipie Street and ordered the house-porter to take the body into the entrance-way. Early the next morning it was taken away. Who the Jew was is not known. According to one source he was called Rozen and was from 24 Elektoralna Street.

The Jewish woman was taken to Nowolipie Street and shot. It is presumed she was brought over from the Aryan side and then murdered. Something similar happened a few weeks ago when two Jewish women who had stayed outside the ghetto walls were shot in Meisels Street.

This week the Germans arrested Zachariasz' only daughter who is aged 18. They have been looking for him quite a while, along with Gancwajch, Szternfeld and Zelman. She is in the Pawiak.

The question frequently surfaces whether a thaw and an easing in the entrenched Polish anti-Semitism has arrived. As with most questions, there are different opinions and polar-opposite views. Many Jews consider that the influence of the war and the terrible blows that the country and all its inhabitants – Jews and Poles – have absorbed from the hand of the Germans has greatly changed relations between Poles and Jews, and the majority of Poles have been gripped by philo-Semitic feelings. Those who hold this opinion base their point of view on a considerable number of incidents that illustrate how from the very first months of the war the Poles showed, and continue to show, pity and kindness to Jews who were destitute, especially towards beggar-children. I have heard many stories of Jews who fled Warsaw on that momentous day, 6 September 1939,[123] and were given shelter, hospitality and food by Polish peasants who did not ask for any payment for their help. It is also known that our children who go begging and appear in their tens and hundreds in the

Christian streets are given generous amounts of bread and potatoes and from this they manage to feed themselves and their families in the ghetto. This is what those who take a bright view think.

Against this those who take a dark view argue that in the matter of anti-Semitism the Poles have received an instructive lesson from the Germans and that hatred of Jews in its active form – that is, the ghetto and the expropriation of property – has penetrated deeply into their bones.[124] These pessimists find support for their view in the different pronouncements of Poles on the Jewish question. In conversation many Poles expressed the opinion that after the Germans had been driven out a grave problem would emerge, that of the confiscated Jewish property. They have not the slightest desire to give up Jewish property that the Germans put into their hands. Jews who take this dark view are also fearful of the transition period when the Germans collapse and retreat. They suspect that the Poles – the masses – will carry out pogroms against us in the ghetto.

I personally incline to the first view. I see Polish–Jewish relations in a bright light. I think that this war will wash this earth of ours clean of much filth and savagery. From East and West will blow towards us winds of freedom and love of humanity. Poland after the war will also adhere to ideals for which the Russians, the English, the Americans, the Free French and the Polish legions have been fighting. There will be no refuge here for anti-Semitism, at least not for public, aggressive anti-Semitism. They will be ashamed to deal in it. I believe that the Polish people too has been purified by the terrible fire that has swept the face of the earth. Let us not forget: the Poles are in second place in the table of tragic losses among the nations, just behind the Jews. They have given, after us, the greatest number of victims to the Gestapo, and this does not take into account the destruction of the country. All this will of necessity leave deep traces in the people and lead to a loathing of the hatred of other races and peoples which is the source of National Socialism and anti-Semitism. Thus I dream of the coming of a time when Jews and Poles will live together in harmony.

This is lent a certain foundation by the good relations prevailing between the groups of Polish and Jewish smugglers. Of course the main thing in business, in the eyes of both sides, is profit. None the less when we consider how these ordinary Poles are capable of acts of humane generosity and great self-sacrifice towards the Jews – we can see that the matter requires further investigation and the reaching of certain conclusions.

I want to record two true stories of this nature:

Next to the 'target' near to where I live operates a smuggler by the name of Artur. It is said of him that he is a former intellectual. Anyone who has been in the army knows that the ordinary people do not like intellectuals and the lot of intellectuals in the army was not a pleasant one. For all that, when this intellectual was arrested on the Aryan side the Polish smugglers raised 5,000 zloty and got him released. And here is the second: a neighbour of mine climbs or crosses over to the Aryan side and stays overnight there with a Christian woman, a former neighbour of hers, who comes from the poorest section of society and is involved with smuggling. A number of days ago this woman was arrested on the other side of the wall. Her former neighbour with whom she was staying paid 800 zloty and got her released. I believe that these small events are also of importance and that they encapsulate within them a deeper meaning.[125]

Today at one o'clock midday an 18-year-old Polish youth was shot at the entrance to the ghetto next to 9 Przejazd Street. He was about to climb over to the Jewish side on some smuggling errand. A gendarme approached, saw him, and as quick as lightning fired once. The boy fell to the ground dead on the Jewish side. At three he was still lying there. Jewish and Polish blood is spilled, it mingles together and, crying to the heavens, it demands revenge!

Tuesday, 9 June

Yesterday there was great nervousness and agitation in the ghetto on account of the political and strategic situation. Widely optimistic exchanges could be heard everywhere: there is chaos in Germany, it is on the verge of revolution. Everyone was waiting in suspense for news of shock events that were to herald the end of the present regime and a radical change in the situation. There were stories of acts of sabotage carried out by paratroops in the area around Lublin, and other fanciful reports, the product of delusions and longings.

To our great distress the surprise did not materialize or rather has not yet happened, and that for which we have been yearning and longing so intensely did not transpire. We continue to choke in the pestilential atmosphere of the Nazi occupation. Instead of events prefiguring our salvation, one can feel it in the air this morning that there was another massacre in the night, on the familiar model of 18 April:[126] people were shot down in the streets like dogs. I could sense this on the street where I live because there was no smuggling going on, as there normally is every morning. Silence reigned, few Jews were passing along the street and even they looked to be hurrying and were anxious and tense. It turned out later that the signs had not been deceptive: I am told that last night and this morning claimed 17 Jewish victims. I managed to identify some of them, who they were and what there names were. At 10–12 Pańska Street lives the former director of the insurance company Europa, Goldman, and his son-in-law, a film director, Henryk Szaro (Szapiro). It is said that they both returned six weeks ago from Wilno. Further, the Leman brothers were murdered, former owners of the Apollo cinema at 6 Marszałkowska Street. It appears that the Leman family had also just come back from Wilno. Then a Jewish woman, Opatowska, was murdered at 7 Ogrodowa Street, a Jew who was a porter at 28 Świętojerska Street and was involved in smuggling, and a whole series of other Jews from among the smugglers.

Day after day, night after night Jewish blood flows like water in the ghetto. When will we see the end of this lawlessness? When?

To the starvation, typhus, tuberculosis and other illnesses that are springing up in the ghetto has been added a further illness known as Volynian fever. The victim suffers from a fever for several months. The fever does not stabilize, it rises and falls. The illness is very dangerous by all accounts because it attacks the lungs in particular. I know a boy who fell sick with this disease, but I also heard that it can attack adults as well. I suppose that it must have come here from Volynia.

Is it possible to see the degree of inequality and tension that existence-levels in the ghetto have reached now from the variety of midday meals on offer and the prices that are paid for them. Before the war an average lunch cost 1 zloty or 1.2. A better lunch of a few courses would cost 1.50. An excellent lunch, for example at Gertner (2 Leszno Street) would cost 8 zloty. A lunch like that was difficult to finish and would last one person a whole day. Bread was served without extra charge and without limit.

What is the position as regards the midday meal in the ghetto? A great percentage of the inhabitants of the ghetto eat no lunch at all. They go hungry or they make do with some small amount of food: a slice of bread, carrot or turnip. Then there comes a long series of levels. The lowest level of consumers, numbering several thousand (3,400), take advantage of what are known as *zupkes* in the community-kitchens and pay 90 groschen for a plate of soup which of course is not enough to satisfy them for even a short time.[127] Then there is the level of about 1,000 Jews who eat at the kitchens at 29 Leszno Street, 30 Nowolipie Street (for officials) and who pay 1.25 zloty for a fuller and more substantial plate of soup. Further there are the kitchens which are termed 'self-supporting'. These are for activists and officials (14 Leszno Street, 6 Orla Street, 13 Zamenhof Street, 32 Nalewki Street and 9 Przejazd Street) and there the price of lunch is 2.25 zloty, consisting of a plate of soup with vegetables, or at 3.50 with a tiny piece of meat. Then there are the private kitchens and once again we can see a long list of different prices and menus. In a private kitchen you can get lunch for 4 zloty consisting of a plate of soup, a minuscule piece of meat and a few vegetables. Then prices go into a steep rise: 4.50–5, 6.50, 10, 14, 17 zloty. At Szulc's Restaurant on Karmelicka Street at the corner with Nowolipie Street a lunch costs 14–15.50 zloty, and as it was described to me, it's pretty impressive: a very large serving of fatty soup, a large portion of meat with vegetables and dessert. This is reminiscent of lunches before the war. There are restaurants where lunch is even more expensive, 17–18 zloty and even 20. Only smugglers, racketeers, important activists, members of the police, and other rich people to whom the times have been good can afford to eat there.

Such are the conditions in the ghetto on the meal-front. In the Mojszeli Restaurant at 1 Nowolipie Street a portion of meat costs 18 zloty. There the customers are mainly smugglers. A very small percentage of housewives cook lunch at home as they did in better days.

According to stories in the German newspapers (*Reich, Novoye Slovo* – the newspaper of the White Russian Guard in Berlin), a committee of Russian Jews has recently been set up in Moscow.[128] According to the *Novoye Slovo* Jewish writers, Kushnirov and others,[129] have made a strong appeal to world Jewry to come to the aid of the Soviet Union in the struggle against Fascism and Hitlerism. To my eyes the thing looks puzzling: they are returning to the impure and heretical notion of the Jewish people. It may be that Moscow officially supports this. At any rate permission was granted for this appeal and note taken of it.

The old adage is confirmed: 'Jak bieda to do żyda' ['when in poverty, go to the Jew'] even though we find ourselves in such a deep pit. Should we see in this a spark of hope and an indication of revival and reawakening?

In the last issue of *Reich* I read a number of articles that demonstrate that conditions in Germany are deteriorating continually and the internal crisis is deepening. It is hard to say when things will come to a head and when the regime will break its neck, but there are signs of a deepening crisis in Hitler's state.

(a) Once again the newspapers are being reduced. *Reich*, which used to appear in 24 pages, is reduced to 12 pages. The food-cards have been reduced in the same way.
(b) All restaurant-cars in German trains have been cancelled.
(c) There has been a collection of old clothes and material. The explanation for this is that stocks of material are exhausted and a shortage is expected of clothes and of shoes even for the army.
(d) The appeal of the Gauleiter of Mecklenberg to all those from Rostock who are temporarily in Pomerania to return to Rostock, since shelters have been prepared for them, demonstrates that the last air-attacks of the English have certainly destroyed whole cities. These air-attacks, if they are carried out systematically and with greater intensity, are capable of bringing the war to a swift end.

Wednesday, 10 June

All the occupants of the building where I am living and of the nearby buildings were witnesses last night to terrible scenes and the whole night passed in the shadow of this horrific event. Yesterday, at 9.20 p.m., while we were eating supper, we heard suddenly the loud echo of continuous shooting below outside the window. The shooting went on for a long time. When silence fell, we saw a man, dressed in civilian clothes, rifle in his hand and sack under his arm. In front of my window a young man lay dead, his head and stomach torn open. It turned out that two German gendarmes arrived in disguise (apparently one of them was the degenerate sadist Frankenstein,[130] who has earned himself a reputation by his butcheries here), their rifles hidden in sacks. As they arrived they spotted a young Christian, who was trying to climb over the wall, and a Jewish woman who was accompanying him to see if he got over safely. The disguised Germans opened fire on them instantly and they were killed. The Jewish woman was 27 years old and her name was Liman. Before the war the Limans had a fruit store in Przejazd Street. Lately the Liman couple has been living from smuggling. The Christian who was killed was supplying them with goods.

It turns out that at the same time acts of terror were being carried out in various locations in the ghetto as part of the war against smuggling. At 30 Świętojerska Street gendarmes fired automatic weapons at two Jews. I have been told that five Jews were shot in Waliców Street; all in all yesterday, Tuesday, was awash with the murder of Jews; on Smocza Street two boys were shot by Junaks while they were observing the confiscation of a store of potatoes and vegetables from the courtyard at 7 Smocza Street; at the corner of Wielka and Pańska Street a Jew was shot by the gendarmes. On Pańska Street two Jews were murdered; on Prosta Street, one Jew. It appears that a large number of Jews were killed in the courtyard of the Pundak Hotel at 32 Grzybowska Street. The occupants of Żelazna Street at the corner of Nowolipie Street heard loud shots between eleven and one in the night under the beam of searchlights. There were also searches carried out with dogs. I don't know the exact number of victims. Different numbers are given: 18, 28, 46 and even over 60. The office at the cemetery probably knows the exact number.

Today at half past twelve midday a young Jew aged 30 by the name of Rosenstrauch was shot at 7 Nowolipie Street (or 8 Mylna Street). He owned a metal-works and wasn't doing badly. Out of friendship he rented part of his basement flat for a small mill.[131] Two gendarmes who were passing spotted traces of the seed scattered around. They went down, took him from behind the door and shot him summarily in the back of the neck. He left behind a wife and a boy of four. Again a night of blood and death was visited upon the ghetto.

An official of the Jewish community, a Mr M., who maintains regular contact with the German Jews who are living in the synagogue building on Tłomackie Street, informed me that he had himself read a letter yesterday that had arrived the same day from Berlin, whose contents – which are almost too good to be true – were as follows: the author of the letter announced that a large air-raid was carried out on Berlin. After the air-raid, riots broke out in the streets and in the course of these 15 SS and SA were killed.[132] On that day a state of emergency was announced through loudspeakers in Berlin. In Moabit[133] movement in the streets was only permitted until five o'clock in the afternoon, and in other parts of the city until seven. Sadly there is no confirmation of these sensational reports from any other source whatsoever.

Thursday, 11 June

It appears that last night there were no fresh victims. A night that passes in the ghetto without blood-letting sounds like something so unusual that it is necessary to take special note of it. We are so accustomed to an unremitting terror that the hour when there is a pause we feel as if we are mistaken, that it is not natural that nothing is happening. It was the same during those terrible days of September in 1939: whenever there was a break in the bombardment of Warsaw from the air and in the heavy artillery fire, we couldn't believe that there was silence. We strained our ears, listened and listened . . . for the cannon and the falling bombs.

When will the war end? How much longer will it last?

This question, one of decisive import for us, which signifies for us to be or not to be, gnaws away at the mind of every one of us and impels us to concentrate all our intellectual and emotional strength to give an answer to it. It is clear to every Jew that if the war finishes soon, there is still a prospect and hope of remaining alive, but if the war drags on, then our hopes of surviving it are almost nil.

I tried posing this question to various Jews. Naturally the answers were all different. Many thought that the war would be over soon.

But there are Jews who hope that the war will be finished by the end of July. They told me about a fortune-teller who foretold the disappearance of the ghetto walls from Warsaw in the course of June, that is, this month. There are those who put the end back to the later autumn months, but think that the whole nightmare will be over by winter. Set against these are those who hold more realistic opinions, since they are preparing themselves for the fact that the end is a long, long way off. They think that the earliest possible date for the end of the war is the summer or autumn of next year. This means that the war has to go on for at least another year.

I should record that the 'lengtheners' of the war are in a decisive majority. Even though Jews are in general optimists, when we come to consider the final conclusion of the war, the proportion of 'lengtheners' to 'shorteners' is of the order of one to five or it may be even one to ten.

If this poll had any influence at all on events, these would be fatal for the Jews. I personally think that the decisive point will fall before winter and the Germans, the German people, will not dare and will not have the strength to continue their campaign for a fourth winter. Their nerve will not hold. That is how I see it.

Recently a community worker received a letter from Zürich which contains the following sentence: 'You can't imagine how close the end of the war is.' May we only be granted the chance to see who is right in their estimates.

It is reported that at four this morning two Jews were shot dead and one wounded on Przebieg Street at the corner with Bonifraterska Street. The murderers were Germans dressed as civilians. The Jews who died were involved with smuggling people and goods through a gap in the bridge that is in that alleyway. It seems that it is not to be granted to us that a night and a day pass in peace.

On Wednesday, after the two had fallen victim on Tuesday evening, the smuggling on Nowolipie and Przejazd Street was halted, almost as if in mourning for the memory of the smugglers from the smuggling groups who died. Today, regardless of the appalling campaign of terror against the smugglers, and in spite of the large number of victims that have fallen in the last few days, the smuggling was going again at full throttle, as if nothing had happened. This shows that under the present conditions smuggling is life's imperative, and that life is stronger than death. In these sad days death and life are walking side by side and death is trying to destroy life. But ultimately life must subjugate death and leave the struggle as victor.

Friday, 12 June

Blood, blood, blood.

This morning at five o'clock at 78 Niska Street, next to the 'target', six Jews were shot. The murder was carried out by Germans disguised in tattered clothes with Jewish armbands and pipes in their mouths. It is said that the murders are being committed by a special unit called: execution unit for the surveillance of the walls.

Yesterday after nine in the evening two Jews were shot in a similar fashion in Ceglana Street at the corner of Walicόw, after seven Jews had already been killed this week. The smugglers have reached the stature of heroes in my eyes, and the day will come when the whole people will surely sing of them in celebration of their great heroism.[134]

I was talking today with a woman from Tłuszcz, where all the Jews were expelled two weeks ago, 750 people in all.[135] The murders that were committed in the course of this expulsion cry out to the heavens. The number of murdered exceeds 60, shot without cause, for any trifling matter. The two Raduszynski brothers, shoemakers, young men, were shot. One of them for taking down the top of his machine and hiding it. And the second because he wanted to slip a small package to a woman who was sitting on a wagon. Three young women aged 18–19 were shot, one because she tried to sit on a wagon, not understanding that her place was among those on foot. An old man of 85, Platkowski (?), whose mind was still clear. The rabbi of Tłuszcz escaped to Jadów, where he was killed by the Germans under horrific torture. They beat him to death. Before the expulsion 12 Jews had already been shot in Tłuszcz. They had been found outside the ghetto. These Jews were executed on the spot without inquiry or investigation.

In other incidents Poles brought about the death of Jews by pointing the finger at them: *Jude*. In fact overall the woman was critical of the behaviour of the Poles towards the Jews: it was generally bad. This state of affairs is puzzling, considering that the position of the Poles is not much better than that of the Jews. They too are afraid to walk in the street. Many of them have had their shops and their goods confiscated.

All the property of the Tłuszcz Jews has been looted by the Germans. Even the parcels that many took with them during the expulsion were lost or thrown away on the road. The Jews made their way on foot to Radzymin, accompanied by gendarmes, soldiers on horseback, policemen on bicycles, and all kinds of Germans from other units. The Jews reached Warsaw barefoot and naked, having lost everything.

The woman I was speaking with was a simple meat-vendor by the name of Zimmerman. Speaking of the expulsion from Tłuszcz, she said: 'There is no way to put into words what happened to us.' I thought over what the woman had said and concluded that she is right. There can be no words, no images, no embellishments – just cold hard facts. The day will come when these facts will shake the world and they will be transformed into an impassioned appeal 'Remember!' against hatred and shame and against the degenerate murderers. As for us – tortured and murdered though we are innocent of any crime – the world will be duty-bound to show love and compassion for our suffering.

One of the most impressive of the books in world literature that engrave themselves deeply on the reader's memory and have a simplicity and directness, a profound tragedy which is quite stunning, is, in my opinion, and I am quite convinced of this, the book 'The War of the Jews and Romans' by Josephus. Anyone who has read this book (I read it in the classic translation into Hebrew by Dr Simkhoni) will never forget, I believe, the terrible and bloody events that took place in Jerusalem, Samaria, Galilee, Trans-Jordan, and Syria, in the days of the fierce struggle between the rebellious mob imbued with an extreme zealotry, who in their blind patriotism said to themselves: freedom or death – and the savage Roman imperialists. Who can forget the bare facts of the slaughter on both sides, both what the Greeks inflicted on the Jews in the places where they had the upper hand, and vice versa, what the Jews did to the Greeks where the Jews were the majority.

I can recall the stories told by Josephus. If we compare them with the slaughters committed by the Germans in our times, then I come to the conclusion that the Germans' deeds today are more bloody, more vicious and more shocking than those of the Greeks and Romans 2,000 years ago. We must not forget that then there was a struggle; today unarmed and innocent people are being brutally killed. And what is more – since then, nearly 19 centuries have passed, and it is 153 years since the French Revolution and the declaration of the rights of man. Do we learn from this that humanity has been regressing for more than 2,000 years and has become more savage instead of progressing and becoming more humane, imbued with greater idealism?

If we are talking about the Germans, there is no doubt that they have regressed dramatically and returned to the moral level of their barbarian forefathers, the inhabitants of the dense forests of central Germany in the day of the Roman Emperors.

Part II
Diary of the Great Deportation

A paper-shop at the corner of Nowy Świat,[136] Daughter of P., Cecylia, was shot.

At 14 Nowolipie Street, P. himself reappeared, miraculously back from the dead ... This I heard from A.

28 Świętojerska Street – Monday – five in the afternoon eight in the evening, the house-porter at 13 Nalewki.[137]

Tuesday[138] – five in the morning – 3 Niska Street, Smocza Street
The shopkeeper who opened for R. before five,
The policeman Ajzensztajn[139]
Dr Sztajnk[140]
The arrests – in the Supply Office (ZZ)[141] and in the Jewish community offices.[142]

15 Chłodna Street – more than 10
The Day of Judgement – whence will come our help?

We are preparing ourselves for death. What will be our fate?
Karmelicka Street – round-up into vehicles.
There is talk of 20 dead since this morning
Szmul of the 'conquerers' – 15 years.[143]
Someone called Rozen and his father and uncle were shot yesterday before ten o'clock going into the shop.

Wednesday, 22 July[144] – *The Day before Tishebov*

A day of turmoil, chaos and fear: the news about the expulsion of Jews is spreading like lightning through the town, Jewish Warsaw has suddenly died, the shops are closed, Jews run by, in confusion, terrified. The Jewish streets are an appalling sight – the gloom is indescribable. There are dead bodies at several places. No one is counting them and no names are being given in this terrifying catastrophe. The expulsion is supposed to begin today from the hostels for the homeless,[145] and from the prisons. There is also talk of an evacuation of the hospital.[146] Beggar children are being rounded up into wagons. I am thinking about my aged mother – it would be better to put her to sleep than to hand her over to those murderers.[147]

Ora brings exaggerated stories from Sweden [that the war is coming to an end].[148]

Thursday, 23 July – *Tishebov*

Disaster after disaster, misfortune after misfortune. The small ghetto has been turned out on to the streets.[149] My nephew Uri arrived at half past seven.[150]

The people were driven out from 42–44 Muranowska Street during the night.

Garbatko, 300 women, 55 children.[151] Last Tuesday in the night. Rain has been falling all day. Weeping. The Jews are weeping. They are hoping for a miracle. The expulsion is continuing. Buildings are blockaded. 23 Twarda Street.[152] Terrible scenes. A woman with beautiful hair. A girl, 20 years old, pretty. They are weeping and tearing at their hair. What would Tolstoy have said to this?

On Zamenhof Street the Germans pulled people out of a tram,[153] and killed them on the spot. (Muranowska Street.)

Friday, 24 July, six in the morning

The turmoil is as it was during the days of the bombardment of Warsaw.[154] Jews are running as if insane, with children and bundles of bedding. Buildings on Karmelicka and Nowolipie Streets are being surrounded. Mothers and children wander around like lost sheep: where is my child? Weeping. Another wet day with heavy skies: rain is falling. The scenes on Nowolipie Street. The huge round-up on the streets. Old men and women, boys and girls are being dragged away.

The police are carrying out the round-up, and officials of the Jewish community wearing white armbands are assisting them.[155]

The death of Czerniaków yesterday at half past eight in the Jewish community building.[156] As for the reasons: during the ceremony at Grzybowska Street,[157] he said: 'Szlag mnie i tak trafi, prozsę pani' [I'll die anyway, Madam].

The round-up was halted at three o'clock. How Jews saved themselves: fictitious marriages with policemen. Guta's marriage to her husband's brother.[158] The savagery of the police during the round-up, the murderous brutality. They drag girls from the rickshaws, empty out flats, and leave the property strewn everywhere. A pogrom and a killing the like of which has never been seen.[159]

Merenlender's visit. She and her father were taken the first day. In what kind of train-wagons are the prisoner's kept? According to her they will not even last a night. Many buildings have received an order to present themselves on their own. The manager of 30 Świętojerska Street, Nadzia, gave himself up. People get attacks of hysteria; 11,000 people have been rounded up; 100 policemen held hostage. One of them let himself down on a rope, fell, and was badly wounded. The policeman Zakhajm has been shot. Terrifying rumours about the night. Will there be a pogrom?

Schultz is dismissing 100 Jews.[160] His explanation for his action. The great hunger in the ghetto. Someone saves his sister and a four-year-old child, passing her off as his wife. The child does not give the secret away. He cries out: 'Daddy!' I am trying to save my mother with a paper from the Jewish Self-help Organization [ŻTOS].[161]

Saturday, 25 July

Last night I couldn't sleep. It passed peacefully. Everything reminds one of September 1939. People rushing through the streets. The day is so long. Packages, mainly of pillows and bedclothes. Noisy movement. The never-ending questions: 'Meken do durkhgen?' ['Can one get through there?'][162] Disaster: Gucia has been thrown out of her flat. Five killed in Dzielna Street in the night. Terrible scenes in the streets. The police are carrying out elegant furniture from the homes of those who have been driven out. *Umschlagplatz*:[163] a policeman is crying.

He is struck. 'Why are you crying?' 'Meine mutter, meine frau!' 'Frau, ja; Mutter, nicht.' ['My mother, my wife!' 'Wife, yes; mother, no.']¹⁶⁴ A smuggler who threw himself out from the fourth floor, I saw him on his sick-bed.

How did Czerniaków die? 10,000!¹⁶⁵ The Wajcblum family. The looting of property. Last night there were a lot of suicides.¹⁶⁶ Conditions at the *Umschlagplatz*. People are dying where they are being held. You can't go in or out. By yesterday 25,000 had been taken away, with today, 30,000.¹⁶⁷ With each day the calamity worsens. Many give themselves up voluntarily. It is supposed that hunger forces them into it.¹⁶⁸

The new proclamation: non-productive elements are being sent to the East.¹⁶⁹ Vast numbers of dead among those being expelled. The German Jews are content to go. For them it is a long journey. The Jewish Self-help Organization is flooded with Jews begging for mercy, stretching out their hands for help – who is there to help them? Then every Jew would come and ask for papers from the organization.

Since Tuesday there has been no newspaper in the ghetto, apart from the very sketchy 'Jewish' paper *Gazeta Żydowska*.¹⁷⁰

Sunday, 26 July

The 'action' continues.¹⁷¹ The buildings at 10–12 Nowolipie Street are surrounded. Shouts and screams. Outside my window they are checking papers and arresting people. Human life is dependent on some little piece of paper. It's really enough to drive you insane. A lovely morning, the sky is wonderfully beautiful: 'the sun is shining, the acacia is blooming and the slaughterer is slaughtering.' The blockade of our courtyard. How it was carried out. Winnik's story.¹⁷² '*Good news*' from Brześć.¹⁷³ The closing of the post office.¹⁷⁴ The seizing of an eight-year-old girl, prettily dressed. She screams: 'Mummy!' Libuszycki, Lejzerowicz.¹⁷⁵ The terrible hunger. Many give themselves up. They are not accepted, so great is the number that are going. Yet they still set up blockades so as to extort money. The terrible corruption of our police and their assistants. An outrage, an outrage!¹⁷⁶

6 Solna Street; 99 victims. Today 12,000 martyrs. The closing of the post office. A kilo of bread – 50 zloty. Potatoes – 20. The violence of the police. Warszawski's son,[177] an official of the Jewish community, was seized and ransomed for 250 zloty. Czudner [Meir Czudner, Hebrew poet, editor and translator, who died in the ghetto]. Kirzner's sister – seven people. The breakup of families – Mendrowski. Pola. It hurts so much. 37,000 martyrs today [till today, that is, in the first five days of the deportation]. The Jewish community and Jewish Self-help Organization workers are also not safe. Only the workers in the 'shops' seem to be still safe.[178]

A new leadership for the community. Lichtenbaum, chairman, the deputies: Wielikowski, Sztolcman, Orliański.[179] The shot in Brustman's window. Lola Kapelusz, the wife of a lawyer from Łódź. She goes twice with her daughter to give herself up because they are starving. 'We haven't eaten now for two days.' They send them away because of huge crowds of people giving themselves up. Confiscations of packages at the post office. First people were given a receipt confirming that the office had received the packages – then, the confiscation.[180]

Monday, 27 July

The 'action' still continuing at full strength. People are being rounded up. Victims on Smozca Street. People were dragged from the trams and shot. One hundred dead (old people and the sick) at the *Umschlagplatz*.[181] Huge numbers of dead at 29 Ogrodowa Street. The remaining occupants were taken out, no notice was taken of their papers. The cause – a piece of glass fell on to the street when there were Germans passing. Shooting all day. Dead on Pawia and other streets.

The terrible hunger. Bread – 60 zloty, potatoes – 20, meat – 80. There are round-ups in the street. The commandant from Lublin is in Warsaw.[182] How high will the numbers of deported become? Opinions differ: 100,000, 200,000. Some will go even further: about 50,000 will be left and these will also be removed to Grochów or Pelcowizna.[183] Today the number of those deported will reach about 44,000. And according to Wielikowski there is no prospect of an end to the 'action'. A break for 48 hours (so people are saying). Auerswald has returned.[184] Perhaps things will get easier? Suicides in great numbers. The Cytryn family, mother and son embracing. The attitude of the Poles. Kalman weeping over the telephone. He calls for revenge. Neustadt has been murdered.[185]

Tuesday, 28 July

The 'action' continues relentlessly. There are many volunteers, two families from 8 Nowolipie left their flats and gave themselves up (10 + 5). The reason – the terrible hunger. Bialer – execution because he didn't remove his hat. The incident with Kirzner. Up to yesterday 45,000. Wealthy Jews have left Warsaw.[186] The Rozencwajgs on a wagon.[187] The seizure of Gutgold. Lazar: taken off a tram. Deaths on Smocza Street. How was a strong young man shot between the eyes? He tried to escape, was wounded in the arm. He begged for mercy, and was killed by two bullets in the head. Gruzalc's mother has been taken away.[188] He works at Többens'.[189]

Pessimism of Kon.[190] The Germans want to leave 60,000 Jews in the town. The fate of those who work for the Jewish Self-help Organization. Some say that their identity papers will only be recognized as valid for another two days.[191] This is what Szeryński is said to have announced.[192] A blockade on our building for the second time. The two Walfisz boys were taken away.

The sight of Nowolipie and Smocza Streets at midday – a hunt for wild animals in the forest. The world has never seen such scenes. People are thrown into wagons like dogs, old people and the sick are taken to the Jewish cemetery and murdered there. I heard that a smuggler who lives on our courtyard wanted to get rid of her old, sick mother: she handed her over to the butchers. Jewish policewomen.[193] The huge numbers of people and sewing-machines assembled in the courtyards of 44–6 Nowolipie Street.[194]

Wednesday, 29 July

The eighth day of the 'action' that is continuing at full strength. At the corner of Karmelicka Street – a 'wagon'. People are thrown up on to it. In the courtyard of 29 Nowolipie Street the furniture of the occupants who were thrown out of the buildings is still standing there. A Jew sleeps in the open air.

Kon recounts: a young woman who returning from work at a *placówka* told of the murder of two 19-year-old boys, shot dead. One was left dying for a whole hour. They were shot for no reason. Ilenman Igla, the daughter from the ZZ [Food Office] walks with her mother. Places of execution: Piaseczno, Pustelnik, Bełżec.[195] People standing at the windows are shot at. A Christian woman on Leszno Street, seeing the wagons with those who have been rounded up, curses the Germans. She presents her chest and is shot. On Nowy Świat a Christian woman stands defiantly, kneels on the pavement and prays to God to turn his sword against the executioners – she had seen how a gendarme killed a Jewish boy.

A meeting of *Oneg Shabbes*.[196] Its tragic character. They discuss the question of ownership and the transfer of the archive to America to the Yivo if we all die.[197]

The terrible news about the Germans' plans. It is being assumed that they intend to deport 250,000. So far, 53,000. The terrible pessimism of G. and K—n.[198] They talk of death as of something that will certainly come. Announcements in the streets: all those who present themselves voluntarily before the first of the next month will receive 3 kg of bread and 1 kg of jam.[199]

'Workshop-mania'.[200] Will that save people? The Germans thank the police for their 'productive efforts'. It is said that they are going to put the police to 'work' in other locations. How are the Jews listening to the loudspeakers?[201] ... So far eight Jewish policemen have committed suicide. Conditions in the streets get worse every day. Many Jews with identity papers from the Jewish Self-help Organization have been arrested.

A bulldog that had been taught to attack only Jews with armbands in Warsaw-Praga. A Jew was seized by him.[202]

How do Jews hide? In couches, in beds, cellars, attics. The Rozencwajgs were set free for 500 zloty. A memorandum has been handed to the authorities, offering a ransom in return for the halting of the expulsion. No reply has yet been received.

No Germans appear until four in the afternoon. The Jews do everything in an orderly fashion. Each day about 1 per cent of those rounded up, between 60 and 70 people, are killed.[203] They throw loaves of bread into the wagons. Those at the front grab even two or three of them, those at the back get none at all. The savage round-ups in the streets will go on until 1 August. Then those who are not working will receive orders. Children will not be separated from their mothers. Someone called our policemen 'gangsters'.

The day after Czerniaków's death the German officer W. came and apologized,[204] justifying himself by saying he was not responsible for the death and giving his word of honour as a German officer that those being deported are not being killed.[205]

At the employment office there are lists of the community workers and employees of the Jewish Self-help Organization. For the moment they are being left alone. It is supposed that they are going to check them. For now they are sorting out the workshop employees.

Sometimes I am quite calm about my life and sometimes a little indifferent, but suddenly I am gripped by fear of death that drives me insane. Everything depends on the news coming in from the street. Blockades in the streets. On Nowolipie Street near the Jewish Self-help Organization they seized a girl aged 15 or 16 who was going with a basket to buy something. Her shouts and screams filled the air. In H. well-dressed women were found. About 95 per cent of the people are sent away without any kind of packing, of linen or clothes.

Thursday, 30 July

The ninth day of the 'action' that is continuing with all its fearfulness and terror. From five in the morning we hear through the window the whistles of Jewish police and the movement and the running of Jews looking for refuge. Opposite my window, in Nowy Zjazd Street, a policeman chases a young woman and catches her. Her cries and screams are heart-breaking. The blockade on our building. How was the Rajchner family saved? How did I save Mrs Minc?

Today the post office was opened again. Brandstetter was seized yesterday afternoon by the Germans.[206] He was released at the *Umschlagplatz*. Dr Fuswerg's wife was seized, as was Klima.[207] They were freed this morning.

From midday yesterday onwards the shooting has not stopped

next to our building. A soldier stands at the corner of Zamenhof and Nowolipie Streets and abuses the passers-by. Terrifying rumours: the authorities have closed the Jewish Self-help Organization. Brandt expresses his condolences to the committee members on Cz.'s death.[208] Höfle defends himself by saying he was not responsible for the death.[209] The terrible appearance of Nalewki Street. A woman shot dead there yesterday when she came out of the courtyard and began to run. Workers were removed and deported from Többens' workshop at 6 Gęsia Street. Community officials were also seized and deported. All the workshops were emptied. Those who hid themselves or refused to go were shot. All the workers have been removed from the workshop of the second section of the Jewish Self-help Organization, which was in the process of being set up. At the corner of Karmelicka and Nowolipie Streets they used axes to break off the locks and open up the shops. By midday 4,000 people had been rounded up, among them 800 volunteers. By yesterday evening the total number passed 60,000.

The notice in the *Deutsche Allgemeine Zeitung*: they are broadcasting continually on London radio, 'SOS Save 400,000 Jews in the Warsaw ghetto whom the Germans are slaughtering. The "lie" of the English propaganda is clear to anyone who saw the film from the Warsaw ghetto.'

A letter from Bialystok that a Polish policeman brought, from a woman to her husband. She and her son are together with several other families and have to work hard in the fields, but they are receiving food. About 2,000 people have been removed from 27–9 Ogrodowa Street. Also a lot of children from the Pnimia children's home.[210] Today many employees of the community were seized (including teachers) and from the Jewish Self-help Organization. The story of Pigowski.

Friday, 31 July

The tenth day of the slaughter that has no parallel in our history. Yesterday a large number of officials were rounded up. The female director of Többens' workshop, Neufeld. At the corner of 11 Mylna Street they stop me and lead me up to an officer. The Jewish Self-help

Organization identity-cards 'have no value any more'. *Odjazd* – ambiguous.[211] I was terrified.

They are driving out the old people from the old people's home at 52 Nowolipki Street. Those rounded up are divided up into: those fit for work (*arbeitsfähig*), those able to survive (*lebensfähig*) and those not fit to be transported (*transportunfähig*). The last group is killed on the spot.[212] About 2,000 people have been removed from the buildings at 27, 29 and 31 Ogrodowa Street. Also from the boarding-school at 27 Ogrodowa Street. The official from the centre,[213] Rozen, and his father taken away. A certain young man, Frydland, who has been working for several months at one of the *placówki* has been seized and deported. Rabbi Nisenbaum's wife was put into the wagon.[214] Mrs Mławer was shot and wounded. They removed the caretaker and his family from Centos.[215]

Yesterday 1,500 reported voluntarily.[216] Today by midday, 750. Among them members of the intelligentsia. There is talk that part of the 'squad' has already left for Radom.[217] The remainder are leaving tomorrow. I have heard that they will be taking 500 Jewish policemen with them from here. At four o'clock they suddenly took those who had been rounded up out of the wagons and announced that the action was being suspended. The joy and hope that this brought forth. At six to half past six the blockades started again.

A woman called Mydlarska jumped up into the wagon after her husband had been taken. In our courtyard a woman threw herself from the third floor – she was starving. Today about 3,000 people were taken away from Waliców and Grzybowska Streets. No attention was paid to identity papers 'Zay gezunt! Zay gezunt!' [Goodbye, goodbye!'] a young Jew shouts from the wagon.

The calamity of the 'dead souls'. 120,000 fictitious food-coupons (*bony*).[218]

Saturday, 1 August

'Outside there is destruction by the sword, and inside there is terror.' The 11th day of the 'action' that gets progressively more terrible and brutal. Germans are in the process of emptying whole buildings and sides of streets. They took about 5,000 people out of 20–2 and other buildings on Nowolipie Street. The turmoil and the terror is appalling. There is a general expulsion of all the occupants of Nowolipie Street between Karmelicka and Smocza Streets. The awful sight: people carrying packages of pillows and bedclothes. No one thinks of moving furniture. Fajnkind says to his sister-in-law: 'Hide yourself and your beautiful child! Into the cellar!'

The nightmare of this day surpasses that of all previous days. There is no escape and no refuge. The round-ups never cease, Sagan[219] and Chilinowicz,[220] Sztajn,[221] Zołotow, Karcewicz, Prync,[222] Opoczynski have been seized.[223] Mothers lose their children. A weak old woman is carried on to the bus. The tragedies cannot be captured in words.

The rabbi from 17 Dzielna Street has been seized and apparently shot. Children walking in the street are seized. The property of those who have been expelled is grabbed by neighbours who are left, or by the new tenants, the 'shop'-workers.

Fifty of the customers, 10 staff were removed from the officials' kitchen at 30 Nowolipie Street.[224] People who have hidden are shot. I spent the whole day at 25 Nowolipki Street and didn't go to eat, so was saved.

Sunday, 2 August

I spent the night at my sister's, at 17 Dzielna Street. The 12th day of the 'action', which becomes more and more intense. From yesterday the parents of police have been excluded from the category of those protected.[225] Last night a lot of people were killed or wounded.

A new proclamation in the streets of the ghetto from the head of the Jewish police: the action will continue. All those who are not employed in organizations or by the German authorities have to report voluntarily on 2, 3 and 4 August and they will receive 3 kg of bread and 1 kg of jam. Families will not be split up.[226]

Today three people were taken away from the kitchen at 22 Nowolipie Street. It looks like they have stopped recognizing the identity papers of the Jewish Self-help Organization.[227] Yesterday evening a large group of hundreds of Jews who have been driven from their homes was taken into the Pawiak. Early today some of them were brought out of the Pawiak, among them old people, young women with small babies on pillows. They were led by Jewish policemen. Jehoszua Zegal has been seized. Among the tragedies: Karcewicz has been taken away; she left behind two children aged four and seven. Magidson. People murdered on Nowolipki Street. The 'action' continues. People are saying that there will be a break for three weeks from 5 August. Those who remain will be able to get themselves fixed up with work. When that period is up, they will return and take away and liquidate anyone who is not working. A large number of people – estimated at 15,000 – have been taken from the small ghetto. Grandmother was killed by a single shot: she was standing at the window that looks over Sienna Street. Mother has gone to Gucia's.

Monday, 3 August

The 13th day of slaughter. A night of horrors. Shooting went on all night. I couldn't sleep. In the morning I went to L.'s sawmill.[228] A mass of people, men, women and children, were gathered in the courtyard and in the garden. They were trying to save themselves. Will they be saved? It is said that from those who were taken to the *Umschlagplatz* yesterday about 2,000 were freed who had various papers. People are consoling themselves with the thought that the savage round-up will stop tomorrow and it will be carried out in an orderly way.

Everyone was taken from TOZ [Society for the Protection of Health] who was found there.[229]

At the cemetery 56 Jewish prisoners were killed. A few days ago more than 100 people were murdered on Nowolipie Street. Today the Germans have surrounded the following streets: Gęsia, Smocza, Pawia, Lubiecka, and took away all the occupants. Yesterday the following were taken away: Kahanowicz,[230] Rusak, and Jehoszua Zegal's whole family.[231]

Tuesday, 4 August

The 14th day of the 'action' that is being continued at full speed. Today the blockades were set up at ten in the morning. The Germans work together with the Jewish police. The small ghetto was surrounded and also Gęsia and Zamenhof Streets. There are stories of terrible lootings and violence during the expulsions. They deport the people and loot and pillage their possessions. Shops are also broken open and the goods carried off. In this participate Jewish police, ordinary Jewish neighbours and Germans.

It was announced that 14 Jews were killed who had sought refuge at the cemetery, those who work in the cemetary organizations, in addition to the 56 sentenced to death, who were killed.[232]

I have heard the following: they found a woman who had recently given birth and her three-day-old child on Szczęśliwa Street. They shot dead both the mother and the child – this is a true story. They are expelling the occupants from the buildings once again: from 45 Nowolipie Street and other buildings. Even if someone is not seized and sent away to die there is no certainty that when they return home they will find a roof over their head.

Again there is talk that the savage round-up will stop today. But we have heard this before and nothing came of it. The workers from the kitchen at 8 Prosta Street have been removed. A Junak was crying: 'Szkoda tych Żydków' [It's a shame about these Jews']. At 9 Nalewki Street a sick woman was murdered. The 'action' will continue until 17 August. Zegal's father has been taken away. How do they get the corpses out? Tozsa Apfel has been taken and sent away.[233] Our feelings have been numbed! We hear of great calamities happening to those closest to us and we do not react. A letter from Baranowicze. The writer is working as a farm-labourer. She asks for underwear. Life is cheap, 7 zloty for white bread, 1.80 for potatoes. It would be good if she could be sent underwear. The letter came by post.[234]

Wednesday, 5 August

The 'action' continues unabated. We have no more strength to suffer. There are many murders. They kill the sick who don't go down to the courtyards. Yesterday about 3,000 volunteers reported. Not all of them were taken. These they sent away. In the town they are rounding up people regardless of the papers they have. Whoever falls into the hands of the Germans or the Jewish police is seized. The Jewish policemen took away Hillel Cajtlin.[235] He was released. Balaban has been taken.[236] At 13 Dzielna Street they killed Mrs Grun who was ill and a girl. Yesterday the 'actions' in Radom began.

Thursday, 6 August

The 16th day of the 'action', which is continuing. Yesterday they took away everyone from the offices of the Jewish Self-help Organization who were there at the time, about 60 or 70 people. Some of them (Dr Bornsztajn,[237] Sztolcman, a girl) were freed. They are predicting a hot day today. Once again there are the theories that the action will be suspended tomorrow because the annihilation squads are about to leave for Radom. Conditions in Landau's sawmill. The expulsion of the occupants of 10–12, 23 and 25 Nowolipki Street. Redoubled savagery and the maltreatment of Jews. While flats are being emptied out and people come to save their belongings, the SS arrive and seize the occupants.

Kohn and Heller have been killed.[238] During a blockade by the Germans the Jewish police storm into Zylberberg's building. They are terrified that they have found them and say: 'Hide and lock yourself in well!' It was then that the whole family of the Radomsko rebbe was killed.[239]

P—wer saw orders with regard to trains and their numbers that were sent to Treblinka (the place of execution?)[240] Starvation haunts the survivors more and more, a kilo of bread – 45 zloty, a kilo of potatoes, 15 zloty. Today they have already taken about 5,000 Jews from the small ghetto. Tosza Apfel has been caught and deported.

Friday, 7 August

The 17th day of the massacres. Yesterday was a horrendous day with a great number of victims. People were brought out from the small ghetto in huge numbers. The number of victims is estimated at 15,000. They emptied Dr Korczak's orphanage with the Doctor at the head.[241] Two hundred orphans. In the evening they drove out the people from the flats in the square bounded by Dzielna, Zamenhof,

Nowolipki and Karmelicka Streets. There are no words to describe the tragedies and disasters. Rozencwajg's two sisters were sent away. One with a child of six months, the other with a four-year-old. Mrs Schweiger is not there.[242] How terrible. Today Germans and Ukrainians came to the sawmill of the L. brothers and they rounded up a large number of women with their children from among the factory-workers, and women who just happened to be there. Wasser,[243] Smolar,[244] with her child, Tintpulwer and others, many others.[245]

The workers turn on the intellectuals. A shocking experience. Many rabbis have been sent away. Mendel Alter from Kalisz,[246] and more, more. During the pogrom on Nowolipie Street about 360 people were killed. At number 30 more than 30 people were killed. Górny's mother has been killed by the Germans,[247] and he came to sell meal-coupons as if nothing had happened. So dulled have our feelings become.

The hunger presses in on us in a terrible way. Today I had no bread for breakfast. I ate pickled cucumber. Today a kilo of bread costs 55 zloty. A new order has been issued that if people report voluntarily for deportation from 7 to 14 August they will receive a kilo of bread and half a kilo of jam. From this it can be deduced that the 'action' will continue for at least a week. Stupnicki has been sent away.[248] Three thousand were brought from Otwock directly to the *Umschlagplatz*. The number who have fallen victim is enormous. The crematorium near Malkinia and Sokołów.[249] I have heard that Erlich (nicknamed *Kapote*) has disappeared.[250] The shooting and the killing flourishes. During the blockade on Leszno Street four people were killed. Hirszhorn has committed suicide.[251] Many kill themselves. It is a miracle that there are people still alive.

Saturday, 8 August

The 'action' continues. The 18th day. There are still reports of our cherished and loved ones who fell victim yesterday: our children. The children of our boarding-schools led away (to be killed): 12–14 Wolność Street,[252] about 1,200, 18 Mylna Street, Koniński with his wife and the children from the boarding-school.[253] They intend to eradicate the whole of Warsaw Jewry. I hear reports today that the Germans are blockading Żelazna and Leszno Streets. They are driving people out of all the buildings on Miła Street. We have lived through a shattering and terrifying day – 30 Gęsia Street.[254]

The numbness of everyone is staggering. Górny loses his mother and sells meal-tickets. Smolar has lost his wife and daughter.[255] Tintpulwer – widowed – goes around in despair, a broken man, and tries to 'find' work so as to be involved in something, not to be superfluous. Terrifying reports from the town. At 64 Lubiecka Street victims, many victims on Miła Street. All the cows were taken away – about 120 – from the 'farm'.[256] A loss of millions: there will no longer be the small amount of milk that was distributed to the children.

In the evening a pogrom in the streets. A great many killed at various locations: Smocza, Pawia, Miła, Zamenhof and others. I was on my way home at half past eight. Hela comes towards me. Luba and Ora are not there.[257] I am sure they have been seized. They come home at nine o'clock. During the blockade they had stayed in the boarding-school at 67 Dzielna Street.[258] What Luba recounted of the children (150) and the women teachers during the blockade. Their packages in their hands, ready to set off – to their deaths. Kon said yesterday: 'I am writing a testament about the events.' Chmielewski's parents were taken away yesterday and he comes to the factory and is still on his feet.

Sunday, 9 August

The 19th day of the 'action' of which human history has not seen the like. From yesterday the expulsion took on the character of a pogrom, or a simple massacre. They roam through the streets and murder people in their dozens, in their hundreds. Today they are pulling endless wagons full of corpses – uncovered – through the streets.

Everything that I have read about the events in 1918–19 pales in comparison with what we are living through now. It is clear to us that 99 per cent of those transported are being taken to their deaths. In addition to the atrocities, hunger haunts us. People who during the war were previously well-fed come to ask for a little soup at a factory kitchen. The 'elite' still get some, but the rabble don't even get that.

Plate 1 Abraham Lewin and his daughter photographed before the war

Plate 2 Lewin's wife, Luba, photographed before the war

Plate 3 A page of the diary manuscript (date 22 November 1942)

וזה בעיקר, ביום ראשון 22/XI.42. להצגה מיוחדת של האסאמבלה
ראשונה של הלהקה Werterfassung וורצלי אותם את
פסקי זמים ותהם את סגל הנוצרי ולהתכונות את
והלוי אמרו כבר בלבד אל הדירקטור. ובעבר כן
אחרית א את כלל. בשעה מלאה והלו אליהן ראיין
הלהקות את תאורה. הלהקה להזהירה אותם. וווו
אמרה, וורן לעצמה וורוה, תחבא ולגזה להבים
שום א הדא שברי לעצור זי ההקרי (ההקר) ולאחת
זורה כי אם וולבה בלבלה אולבנה תאל וקלה אם
א אולהא הן ולה. אך לב אלא ושבן כא ולהה א
וגורן הוציאם בלאחבם להולל את ריוצן הוציאם
פסק ווים ותהם בצאים בלצון פלוון אל אם א
הוש אולון שמ לעשה ווהלי פל לאברה.
וחוו היה הרהרה זדא לאת ואני גוזל, בחוה
הוצל כה, אלא להשל וא החקקה האחוות.
וכל, ואבלון והן רך. רצטה ", (לא ווחו
ווחה הם אחני, ההיה וברו שורה סבא א וות
א זה (א) הב ! ורם קלוו וזן לזו, ההוחו
אב. (וא) לחחות אלוח אן המות.
וולון " כלוה חול האלא בכללה וטחו. לב וחלו

Plate 4 Tin trunks and milk churns in which parts of the *Oneg Shabbes*
archive (including Lewin's diary) were found

Plate 5 Building the wall of the ghetto at Świętokrzyska Street and
Elektoralna Street, October 1940

Plate 6 A Jewish policeman directing the traffic (including the tram which ran through the ghetto)

Plate 7 Men being taken for forced labour
Plate 8 Street vendors

Plate 9 The bridge over Chłodna Street linking the 'larger' and 'smaller' ghettos

Plate 10 A view over the ghetto wall

Plate 11 Children in the ghetto

Twenty Ukrainians, Jewish policemen (a few dozen) and a small number of Germans lead a crowd of 3,000 Jews to the slaughter. One hears only of isolated cases of resistance.[259] One Jew took on a German and was shot on the spot. A second Jew fought with a Ukrainian and escaped after being wounded. And other cases of this kind. The Jews are going like lambs to the slaughter. Yesterday 23 Jews were killed in one flat.

I have heard that the 'action' in Radom is already over after a week and three days – 7,000 victims.[260] That is the target they set in advance. And here we have no idea when they will say – enough. I have heard about letters that arrive from France telling of expulsions of Jews there. They also say that they will be brought to the Warsaw ghetto. It is a wonder that people can endure so much suffering, living the whole day on a knife-edge between life and death and clinging with all their might to life in the hope that they may be among the ten survivors.

Monday, 10 August

Yesterday was horrific in the full sense of the word. The slaughter went on from early morning until nine and half past nine at night. This was a pogrom with all the traits familiar from the Tsarist pogroms of the years 1905–6. A mixed crowd of soldiers of various nationalities, Ukrainians, Lithuanians and over them the Germans, stormed into flats and shops, looting and killing without mercy. I have heard that people are being slaughtered with bayonets. Yesterday there were vast numbers of deaths.

In the town, proclamations have been published ordering the occupants of the small ghetto to leave their homes today by six o'clock.[261] This is a further terrible calamity. Firstly for all those who have remained there. There is no possibility for them to take out with them a few of their possessions, clothes and bedding, because there is a danger of being seized while moving. And secondly, where can they move to? A great many streets and blocks of buildings have been emptied by German factory-owners. The number of buildings still in Jewish hands is very low.

The number of those deported out (read: murdered) is estimated at

150,000. Yesterday the Guzik family was seized. He was freed, his family not.[262]

It is reported that the community organization is to be dismantled[263] and a commissar appointed. I have heard that Gancwajch, whom they wanted to kill a few weeks ago, has climbed back to prominence.

I was unable to go home. We all spent the night at 30 Gęsia Street. It was a very difficult night. Until two we sat on chairs, from two to five – we lay on plywood boards. We were told that 2,500 officials of the Jewish community and two members of the *Judenrat* have to present themselves at the *Umschlagplatz*. Later this was denied. The embitterment of the workers against the unwelcome intelligentsia is growing continually. They feel they have been wronged by them. The wife of the editor Wolkowicz has killed herself.[264]

The terrible hunger: bread, 88 zloty, potatoes, 30. The appalling appearance of the Jewish streets. The shops and flats stand open, the Jewish crowds have remained – looting. In a building on Leszno Street, where 150 people used to live, there are now 30 left. Of these eight were killed yesterday.

I have heard that in the course of the massacres yesterday the famous Warsaw singer Marisia Ajzensztat, the only daughter of her parents and a former pupil at the Yehudia School, was attacked and killed.[265] I have heard that yesterday Kohn's sister and her husband were killed. And she who had celebrated her recent marriage so exuberantly. A worker sat weeping, Jewish policemen had come to his home and taken away his 16-year-old son. What brutality!

Tuesday, 11 August

Things are deteriorating fast. Appalling, horrendous. The brutal expulsion from the small ghetto. Whole buildings have been emptied of their occupants and all their possessions left behind. Christians are already beginning to loot. 24 Sienna Street, 28 Śliska Street. Except for Jakub's family,[266] there is not even a single tenant remaining in the building; the house-porter is also gone. Aunt Chawa and Dora Fejga have been seized and deported. The destruction of families. Early this morning the Germans and the rioters spread through the ghetto. By the evening they were distributed throughout the ghetto and were seizing people. In the course of five minutes they drove out all the occupants on Gęsia Street between Zamenhof and Lubiecka Streets. They pay no attention to papers.

The Jewish community offices have moved to 19 Zamenhof Street, the post office building.[267] They have reduced their personnel by half. The number of victims has already risen above 150,000. Today they will complete three weeks since the beginning of the terrible massacre. In the night a large number of women who worked at Többens' were removed. It looks like there is a policy to liquidate women and children. Yesterday at Többens' three Jews died at their work. Blockades and murders in the streets that still belong to the ghetto. The heavy blockade on the entrance to the buildings of the Warschauer Union, with two killed and a vast number seized, nearly 100 women, children and men. The mortal terror that gripped us as we sat in the office.

Smolar rang Sokołów. He was told that those that are deported, or if they are to deported to Tr., are going to their 'death'.[268] The news that K. brought. In Warsaw there is a Jew by the name of Slawa who has brought reports of Treblinka. Fifteen kilometres before the station at Treblinka the Germans take over the train. When people get out of the train they are beaten viciously. Then they are driven into huge barracks. For five minutes heart-rending screams are heard, then silence. The bodies that are taken out are swollen horribly. One person cannot get their arms round one of these bodies, so distended are they. Young men from among the prisoners are the gravediggers, the next day they too are killed. What horror!

Wednesday, 12 August

Eclipse of the sun, universal blackness. My Luba was taken away during a blockade on 30 Gęsia Street. There is still a glimmer of hope in front of me. Perhaps she will be saved. And if, God forbid, she is not? My journey to the *Umschlagplatz* – the appearance of the streets – fills me with dread. To my anguish there is no prospect of rescuing her. It looks like she was taken directly into the train. Her fate is to be a victim of the Nazi bestiality, along with hundreds of thousands of

Jews. I have no words to describe my desolation. I ought to go after her, to die. But I have no strength to take such a step. Ora – her calamity. A child who was so tied to her mother, and how she loved her.

The 'action' goes on in the town at full throttle. All the streets are being emptied of their occupants. Total chaos. Each German factory will be closed off in its block and the people will be locked in their building. Terror and blackness. And over all this disaster hangs my own private anguish.

Thursday, 13 August

The 23rd day of the slaughter of the Jews of Warsaw. Today about 3,600 people were removed from Többens' buildings, mainly women and children. Today is Ora's fifteenth birthday. What a black day in her life and in my life. I have never experienced such a day as this. Since yesterday I have not shed a single tear. In my pain I lay in the attic and could not sleep. Ora was talking in her sleep: 'mamo, mamusiu, nie odchódź beze mnie!' ['Mother, Mama, don't leave me']. Today I cried a lot, when Gucia came to visit me. I am being thrown out of the flat at 2 Mylna Street: they have already taken most of my things. Those who have survived are thieving and looting insatiably. Our lives have been turned upside down, a total and utter destruction in every sense of the word.

I will never be consoled as long as I live. If she had died a natural death, I would not have been so stricken, so broken. But to fall into the hands of such butchers! Have they already murdered her? She went out in a light dress, without stockings, with my leather brief-case. How tragic it is! A life together of over 21 years (I became close to her beginning in 1920) has met with such a tragic end.

Friday, 14 August

The last night that I will spend in my war-time flat at 2 Mylna Street. The sight of the streets: the pavements are fenced off, you walk in the middle of the road. Certain streets, such as Nowolipie (on both sides of Karmelicka), Mylna and others are completely closed off with fences and gates and you can't get in there. The impression is of cages. The whole of Jewish Warsaw has been thrown out of the buildings.[269] There is a full-scale relocation of all Jews who have not yet been rounded up and are still in the town. Whole streets that have been given over to the German firms: Müller, Többens, Schultz, Zimmerman, Brauer and others.[270] We have been sold as slaves to a load of German manufacturers. The living-conditions of those in the workshops: hunger and hard labour. Their ration: a quarter kilo of bread a day and a bowl of soup.

The 'action' continues – today is the 23rd day. Yesterday they took away from Többens' workshops about 3,000–4,000 men and women, mostly women and children. This morning the Jewish community-council posted a new announcement: all Jews who live in Biała, Elektoralna, Zielna, Orla, Solna, Leszno, odd numbers in Ogrodowa, Chłodna Streets have to leave their flats by tomorrow, 15 August. Yesterday and today, a huge number of people killed – victims of the blockades. I am moving my things over to Nacia's at 14 Pawia Street.

Setting up of blockades on Nowolipie and Karmelicka Streets. Further victims – there are more deaths today, and very many driven out. There is talk of 15,000. I have heard that measures decreed in the expulsion orders are directed mainly against women and children. The police commandant of the second district is trying to save his wife and children. A new raid on the Jewish Self-help Organization at 25 Nowolipki Street. Dr Bornsztajn and his wife taken away, Elhonen Cajtlin with his son and others.[271] This was carried out by Jewish policemen without the Germans, that is, on their own initiative. Renja Sztajnwajs. I have heard that Yitshak Katznelson's wife and one of his children have been seized.[272] The second day that I am without Luba. I am now also without a place to live. I have nowhere to lay my head. The number rounded up has reached 190,000, just counting those expelled, excluding those who have been killed and those who have been sent to the *Dulag* at 109 Leszno Street.[273]

Every crime in history, like the burning of Rome by Nero, pales into insignificance in comparison with this. Kirzhner has been taken away from work and deported. Together with him they took away a further 28 people. All were aged 35 and over. The same thing has happened, I have learnt, in another *placówka*: 29 people were taken away and deported.

Saturday, 15 August

Today is the 25th day of the bloody 'action' carried out by the butchers. I spent the night at 17 Dzielna Street. The rain of shooting started at half past nine in the evening. Deaths in the street. The whole night incessant movement in and out of the Pawiak. Gutkowski sends his only son, three and a half years old, to the cemetery to have him taken to Czerniaków.[274]

I have nowhere to rest my head at night. Gucia is being thrown out of her flat. Nacia and Frume are not allowed to enter. All the orphanages have been emptied.[275] Korczak went at the head of his children. The pain because of the loss of L. is becoming more intense. My soul can find no peace, for not having gone after her when she was in danger, even though I could also have disappeared and Ora would have been left an orphan. The most terrible thing is that Landau and Sonszajn misled me by saying that Luba wasn't in the queue. Be that as it may, the anguish is terrible and it will never be dimmed.

Rumours about reports arriving from women who were deported from Biała-Podlaska and Białystok.

Today by eight o'clock there was a blockade on Miła, Gęsia, Zamenhof and other streets. 'Our spirit is weary of the killing.' How much longer? Yesterday a huge number of bodies were brought to the cemetery, victims of the blockade of Többens' workshops. Today they were also taking people from the 'shops'. It will soon be seven o'clock and the blockade on Gęsia is still continuing, around our factory. The Jewish police have been looting, breaking open flats, emptying cupboards, smashing crockery and destroying property, just for the fun of it. More people were killed today in the course of blockades. People killed during the blockade. Mirka Priwes, her mother and brother have been deported. Yitshak Katznelson's wife and two of his children have been seized and deported.

The desolation and chaos is greatest on the streets from Chłodna to Leszno Streets, all the Jewish possessions have been abandoned and Polish thugs with the Germans will loot everything. The whole of Jewish Warsaw has been laid waste. That which remains is a shadow of what was, a shadow that tells of death and ruin.

Sunday, 16 August

Today is the 26th day of the 'action', which is continuing with all its atrocities and animal savagery, a slaughter the like of which human history has not seen. Even in the legend of Pharaoh and his decree: every newborn boy will be thrown into the river.

People who have returned from the *Umschlagplatz* have told of women who were seized yesterday who were freed if they sacrificed their children. To our pain and sorrow many women saved themselves in this way – they were separated from their children, aged 3 to 12 to 14, and if they had identity papers, they were freed. Any woman carrying a child or with a child next to her was not freed. The Germans' lust for Jewish blood knows no bounds, it is a bottomless pit. Future generations will not believe it. But this is the un-embellished truth, plain and simple. A bitter, horrifying truth.

The Jewish police have received an order that each one of them must bring five people to be transported. Since there are 2,000 police, they will have to find 10,000 victims. If they do not fulfil their quotas they are liable to the death-penalty. Some of them have already received confirmation that they have presented the required number. Since every Jew has some kind of documentation – in the main valid ones – they tear up every document they are shown and round up the passers-by. It is now dangerous for every Jew to go out on to the street. No one goes out.

Rumours have reached me again that letters have allegedly arrived from the deportees saying that they are working in the area of Siedlce and conditions are not bad. Lifschitz's son (my friend from elementary school) told me that his daughter herself had read one of these letters from an elderly couple.

As things are developing, a handful of Jews will be left, those of a designated age. Apart from this there will be no way for a Jew to survive: there will be nowhere to live and no bread. The position of the old is especially tragic: they have no way out. They can either give themselves up into the hands of the butchers, or take their lives themselves, or hide out and live in dark corners and cellars, which is also very difficult because of the general expulsions from the buildings and the upheaval of the residents. In those buildings that have been taken over by new occupants, no strangers are let in. It is easier for an animal to find a hiding place and a refuge in the forest than for a Jew to hide in the ghetto.

Now (four in the afternoon) I have heard that there are no Germans at all in the *Umschlagplatz*. There are only Jews there and they are carrying out the bloody and terrible operation. Today rumours are going round that an order has been issued that all wives and children of officials have to report at the *Umschlagplatz*. Josef Erlich and his family have been killed, so I have heard. According to certain reports, Czerniaków's place here with us – à la Rumkowski[276] – will be inherited by Gancwajch, the man they had been hunting and trying to kill. He is outside the ghetto at the moment.

Monday, 17 August

The 27th day of the annihilation. Yesterday I came to 14 Pawia Street very late at night by a round-about route (via Zamenhof) and was anguished to hear the terrible news about Jakub, Frume and Uri. A very great blow. There is still a faint hope that they can be saved, since there were no train-wagons yesterday and they weren't taken straight to the train. This morning I saw in the streets an announcement about a new reduction in size of the ghetto. Very many streets and sides of streets (the odd or the even numbers) must be vacated by the Jews by 20 August, at four in the afternoon. The ghetto will be a third or a quarter of its original size, if there are no further decrees of this kind. They are emptying those streets that had already been handed over to the German firms, and been fenced off, for example Mylna, Nowolipie, Dzielna Streets and many others. The enemy's claw is reaching out for us and it is still not sated.

Yesterday hundreds of officials of the community and of the Jewish Self-help Organization were taken away. The Gestapo commandant Brandt stood there and struck the detainees with his own hands. Jakub, Uri and Frume were hit. The 'action' is continuing today. There was a blockade on the cemetery. Ora, who works with the group from Hashomer Hatsair, was in great danger. The group was saved today thanks to the intervention of Commissar Hensel.[277]

Jewish policemen round up people all day. It is said that they have received an order that each policeman must find six Jews. They abuse those who are rounded up, and smash and loot the empty flats. I have heard that a thousand policemen have received an order to report at the *Umschlagplatz*. This report turns out to be false – for the time being.

Harsh conditions at the factory. Before 80 people were employed there and now almost a thousand are registered there. Hundreds of people wander around bored with nothing to do. They sit around in dread of German blockades and many hide themselves in all kinds of dark corners.

The pain over the loss of L. is getting more and more intense. During the day I am often choked with tears. The fact there is no news about her suffering and torment, whether she is alive or dead, how she died – gives me no peace. If I knew that she was alive and that she was not suffering too much, I would be calm. And if I knew that she had died but did not suffer much at her death – then I would also be calm.

I have been told that Yitshak Katznelson shows great inner strength and endurance, keeping hold of himself after the terrible disaster that has befallen him.

The Ejdus's have been seized. Every day there are killings. When Jakub, Frume and Uri were taken away, someone tried to escape. He was killed on the spot. For a week now we have had no news of the progress of the war. The last report was a few days ago of the heavy bombardment of Mainz. The story about the Jew Chunkis (one of the directors of Adriatika).

Frume and Uri have returned. What they have told me about what is going on at the *Umschlagplatz*. Hell, pure hell. The rich save themselves, if they are not shut into the wagons straight away. The tragic fate of the Taubers. He was killed on the spot, his wife and beautiful and charming son (with statuesque features) – Rapusz – were deported.

Tuesday, 18 August

Today marks 4 weeks or 28 days of this blood operation, which has no parallel in history. The Germans and the Jewish police have been carrying out further blockades. Disaster has struck our family once again. Gucia and Hela have been taken away by the Germans, who entered their building. This is a very heavy blow for me. She had been so concerned for us and helped us in the war-years. I have heard talk again about the new rise of Gancwajch. He will take over Lichtenbaum's place and become commissar of the Jewish community.

Today I went with three friends to collect up the books that are in the flats that our firm has been allocated on Miła Street. We set eyes on an appalling vision, all the doors broken open, all the goods and property smashed and scattered through the courtyards. Russian pogromists would have been unable to make a more thorough and shattering pogrom than that carried out by the Jewish police. This sight, which is everywhere to be seen, stunned us. The destruction and the annihilation of the greatest Jewish community in Europe.

New proclamations from the *Judenrat* have been hung up which have caused panic among the Jews. Jews who are not employed are not permitted south of Leszno Street. Those who are caught there will be shot.[278] The families of those working are no longer protected. In fact all those who are not working, even the families of those who are employed, have to report voluntarily at the *Umschlagplatz*. Otherwise their food-cards will be taken away and they will be driven out by force. We can see that the Germans are playing a game of cat and mouse with us. Those employed have protected their families, now the families are being deported (killed) and they want to leave behind the working slaves for the time being. *What horror!* They are preparing to destroy us utterly.

Wednesday, 19 August

The 29th day of the bloody action. Last evening ended in a massacre and with a large raid on the brush workshop on Franciszkańska and Świętojerska Streets.[279] About 1,600 people were removed. Eight were killed. Among those taken away were large numbers of well-known and cherished individuals such as Mrs Mokarska,[280] Rabbi Huberband and others.[281] I have been informed that Nisenbaum's father and Szczeranski have been seized.[282] Rokhl Sztajn poisoned herself at the *Platz*.[283] Hillel Cajtlin's wife was taken. Last night the terrible news reached me that Mrs Schweiger has been taken away.[284] Inka tried to poison herself, but they saved her.

There is no 'action' in Warsaw itself today. The squad has left for Otwock.[285] And there is an 'action' there, according to reports. The Jewish police is carrying out checks in the buildings in search of 'outsiders' who are certain to be hiding there hidden in dark corners and cellars. Large numbers of Jews commit suicide.[286] The number of victims of the expulsion has reached approximately a quarter of a million. Today is the seventh day since the great calamity that befell me. If only I could die and be free of the whole nightmare. But I am still tied to life and it is still difficult for me to take my own life.

The squad is running riot in Otwock. I have heard that they have emptied Brius and Sofjówka.[287] Who knows how many cherished and beloved victims we have lost today. And to think that many had gone to Otwock to find an escape from death.

Thursday, 20 August

There was no 'action' yesterday in Warsaw. However, it is reported that there was a hunt on the Aryan side for Jews who had fled there. The squad carried out the action in Otwock with the help of 500 Jewish police from Warsaw (so it is said). I have heard that those rounded up have been marched to Warsaw on foot.

My sister Gucia is lost and her daughter Hela killed. This new disaster adds still further to the weight of my gloom. She was the best of sisters and was very concerned for me during the war-years. It is such anguish and only death will end my suffering.

An order for the caretakers in the buildings has been issued: to collect up and gather in one place all the goods and possessions of those who have been driven out and hand them over to the community representative who will call. A great looting is being prepared, Nazi-style; the Germans are preparing to remove all the Jews' possessions.

Friday, 21 August

Yesterday evening after six the Jewish police moved into the buildings which were supposed to have been evacuated by the occupants. They drove out the occupants by force, broke into locked flats, robbed and looted and smashed whatever they found and at the same time seized women, especially those who had no papers (*Meldekarten* – population registration coupons). Where did the Jews get this brutality from? The Germans' spirit has passed into them. They also entered our workshop at eight and caused panic among the women. They were bribed and left. I was worried about Ora and walked with her late to Frume's.

At eleven in the evening the air-raid on Warsaw began. It was as bright as on a clear, moonlit night, because of the bombardment. Bombs were dropped. In spite of the danger we welcomed the raid with a feeling of great satisfaction.[288] Perhaps our salvation will come, perhaps this evil power will be broken. There is talk of a second front in France and Holland. If these things had happened four or five weeks ago, perhaps we would have been saved from the catastrophe.

I have heard there was an assassination attempt on the chief of police Szeryński.[289] He was wounded in the cheek. According to rumours he was wounded by a Pole from the Polish Socialist Party disguised as a Jewish policeman. Today leaflets were distributed against the Jewish police, who have helped to send 200,000 Jews to their deaths. The whole police force has been sentenced to death.[290]

What should I do with my mother? Old people have nowhere to turn. They have nowhere to hide. They have been driven out of their former flats and are not let into the new blocks. The entrances are closed and the caretakers will not admit strangers. There are those who go to the *Umschlagplatz* and hand themselves over to the butchers to die a martyr's death.

Saturday, 22 August

Yesterday there was no 'action', but the squad is active in the Warsaw area. Yesterday, it is said, it was in Mińsk Mazowiecki.[291] The heavy and gloomy scene that I had at Nacia's because of mother. The Tombecks will not let her sleep there.[292] She has nowhere to go, except to go and give herself up to the executioners. How horrifying. Ora is ill and she has nowhere to lie down and no medicine. We have no roof over our heads. I leave her at Nacia's. I am deeply worried and frightened.

Sunday, 23 August

Yesterday was the 33rd day of the bloody 'action' in Warsaw, which has not been discontinued; on the contrary, it is still continuing. Yesterday the Germans rounded up mainly women and children with rampant viciousness and savagery. I was told that a prettily dressed 10-year-old girl was seized. The girl screamed in anguish and cried out: 'Mr Policeman!' but her pleas were of no avail. He was deaf to her screams and put her in a rickshaw to the *Umschlagplatz*. Yesterday the two Ostrowiec girls from Hashomer Hatsair who work at our office were seized. I have heard that the Jewish police have been ordered to round up 1,000 victims a day, and that the hunt will continue for another 14 days. In short, not one of us is sure to survive, especially women and children, who are left living with the threat of destruction, every day, every minute. The knowledge of this so preys on their nerves that many nearly go insane.

There is talk of an 'action' in Piotrków.[293] The group (from Hashomer Hatsair) that works at the Jewish cemetery, and the 'business' that is carried on with the Christians. The Germans are looting Jewish property. Yesterday they came to the Tepicyn factory and took away the best suitcases and everything of value. They even pillage from the wagons in the street. Life in the ghetto has become quiet. The few who have survived wander the streets like shadows, like corpses, and their number diminishes from day to day.

R. told me something he had heard from some German woman that in the area around the station at Kosow you can hear the screams of them being tortured to death 3 km away.[294] The savagery of the Jewish police against their unfortunate victims: they beat viciously, they steal, and they loot and pillage like bandits in the forest. What degeneracy! Who has raised these bitter fruits among us?

I have heard that in Falenica all the Jews left their homes, dispersed in the nearby small towns and the woods, and not a single one remained behind. The executioners were left without prey. Apparently they massacred everyone in Otwock and didn't deport people. In Falenica the Jews tried to resist the Germans and they were slaughtered.[295] Anyone who was found was killed. The remainder ran off into the woods. Today the butchers are supposed to return to

Warsaw and there are terrible rumours circulating because of this: that they intend to liquidate the whole of Jewish Warsaw and empty it of Jews. Horrific.

Fela has returned from the *Umschlagplatz* and told me that Suchowolska has been seized. A few hours later I learned the end of the story. The neighbours collected a little money, clothing and food . . . and sent the mother and her two children, boys aged 10–12. Asch's brother-in-law has died – Alberg.[296] Yesterday he was still walking around, and today he died because his strength gave out.

Today the Jewish police carried out the 'action' with savage brutality. They simply ran riot. There is a dread of tomorrow, of an 'action' with the participation of the Germans. The firm [Ostdeutsche Bautischlerei Werkstätte] has set up a confiscation-team, which drives around carts with beds, couches and other valuable goods. The whole society has been pillaged from top to bottom. God, is there any help or salvation for us? Will the survivors stay alive, or will our end be the same as that of the hundreds and thousands who have already died?

Monday, 24 August

A meeting of *Oneg Shabbes* at the Hashomer Hatsair with the participation of R—m, G—n, G—k, B—ch, L—n, G—ski, W—r, Szmul, Josef, B—au. Rabbi H. was missing, he was seized at the broom factory.[297] The place, the time, and the appearance of the participants underline the special tragedy of the meeting.

The 'action', as I have already mentioned, was carried out yesterday without the Germans, and is continuing today as well. The centre where bread and soup is distributed has been reopened and orders have been issued for 1,100 portions to be prepared. An indication that they are expecting to round up that number. Rumours are going around that the Germans have allowed 120,000 food-cards to be prepared and distributed for September. This would seem to indicate that they are going to leave behind that number of Jews. But this is only a rumour and nothing more. On the other hand, there are other rumours, much more pessimistic. There is talk again that the 'action' will be extended for another week. Today is now the 34th day. Rumours have arrived that A. I. Einhorn, one of the editors of

Haynt, has been murdered or died on the way from Otwock to Warsaw.[298] He didn't have the strength for such a long walk. He had gone there to improve his health and met with his death. The business that the Toporol-group are doing with the Christians in the cemetery.[299] It is said that Szeryński, the head of the police, a convert, who was wounded a few days ago, died from his wounds yesterday.[300] This piece of news has still to be confirmed.

Ora is ill again. The fever reached 40 degrees yesterday. I had to leave her at Nacia's even though she is in great danger. For the first time in her life her mother is not at her side when she is sick. How can such a situation be described? Also the matter of my mother is causing me great anguish. What can be done with her? I have given my permission to put her to sleep, eternal rest, rather than give her over to the executioners. But J. refuses to carry it out.[301] Even the devil could not have conceived of such a situation.

Two in the afternoon. The day passes, unexpectedly quiet. Have events taken a new turn? I have heard that today they have taken out of the Pawiak the foreign citizens who were put in there six days before the events began and the members of the *Judenrat* who were imprisoned as hostages. If these stories are true, then they herald the cessation of the 'action'.

The young man Shmuel, passing by 101 Żelazna Street, saw with his own eyes how the squad was packing up its booty in separate boxes and loading it up into lorries.[302] It is possible to conclude that they are preparing to take their leave. But even cessation of the 'action' can be of little comfort after the appalling slaughter of two-thirds of Warsaw Jewry. The mourning of our losses will continue to accompany us, especially those of us who mourn for their loved ones from the depths of their soul. In any case the survivors will be able to recover a little and continue their wretched existence until the end of the war. When will the end come? There is no sign of it.

A rumour is going around that Brazil had joined the war against the Axis powers. Does this not show the terrible duration of this war?[303] Has Brazil come in at the end? There is also pressure on Chile and Argentina for them to join the war. It is possible that the main thrust of these nations will be turned against Japan, and the war over here could even be over this year.

Abroad, as it turns out, they are unaware of our great disaster.

Roosevelt, who threatened Germany with revenge for murdering the hostages, is completely silent about the great tragedy, about the great slaughter that has been perpetrated against us.[304] Apparently he has had no precise and authentic reports, since he passes over all this in silence.[305]

Six in the evening. Jewish policemen have returned from the town and said that the action is continuing. So, all our hopes that the bloody action had ceased now, that we would be allowed a little breathing-space, have been swept away. How will we survive? How will we be able to bear it? Of the rumours from this morning only one has been confirmed, namely that the members of the *Judenrat*, Ekerman, Zundelewicz and others, who were in prison as hostages, have been released.[306] It might have been possible to conclude from this that the 'action' was over. But we are none the less not to be left in peace. People talk of the special danger that now threatens children. A terrible dread seizes me, when I think of the fate of Ora. She has no documents and is in danger.

Since Friday the loudspeakers have not been operating. No newspapers reach us. No newspapers are allowed into the ghetto. The guards at the gate confiscate them. Thus we find ourselves in a special prison where we live each minute with the threat of seizure and execution, and no news reaches us from the other side of the wall. And perhaps it will be granted to us one bright morning that our eyes will be opened to the light of the sun of freedom in all its strength and splendour.

How can we live like this? We never know from one day to the next if the day will pass safely. We have no roof over our head. We have no flat and our sleeping at Nacia's is already becoming burdensome to me. And Ora's illness?

Tuesday, 25 August

Today it is five weeks since the beginning of the slaughter that is being carried out without respite against the Jews of Warsaw and the surrounding area. The 'action' itself is continuing. Germans and Ukrainians carried out a round-up today in the block where the community offices are. This means Zamenhof, Pawia, Gęsia and Lubiecka

Streets. I am terrified for Ora, for mother, and for all the relations I left at 14 Pawia Street. I have heard that they took community employees, from the supply division, and others. All the workshops have received instructions as to the maximum number of workers that they have the right to employ. L's factory has been allocated 900. At our workplace the number is not so small, but other workshops feel themselves hard done by and are threatening to stop work and return the materials, as they cannot produce the goods with such a small number of workers. Yesterday there was a meeting at the office of employment with the manufacturers and the SS present.

This morning, I saw an announcement on Lubiecka Street written with a typewriter (in Polish) to the following effect: 'In the light of the accusations raised against the head of police, the officers and the ordinary policemen who have been found guilty of criminal acts – the assassination attempt was carried out against Szeryński Jakub. Further acts of this nature will be carried out with the full severity of the judgement.'[307]

Telephone calls from Radomsko yesterday and today with the news that everything is quiet there. Gancwajch is there. However there are rumours that things are not quiet in Częstochowa.

Six in the evening. Once again a difficult and terrible day that freezes the blood in our veins. The whole day the Ukrainians and the Germans run riot in the blocks, because that is where the small crowd of survivors is concentrated. People are also being taken away from there. The impression is that they want to exterminate us entirely. My own position is even more difficult now. It is very dangerous to go from here, 30 Gęsia Street, to 14 Pawia Street. And how can I not go and see Ora? Especially when I am tortured with worry over her fate and that of the remainder of my family. I will certainly go and take the risk.

Wednesday, 26 August

Yesterday evening two announcements were posted in the streets.[308] The first: after eight, rickshaws may not be in the streets, and after nine, Jews are not permitted in the streets, except for police. Signed the Jewish community-council (*Judenrat*). The second announcement is from the office of employment. It states that a Jew may not change place of work without the permission of the *Arbeitsamt* [Office of Employment]. The penalty for disobeying the instruction is immediate removal from Warsaw. It is interesting that a few days before the onset of the events, the curfew was extended until ten o'clock in the evening and the decree was valid until the end of September.

Yesterday was one of the most difficult since the events began. The Germans and Ukrainians (a band of thugs) ran riot among the few remaining Jews in the blocks and factories. Yesterday there were renewed round-ups in the community-buildings of the Jewish community.[309] Especially – so I have been told – of young people – all the messenger-boys and others. People were also taken from the blocks on Pawia and Zamenhof Streets, among them 15 doctors from 14 Pawia Street. Large numbers of those rounded up were shut into the wagons directly and it was impossible to save them. Workers were also taken from certain factories (Schmidt). Those remaining are in fear of their lives, the nightmare is worsening, turning our lives into a living hell.

A list of the number of workers permitted to be employed in the Jewish workshops has been published, in total 24,980 people, and, together with officials, of the Jewish community, the police and the JHK [Jewish Self-help Organization].[310] This will mean that they intend to leave 25,000 Jews in Warsaw, or 6–7 per cent of the former number.[311] History has not witnessed a greater destruction of an ethnic or national population. Yesterday a large number of people were taken from Müller's workshop. Szymon Heller's parents, Zelmanowski and others.[312] I have been told that Mrs Pulman has been seized.[313] I feel very sorry for him. Szternberg and his family have been deported. Cytrinowski, and others, many others.[314]

The streets are terrible to behold today: they are deserted with not a living soul in sight. The butchers roam the streets looking for victims.

Thursday, 27 August

Today is the 37th day of the greatest slaughter in human history. Yesterday the 'action' was carried out in the workshops and the blocks. Men, women and children were taken away. The day before yesterday about 45,000 people were deported. I have learnt of the death of the person who has been my closest friend during the war, David Pulman, and his daughter Henja.[315] His wife and youngest daughter had been taken earlier. This news was a terrible blow. Ajnhorn's wife was also taken away the day before yesterday from Müller's workshop. I talked with her in the morning on the way to work. The destruction of a whole family.

The appearance of the streets at five in the morning. At five o'clock a few isolated people begin to appear. The 'dealers' go about with their 'wares'. They sell saccharin (fake), bread, potatoes and so on. Later the streets are deserted until 7 in the evening. The prices: bread – 28–30 zloty, potatoes – 12–14 zloty, butter – 300 zloty, meat – up to 100 zloty. Cigarettes (hard to get) – a packet of 20 – 20 zloty.

Today we are expecting a visit from the murderers to our workshop and everyone is waiting nervously and in a state of agitation. At two o'clock in the afternoon there was an inspection at our workshop and it passed off peacefully. Two men from the *Sicherheitsdienst* [the German Secret Service] sat in the director's office and drank and ate and looked over the list of employees, without checking documents or going to see the workers for themselves. At the same time there was a blockade on our block on Miła Street. About 40 (39) people were taken away, mainly women and children. The 'action' is directed against women and children. One sees weeping mothers whose children have been taken away (I saw this with my own eyes). There was also a blockade on other streets. We are drowning and the water is already up to our mouths.

The meeting of all the workers and the speech of commissar Hensel and the words of thanks to him from the Landau brothers. He spoke of the benefits for us and of his efforts on behalf of the workers during the terrible 'action' which was now coming to an end for us. His efforts had met with partial success and partial failure, perhaps because of a lack of understanding on our part. In return for these benefits he appealed for dedication to the work and loyalty to the firm. He would hunt down saboteurs. The workers applauded and thanked him, as did the Landau brothers. This was a performance, prepared in every detail. Unfortunate slaves – when they hear an encouraging word – it goes to their heads and they get excited and enthusiastic.

Among the children who were rounded up today were ten-month-old babies and eight-year-olds.

Friday, 28 August

The acts of terror are continuing. I have heard that yesterday evening a group of workers was returning from work at Oschman's factory, in procession. The SS divided the group in two. Half were allowed to keep walking, and the second group was led away straight to the *Umschlagplatz*.

The children who were seized yesterday were not rescued. They have perished, perished.

Today we had a long talk with Dowid Nowodworski, who returned from Treblinka.[316] He gave us the complete story of the sufferings that he endured from the first moment that he was seized to the escape from the death-camp and up to his return to Warsaw. His words confirm once again and leave no room for doubt that all the deportees, both those who have been seized and those who reported voluntarily, are taken to be killed and that no one is saved. This is the naked truth, and how terrible, when we remember that in the last weeks at least 300,000 Jews have been exterminated, from Warsaw and other towns: Radom, Siedlce, and many, many others. From his words we put together a testimony of such stark anguish, so shattering, that it cannot be grasped and put into words. This is without doubt the greatest crime ever committed in the whole of history.

Yesterday about 4,000 people were driven from Warsaw to their deaths, men, women and children. The 'action' is continuing today. Workshops are surrounded and besieged. But – I have heard – there are no wagons. They will be held until evening, or until tomorrow and then another large group will be sent away. This is the 38th day of the great slaughter. From the poison cup have so far drunk – apart from Warsaw – Siedlce, Rembertów, Radom and many, many more.[317]

Yesterday I heard that the large factory owners, Schultz, Többens, are negotiating with leaders of the murder squads. They are promising them millions in bribes if they leave the rest of the Jews in

Warsaw, which they estimate at 100,000, and if they leave the city. In this connection there are rumours going around that the 'action' will continue until Saturday or Sunday, and after that they will leave Warsaw and the town will be quiet. We have so often had our hopes raised of an end to the bloody action, and they have turned out to be false and we have been disappointed. No doubt this time we will also be let down, and blood will continue to be spilled.

God! Are we really to be exterminated down to the very last of us? Now it is certain that all those deported from Warsaw have been killed.

Saturday, 29 August

The 39th day of the bloody extermination that still continues in all its terror and fearfulness. Yesterday in the course of the evening, when the workers at various German workplaces, the so-called *placowkarze*,[37] were returning home they were attacked by SS men who shot or seized many of them and took them off to the *Umschlag-platz*. Who was seized? I have heard various accounts: some say that they took away the very young and the old, those over 50; others say that they took people away at random. There was turmoil and screaming at the *Umschlagplatz*. Many were shot. Two doctors from 14 Pawia Street, who worked at a location outside the ghetto, did not return home to sleep. We must assume they have been seized.

With regard to the numbers killed during the 'action' so far,[318] there are different opinions. Some say, Dr R. for example, that 15,000 have been killed. Others believe – the head of the police, Brz.[319] – that the number is 'only' 6,000. As far as the number of those deported (read: murdered) is concerned, there are also different estimates: some say that the number is over 230,000, others believe that it is smaller, about 190,000. This is according to the Germans' figures. The number of Jews remaining in Warsaw is estimated at about 100,000.

The number of hostages who were held in prison until the 24th of this month was 53. They were treated very badly. Some of them came back and could not find their families. Ekerman, for example, found only a son left out of his numerous relations.[320]

One gendarme said that the action will be extended until 1 September; after that, according to him, the execution-squad will leave for France. To the question as to why it is going to France, there not being many Jews there, the gendarme replied that the unit's activities, the extermination squad, were not only directed against Jews. However, it seems that he doesn't know what he is talking about. For the moment all the bloodlust and the animal violence in the form of these human butchers is directed exclusively against us. It is possible that they will leave Warsaw, but they will turn their attention to those places that have not as yet tasted the poison chalice.

Among the prominent people and those near to me who have fallen victim: Rabbi Huberband, Mrs Słapak and her daughter, Celina Lewin and her son, the poetess Lazowert, Winnik.[321] Mojsze Lewita or Levitas, from 4 Twarda Street, went to look for his wife three weeks ago at the *Umschlagplatz* and was himself seized and sent away to Kosow. Two days ago he returned from there. The Germans freed him as he was a carpenter. He said that Kosow, which was emptied of its Jews, is now full of deportees. The Jews who have money buy food from the peasants and distribute it among those who have none. The matter must in any case be investigated. It would mean that not all of those deported have been murdered.

Sunday, 30 August

Yesterday, the 39th day of these bloody events, the 'action' was carried out in the workshops. Several hundred people were removed from Bauer's workshop on Nalewki Street. Czerski and Rakowski were taken away, but freed later.[322] In the evening at about nine o'clock there were loud shots in the streets of the new ghetto. There were many deaths. Seven bodies were found at the corner of Smocza and Wołyńska. They were Jews who were found on the streets at nightfall. It is dangerous for Jews to show themselves on the street in the day, when the streets are completely deserted, and it is dangerous to go out after dark. This means that a Jew can go out only from half past five to seven in the morning and from seven or half past seven to eight in the evening.

The large number of fictitious marriages. G. P.'s husband arrived from Paris and had told us that the same deceptions are being carried out there as here. He does not know where G. is. There they are preparing another expulsion of 200,000 or more.[323] Where will they be sent, and will they do to them what they are doing to us? God only knows.

I have heard that the squad have booked the orchestra of the Jewish police for today.[324] It looks as though they are celebrating a holiday today, are making merry and want to relax to music. From this it might be deduced that they are preparing to take their leave.

Today terrible rumours were going around that from midday today until tomorrow evening the ghetto would be closed to Christians. In the end it turned out that the rumour was false and without foundation.

I have heard that Rabbi Kanal of Warsaw decided to die so as to be buried as a Jew. When he was seized, he refused to enter the wagon. He was shot and killed by a gendarme. His wish was fulfilled, he was given a Jewish burial.[325] I have heard that the day before yesterday a group of workers returning from their workplace outside the ghetto were murdered by Ukrainians. Hence the large number of bodies found at the corner of Wołyńska and Smocza Streets.

Monday, 31 August

The last day of the third year of war and the 41st day of the terrible slaughter that is being carried out against us. Today was once again a difficult day. Many workshops were blockaded. I have been told that 80 people were removed from Hallman's factory. The details are not yet known. I have been told of rewards of 5,000 zloty being offered for each Jew who is discovered on the Aryan side. I have heard of a large massacre that took place between 25 and 28 August in Międzyrzec Podlaski.[326] One of the days – the 25th – was horrendously bloody. All the Jews were driven onto the street and mown down with machine-guns. An 'action' was supposed to have begun in Częstochowa, but it has been delayed or postponed.

Yesterday 54 people were taken away from Schilling's factory, and from Hallmann's factory people with small defects such as the lame, the undersized, the weak were taken, even if they are specialists or excellent at their work.

Wednesday, 2 September

Yesterday marked six weeks since the beginning of the 'action' that still continues, as if it is only to be ended along with the last Jew. The tempo of the 'action' was yesterday a little less frenetic, but it was still continuing. The Jewish police have, as mentioned, received an order each to bring 'two heads'. At 6 Pawia Street women were queuing to buy green vegetables. The Jewish police swooped and took several of them away. The Germans have blockaded several factories. In the evening they led away groups of prisoners. I have heard that these are from the *placówki*. They had been going home from work and were seized. Yesterday there were 1,400 people held at the *Umschlagplatz*, so R—m, who lives at 3 Dzika Street, told me.[327]

Last night from quarter past ten to twelve o'clock there was a second air-raid after a break of 12 days.[328] This time more bombs were dropped than the previous time and many buildings in the ghetto were hit. In the building on 7 Dzielna Street (the Moriah synagogue) – which has been occupied by the Jewish police – a fire broke out which lasted a whole night. The building at 35a Gęsia Street was also damaged, the roof and the façade is in danger of collapse. Many windows were broken in the nearby streets, Lubiecka, Pawia. On Wołyńska, Miła and Smocza Streets there were also fires and several wooden buildings were burned down. The air-raid also hit the Jews hard. But the Jews welcomed it with feelings of satisfaction. We are waiting for events that will change our fate. Today – on the first day of the seventh week of the bloody events – there are already reports that they are blockading Schultz's factories.

Thursday, 3 September

Yesterday there were heavy blockades of Schultz's and Többens' workshops. From Schultz's alone they took out several thousand workers. Workers were also removed from other workshops. There is no end to the disaster that is devouring us relentlessly. Today was a day of calamity, and disaster. Josef K. was arrested this morning.[329] Later Shmuel Br. was shot.[330] In the afternoon there was a heavy blockade of our shop: 100 men and women were taken away. By a miracle Ora and myself were saved. God! What terror, what a feeling of imminent death! And the visages of the executioners – the Germans and the Ukrainians! Rumours about the transferring of the remainder of the ghetto that is outside Warsaw across to Wola.[331] The supply-division has received permission to distribute 105,000 food-cards.

Friday, 4 September

The 45th day of the bloody operation against us, which is being carried on with great savagery. In addition to the blockades on our factory, they also took 400 people away yesterday from HG Zimmerman and the whole factory is being liquidated.[332] The same fate awaits our workshop as well. Yesterday 100 people were taken from our factory itself and 70 from the buildings. Today the same thugs came back completely unexpectedly, set up another heavy blockade, and took away 100 people from the factory. Among them people dear to me – As., Gut—ski, Zilber—g, Mazur and others.[333] They were also at the broom-manufacturer's this morning and took away 250 people. Considering the large number in the work-force, that is not many. The role of the Jewish police today during the blockade: they extorted money from those they set free. Sze—g was freed in the street for 800 zloty. Someone else was also freed for money.

Shmuel's funeral attended by the members of Hashomer Hatsair who worked at the cemetery, at Toporol [The Association for the Advancement of Agriculture, see n. 299].[334] Our tragedy expressed in Ora's story. God!

Saturday, 5 September

The enemy shows no mercy and continues to torture and murder us. I spent the day in the workshop in dread of a blockade and of death.

In the morning blockades were set up at Többens', so I heard, and they took away about 2,000 people. Once again they took everyone away from Frank–Schultz's and left behind only 50.[335] There was also a blockade at Hallman's. Several hundred people were taken away from there. It seems that their plan is to destroy the Jewish community in Warsaw utterly.

Our factory is threatened with liquidation. Then we will be left hanging in limbo. The whole day passed with a heavy presentiment of imminent death. I would like to die peacefully and with the knowledge that it had to be and nothing could prevent it. I have not forgotten Stolypin's last words: he said on his death-bed: 'Chemu byt tavo nie minovat' (russ.) ['Something that is decreed in advance will happen. There is no escape']. This is our bitter fate – to fall into the hands of the butchers and to be the sacrificial blood of a new era. I believe that there is no way out of the clutches of the savage animal and that we are only drawing out our death-agony.

Gutk. and Zilberb. have managed to save themselves in a quite miraculous and heroic fashion. News from As. has reached us from Wołomin.

Friday, 11 September – *The Eve of Rosh Hashanah*

Since last Saturday I have had neither the inclination, the time nor the opportunity to write anything.[337] The human hand and pen are weary of describing all that has happened to the handful of Jews who are for the time being still alive, myself among them. The cup of our sorrows has no parallel in our history.

The horrific and brutal week began on the Saturday night, Sunday morning. A Jewish policeman knocked on the door at three in the morning and gave us the terrible news that all Jews were to be concentrated within the boundary formed by Gęsia, Miła and Ostrowska Streets, for a new registration. Enough food for two days should be taken, and something to hold water. The panic that gripped the Jews of Warsaw on Sunday morning. We all believed that our time had come to depart this life.[338] With tears in my eyes I said goodbye to my whole family: to mother, Frume, Nacia, Jakub and the children.

The terrible and particular appearance of the streets: Miła, Wołyńska, the rectangle that has been transformed into an *Umschlagplatz*. The crowds of Jews with packs on their backs, streaming from the streets of the ghetto. Everyone is camped out on the street. In this way we spend the whole of Sunday. In the evening the inspections begin by the workshops, and certain groups return back to their factories or to their blocks. On Monday the return to the blocks continues. The inspection brings new victims: children do not pass. The old, women, do not pass. However, everything depends on chance. With some groups the inspection is not so severe, other groups on the other hand have enormous losses.

Murders in the streets. I saw with my own eyes how a young, strong man and a young, attractive woman were shot. A sight that I will never forget as long as I live: five tiny children, two- and three-year-olds, sit on a camp-bed in the open from Monday to Tuesday and cry and cry and scream without stopping – 'mama, mama, chce jeść!' ['Mummy, mummy, I want to eat!']. The soldiers are shooting continually and the shots silence the children for a moment. The children lay there for 24 hours, sobbing and screaming: Mummy, Mummy. Tuesday afternoon a middle-aged man, aged about 50, went up to them, broke down into a continual, choking sobbing and gave the children a little something to eat. Earlier, women had come up and given them food. Our hearts have turned to stone and there was no way to save them. What are we saving them for if we are all sentenced to die?

We were waiting for the commissar of the firm, Hensel, to come and take us to the factory. He doesn't come. Our mood becomes more and more despairing. The feeling that death, in the form of the *Umschlagplatz*, is getting slowly nearer and nearer, chokes us and is throttling us to death. A rumour went round that our firm had been closed by the Warsaw SS. The people's mood swings between hope and despair. Meanwhile there are blockades in the nearby streets and in Miła Street.

Several dozen of our people are removed from the buildings at number 61 Miła[339] and from the *Werksschutz* [factory guard]:[340] Rozenowicz and his father, Ryba and his family. This happened on Monday. Our despair, and the suffering of the hundreds of people, shut in the alleyway, reaches the ultimate limits of endurance. The shooting that goes on all day and, especially, all night shatters the nerves, bringing a deathly depression. Midday Tuesday a glimmer of hope appears, but is immediately extinguished. Hensel arrives for a short visit at ten till eleven in the morning and promises he will soon come to take us away. He leaves, the hours go by and he doesn't return. Once again our resolve is weakened and we fall into deep despair that is many times worse. We wait for the end that is inevitable: to be taken to the *Umschlagplatz*.

It is hard to keep going. I have no food, nothing to sleep on. I am sleeping (a) at 3a Dzielna Street, (b) at Rabinowicz's, on the floor,[341] (c) with Recymer. People are quarrelling with each other. Anyone who has anything left, cooks and eats and watches over their property. People steal everything they can lay their hands on, especially food; there is no feeling of common fate, of mutual aid. People wander around aimlessly like shadows.

Ora with the members of Hashomer Hatsair. These young people are more mature, more united. Tuesday night was bitterly sad for me. I tried very hard to acknowledge the idea that death is inevitable and to prepare myself. I thought: the whole thing will only last 10–15 minutes, the execution, that is, and it will all be over. The lack of news from my sisters and my mother weighs oppressively.

There is also an oppressive plague of fleas. Hunger forces us to beg, to ask for a little food. Even in such terrible hours as these a hungry person wants to still the hunger. Wednesday morning: once again a rumour that brings hope. Hensel is coming to get us. He really has come. Joy grips all those who are shut in the street. Straight away most of those who work in the workshop come down, men and women. Left behind in their homes, that is, in their hiding places, old women and children. We stand and sit in the street from ten in the morning until six in the evening. The mood is almost joyful. A crowd of women, like some unit, is standing in front of us. The hours pass. But still everyone waits patiently. They want to get to the factory. Suddenly four or five SS officers appear and . . . a pogrom begins, the like of which I have never seen. Even the marauding of the Cossacks in the first revolution of 1905–6 bore no resemblance to what the Germans did. They beat men and women with whips, sticks and strips of wood. They took all the women away to the *Umschlagplatz* (except for a few with metal numbers) [that is, those exempt from deportation] and large numbers of the men, who had by chance not obtained a metal number, thinking them to be worthless.[342] The best-looking and the most elegant women perished. Whole families were cut down. A young officer hit out with murderous blows and shouting wildly: 'Über euch, verfluchte, verdammte, kräzige Juden habe ich 3 Jahren Lebens verloren. Schon 3 Jahren plaget ihr uns, ihr Hunde . . .' ['Because of you, accursed, damned, leprous Jews I have already lost three years of my life, for three years we have been plagued, you dogs . . .'] and so on. I have never before seen such bestial hatred. There was also killing.

We go towards 30 Gęsia Street and there is a round-up going on there, that is still continuing today. Yesterday and today there were blockades on our blocks; people have been taken again. The Świeca family has perished. He gave himself up after seeing how his wife and two children were taken. Initially he went with us to Gęsia Street, later he went back, gave himself up and was sent away. I feel a great compassion and admiration for this straightforward person. Strong in mind as well as strong in body. I think that Luba would have done the same, but I didn't have enough strength to die together with her, with the one that I loved so much.

Apart from the hunt for people, the Germans are looting openly, as something quite legal. They take away everything from the buildings that appeals to them. The Ukrainians are common bandits. They break into the buildings at night and steal everything they find, with revolvers and rifles in their hands. The Jews are also in the grip of a frenzied looting and thieving. They loot and steal everything that they can lay their hands on.

Since the day before yesterday we have been shut in the factory. We tremble at every noise and shot that comes from the street. Yesterday the SS visited us for the purpose of looting. Today is the eve of Rosh Hashanah. May the coming year bring salvation for those who have survived. Today is the 52nd day in the greatest and most terrible slaughter in history. We are the tiny remnants of the greatest Jewish community in the world.

Tuesday, 15 September

The days go by without the shattering upheavals of the previous weeks. Yesterday I was told that the *Umschlagplatz* has been totally cleared. Those who were still there, who were hiding, have been freed. Thus the bloody 'action', of which history has not seen the like, lasted 54 days. The conclusion was the deportation from the hospitals of their patients and their doctors, nurses and staff.[343] Nor did they spare in this those patients whose days are numbered. According to officials of the Jewish community the number of Jews remaining legally in Warsaw is 34,000, together with those in hiding, as many as 50,000. This is the sum total of the greatest Jewish community in Europe, in actual fact, in the whole world. More than 300,000 Jews have been exterminated in the course of seven and a half weeks. Jewish Warsaw now has the air of a cemetery.[344]

In the last days of the action, on Saturday, more than 20 people were killed in the building at 3 Dzika Street, the only building where there had not been a blockade. Two Jews were having an argument, Gorilow and one other.[345] At that moment two Junaks were passing; they stormed in and led out more than 20 Jews. Among the dead was the family of Leon Ringelblum: Leon, his wife and their three-year-old child.[346]

I have great respect for those Jews such as Świeca, Dr Wislicki, Dr Plonsker,[347] and others, who sacrificed themselves, not wishing to survive the death of their wives and children. The greatest admiration and awe is awakened in me by the Jew Świeca, a giant in physical stature, who stood with us in the square, came with us to the factory and then went back and gave himself up to the butchers, because he could not part from his wife and children, who were seized that day during the slaughter. The next day his two other children were taken away, so the whole family perished. Only his aged father is left, for whom we have great compassion in his loss and loneliness.

Word has it that the 'action' has begun in Częstochowa.[348] It is already in its second day. We, who have been through the ordeal, feel what our brothers are going through there. I have heard the following about Kielce:[349] when the thugs arrived there, they approached the Jewish community leaders with a request for help in the 'action'.

They refused to help. They were given 24 hours to think it over. After the deadline they gave another negative answer. In reply to this the thugs murdered all the council members and the members of the police, and then carried out a large-scale massacre in the streets. They killed about 1,000 Jews and expelled the remainder in familiar fashion. According to what I have heard, not a single Jew is left in Kielce. According to another rumour, there are still about 1,000 left out of about 30,000.

Josef Kaplan is now no longer alive. He was buried last Saturday at the cemetery, the first day of the new year. It turns out that he was murdered in the Pawiak. Those two fine boys Josef and Shmuel have paid the highest price for their strivings and their ideals: with their lives.[350]

Wednesday, 16 September

Once again we have been through two days of misfortune and abuse at our factory. Yesterday the SS raided it and took away 50 people to work in Smolensk. During this incident they killed Rabbi Blumenfeld.[351] He wanted to go up to the officer to ask that his life be spared. He was shot seven times over several seconds. Slowly, slowly. The events yesterday shook me up terribly. Today there was another formal blockade. A whole squad of SS raided the factory and again they took away a further 50 men and several dozen women. I was lucky yesterday and today and remained alive. But how much can we bear? Of those rounded up today, those with money came back. In the evening nine Jews in the factory were rounded up and sent to the *Umschlagplatz* in the place of the nine Jews who were taken this morning and freed. Things that we would not believe if we were told about them.

Friday, 18 September

New and extreme difficulties are besetting us. The ghetto boundaries are being reduced further. The whole rectangle: Pawia, Lubiecka, Gęsia, Zamenhof Streets is being removed from the ghetto. My two remaining sisters are losing their flats. In any case they have no right to be alive, since they have not received a number from the community authorities. All my belongings are over there. If they lose the flats, what little clothing and bedclothes I have will be endangered and I will be naked and destitute. This disturbs me deeply, even though we are in mortal danger and there is no need to get upset at the prospect of having nothing to wear or no pillow for our head, at a time when our very survival is in doubt. But perhaps a miracle will happen and our salvation will come suddenly?

Sunday, 20 September – *The Eve of Yom Kippur*

Such bleak and gloomy days go by, our spirits are being crushed. In our workshop, 30 Gęsia Street, at the Ostdeutsche Bautischlerei: Werkstätte, nothing out of the ordinary has happened. People work a little, become tired and hungry. A few individuals who have a lot of money or pilfered goods make murky deals, eat and drink. The rest suffer. My position is very difficult. I have no money. The general state of things is indescribable. It is as if they want to destroy all the Jews down to the very last one. The 'action' is still not yet over. Yesterday a blockade was suddenly set up on Miła Street at HG Zimmerman. A lot of people were taken away. I heard that it was 600. The *Umschlagplatz* has been set up again, so people are saying. Yesterday an order was issued that one doctor and two nurses were to report to work there. Unless a miracle happens, we will all die. Will there be a miracle? Will it happen?

My meeting with my girl students from Yehudia: Hochberg, Adina Schweiger[352] – I receive the shattering news that the whole of Yehudia has perished: her mother, Brotmacher, Złotowska, Weinberger and everyone, everyone.[353] A terrible scene. Najburg.

The difficult and dangerous position of the employees of the Jewish community who have been dismissed. Among them my brothers-in-law, Mojsze and Jakub. They have no numbers from the community authorities and have no refuge of any kind. They will not receive a flat, they have now to move out of Pawia Street, and in general they have no 'right' to live. What will happen? What will happen?

I went to bed at nine, half past nine. There was a knock at the door. Thugs – Junaks or soldiers – who roam around at night thieving and looting. We didn't open up for them. They hammered on the door and fired a lot of shots. I lay in terror, sweating. Days of terror and nights of terror. The Kassel family is no longer here. More than 300,000 Warsaw Jews have been struck out from the book of life, that is five-sixths of the Warsaw Jewish community. For each six Jews, five have gone. This is for the time being, the enemy is still not yet sated.

Monday, 21 September – *Yom Kippur*

We are not allowed into the factory. I spent the day at Nacia's and Frume's. There were blockades on Miła Street, in the building where the office of employment is, and others. Already a large group has been led away, most of them women. According to the rumours these are women from Többens', from the small ghetto. They were tricked: they were asked who would like to transfer from the small to the large ghetto: living conditions are very, very difficult in the small ghetto. Three hundred women volunteered, and they were taken straight to the *Umschlagplatz*. Anyway it should be set down that the 'action' is still continuing and today is the 62nd day. Warsaw's fate is more tragic than that of other towns that have been touched by this evil.

Those who are far away cannot imagine our bitter situation. They will not understand and will not believe that day after day thousands of men, women and children, innocent of any crime, were taken to their death. And the handful of those remaining after nine weeks is in mortal danger and, it seems, can expect the same fate. Almighty God! Why did this happen? And why is the whole world deaf to our screams?

Earth, earth, do not cover our blood, and let no place be free from our cries!

A Jew has returned to our workshop who was taken away from here three weeks ago and worked as a gravedigger in Treblinka for nine or eleven days before escaping in a train-wagon in which the martyrs' belongings were being taken away. He tells horrific and shattering things. In any case we have another eyewitness to the fate of those who are deported. According to what he said, not only Jews from Warsaw and of the *gubernia* are being exterminated in Treblinka, but Jews from all over Europe – from France, Belgium, Holland, among others. Such a calamity has never before befallen us in all the bitter experiences of our history. In our courtyard Jews are praying, pouring out their cares to the Creator.

Wednesday, 23 September

Yesterday I was quite unable to set down what happened in the ghetto on Monday, Yom Kippur. All the heads of the factories made an inspection or selection on their own initiative and themselves sent those they had picked out away to the *Umschlagplatz*, with the help of the *Werksschutz* [factory guard]. There was also a new registration at our factory after I had gone to Pawia Street. After the registration the commissar himself made an inspection of the flats and found 13 people hiding there. Six of them were workers who have numbers, completely legal workers, who didn't go down to the registration out of fear, and seven outsiders, who were hiding in the block. These 13 people he sent off to the *Umschlagplatz*. Grosberg's elderly mother has perished. The same thing happened in other workshops. In M. Kirschenbaum's workshop at 81 Gęsia Street, the director threw out all those he didn't like. After he had reached the letter 'T', he sent everyone to the *Umschlagplatz*. A large number from the ranks of the Jewish police have also been sent to the *Umschlagplatz*, together with their wives and children. The Jews who watched this scene felt a definite satisfaction. This is the reward for their brutal acts against the Jews of Warsaw.[354]

Thursday, 24 September

A day of turmoil and unrest among the few Jews who for the time being are left. Yesterday the new phase of moving out from the buildings on Pawia, Gęsia, Zamenhof and Lubiecka Streets began. No one gave the order for us to leave the streets, no one has set the deadline by which the move had to be completed, but there has been a feverish exodus from the streets since yesterday. Instead of the 36 buildings that the earlier block consisted of, only half this number have been allocated to us and they are in very poor condition. Another problem: many officials of the Jewish community and doctors have no numbers, that is, they are not 'legal' and didn't receive a flat, and they move in as guests with the legal workers. The crush that there will be in the new flats can easily be imagined. And over us hangs the sword of the SS. Everyone lives in dread of a new blockade and of deportation to Treblinka and death. Even yesterday, which seemed to us to be a quiet day, there was a blockade at von Schön's factory and people were taken away. Norbert Mandzicki's wife was taken away. Accursed are we whom they are torturing so.

Friday, 25 September

Terrible things happened yesterday. The commissar himself and his assistant rounded up women from among the workers, like Jerachmiel Rabinowicz's wife, and sent them to the *Umschlagplatz*. The same happened in the evening. The thugs of the *Werksschutz* [factory guard] allowed themselves a further terrible outrage. They went out into the street, seized passing women and freed those they had already taken in their place. Also: the husbands of two women who had been rounded up pointed the finger at two women hiding in the block. They were seized and their two wives freed. The hunt for people has started up again, especially for women. The deathly grip is tightening. Someone else has come back from Treblinka, a certain Rabinowicz, and what he told us made our hair stand on end.[355] Everyone without exception is exterminated. The proclamation with seven sections in the courtyard that begins with the announcement: 'Attention, emigrants from Warsaw!'[356]

Sunday, 27 September

The days pass by, in all their gloom and oppressiveness. Yesterday morning I was racked and tortured by hunger. There was no bread to eat. I filled my stomach with green vegetables, but the hunger did not go away. For two days running now there has been no bread at the workshop. Next to me was sitting the L. family, the owners of the factory, eating white bread and butter, eggs and other things.[357] This was hard to bear, especially as I like Mr Landau. It is hard for someone going hungry to sit next to someone who is eating their fill.

In the morning there was an announcement of the closing down of the Diehl workshop. There was a blockade and people were taken away, it is estimated about 150. The whole factory has been put out of action, hundreds of people have been left without legal protection. I visited Nacia for the first time at 44 Muranowska Street, a building that I lived in when I was seven. The terrible appearance of Miła and Zamenhof Streets. On my way back I spent the evening with the Wassers.[358] Rabinowicz was there, a relative of the Rabinowicz's, who escaped from Treblinka. For hours on end he recounted the horrors of Treblinka. His central observation: it has nearly reached the point that the Jews are more afraid of a German than of death. The facts that he recounted show that his observation was correct. 'Graves for the *Führer*'. The women go naked into the bath-house – to their death. The condition of the dead bodies. What are they killing them with? With simple vapour (steam).[359] Death comes after seven or eight minutes. On their arrival they take away the shoes of the unfortunates. The proclamation in the square: 'Emigrants from Warsaw . . .'

Thursday, 1 October

The devastation in the streets of the reduced ghetto which now only extends over a few streets: Miła, Zamenof, Franciszkańska and a few alleyways: Ostrowska, Wołyńska, Niska among others, are desolate. It is forbidden to be on the street. Not a single Jew to be seen. Every factory is a prison, locked and bolted. One can't go from Schultz's factory on Nowolipie Street to Többens' factories on Leszno Street. We are shut in the whole day at 30 Gęsia Street. We go in a group to and from work, before seven in the morning and at six in the evening. Most of the Jews who have survived are still living by selling their possessions. The prices are incredibly low. A dress is sold for 50 zloty (a new, good quality dress), that is for two kilos of black bread or for one kilo of white bread. The smuggling is carried out by the groups who go to work outside the ghetto. The smugglers can sustain themselves: they eat and feed their families. The vast majority goes hungry.

The 'action' has in fact still not been completely halted. The *Umschlagplatz* is still in existence. Hundreds of Jews are sitting there waiting for their fate. In the last few days there have been no wagons, and they have not been transported to Treblinka. I have heard that it is very difficult to get oneself freed. In any case it costs a great deal of money. The day before yesterday a member of our *Werksschutz* [factory guard] at OBW grabbed two people, an old man and woman – and sent them to the inferno (*Umschlagplatz*). Oppenhajm, who sleeps at Leszno Street with his wife who works at Többens' told me today that people were taken away from there yesterday to the *Umschlagplatz*. The sword of destruction hangs continually over our heads.

Last Sunday, the first day of Sukkot, the infamous Frankenstein killed two Jewish policemen at the cemetery and mortally wounded a third.[360] Wasser was at the burial. A Christian girl was weeping bitterly: 'moj kochasiu' ['my little sweetheart'].

Monday, 5 October

The days pass in gloom, without upheaval, bleak, full of grief and sorrow. We spend the whole day at the 'shop'. We are not allowed on the street during the day at all. The street casts a pall over the chance passer-by or over those who march in groups. Not a living soul to be seen. The streets are deserted, streets that were once humming with bustling crowds of Jews, like a bee-hive.

The head of the Jewish community has issued an order that no one at all is permitted south of Leszno Street and during working hours no one is permitted into the small ghetto. Anyone found in the street without a special permit will be deported from Warsaw, to their death.[361]

The few who remain in Warsaw tremble like leaves in an autumn wind. Each passing hour brings new and terrible rumours about the end that is imminent for the remaining Jews in Warsaw. There are also those who, quoting some German or other, say that this small group of Jews will be left in Warsaw until the end of the year. But in fact no one knows what tomorrow will bring and we all live in perpetual fear and terror.

Yesterday I had a short talk with the official G—n.[362] He said that no one knows what plans the authorities have for us and that our fate is dependent not on economic but on political factors. The question is: have they decided to leave us alive or to exterminate us? He also told me that he had an explicit order to leave 60,000 Jews in Warsaw, and they have only 50,000 left. The SS commandant Brandt admitted that they deported more people than necessary. They exterminated 10,000 extra Jews: either because they wanted to excel themselves and show their devotion to duty, or through an error in the calculation. How appalling!

Today a policeman informed us that there are 829 Jews at the *Umschlagplatz*. They are not being sent to Treblinka, nor are they being set free. In general it is difficult to get someone freed, because they are signed in and registered there with their full name. Thus to get a Jew freed costs a great deal of money. Dr Ringel. told me that in 'Hallmannowa' they offered to give 15,000 zloty for the release of Brandl (of the family of bakers) and have had no success.[363]

The 'plague' is now ravaging the small towns around Warsaw. In the past few days they have wiped out Wołomin, Jabłonna.[364] Similar news has reached us from Skarżysko.[365] The Jews dream of escaping to the Aryan side, to the Poles, or to the 'East' in the area of Białystok.[366] Each day someone leaves the shop secretly and gets out of the town. Yesterday the Margolises left, among others. Friends around me are having photographs made and are trying to negotiate papers of various kinds, *Kennkarten*,[367] and are preparing to leave Warsaw. I, having no money, do not involve myself with these matters. The member of the *Judenrat* with responsibility for the cemetery, Hurwicz, was here and said that since the beginning of the bloody events 12,000 murdered Jews have been buried at the cemetery.[368]

Wednesday, 14 October

Nothing new is happening. The days drag by in tedium and desolation, filling the Jews with terror and despair. Since yesterday the feeling of being caged in has become unbearable. An order was issued yesterday absolutely forbidding us to walk alone in the street, irrespective of the hour, that is, before and after work. This applies here too – that is, even in the small and much reduced ghetto a Jew is not allowed to walk alone, with the result that we are shut up all day in the workshop to which we have come marching in a group and which we will also leave in a group when we go back to the block. This is all our exercise the whole day, no more. The other streets of the ghetto are completely deserted all day and all night. This new order was issued in conjunction with the arrival of the SS comman- dant Krieger in Warsaw.[369] Word has it that Himmler has arrived or is due to arrive today. At any event, our existence is very hard, we are being throttled until we perish.

Over us hangs the threat of destruction. The Warsaw workshops have authorizations only until the 20th of this month; the 20th falls in six days and we still do not know what will be the fate of the handful of surviving Jews. The workers at our workshop (OBW) are especially afraid and despondent, as its existence is less sure than that of the others.[370]

Since I made the last entry on 5 October, we have lived in perpetual fear for our fate. We have made several visits to the Jewish community official Git—n to discuss this and are making efforts to secure our future should our factory be closed down. Day after day there is also talk of dismissals and of a considerable reduction in the work-force. To this day we do not know what tomorrow will bring.

Friday, 16 October

Nothing new has happened to us, everything is quiet, life is mono- tonous, but there is something heavy about the stillness that is oppressive and suffocating. We are still never free from fear about our fate in the immediate future, that is, 20 October and thereafter. There are some who are reassuring, who say: it is clear that the Jews left in Warsaw will be left alive and there is no need to worry about our fate. On the other hand there are those who never stop worrying and live in continual dread of tomorrow. When the first argue: look, we are being surrounded with a new wall along Smozca Street up to Gęsia, the others – the pessimists – reply: were we not also surrounded by walls even before the great 'action', and what good was that to us?

Furthermore, there are terrible reports reaching us from the provinces. The whole of the Kielce district has been completely cleared of Jews. Today I heard that in Białystok, which had been an oasis in the desert, as far as the behaviour of the authorities towards the Jews was concerned, an 'action' has started. The sword of death and destruction is cutting through the whole of the *gubernia* and thus those who see everything through dark glasses are troubled and have no faith in our survival.

The position of our 'shop' has still not yet been clarified. Every hour brings a different rumour. Some say that the confirmation has already been granted, and even if it is not yet in black and white, it is as good as in the drawer. They point to an order for 1,500 new boxes in support of their argument. The sceptics retort by saying that the prospects for our workshop are extremely poor and we are faced with a danger of closure and liquidation. And even if it is not closed, we will have the scourge of dismissals and a large number of workers will be sacked. What will they do? Where will they turn? Will they be allowed to live? All these fears and doubts are consuming us like fire.

The prohibition on walking alone in the street is in force and means that the whole day there is not a Jew to be seen outside. The streets of Warsaw are deserted and desolate without their inhabitants. A cold shudder goes through me as I march to work in the morning, and especially in the evening, through the deserted streets. A 'dead city' in the fullest meaning of the word. Even three weeks ago these same streets, in spite of the terror and the Germans' persecutions, were bustling with people and the buildings were full of Jews, women and children, young and old. What has become of them all? Have they really murdered a community of over 300,000 (more precisely: 310,000–320,000) Jews in Treblinka? It is so hard to believe in this appalling and terrible truth, but we cannot escape the knowledge that it is the truth: more than 300,000 Jews have been murdered in the course of eight weeks, dying such a cruel and terrible death. The best of our blood has been spilled by these thugs.[371]

Earth, earth, may you never cover this blood!

In the streets of Aryan Warsaw proclamations have been pasted up to the following effect: As punishment for the damage that was inflicted by criminal elements on the railway-track on 7 October in the area of Warsaw, 50 Polish communists have been hanged.[372] If similar acts are carried out, then even more severe punishments will follow. There is talk of an action against the Poles, similar to that which was carried out against us. In general there are rumours going around of acts of sabotage in various locations, about acts of revenge, severe retribution exacted, and self-defence and resistance by the Poles. It is hard to know how much truth there is in all these rumours.

It is too early to add up the total number of those who have fallen, but every time that a new report reaches me of our cherished martyrs, a shudder passes through me. I had this feeling when I heard recently of the deaths of Hillel Cajtlin and Gawze.[373] They were both seized during the 'action'. I have heard that Cajtlin was shot standing in front of the train-wagon.

God! Will revenge be taken for our innocent and cherished blood? May the day come quickly when our suffering and our humiliation will be washed away in the blood of these degenerates and barbarians.

Tuesday, 20 October

Days of turmoil and great fear have gone by at the workshop. A number of days ago a representative of the management of the German company, Kazparek, announced the sad news that the SS were reducing the number of workers in the OBW to 140 people. It became clear that they are to leave behind in the first instance only the carpenters and the family members, that is, the Landau family and their relatives. Then they spoke about efforts to raise the number of workers to 250. There was also talk that the factory would be closed altogether.

The mood of the workers was one of deep despair. People are walking around like shadows. They ask each other: what will happen to us if the factory is closed, or if the work-force is reduced? Will we be allowed to go on living in the block? Or will they come and take us to the *Umschlagplatz*? And what will we do then? What protection is there for our lives in these circumstances? We have begun running to the Jewish community official G—man, to ask him to intervene for us, that is, for the group from *Oneg Shabbes* and the Self-help Committee who are here.[374] The danger threatens us in the first instance, the leaders of the idle intellectuals, since people without a skill are certainly not required in a carpentry workshop if only 140 or 250 workers are to be employed.

As I described, we are going around in anguish and despair, helpless. The assistance that Mr G. was able to give was as follows: to find for some of us a second German place of work (at a so-called *placówka*). For some of us, for me, for example, this was practically a death-sentence. Suddenly a day of relief. A way out was found: collect money (350,000 zloty) and buy out the firm and its present owners, on condition that it pass to the Jewish community, and then all the workers will be able to stay registered. Today our position improved still further, since meantime everything will be unchanged, until the end of November. The collection of money is being carried out with great urgency. In any case we have been saved for the time being and the joy (if joy it can be called) is great in our wretched and desolate abode.

The mood of the small group of Jews is in general sombre and embittered, as there are fresh rumours about a renewal of the 'action', of the bloody operation. It has been said that they will begin by clearing out all the 'illegal' women, children and men in the Jewish population, that is, those who are not registered in any factory or as officials of the Jewish community. Many of us did not sleep last night and many have hidden themselves in advance. To our great relief the night passed peacefully. The fears were groundless.

The walls around the ghetto, that is, around the few streets still occupied by us, are nearing completion. The new ghetto – even more than the old – is like a small cage. It will be even harder to live here than in the old ghetto. The hunger, the cold – there is no fuel – will bring destruction upon us. Typhus has already appeared in our block.

Last Saturday the victims of the German terror were buried at the Jewish cemetery, the 50 who were recently hanged in public as a punishment for the acts of sabotage against the railway. The bodies of the executed were displayed for several days in various locations for public view.

Friday, 23 October

The days go by in superficial calm. Without 'actions' and without blockades, but none the less they have cost us – the workers at OBW – a large number of victims. I can't give the exact number, but it is as high as 30.

A group of people, mostly women, goes to the cemetery each day, supposedly to labour there, a remnant of the days of Toporol, but in reality not work but business is in prospect. They bring clothes and linen and sell them to the Christians who come there every day. The Christians bring food produce to sell to the Jews. The group is about 60–70 in number. The firm has been exploiting the situation and has been taking 30 to 50 zloty from each of them per day.

Yesterday morning, when the dealing was in full swing, the SS raided the cemetery, with the infamous Brandt at their head, and renewed their practice of a few weeks ago. All the Poles, 20 in total, that they found there were arrested and taken away – they claimed – to Prussia to work (certainly to Treblinka). The Jews they divided into two groups: one was set free, and the second – about 30 people – was led away to the *Umschlagplatz*. Among the second group there were also children aged 13–14. Since yesterday they have been at the *Umschlagplatz*. What will happen to them – is not yet known.

Friday, 30 October

The days themselves are full of radiance and light, glorious, sun-filled days at the close of autumn, golden autumn days of which Poland used to be so proud. But for us, here in our cramped and gloomy little world, the days are black, desolate, with a tedium which is in itself almost deadly.

My life and that of all my companions is passed between the 'shop' and the 'block'. At seven o'clock in the morning we walk to 30 Gęsia Street and there we spend the day. Everyone does something, or gets out of work and idles the day away somehow. At five in the evening we return home to Miła Street to our block and kill time in the evening and spend the night there, only to get up at five or half past six, and so on continually. We have no holidays or rest-days. We work both Saturday and Sunday. There is only the concession that on Saturday we finish work at four in the afternoon and on Sunday at two.

When will our suffering end? When will our situation and that of the whole of Europe change? If in the future someone should inquire what the select few who remained alive lived on, it would be very difficult to give them a clear and satisfactory answer. We live mainly from selling things, that is, mainly from clothes. But the selling of clothes is also no simple and straightforward matter. In the ghetto people pay very low prices. Ultimately they are not needed there. Their value is realized outside the ghetto. The Poles buy our clothes and linens, pay their low prices, and the vast majority of the Jews live from this.

The amount of Jewish property that the Germans confiscate through their office known as *Werterfassung*, which is part of the *Umsiedlungsstab* (this is the name of the department of extermination, whose head is here and everywhere and whose rear-end or nether-organ is in Treblinka),[375] is so vast that this alone fills the Jews with terror. The empty houses with the air of a graveyard shake me to the core every time that I pass by them on the way to my quarters from the factory.

The pain for the loss of the person dearest to me grows from day to day. Only now do I understand the full meaning of the words of the Bible: 'Thus a man leaves his father and his mother and goes unto his wife and they become of one body.' I have lost a good sister whom I loved dearly, I have lost so many who were close to me. But their absence does not hurt me as much as that of my life's companion who shared my life with me for more than 22 years. And what makes the pain more intense – until I almost go insane – is the way in which she left this vale of tears. It is not easy to make peace with this thought and with the images that accompany it. How was this gentle and delicate woman killed, whom I used to call 'child'? And when I wake at night this thought drills into my head and my whole being cries out the cruel piercing sentence: 'My child is no longer with me. Wild animals have appeared and murdered her! Where are you, child of mine?'

Five of the women who were taken away a week ago were freed

today at a price of 6,000 zloty for each. There are still 15 being held there, and their husbands are making efforts to free them. Of course it will be at the same price.

At about five o'clock yesterday evening at 10 Gęsia Street, the deputy-head of the Jewish police, the lawyer Lejkin, was shot dead.[376] His adjutant Czapliński was wounded in the leg.[377] There is not much precise information about the killing. It is assumed that this is an act of revenge and retribution against those Jews whose hands are stained with Jewish blood, who have sent hundreds and thousands of Jews to the *Umschlagplatz* and to Treblinka. A while ago the police-commandant, the convert Szeryński, was wounded but only slightly and he is already better. This time – so it is thought – his chief assistant has been punished, Lejkin.[378]

Saturday, 31 October

Yesterday the community official Gi—man informed us that children aged 14 who have somewhere to go are being freed at the *Umschlag-platz*, and are sent to their relations, and those who have no one will be taken into educational institutes of Centos. The adults are divided into those fit for work and those unfit for work. It is not yet completely clear what will be done with them, either with the first or the second group. Things for the moment are very quiet here: there are no murders and no one is sent to their death in Treblinka. I heard a very sad piece of news today that in Kraków and Sandomierz all the Jews are being liqui-dated.[379] Terrible, terrible, what disasters have befallen us!

Sunday, 1 November

The weather in this period is unusually warm and bright. Not like autumn, like spring. The sun shines and warms. The air is so clear. A warm, caressing breeze. You can walk around in summer clothes. We are not used to being spoiled in this way by nature. As far as I can remember, this day, the Christian day of remembrance of the dead – *zaduszki* – has always been a rainy one, with cold winds and even snow. This year is such a pleasant surprise.

Among the Jews as well there was an air of relaxation. The streets were full of strollers. The few Jews who have remained alive came down from their cramped flats and went outside. Miła and Zamenhof Streets have filled up with these few Jews. True – they are gloomy, broken, emaciated, but they have dared to show themselves in the streets, something that has not been seen for weeks and months, since the intensification of the 'action'.

What has affected the Jews' spirits? First of all the release of the children from the *Umschlagplatz*. It actually came about: yesterday they decided to free children up to the ages of 14–16. Officially they were freeing 14-year-olds, but because they didn't require any kind of papers, 15- and 16-year-olds were able to get released, if they were small. Two children of our neighbour Racimor's family (out of six boys and girls, only a 14-year-old girl remained), the daughter and a nephew, came home yesterday. Those who have no one to go to are being taken into the orphanages run by the Jewish community. The number of freed children was 118.

The release of adults has also become easier and cheaper. I have heard that one can buy one's freedom for 2,000 zloty instead of 6,000. It seems as though they really have stopped sending people to Treblinka and the *Umschlagplatz* is on the point of being closed. In the ghetto there is a rumour going around that an international commission (of the Red Cross) is supposed to come here and the Germans want to prove that there are Jews still here and that they are working. We must take this as a fabrication. Our spirits were also lifted by the double-holiday: it is Sunday and the day of remembrance for the dead (*zaduszki*). I have been told that in general optimism has increased among us. There is a belief that important new developments will take place this month. If only!

Mr Rabinowicz told me something unbelievable today. The SS commandant, the one who has carried out the murder of 300,000 of us, excluding the victims in the provincial towns in the area of the *gubernia*, came to the offices of the Jewish community yesterday and gave an 'address' to the effect that children are the future of a people, that the old are dying off, and that therefore our hope and future is just with the children, and that because of this we should take excellent care of them.[380] He called on the leaders of the community to look after the children and to put them into educational establishments for orphaned children.

What words are there for such hypocrisy, such cynicism? In our language, in human speech, there are no expressions that can describe the behaviour of the sick and savage butcher, Brandt, just as there are no words in our human tongue to capture the devilishness of their ghoulish acts during the three months of the 'action' – the extermination action.

There is no communication or contact whatsoever between Warsaw and the towns outside it. We do not know what is happening now on the streets of Poland, in the areas that have been absorbed by the Reich, and in those that belong within the borders of the *gubernia*. We know that whole communities have been wiped off the face of the earth and torn root and branch from the ground. In certain areas of the country 10 per cent survive. There is talk of new expulsions in Kraków, Lublin and elsewhere. At a rough estimate we can say that of the two million Jews of the *gubernia* about 10 per cent are left. But it is difficult to say anything precise.

No one leaves here or comes in from the outside. If anyone manages to steal into the ghetto, it is someone who was seized and taken to Treblinka and managed to escape. Such a person has spent several weeks on the road, has seen or heard about the destruction of Jewish communities, stayed at night on the peasants' farms or in the fields and then finally returned. All that they can utter is sighs and lamentations, but precise accounts of the extent of the slaughter and of the number of survivors and their fate – are difficult to get from them. But there is no doubt that Polish Jewry is finished, it exists no more. Hitler has put an end to it. And the reaper has raised his scythe over all of Jewry . . .

Tuesday, 3 November

I have heard, and it seems that the report is true, that the SS commandant Brandt announced during his visit to the community offices that he would return the Torah scrolls that were found in the streets that Jews have moved out of and that he will permit the allocation of space for prayers, not a synagogue, but *minyonim* (*kleine Gebethäuser* [small houses of prayer]).

There is also talk that a theatre and a cinema will soon be opening in the new, miniature ghetto. I have also heard it said that permission has been given for shops to open. The day before yesterday it was a surprise to see a barber-shop open at Miła in the miniature ghetto, in which Jews were sitting and having a shave. One gets the impression that the Germans want to create the illusion of life and movement in the ghetto. Why do they need it? The devil only knows. Perhaps a commission really will be coming from abroad? According to rumour there will soon be a cabaret opening on Wołyńska Street.

Yesterday I was told that Treblinka, which has been a place of execution for hundreds of thousands of Jews, no longer exists. Supposedly there is a huge work-camp there now. Perhaps this story is true as well?[381]

In our block there is an epidemic of stomach-typhus. Among the seriously ill are the engineer Perlrot, and Josef Landau, of the factory owners. Silberberg's wife and others are also ill. And no wonder.

Wednesday, 4 November

The few remaining Jews who have survived the massacres are perplexed. Things have become a little easier, there is continual talk of shops, cinema, theatre, about this and that, from which we can infer that we will be allowed a breathing-space in the coming weeks and months. Thus I have heard that we will be allowed to take flats in any building of the ghetto. True, the number of buildings is limited, but we will all be able to move in where we can find somewhere, not as now, when every 'shop' has its own building or block where all the workers are concentrated. For example, we are concentrated on Miła Street in the buildings at numbers 54, 56, 64, 68, 61 and 59. They will start to demand rent once again. This all creates the impression that the Germans intend to let the tiny ghetto come to life.

At the same time, reports are arriving that the horrific extermination operation against the Jews is continuing in the provinces, and town after town is falling victim to these brutal animals who show no mercy in their thirst for Jewish blood. Yesterday or the day before yesterday a refugee arrived from Sandomierz [Zuzmir in Yiddish]. He recounted the following: the butchers had raided during the night and attacked the Jewish quarter. But the Jews had known in advance what was coming. The members of the *Judenrat*, the policemen and three-quarters of them had fled for their lives and were in hiding. The butchers were unable to carry out their plan, that is, to execute the expulsion as was set up and ordained in advance. The few Jews who had remained there they murdered on the spot. The town has been left empty of Jews for the time being. There is further talk of Kraków: there too they raided the Jewish quarter in the night and took out or 'expelled' 5,000 Jews. These reports fill us with terror, forcing us to fear for our fate and to reflect on what terrible plans the Germans have for this tiny and ragged community, the remnants of the great Jewish centre that Warsaw once was.

It is worth recording that there is a rumour that soon 25,000 Jews will be returning from Treblinka to Warsaw. The same report tells of a large number of Jews being gathered together in Treblinka; exaggerated figures in the hundreds of thousands are being mentioned. It is hard to tell who is spreading these fantasies. We have spoken face to face with escapees from Treblinka and know very well that one can find bones there, the bones of hundreds of thousands of Jewish martyrs, but no living Jews, if we exclude the few who are employed in sorting out the clothes and belongings of the dead.

Just today I heard the bitter news of the death of Yisroel Zeltser, one of the leaders of Gordonia in Poland.[382] He was buried together with Josef Kaplan from the Pawiak. I remember meeting him on Pawia Street in early autumn on my way to work at the OBW factory. He was carrying a pair of boots under his arm. He said that he was leaving Warsaw. Now I have learnt that he really did leave Warsaw, but was caught and imprisoned in the Pawiak, where he was murdered, apparently on Yom Kippur, together with Kaplan.

Ostrowicz, who goes to the cemetery each day to do business, told me about two funerals that took place yesterday. Two martyrs were buried who had been killed in the Pawiak. One of them was hanged. He was a strong man, well-built and white as alabaster. The second was shot. He was a policeman. Why they were murdered and who they were – their names – is not known. There are days when there is not even a single funeral at the cemetery, something which has never happened before in Warsaw. This can be explained by the nature of the human material that has survived: that is, the young and strong, in the main, the workers, and also the number of Jewish inhabitants is small. Yesterday no one was buried either, apart from the two murdered men.

I have heard that yesterday the bloody 'action' began in Białystok. This was also once a great Jewish centre.[383] A young woman who has arrived from Kraków has said that an 'operation' was carried out there last week from Monday to Thursday. Six thousand Jews were taken away. According to the Germans' calculations there are about 6,000 Jews left in the Kraków ghetto. According to the Jews' calculations, about 10,000–12,000.

Friday, 6 November

Yesterday in the Polish newspaper a decree was published concerning the locations where ghettos for Jews will be situated. In the district of Warsaw the following places have been designated: Warsaw, Rembertów, Siedlce, and Sokołów. I didn't see the decree myself because it is very difficult to get hold of a newspaper, but I was told about the contents.[384] All Jews (that is, those who are still alive and hiding or are living with Christians) must choose one of the designated places by 1 December. After this deadline any Jew found outside a ghetto will be sentenced to death. Christians (Aryans) are forbidden to be in or to enter the ghettos, under penalty of a fine of 100,000 zloty. What is the purpose of this decree? Is it not a trick to get hold of those Jews who are hiding with Christians and shut them in a cage, so as to be in a better position to destroy them too one morning? Or perhaps they intend to allow the remainder to live and to shut them into these five holes. The coming days and months will show the intentions of the murderers and looters.[385]

Yesterday large proclamations in enormous letters were posted in the streets of the ghetto announcing that 700 male and female workers are required for those who are looting the Jewish property (*Werterfassung*). They are being promised accommodation in the community buildings and the food that workers receive, that is half or three-quarters of a kilo of bread and soup every day. I doubt if there will be 700 men and women in the ghetto of working age who will be prepared to accept this work. True it is not strenuous work, but it is humiliating and depressing work, because it involves gathering up all the property in the buildings that belonged to Jews and handing it over to the murderers and looters. Each home tells of living people who once lived and worked there and who were murdered in such a horrific fashion. To be busy the whole day with such work as that – is surely not particularly pleasant. The announcement was published yesterday. The day before yesterday I heard that they are again rounding up people for work. It seems that the hunt in the street was not successful, because there is no one to round up and so they decided to devise a scheme to find another 700 slaves. The announcement was signed by the employment section of the *Judenrat*.[386]

Monday, 9 November

The exact list of the locations where there will be ghettos is the following. In the district of Warsaw: Warsaw, Kałuszyn, Siedlce, Rembertów, Kosow. In the district of Sokołów, Sobolew – altogether six places. In the district of Lublin: Łuków, Parczew, Międzyrzec, Włodawa, Końskowola, Piaski, Zaklików, Izbica – in total eight locations. In addition there may be closed work-camps established for Jews.

In connection with this decree there was a rumour going round in the ghetto yesterday that there will soon be 20,000 new Jews arriving in the ghetto. Apparently from those places where there are still surviving Jews and where Jews will be forbidden to live from 1 December. People are saying also that all the 'shops' that are situated outside the ghetto walls such as Többens' and Schultz's will be incorporated into the ghetto. There is no way of knowing at the moment how much truth there is in these rumours.

Borowski's son has returned to Warsaw to our workshop. He was seized on 9 September during the selection and was sent to 7 Lipowa Street in Lublin.[387] There are thousands of Jews there. The working conditions are hard. Each receives 190 g [6 oz] of bread and soup twice a day. In the camp there are very many Jewish prisoners who took part in the deportation of the Jews from Lublin at the end of March this year, and filled their pockets with Jewish booty. These prisoners live well. They have a lot of money (and gold) and they eat the very best food. According to him it was possible in that camp (7 Lipowa) for prisoners who did not need soup to give their numbers for the soup-ration to workers who came from nearby.

Lately Jewish workers who had been given positions of authority, the squad-leaders, have been running away. Rumours were going round there that the work-camp was to be shut down and the workers were to be sent away to a punishment-camp known as KL [*Konzentrationslager*] where death or a prolonged death-agony awaits all the prisoners. Living conditions are so hard there that even the strongest person can survive there just a few days. If he falls slightly ill, he is sent directly to a place of extermination where he is murdered with vapour.[388] Out of fear of such a fate many of them ran away, among them this young man. He wandered for eight days before reaching Warsaw on foot. On the way two Polish policemen took away his coat and threatened to shoot him. A Pole who allowed him to spend the night in a hay-rick stole his boots. Barefoot and his clothes in rags, he managed to reach Warsaw by the back-lanes. He said that he had passed places where many Jews who had been in hiding were murdered. On some Jews money was found. On one woman who was murdered by the Germans 30 roubles in gold was found. The young man gave the policemen his last 100 zloty. In Mińsk Mazowiecki there are no Jews, except in the several work-camps outside the ghetto, where a small number of Jews are working. The whole Mińsk ghetto has been sold to someone by the SS and now all the possessions are taken to the market. On his way the peasants gave him pieces of bread, thanks to which he managed to survive and not die of hunger. He spent a few nights in the fields. In spite of the fact that he had no overcoat and no shoes, he arrived in good physical shape and doesn't look bad.

We have reached a point where we have become indifferent to death. We are led to our deaths and we go without any attempt at resistance or self-defence. This young man says matter-of-factly: when the police were threatening that they would kill him, he was sure that they would carry out their threat, because he knew that on that same spot nine Jews had been killed the day before. He was going with them to his *death*. On the way, as they were walking with him, they reconsidered and gave him back the bread they had found on him and taken away at the beginning. The young man could not understand why they were giving him back the bread and asked: What use is bread to me if I'm going to my death? The police replied that he would sooner or later fall into the Germans' hands and they would kill him, so why should they bother with him and get their hands dirty with such messy work? It seems that they took pity on the young boy who is still wet behind the ears, as the saying goes. In Praga he managed to slip into a group of Jewish workers who are working on the tracks of the Eastern Station,[389] and entered the ghetto with them.

Tuesday, 10 November

Unrest and nervous agitation have taken hold of the ghetto once again. The reason is the political events of the past few days: the English offensive in Egypt, the American occupation [their landing] on the coast of French Africa – Algeria and Morocco – and in particular Hitler's latest speech on the anniversary of the foundation of the Nazi Party, 9 November 1922, 20 years ago.[390] As yet we have not received a copy of this speech in print, but the Jews already *know* that it is steeped in venomous hatred and full of terrible threats against the Jews, that he talked of the total annihilation of the Jews of Europe, from the youngest to the very old. If any of us manage to escape – then they will be brought low subsequently. This is what the Jews are saying and they add that his speech was mainly devoted to us, that it lasted 40 minutes and 25 of them were devoted to the Jews.

There are further developments here that are intensifying the tension and increasing our terror and dread. Word has it that more gendarmes have arrived in Warsaw and that there is activity starting up at the *Umschlagplatz*: they are clearing out further large rooms there. We should bear in mind that the days of 10, 11 and 12 November are the holidays celebrating Polish independence,[391] and that they are capable – especially during English and American attacks and at the beginning of a second front[392] – of raising the level of disorientation and turmoil among us, in Warsaw in general and among the Jews in particular.

There is another event to report in our tiny little world: half of Hoffmann's 'shop' is being closed [tailors were employed there sewing coats for the army and also for civilians], that is it is being liquidated. The number of those made idle or dismissed is as high as 500. The reason may be, so people are saying, the demand from the authorities (SS) for 2,000 highly qualified tailors (or even tailors with fewer qualifications) to be handed over to them to be sent to Lublin, as they are needed there in the workshops.

Yesterday they registered the highly qualified tailors, without giving an explanation or a reason. Last night at half past one there was a commotion among those who work at 52 Nowolipie Street. Early in the morning, at five o'clock, they began to make their escape. The workers have scattered in all directions. They are afraid that they will be rounded up and sent somewhere from which there is no return. It's all the same, Lublin or Treblinka. In fact in the course of the morning a large number of SS entered the block. What they will do there and what their plans are – I do not know as yet. Do they intend to hunt down people as they did a few weeks ago during the 'expulsion'? Who will they take? Will they take the specialist tailors or just anyone? Who can say? I have heard that for the moment they are removing sewing-machines from Hoffmann's workshop number 2.

Yesterday they ordered the Jewish authorities to find 15 carts for them, apparently for the purpose of removing the sewing-machines from Hoffmann's.

People are living in dread of persecutions and new massacres. My own daughter – 15 years old – has registered with the group of 700 who are to collect the Jewish property and hand it over to the murderers. It hurts me very much that girls of this age have to be involved in this kind of work. Many girls of this age will be employed in this degrading work.

At this moment, eleven o'clock, I have heard that an 'action' has begun on Prosta Street at Többens'. They require 1,000 people. It is not yet known how much truth there is in this rumour. These reports are from a Jewish policeman who said that he had seen a group of Jews on Zamenhof Street – among them women and children – who were being led in the direction of the *Umschlagplatz*.

Wednesday, 11 November

Once again the survivors in the ghetto have lived through an extremely difficult day, a day of fear and trembling. The wings of death have been beating over the heads of the few remaining Jews, and all of us live with fear in our heart. It is hard to describe this feeling. Only someone who is familiar with Russian literature, especially Dostoyevsky, will be able to imagine what kind of life they are living, with the *Umschlag*-sword hanging over their heads. There are no precise details about the 'action' that was carried out yesterday. We only know that it was carried out in the 'shops' of Hoffmann, Többens, Oschman and Brauer. In total 1,000 were taken, according to those who give larger, more inflated numbers, and 600–700, according to those who give lower figures. Among those rounded up were also women and children.

No one knows what all this means. It can be interpreted in various ways: (a) that this is a renewal of the old 'action'. Its purpose is to liquidate the small community that has remained. If this is the case then we have no hope of escaping with our lives. Where can we escape to and where can we hide? Hitler's last speech with his threatening words against the Jews ('the few who are still laughing at my words will soon lose the desire to laugh . . .') seems to give credence to the idea that a new extermination of Jews really has started;[393] (b) that this is a punishment for the fact that the tailors were not handed over as they had ordered. Those who believe this is the case base their argument on the fact that when the SS arrived at Hoffmann's they found in two sections instead of 1,000 workers just 42. As a punishment for this sin they carried out the 'action' in all the 'shops' where there are tailors or needleworkers: Többens, Hoffmann, Oschman and Brauer.[394]

There are further reports that a certain number of people were freed from the *Umschlagplatz* yesterday. According to one opinion the number of those freed was 100. Who was freed? It is hard to say exactly who. One version was that it was the women. The director of Többens' drove to the *Umschlagplatz* and took them away. Someone else said that they freed everyone who did not have a skill, and the skilled workers were left there, that is, the tailors. In spite of the fact that the ghetto has become so small, it is impossible to collect precise information and it is impossible to determine which events really happened and to sort out the truth from the lies, reality from fantasy.

At this moment, at nine o'clock, a report has reached me that an 'action' is also being carried out today on Leszno Street in the blocks of flats. So we are therefore dealing with a new 'purge' of the community. We are all in the gravest danger. It all depends on how far the 'purging' will go. Will it include the whole ghetto, or will it be confined to the 'shops' of the garment workers? Whatever the case, we are desperate for mercy and for the 'miracle'.

Yesterday at half past two, five or six German officers from the army and the SS came to our factory. Their arrival caused great terror among the workers. The people have been alarmed and shocked by the latest happenings in the town. They passed through the carpentry-shop, on their way out handing out a few blows across the face to one of the guards from the so-called *Werksschutz*, because an answer he had given them did not find favour with the questioner. According to the factory management, they had come to see which machines are standing idle and are not needed by the factory, and so can be taken away. This visit, which for the time being has had no tragic consequences, shook everyone up very badly. All Hoffmann's workers have fled in all directions. The workshop looks just as if it had been closed down completely. This is a bad sign. It is said that Hoffmann [a German] had himself advised the Jewish management to hide until Saturday. If they have shut down this 'shop', which was held to be among the safest and most secure (not a single blockade was carried out there, except for the last selection on 6 September, because of the good relations between Hoffmann and the SS commandant – so this particular good fortune has been interpreted), then why should they treat the remaining workshops any better? Very depressing.

This last night was filled for me with nightmares and horrors. I tossed and turned on my bed, my sleep was disturbed, and my torments reached the unbearable. Nights such as these are endured by those who are sentenced to death and who do not know exactly when the terrible sentence will be carried out. How terrible it is that a whole generation – millions of Jews – has suddenly become a community of 'martyrs', who have had to die in such a cruel, degrading and painful manner and go through the torments of hell before going to the gallows. Earth, earth do not cover our blood and do not keep silent, so that our blood will cry out until the ends of time and demand revenge for this crime that has no parallel in our history and in the whole of human history.

The 'action' on Leszno Street, that is, outside the ghetto walls, is continuing.

Thursday, 12 November

Everything was quiet in our 'shop' yesterday. The day passed peacefully. But in the town the 'action' continues. It involved Shultz's, 'Oksako', Röhrig and perhaps others. Again hundreds of Jewish victims have been taken, among them women and children. In the evening they shut people into train-wagons. They put 60 people into trains. According to rumours all those rounded up were skilled workers: tailors, leather-workers, seamstresses and linen-workers. Word has it that no children were taken. A group of 50 men (among them the young man Senenski) was freed in the evening. The SS commandant, Witossek, tried to persuade them to go voluntarily to Lublin, because all Jews will be removed from Warsaw. However, when no one stepped forward to volunteer to go to Lublin, he set them all free. This group came from Schultz's workshops. On the other hand they grabbed young girls and women out of the groups who are working for the SS at the *Werterfassung*, where Ora is working as well. Overall yesterday was a difficult day.

Terrifying rumours are going round among us that weigh heavily on our hearts and break and destroy our spirits. I have heard that it is quite certain that the children who were rounded up yesterday at Többens' have been transferred to the orphanages run by the Jewish community or have been set free, if they had a home or someone to go to. From this it can be inferred that those who were rounded up were not sent to Treblinka to be murdered, but to work, apparently to Lublin.

We know already that there was an 'action' today at Schultz's. I was told that they were looking for outsiders there, those not connected with the 'shop'. Seven or eight people were seized. From today there will be a guard of gendarmes at the ghetto wall at the corner of Gęsia and Zamenhof Streets. From now on we really will be shut up inside a tiny, cramped cage.

Friday, 13 November

Overall there was no 'action' yesterday. There was some kind of commission at Schultz's – an inspection committee, which arrested seven people not for 'resettlement' (*Umsiedlung*) but to be held by the police (*Nebenstelle*).[395] But the unrest in the tiny ghetto has grown because of the gendarmes, who have filled the streets that used to belong to the ghetto (before the great slaughter). In the evening rumours were going round that we are to be finished off this evening. Some people didn't go to bed at all and did not get undressed. In the evening people were seized from the groups of workers returning to the ghetto, to work at the fort of Wola. This morning on my way to the factory I took a look at the gendarmes. All of them are old with good-humoured faces. I felt a little calmer.

Saturday, 14 November

The tension among the Jews lessened a little yesterday. There was no 'action', and various people were released from the *Umschlagplatz* by various means – by people's intervention, or by some other means. A telegram arrived from the group who were sent to Lublin that they arrived there safely. From the community authorities we hear that they have been invited to a meeting with the SS today. The community authorities will be represented by Sztolcman. The Jewish Council was invited to the meeting by the former ghetto commissar Auerswald.[396] It is not yet known if he will also be at the meeting. In this connection rumours have been going around that Auerswald has become ghetto commissar again, and the situation will be back to what it was before the 'expulsion' or destruction, but these are just rumours and we do not know if they have any substance.

It turns out that the 500 or 1,000 new gendarmes have been brought here to work for the *Werterfassung*, to clear out and collect up the booty in the ghetto, the booty of our 300,000 Jewish martyrs who died an agonizing death in Treblinka. It is said that this work is to be finished in a month. At the moment there are more than 700 men and women working at it (my daughter Ora is also working at this shameful and painful work – how terrible, that I have come to this). I have heard that the SS are demanding another 1,000 people for this work, so great is the amount of property that is left in the 'dead buildings'. My heart trembles as if it will burst with pain. The people from our 'shop' who were seized the day before yesterday to work at the fort of Wola were freed yesterday, as a result of the efforts on their behalf made by the inspector of the hospital where they were working – Holzheimer.

According to reports that have reached us in roundabout ways there were recently 'actions' in Białystok and in Grodno.[397] There are reports that the course of the 'action' in Białystok was particularly tragic, since it took the form of a large-scale massacre on the spot when the Jews resisted. We have no details.

Sunday, 15 November

I have heard the following account of the meeting that took place yesterday between the representatives of the *Judenrat* and the SS.[398] The Germans say they intend to extend the ghetto, that is, add on buildings and streets, so as to be able to increase the number of inhabitants. Who will they bring here? This is as yet unknown. Perhaps they mean the Jews who are working in the 'shops' outside the ghetto (Többens', Schultz's and others) who are living in blocks next to their workplaces, and perhaps those who are still in various small towns – the few stray ears of corn – where Jews are now absolutely forbidden to live according to the latest decree about the ghettos in the *gubernia*. If we can rely at all on the promises of degenerate murderers and if they carry out the promises they made yesterday, we will find out who they have in mind for their planned ghetto-extension.

Then the Germans promised to give out food-cards again for the coming months for all Jews, both for those who have numbers (officials of the Jewish community, 'shop'-workers, SS-employees) and those who do not, that is, those who are not working. The latter will receive smaller rations than those who are working. This must be seen as a legalization of all those Jews who have hitherto been considered as illegal and who have not been sent away to Treblinka only because they were hiding in various dark corners. In addition an amnesty was declared for all Jews who are outside the ghetto among the Poles. They are permitted to return to the ghetto before 1 December without any punishment and to bring all their belongings and property with them. According to what one Jew told me, the Germans put it as follows: from today onwards – that is from 15 November – we have been granted the right to life once again.

These reports spread fast among us and set people talking. In general, though, the Jews – quite rightly – have no faith at all in the promises made yesterday. In fact, most Jews believe that this is a cunning strategy of the Germans, the purpose of which is to gather together the remaining Jews in one place so that it will be easier to annihilate them at some point in the near future. If we recall and consider everything that our mortal enemy has done to us, one must admit that were we to believe these people – the like of which history has never seen – it would be very foolish of us. Hitler's latest speech weighs on us heavily where he said that *soon* those Jews will stop laughing who up to now have felt like laughing. In these words there was an explicit threat of extermination for the few surviving Jews. How can we, after all that has happened, all that we have lived through in the months of July, August, September and after the speech of 8 November, still have any belief in the words that are passed on in the name of the leader and in the name of those who carry out his plans and orders? Only a miracle can save us.

Tuesday, 17 November

There are reports of announcements posted up on the walls of Warsaw that concern the Jews. They state that ghettos have been created for the Jews in those places that were listed in the well-known decree. Furthermore they state that Jews are allowed to enter one of these locations before 1 December and transfer their property without any form of punishment. Any Jew who remains outside the ghetto after 1 December will be liable to the death-penalty. Also those Poles and *Germans* who allow Jews to stay in their homes will be punished with death. From this order it is clear that 'they' are concerned to clear out the Jews from the 'Aryan' side and concentrate the last ones in the ghetto. For what purpose? In order to destroy us in one go – as the pessimists believe. How horrific!

It has emerged from a telephone conversation with Christians in *Lublin* that the Jewish community there, which has been uprooted through deportations over the course of the year, with the remaining 10 per cent moved to the suburb of Majdan-Tatarski, has now been completely liquidated. A certain woman named Silber (the daughter of the alcohol manufacturer) telephoned there in the presence of Mr 'Water',[399] and asked after her brother and various relatives who were working in different factories in the town. To each question she received the answer that the person had 'fallen ill' the previous week and had left the town. The meaning of such an answer is clear and leaves no room for doubt. A few days ago a Jew in our 'shop' said that the Jewish community in Lublin had been totally destroyed and no longer exists.[400] In my heart I have been still unsure and have not wanted to believe the appalling news. Of the 40,000 Jews of Lublin 3,000–4,000 were spared and moved to Majdan. In the course of time their number grew to 6,000–8,000 and their position was more or less tolerable. And now the end has come for this historic Jewish community. Is this not a reminder for all the other Jewish communities in the *gubernia*, as well as those in the recently sanctioned ghettos? Who can be certain?

Today the gendarmes raided the cemetery and took away all the goods that they found on the Jews and Poles. The value of these goods runs into hundreds and thousands of zloty. During this incident two Poles were shot dead.

Thursday, 19 November

The last few days have passed without disasters and without terrible incidents in this tiny ghetto of ours. Something even happened that might have reassured the troubled spirits of the survivors and suggested that we will live a little longer, that our life will not be under threat day in and day out, were we not familiar with the Nazis' methods of dealing with the Jews. Every lie, every strategem, every betrayal and every act of common trickery, if they lead to the extermination of the Jews, is permissible in their eyes. The rule is: one shouldn't believe them and one shouldn't rely on them if they do anything that is supposedly beneficial for us.

Yesterday about 150 women and children were freed from the *Umschlagplatz*. Rumours circulated saying that all those detained had been released. It turned out that for the time being only 150 women and children had been released, but all those detained are to be released by Saturday. So I have heard from a very reliable source. From this one might infer that we are about to see the closing of the *Umschlagplatz* in Warsaw. If this had not happened together with the fierce agitation against the Jews in the German press (in connection with the news of a celebration and blessings with the Torah scroll by the Jewish community in Moscow on the anniversary of the revolution: in this report, which was drafted by the ministry of propaganda and appeared in all the German press, it is explicitly stated that Jews want to rule the world but the war against them and their *extermination* is already far advanced), if it were not for this, then one might think that the campaign against us had eased up a little, that the surviving *10 per cent* will be spared. But now we know not to get our hopes up. Death will always be hanging over us – unless something out of the ordinary happens. And indeed the mood of the Jews, especially those in Schultz's and Többens' workshops that are outside the ghetto, is one of extreme gloom and depression. We live in dread of sudden annihilation.

I have been told that representatives of the Jewish community have gone to Łódź in order to inspect the ghetto and to study its economic structure, in order to construct our life here on the Łódź model. It has not been confirmed whether this report is true.[401]

The tidings of Job are reaching us from various places in the *gubernia* and from the areas that have been incorporated into the Reich. I have heard of the total extermination of the Jewish communities in Mława and Płońsk. These towns belong to the Reich. From Częstochowa have arrived – or more accurately – fled members of Hashomer Hatsair who said that from the whole of that community (40,000) people only about 4,500 are left, and the 'action' is continuing.[402] They said that the town will be *judenrein* by 18 November. That is why they fled to Warsaw. Many of our nationalist and pioneer Jewish youth have perished. There were many youth organizations there.

Sunday, 22 November

Lejke Tenenbaum, who works with my daughter Ora at the *Werterfassung*, came across the dead body of a Jew in a building on Ogrodowa Street, already in a state of decay. He was lying in a pool of congealed blood. Apparently the body has been lying there a long time, since the time of the blockades. The girl was terribly frightened. Ora said that she was not afraid of dead bodies and she wanted to go into the dead man's flat where it was lying to take advantage of the abandoned property and take out some things. But when she went up to the door she was gripped with terror and she too was unable to go inside. These are the experiences of our children who are helping the bandits to collect up the great booty.

A few days ago on the way home from the 'shop' in the evening we found a Jew in Gęsia Street who was wounded in the head. He was conscious. He asked us not to stand next to him because he was pretending to be dead, but for us to call the emergency services. I heard that the wounded man is the owner of a rickshaw, and the German who has been his passenger for four months had wounded him. Apparently the Jew knew more than he was supposed to and he (the German) wanted to get him out of the way.

The *Umschlagplatz* really has been closed down in Warsaw. All those detained have been freed. Not only that, all Jewish prisoners in the prisons of Warsaw have been freed: from the Motokowska, from the Pawiak, from the special prison on Gęsia Street (60 Jews and 100 Gypsies). The *Umschlagplatz* has been handed over to the control of the *Werterfassung*, in which the former arrestees are now employed. In the ghetto proclamations have been posted up stating that all Jews who are not working must register for work with the *Werterfassung*. Stern measures will be taken against those who have no occupation, beginning 23 November.

Word has it that tomorrow the Jewish police is going to round up everyone who is not working. The Jewish police and the members of the *Werksschutz* in each 'shop' have received an order to hand over half of their workers to the *Werterfassung*. It looks like they are concerned to get the Jewish property out of here as quickly as possible.

What is the reason for all this haste? No one can give an answer to this question, but the 'Jewish heart' is deeply afraid and anxious. Those who look through dark glasses say that 'they' want to finish the clearing out with our help, so as to be able to put an end to us suddenly and at one go. This is why they announced on the outside that Jews may return to the ghetto without suffering any form of punishment. Their aim is therefore to concentrate all Jews here and destroy them. Aside from these prophets of doom, there are also re-assuring voices, who want to believe that the few remaining Jews will remain in locations that have been designated by the Germans, including Warsaw. They think that a Jewish community will survive in Warsaw. These are people in whom a spark of hope has not been extinguished, in spite of all the terrible disasters that have befallen us since 22 July, since the mass-slaughter began exactly four months ago.

Yesterday a rumour went round that the annihilation-machine in Treblinka has been halted (this news was passed on to me in Git's [Yitshak Giterman's] name). Because of this there is talk that an inter-national commission is to come here to research and investigate and inquire into the Jewish question. Some people actually connect the latest measures of the authorities with regard to the Jews with the commission that is supposedly about to arrive. The report from Treblinka (that it has been shut down) is also supposed to be related to the 'commission'. It would be possible to believe the news if we had heard that the treatment of Jews had improved anywhere, if we had at least heard that we have ceased to be lambs for the slaughter, and that they had stopped murdering us systematically and in vast numbers. To our terrible despair, horrifying news has been reaching us from the provinces. Whole communities are being wiped out, torn up by the roots: Częstochowa, Mława,[403] Płońsk, Białystok, Grodno are sad proof that the gloomy views of those who are pessimistic are closer to the truth about our existence. What a calamity has befallen us!

A Jewish young man, who was a policeman, told me the following illustrative story: the Christians are being given packed meat (in cans).

We also received a ration. Among the Polish masses there is a rumour that this meat has been made from our flesh, that is, from the flesh of Jews who have been murdered. Because of this the Poles are revolted by the meat and refuse to eat it. Let this be set down and recorded: this is what the Polish masses thought of the Nazis. And it is undeniable that the Nazis are cannibals in the fullest sense of the word.

Tuesday, 24 November

Yesterday there was a renewed hunt in the streets. The SS were stopping people in the early morning and the afternoon. They were inspecting work-papers. Those detained they handed over to the control of the employment office of the Jewish community and to the *Werterfassung*. Two people were killed. There are two versions of how they died: one that they were ordered to stand on the spot and they didn't stand, but tried to run away; the second is that they were trading in the streets. Whatever the truth of the matter – after a short pause fresh victims have fallen in the ghetto and innocent Jewish blood has been spilled once again.

The anti-Jewish agitation is being carried on in the German press with vigour and extreme intensity. The newspapers are still continuing to write about the return of rights to the Jews of Algeria and Morocco and are using this to spice up their campaign of agitation and incitement against the Jews.[404] This awakens a fear and dread in the Jews. We are living once again balanced between hope and fear. Each day, each hour we ask ourselves: will they let us live or will they suddenly destroy us?

Thursday, 26 November

Yesterday was another day of blood-letting for our small community in Warsaw. Many victims fell in the streets. How many? From the community official G., we were given the number 26, but this does not reflect the true figure. It is possible that there were more deaths than this. On the way to the factory in the morning (yesterday) we came across a dead body at the corner of Gęsia and Lubiecka Streets and returning home from work at half past four we witnessed another murder. Coming into Miła Street (at the corner of Zamenhof Street) we heard a dull shot from nearby. As we approached the corner of Zamenhof and Lubiecka we heard the bitter sobbing of a woman next to the body of a man. We were told that a soldier had been speaking with him and then shot him once, killing him. Going to work in the morning we could still see the pool of the blood of the murdered man.

These murders have hit the morale of the Jews hard and plunged them into a bitter, black despair. Are they starting on the survivors now? Were we not told, just a few days ago, through Git., that the Germans gave assurances to the *Judenrat* that no harm would come to the survivors, and life in the ghetto would take on a fixed pattern (stabilization) and so on? And now suddenly a new slaughter, in miniature. Officially this is explained as punishment for the avoidance of work, especially for evading employment in the *Werterfassung*.

Today – Thursday – I heard that there had been three murders on Franciszkańska Street. They were three brothers who sold meat in some kind of shop. One shudders to think of everything that is being done to us. I have heard that the SS have passed on to the Jewish Council the numbers involved in the blood 'action' that was carried out from 22 July onwards. It goes as follows: transported (read: annihilated in Treblinka) 254,000; murdered during the blockades – 5,000; and those sent to work in *Dulag* [*Durchgangslager*] – 11,000. In total therefore according to the Germans' figures 270,000 people have been taken from us.[405] We must assume that these numbers are incomplete and do not reflect the true extent of our losses – the number of martyrs. And these are only the victims from Warsaw, and where are all the other towns, townlets and villages throughout Europe, on which – that is, on the Jews – Hitler's avenging sword of destruction has fallen? God! How is it possible?

The three brothers who were killed for selling meat were called Suchecki and were involved in smuggling.

Friday, 27 November

Yesterday the number of victims, according to what I have heard, was six. In addition to the three Suchecki brothers, a further three Jews were killed.

The workers from our 'shop' on their way to work at the court-house at Ogrodowa Street saw two murdered Jews at the corner of Pawia and Smocza. Apparently the three Suchecki brothers were killed on account of a slander. They really were selling meat products. The murderers first took a large sum of money off them, about 30,000 zloty (according to rumour) and then they were shot dead.

The chairman of the *Judenrat*, engineer Lichtenbaum, has issued a proclamation to the Jews that everyone aged between 16 and 45 must be registered with the employment office and must work.[406] In the main Jews are now employed by the *Werterfassung*. Walls are being built up around the 'shops' that are outside the new, miniature ghetto, and almost all of the 'shops' are located outside the ghetto. In this way each Jewish workshop will be turned into a separate prison. No one will get in or out. The issue of survival, that is, the question of bread, is a very pressing one in the ghetto. Those who work in the factories or for the Germans in the *placówki* or in the *Werterfassung* receive a quarter or half a kilo of bread and one or two portions of soup six times a week. No working person can live on this, especially if they have a child or elderly parents who by some miracle have not been killed and not been deported to Treblinka. What are those Jews who are still alive supposed to do and how are they supposed to live? This is a very difficult and serious problem. A certain percentage of the Jews are still living on the proceeds of looting during the 'action', when all our property worth millions and millions was abandoned; a certain percentage live from smuggling or from 'trading', that is, from selling things outside the ghetto. They dress up in all kinds of rags and conceal things from the gendarmes. Often everything they are taking out or trying to bring in is confiscated, mainly food. Sometimes the Jew is stripped in the search for money or objects of value and made to stand there as naked as the day he was born. But this group still manages to earn something. There are Jews who still have saved clothing and linen. They sell whatever they have left and live on the proceeds. But in addition to all these there are very many Jews (and they are the majority of those left from the Treblinka slaughter) who do not belong to any of the above-mentioned groups and they quite simply do not have a crust to bite on.

What are we to eat? Even if the murderers do not slaughter us, there still remains the stark question of our daily bread.

In our factory, the OBW, there is new talk of dismissals or a reduction in numbers. There are too many people there. The German owners, into whose hands the property of the Landau brothers fell, are demanding the dismissal of 150 workers. They don't need 500. Even 100 would be enough. They perhaps wouldn't have minded, but because they have to pay 7 zloty a day for each worker, they don't want to carry the burden and waste money.

The sword is hanging over our heads once again. What will become of us?

Monday, 30 November

Yesterday a political assassination was carried out in the ghetto: Israel First, the head of the economic division of the Jewish community, and a close associate of the 'regime', one of the Jews whom the Germans prized greatly, was killed by two shots in Muranowska Street. This Jew was involved in large-scale dealings in partnership with and under the aegis of the German authorities. He had certainly become very wealthy. Who killed him? I can't give a definite answer to this question. There are two possibilities. Firstly, the Germans disposed of him as they have previously disposed of their assistants who have become superfluous: Kohn, Heller, Erlich, and many, many others.[407] I also heard that Szymon or Syzmszon Grajak from Lublin has now been disposed of. Perhaps they also killed First.

But there is also a second possibility. He may have been cut down by either a Jew or a Pole, and killed as a traitor, because he had sold his soul to the Germans and assisted them during the 'action'. In fact I do not know if he took part in the terrible events of those days, but at any rate he continually associated with them and mixed in their circles. In the ghetto I have heard that the PPS [Polish Socialist Party] has issued a proclamation, announcing that it has sentenced to death 150 Jews for leading their brothers to their death. Among those who have been sentenced are Lejkin and First. Lejkin was shot dead a few weeks ago, now First's turn has arrived. According to this version he was shot by a Pole from the PPS or a Jew. This event has made a deep impression on the Jews and terrified those who do not have a clear conscience and whose hands are stained with the blood of our martyrs. For myself I incline more to the first possibility, that like the others, First fell victim to these new Huns, as the modern barbarians are called in England.[408]

Yesterday I met Yakir Warzsawski's son, Aaron. He told me that during the events his father, mother and younger brother, Amram, all perished. In Yakir I have lost a very dear friend. We got to know each other in 1915 at the Zionist school where we were both working. We became friends. He felt a sympathy and kindness towards me, and showed this at various times in my life, like a spark of love that is not dependent on anything. I was also deeply attached to him. He was a pure spirit, a man of sensibility and nobility. Hebrew and Jewish literature has lost a talent of perhaps only the second rank, but many of his figures, especially the characters of the Jewish shtetl [small town], who are no longer with us, and who have been captured by Warszawski's stories, belong in my opinion to the pearls of our literature and can take their place at the forefront of our classic literature. His novellas [published under the title *The Last Ones*] belong without doubt to our literary canon and immortalize him in the annals of our people.[409]

I grieve for you, my brother Yakir! You have fallen at the hands of degenerates and murderers.

Sunday, 6 December

The days go by without special incident, in a deep and stifling gloom. There is not a single ray of light to brighten our darkness here and that of the world outside. Almost every day there is a rumour that we are about to see a new expulsion, or a new 'action'. Lately people have been saying that it is certain that the 'action' will begin on the sixth of this month, and will continue through the seventh. These rumours have come to the attention of the SS authorities and the commander of the division in Warsaw, Mende,[410] has instructed his officials to inform the chairman of the *Judenrat* that there is no substance to these reports and that he should reassure the Jews on this score. Today Lichtenbaum, Czerniaków's replacement, issued a proclamation along these lines. In the announcement he states that he has received a telegram from the SS commandant Mende saying that the Germans have heard the rumours that are going round in the ghetto about an 'action' or a new expulsion and changes in the workplaces where Jews are employed (that is, rumours that the Jews' work will be changed around and they will be sent from place to place) and that they even know who is spreading these rumours. They authorize the chairman of the *Judenrat* to inform the Jews that the rumours are false, and that they should carry on in complete security.

Of course proclamations of this kind cannot reassure us or calm us down. On the contrary, they increase our fear and agitation. We still remember well how on 19 July, three days before the start of the extermination of the Jews, Commissar Auerswald assured the late Czerniaków that the worrying rumours were false and that nothing would happen. Three days later the terrible disaster fell. We cannot have any faith in the promises of these murderers of children, women and old people. There are no crimes, degradations and brutalities of which they are not capable. So the surviving Jews live on in the confinement of the ghetto literally between life and death. Every day our lives are in the balance.

In the last few days several work-camps at various locations around Warsaw have been closed down and the inmates brought into Warsaw.[411] These people are a terrible and horrifying sight. Many are swollen with starvation, covered with sores, many black and festering. They are wearing clothes that are rags in the fullest sense of the word. It is hard to look at these people who have death so close behind them. Many of them beg in the streets. Since the streets are busy first thing in the morning as people go to work, one can see these unfortunates as they walk along with each group, begging. In general people give to them generously. Perhaps because we haven't seen any beggars in the streets for the past two months and the ordinary Jew – a child of the people of compassion – feels the urge now to fulfil the commandment of giving to charity, and perhaps the terrible condition of these Jews, who are naked and swollen with hunger, has opened the clenched hands of our brothers. Each day, on the way to the factory at 30 Gęsia Street, I see these people and my guts churn within me. It is hard to contain oneself. Once again we reflect and ask ourselves: why have they closed down the work-camps and for what purpose have they sent these people here, why this concentration in the ghetto? And now at the beginning of winter? There is no answer to these questions. Even the devil himself could not have hatched a more horrific scheme against us.

Tuesday, 8 December

There is nothing new to report here. There has been no change for the better or for the worse. Only a dread of what can come at any moment, and anxiety that weighs heavily on our hearts. Isolated Jews arrive here who have escaped from the field of slaughter of Treblinka. I was told about one of them who arrived the day before yesterday and who had left Treblinka ten days ago. According to what he says, the annihilation machine there is still working at full throttle. Jews are brought in from Western Europe and from the Balkans, that is, from Serbia, Croatia, Greece, and of course from the various districts of the former *gubernia* and from various parts of the former Polish territories. News such as this casts a black shadow over us and grinds us down with despair. To judge by Hitler and Rosenberg's speeches we have to face the possibility of the complete annihilation of every Jew in Europe. Where will help come from? At the moment there is not a ray of light reaching in to save us from any quarter. What human society has ever been through such hellish torments?

Yesterday I heard that in England and America last Sunday two hours were given over to the Jewish question on the radio and in the synagogues. They spoke of the annihilation of five million European Jews. We should be happy at this 'concern' for our fate, but will it be of any use to us? Will these savage killers pay any heed to public opinion in hostile nations? I very much doubt it.

There is the following strange rumour going round in the ghetto today: the government of the United States of America has announced that all Jews surviving in Europe are automatically to be considered its citizens and to benefit from its protection. If these Jews are harmed, then retribution will be exacted in a similar manner on Germans in America. I don't know where this fantastic story has suddenly sprung from, among the Jews over whom the sword of destruction hangs day and night. But I can recall that in the summer of 1933 a member of parliament introduced a bill into the English parliament similar to the order which the government of America has supposedly issued. The bill stated that every Jew can become and be considered as a citizen of Palestine! And on the basis of this they would be under the protection of the government of England. This bill was passed by the House of Commons on the first reading, as far as I remember. After that they didn't return to the bill. The Jewish press wrote at that time that this was of no use, except as a kind of demonstration, of which there are many in the English parliamentary life. It was, that is, a bill in theory but not in practice or, as we used to say at home: 'a law that though prescribed is not necessarily obeyed'. Who started this rumour and on what basis – we cannot know. It seems that a bitter despair and perpetual terror bring about all the rumours of this kind, those that tell of an imminent salvation following in their wake. How we thirst and long for deliverance!

Thursday, 10 December

Today I heard the following story from a reliable source: a meeting has been held in Berlin to discuss the Jewish question. Participating were representatives of all the German ministries and a large number of representatives of the Party and the military. Two proposals were put to the meeting: the first, to destroy survivors, the last handful of Jews that have been left scattered here and there. This proposal was supported by the ministries for agriculture and finance. They took the position that in this way they would get rid of superfluous 'eaters' and a great deal of bread and food in general would be saved. This proposal was opposed by a second: not to kill the Jews who are still alive. This was supported by the ministries for public works and supply. They argued that young Jews are necessary as workers in German manufacture. According to this report, the argument that Jews are useful for the German economy won the day, and it was decided to allow them to live for the time being.[412]

A further report was passed on to me: the *Daily Herald* in London has published a long article of two columns describing the plan of extermination that is being carried out against us, that is, against every Jew in Europe. This article gives a precise and detailed account of all aspects of the hell that the Germans have constructed for the slaughter of the Jews.[413] Overall therefore precise information has reached countries abroad of the appalling catastrophe which has no parallel in human history. I have heard that Roosevelt has made a speech on this topic and said more or less the following: we will not follow in the Germans' footsteps and will not copy their actions and their methods, but we too will take counter-measures (repressive measures) against the Germans.

What good is this to us? Will we be saved? Will someone appear and hurry to our rescue and to bring us relief? My God, my God. Why has all this come upon us?

Yesterday I heard that Riszek Berger was sent to Treblinka during the 'action' and that the next morning his mother poisoned herself. Riszek was a gentle and sensitive young man, and very talented in technical matters. Who can know how many fine and talented children Treblinka has taken from us?

Friday, 11 December

Yesterday members of Hehalutz were brought into the ghetto (to the *Judenrat* at 19 Zamenhof Street) who had been working on an agricultural settlement outside Warsaw – at Czerniaków.[414] They are about 150 in number. They have been working there a long time, have been fortunate throughout all the blockades, and no misfortune has befallen them. Their living conditions were not excellent by any means, but in comparison with our conditions in the gloomy, crowded ghetto they were good. Firstly they enjoyed light and fresh air in sufficient quantities. This is now even more important than bread – which they had in limited amounts. Now all this has come to an end. They will share the bitter fate of the ghetto with us. This also points to the fact that the Jews are being concentrated in one place for some particular purpose. What is the intention? What evil plans and schemes lie behind these orders and actions? Our hearts are filled with dread. Who knows if 'they' are not preparing a fresh slaughter for us?

I have heard a report that the Archbishop of York made a speech in the English House of Lords concerning the Jews. He gave the Lords all the details of the 'expulsion' and all the appalling things that took place. He demanded punishment not only for those who gave the orders, but also for those who put them into practice. At his proposal a committee was set up to deal with this matter. This commission has already had its first session. The meeting was also attended by representatives of the Polish National Assembly, members of the Polish government in exile in England. They gave the commission clarifications and further details concerning the murder and the slaughter of the Jews of Poland.[415] For all the feelings of satisfaction and encouragement that this news awakens in us, doubt continues to eat away at us and the bitter question surfaces in our minds, sapping our strength and will – what will save us? Will we be saved? Will we survive?

Wednesday, 16 December

In our abandoned little corner of the world there is no news to report, but from various locations around Warsaw there are horrific and terrifying reports reaching us. Nowy Dwór near Warsaw has been emptied of all the Jews who were there, about 6,000 in number. Recently the Jews from Czerwińsk were moved there. All the Jews have also been driven out of Płońsk ['Plinsk' in Yiddish], altogether 9,000. I have heard that they were sent away by train in passenger-cars [*pasażerskie*] to Oświęcim. Similar reports have also arrived from Kałuszyn and Siedlce.[416] In these towns the Jewish communities that were there until recently – left behind by the expulsions (the murders) – have likewise been completely destroyed. Kałuszyn and Siedlce were at the top of the list of ghettos that was published a few weeks ago. We had thought that they would leave a handful of Jews in those locations. Did they not state explicitly that there would be Jewish communities at these locations and that all those who were displaced or in hiding could go and live there?

These facts show that the wild animals have decided to exterminate the Jewish race wherever their power extends, that is, over almost the whole of Europe. And there are no methods that are too base for them, nothing they would not stoop to in order to trick as large a number of Jews as possible and bring them to the slaughter. Some Jews have fled from Nowy Dwór to Warsaw, but they are members of the *Judenrat*, about whom people are saying a lot of shameful things.

These reports awaken in us a trembling and mortal terror, which is perhaps worse than death itself. Departing this life is a matter of 10 or 15 minutes in Treblinka or in Oświęcim and our existence is exactly that of someone sentenced to death, whose appeal for mercy has already been refused, who is waiting in a prison-cell for the death that is being delayed for some reason unknown to him. A miracle could happen to save him. Perhaps at certain moments he lives in hope of this, but only for those few moments. For most of the hours of the day and night he tosses and turns in torment and in terror of death. We too are in this position, the few isolated ears of corn, dried out and emaciated, that for the time being remain in the cramped and gloomy ghetto.

There is also a tragic report from Lwów of the total destruction of the community there. A telephone call was made from here, from the OBW, to the Lwów *Judenrat*, but we couldn't get a connection. The telephone-exchange reported that the *Judenrat* was not answering. This means that it no longer exists.[417]

Sunday, 21 December

Life drags on without changes and upheavals of any kind. The same heavy gloom and the same wings of death hover over the remaining few who have survived the murderous enemy.

Yesterday a wave of good and unexpected reports swept through the ghetto. According to these reports, Jews in Kraków and Lwów were permitted to remove their Star of David armbands, and in their place they will wear a symbol of their place of employment, and if they are employed by the military, a symbol of the *Wehrmacht* or some other service. The reports go even further. It is said that Jews of Kraków have been granted permission to live together with the Poles, that is, the ghetto has been abolished. Of course one must approach these reports with deep suspicion and with caution. There is also a story that yesterday, in Blank's Palace[418] there was a meeting to discuss the Jews, in the presence of military intelligence officers [*Sicherheitsdienst*]. Moderate views about us were expressed there, for instance that the Jews who remain are necessary as workers for the German economy and that they should be left alive.

I have heard that tomorrow, 22 December, protest meetings have been planned throughout the world to protest at the slaughter that has been and is being carried out against us. The Pope apparently appealed directly to Hitler on our behalf. Are we really about to see a change for the better in these barbarians' treatment of us? The coming few days will show. Some say that here in Warsaw the ghetto will also be abolished, on the first day of the new year, 1943. Where do these stories come from all of a sudden?

A certain Jew – Ludina by name – who had family in Płońsk has just told me that in spite of all his efforts he failed to save his wife and children. The Poles that he hired and sent there to bring them to Warsaw were not able to get through to them, as the whole town was surrounded by the SS. His whole family numbering about 20 was sent away by train in ordinary [*pasażerskie*] cars and last Wednesday they passed by Warsaw and the train stopped at the Eastern Station. The Jews had not come to the conclusion that they were being taken to their death. They could also have jumped out of the train. The guard was light, but they still made no attempt to save themselves. It seems that there is a strong feeling of resignation among those who are being deported. They are lulled by the mild treatment on the way, by the fact that they are travelling in passenger-cars and not in cattle or freight trucks and by the absence of heavy guard. It appears that they believe that they are being transported to another location where they will have to do hard labour, but that they will be left alive. What unfortunates! They have not yet discovered the true nature of this wild and vicious animal that knows no mercy in its thirst for our blood.

Avenging God! Take vengeance for our blood that has been shed, and whatever may be, let them never be forgiven the blood of our innocent children, of our mothers and of our parents. May they reap their just reward!

Monday, 28 December

Once again day after tedious day has passed without any change in our dark and miserable lives. During Christmas the Jews did not have to work, and the few ghetto streets were filled with strollers. We heard through the Jewish police that it enraged the Germans. How comes it that the Jews dare to walk through the streets instead of hiding in their homes? Rumours were even going round to the effect that the butchers were threatening to carry out a new slaughter because of this Jewish 'impudence'.

The dread of what might happen, of a new 'action', robs us of our peace of mind and leaves us not a moment's peace. The reports that are reaching us from various towns are so terrible and horrifying that they fill our eyes with gloom and drive the sleep from our eyes, in the simple meaning of these words, not as some poetic imagery.

People who have returned here having escaped with their lives from Treblinka report that the annihilation machine was in operation up to the day of their escape. They arrived in the ghetto about 10 days ago. Recently they were bringing in large groups of Jews from Grodno and other places twice a week. These Jews are held in a concentration camp for three weeks and then they are brought to Treblinka where they are exterminated.[419]

From the district of Zamość there are reports that there Poles too are being driven from their homes and they are being sent off to unknown destinations. It looks as though they also have evil intentions with regard to the Poles.[420]

About a week ago there was a case of robbery and murder in the ghetto. A Jew was murdered in the course of a robbery. He was thought to have money on him and the thieves tricked him into going into a building (at 51 Mylna Street) to buy gold. On the dead man they found a total of 400 zloty. At today's prices this is such a trivial sum that it was not worthwhile for the killers to spill innocent blood for it. The Jewish police arrested five suspects in the murder and handed them over to the Germans. The Germans killed all five men, without carrying out any kind of investigation. An officer in the Jewish police told me that two of the five had absolutely no part in the murder, and not even the other three carried out the murder directly. On the one hand we see our moral decline – on the other the Germans' savagery and the thirst for Jewish blood.

Recently there have been Jews caught outside the ghetto walls. The Germans deal with them differently than before the 'expulsions'. Previously, they had sent them to the Jewish prison, brought them up before a special court (*Sondergericht*) and sentenced them to death. Sometimes these Jews were murdered in the prison at 24 Gęsia Street. On one occasion the names of the martyrs were published in special proclamations in the streets. In the past few days those arrested have been handed over to the *Judenrat* to be employed in the *Werter-fassung*. Once again we are confused and are unsure how to solve the mystery. Where has this sudden leniency come from in these savage killers? What kind of evil trick lurks beneath this gracious behaviour?

In the past few days 16 such Jews have been brought in. The special authorities that deal with Jews – known as the *Umsiedlungsdienst* – has announced that they are not involved in hunting for Jews on the other side of the wall. But if Jews are pointed out to them, then they grab them. Incidentally, it is said that a large number of Jews have been employed as agents, their only task being to look for and uncover Jews on the Aryan side. Those who try and justify these Jews say that they only want to get a permit to cross over to the 'other side' and are just exploiting the opportunity.

A strange thing happened recently. They suddenly discovered a Jew in the German army, or a half-Jew or perhaps even a quarter-Jew. His name is Josefowicz. Mende of the SS ordered that a civilian suit be provided. The Jewish community supplied him with a suit. This 'Jew' was also handed over to the community, with instructions that he should be given some kind of employment. I think that he has become some kind of caretaker [*wóźny*] in the community-buildings. This man served two years in the army.

The day before yesterday at half past two in the morning the scholar and historian Dr Majer Balaban died suddenly from a heart attack.[421] He was 65 years old at his death but looked a lot older. The remains of the Jewish intelligentsia came to pay their last respects to the deceased. God! What a tragic and depressing sight the gathering at the funeral made. Firstly the small number who came. It was plain to see that very few of us are left, just a handful. And secondly: the appearance of the people! What impoverishment, what gloom, what weariness filled their faces! In this small gathering was expressed our total destruction in its most tragic and appalling form, the destruction of the greatest Jewish community in Europe. I was shaken to the core, looking at the extinguished and despairing eyes, and the lined faces and the torn and ragged clothes. Utter annihilation.

One of the ghetto-jokes (the exchange takes place outside the ghetto – in the Aryan section – and in Polish):

A small boy asks his father: 'Kiedy się zapała świeczki chanukowe?' The father replies, correcting him: 'Nie mówi się chanukowe tylko choinkowe.'
The child asks: 'Daddy! When do we light the candles for Chanuka?' [the Jewish festival which takes place at approximately the same time as Christmas].
Correcting the child, the father says: 'We don't say Chanuka candles but "choinka" [Christmas tree] candles.'[422]
New Marranos [crypto-Jews].

Another joke: Jews are leaving some Polish or German eating-place or café and a small child – perhaps Jewish, perhaps not – latches on to them. The child is selling newspapers and sticks to them like glue. The Jews approach a tram-stop. In their anxiety to get rid of the small pest and, fearing some kind of German trap, they buy a paper from him. The boy seizes this chance and slips a note to them. Unrolling the note, the Jews read the following text: 'Cholent with kishka [a popular Jewish dish], kosher, at affordable prices, obtainable at such and such an address.'

On the first day of the Christmas holiday a few Jews were killed on Leszno and Smocza Streets because they were 'wandering around' on their own in the streets. They had left the ghetto to go and visit their relatives who are locked in in Schultz's and Többens' workshops. Cholodenko's[423] son-in-law – Biberstajn – was killed last Thursday at eleven o'clock in the evening in the broom factory. His wife was injured and is in hospital. Their sin consisting in having crossed the boundary of the workshop from one building to the next, from 28 Swiętojerska Street to 30 Świętojerska Street. They were accompanying a woman. One of the German supervisors opened fire on them.

An officer in the Jewish police told me a story which is worth recording for future generations. During the first days of the expulsions they would select the old people from all the others held at the *Umschlagplatz*, characterizing them as *transportunfähig* ['not fit for transportation'], and put them into Kohn–Heller wagons (*konhelerówki*).[424] The old people were taken to the Jewish cemetery and shot with machine-guns. Later they stopped killing the old people here in Warsaw, and allocated them the last two cars in the trains that were going to Treblinka. On the fourth day of the expulsion, Saturday 26 July, a car drove to the Jewish cemetery and a middle-aged German woman with two young children got out. She took them inside the cemetery and led them to the place where our old people were being murdered. She wanted to show the children how the Jews were dying. A typical illustration of the character of this evil and brutal people. New Amalekites.

Tuesday, 29 December

The woman who was wounded last Friday sometime before midnight died from her wounds. Her name is Kadiszewicz, the wife of the doctor of the same name. It turns out that Biberstajn, who was also killed, was accompanying her from one lobby to another on the same courtyard. It was half past ten. One of the German owners of the workshop – Brenner – went up to them and shot five times at them. Four bullets hit the woman, and one struck Biberstajn. He died on the spot and she a day or two later. Yesterday I learnt that about a month ago in mid-November, or a few days after, 40 Jews were shot in the Pawiak. Among those killed was a Jew by the name of Osnus, the husband of a woman who works in the OBW workshop, and a close relative of one of the owners of the factory, Al. Landau. The dead man had also been working in the workshop since the beginning of the expulsions. At the beginning of August he had been standing in the courtyard smoking a cigarette, and was caught in the act – it is forbidden to smoke in the carpentry-shop – by Commissar Hensel, the man who later caused the deaths of hundreds of us, and he telephoned the SS. The butchers came immediately, arrested Osnus and took away the 'offender' to the Pawiak. There he was held for almost four months and finally murdered.

I have been told that they have recently begun killing the prisoners in the Pawiak who have foreign citizenship and who were arrested a number of days before the expulsion. At that time it was thought that their lives were safe, and that they had been arrested only for their own security, a sort of protective custody, *Schutzverhaltung*. Among them was one of the leaders of the 'Joint' in Warsaw, Neustadt, and the well-known lawyer A. Margolis,[425] both of whom held passports of one of the South American countries. Among those arrested at the same time were Herman and his wife Fela Eckheiser, a pupil of mine from Yehudia – as Palestinian citizens (he took out citizenship there). Who knows if they are still alive?[426]

The main ways of making a living, on which depends the greater part of the Jewish community in Warsaw, are described by two newly created expressions or words:

1 *shabreven*, in Polish *szabrować*
2 *tshukhes*, or *ciuchy*.

The first means: taking valuable items (mainly bedclothes and counterpanes) from Jewish flats that have been abandoned and which are being emptied by the Germans, who are taking everything that is left there. As is known, there are 4,000 Jews employed in this 'clean' work – boys and girls, men and women of various ages. These Jews take some things for themselves and sell them to those who go to work outside the ghetto (in the so-called *placówkarze*). From this – looting from looters – large numbers of Jews support themselves. The word is derived – so I have been told – from German, and is frequently used by the Polish craftsmen, the lathe workers, with the meaning: 'scratch, clean off'. A young Jew tried to prove to me that the word derives from Hebrew and consists of two words joined together: *lishbor* and *bar*: ('Vayerdu bney yaakov mitsrayma lishbor bar' ['The children of Jacob went down to Egypt to buy grain']).

The second means of earning a living, from which even more Jews support themselves, is the selling of *tshukhes*. This word refers to all kinds of old clothes, and above all to bedclothes. Almost all the Jews live by selling what they have, whether it is theirs or not. The sense of property, of possession – mine–yours – has become much less definite. A Jew who would never have taken something that belonged to somebody else thinks little today of putting into his bag anything that comes into his hand. Those who do not sell their own things buy *tshukhes* and sell them to others who sell them to the Poles outside the ghetto, and from this a large percentage of the surviving inhabitants supports itself. The etymology of this word is Yiddish: from the word *tsikhlekh* [covers, such as for pillows and duvets]. The word *tsikhn* was altered by the Poles to *ciuchy* and became widely used by young and old (though there are hardly any of the latter left here) in the ghetto.

If one looks closely at the passers-by in the streets of the Warsaw ghetto one can see that the overwhelming majority of them are not originally from Warsaw, but are from small towns. They were driven out from their homes a long time ago and saved themselves during the expulsion by hiding out in various dark corners. In general one sees rough faces and vulgar types from the common folk. Members of the middle classes, intelligentsia, the more educated elements, are not to be seen. Very few have survived from bourgeois and cultivated Jewish Warsaw.[427] Teachers, for example, have been almost completely wiped out. I am the only survivor from my school. Out of all the female teachers, the directress, and the male teachers who were working in the classroom until recently, none survive.[428] The same situation can be found at practically all levels of Warsaw Jewry.

Warsaw was in fact the backbone of Polish Jewry, its heart, one could say. The destruction of Warsaw would have meant the destruction of the whole of Polish Jewry, even if the provinces had been spared this evil. Now that the enemy's sword of destruction has run amok through the small towns and villages and is cutting them down with murderous blows – with the death-agony of the metropolis, the entire body is dying and plunging into hell. One can say that with the setting of the sun of Polish Jewry the splendour and the glory of world Jewry has vanished. We, the Polish Jews, were after all the most vibrant nerve of our people.

In terms of the number of victims, Hitler has murdered an entire people. There are many peoples in Europe who number fewer than the number of our martyrs. The Danes and the Norwegians are no more than three million. The Lithuanians, the Letts and the Estonians have far fewer. The Swedes – six million. The Slovaks fewer than two million, and so on. And Hitler has already killed five, six million Jews. Our language has no words with which to express the calamity and disaster that has struck us.

Monday, 4 January 1943

Once again a few dark, melancholy and very, very gloomy days have gone by. The few who have survived continue to live their lives, which are filled with baseness and bitterness. On the surface everything is quiet and it seems that they do not want to disturb the peace of those who have been left alive. But deep in our hearts is gnawing away the perpetual dread that never lets up for one moment and eats away at us like a moth.

In the past few days we have been seized with anxiety and with a terrible dread. The cause of our disquiet is the arrival of Ukrainians in Warsaw. I have heard that a group of 600 men – Ukrainians – has arrived here. All kinds of theories have been put forward to explain their presence. The Jews have been walking around in gloom and despair. We were afraid that they had come for us, that we were on the brink of a new liquidation, this time a complete one. There were those who reassured themselves and others. They say that their arrival is connected with the 'action' against the Poles that is due to begin shortly. In fact there are reports of unrest and turmoil among the Poles over the mass-expulsions of Poles in the Zamość area. There are also those who say that the Ukrainians have only been sent here for a short period. They are just passing through Warsaw. Whatever the truth may be, the Jews entered the new year – 1943 – in a depressed and agitated state of mind.

I heard today that the murderers have already left town. As to the reason for their short visit: the same source told me the following: they brought a transport of Poles from Słonim and the surrounding area here. The transport was escorted by the Ukrainians. The town of Słonim, which was once a great Jewish centre, is now 'completely *judenfrei*'.[429] All the Jews have also been expelled. What became of them, whether they were taken to a second location and kept alive, or if they were brought to Treblinka – is not known. One must accept and tell oneself the bitter truth that if the town of Słonim has been emptied of Jews, then these Jews have been wiped off the face of the earth.

The campaign of incitement against Jews in the German press is still continuing and has become even more intense. Much is written about such countries as Romania, Slovakia and Hungary, and about the 'solution' of the Jewish question in these countries. According to what they write, three-quarters of the Jews of Romania and Slovakia have already been exterminated, nearly one million. Hungary is oppressing its Jews economically, but has not yet followed in the footsteps of the Nazis, that is they have not exterminated Jews on a mass scale. All the remaining Jewish communities in Europe face complete annihilation. This is the fate of those countries that find themselves under the rule of these Teutonic butchers: France, Belgium, Holland, Norway, Germany, Denmark, Poland, Czechoslovakia (Bohemia and Moravia), the Baltic countries – Lithuania, Latvia, and Estonia – and the occupied territories of Soviet Russia, as well as Romania, Yugoslavia, Slovakia and Greece. It is to be assumed that about 90 per cent of the whole of European Jewry has been destroyed in the ovens of hell that these twentieth-century Huns have erected.

I was told by a certain Jew that a group of Swiss and Swedish journalists have approached German journalists with the question: is there any truth in the stories about the mass-destruction of Jews in German-occupied countries? The Nazi journalists are supposed to have replied that they would give an answer after investigating the matter and researching their sources. A few days later they gave the reply that there had been no mass-murders, but that for economic and supply reasons it has been necessary to shift a percentage of the population to the Eastern territories and resettle them. A certain proportion, especially children, women and old people, had been unable to survive the arduous journey to the new locations and had died. The number of dead is put at only 110,000.

It may be that there is a kernel of truth in this report.[430]

In the proclamations that Hitler has been issuing for the new year he repeats the slanderous lie that Jews were responsible for the outbreak of the war, and that it was only through the Jews that an alliance between the capitalist countries and the Soviet Union became possible. His prophecy of the extermination of European Jewry has already been realized. From his words and from the whole campaign of incitement against Jews in the German press we can see that the active war against us has not eased up in the least.

Thursday, 7 January

Conditions have not changed here either for the better or for the worse. Nothing. We are continually consumed by fear and anxiety. We do not know if today will be our last day, if they will come, surround the ghetto and take us out to our death. Contact with other towns has been almost completely broken. We have no precise idea where there are any other Jewish communities and where they have been completely wiped out. Today I heard a rumour that the whole Jewish community of Lwów has been liquidated and the town has become *judenfrei*. However, it is hard to know how much truth there is in this rumour. We do not even know what is happening on the next street. Just yesterday a rumour went around that the Poles were being driven out of Praga and that they are being brought into the streets that have been left empty by the Jews. Similarly there was also a rumour that at the Eastern Station in Warsaw there are trains standing full of Polish children and that many of them (200) died on the way.

It is hard to determine how much truth there is in either of these reports. We are locked in a cramped and tiny prison and we have no idea what is happening outside the walls of our prison, except in the form of sickening and confused rumours. Indeed there is under present conditions no crime of which the Germans would not be capable. They are turning the whole of Europe outside the Reich into a wilderness. I am talking about the populations of these areas. They have almost completely wiped out the Jews, now it looks as if it is the turn of the Poles. The Russians are being exterminated, the Czechs are being murdered. The Teutonic sword is destroying the peoples of Europe.

When will this nightmare through which we are living come to an end?

Whole wooden buildings are disappearing from our ghetto. In the course of one or two days they are dismantled and the wood used to heat the homes. Those who have returned from the work-camps (*obozowicze*) are particularly busy at this. The wood-trade is flourishing at the moment in the ghetto. Prices are low, half of what they were a year ago. And it is only thanks to this that we manage not to freeze, and a certain number of unfortunate Jews can support themselves.

Saturday, 9 January

Since yesterday renewed tensions can be felt in the ghetto. The day before yesterday proclamations were posted on the walls forbidding entry or exit from the old ghetto into the new ghetto, or from the new ghetto into the old ghetto without special permission from the *Sonderkommando* at 103 Żelazna Street. This decree, which is signed by the *Judenrat*, is causing great alarm. Once again there is a dread of increased persecutions. In addition, the order issued by the local *Führer* Brandt concerning the buildings at the *Umschlagplatz* that in the course of the summer swallowed around 300,000 Jewish souls has awakened a deep and agitated disquiet. According to Brandt's announcement they plan to make these buildings into a prison or some kind of camp for the Jews who are arrested each day on the Aryan side or in the streets of the old ghetto. These Jews are brought to 103 Żelazna Street. Their quarters are very cramped there and they want to prepare more spacious facilities. This whole business makes every Jew's heart beat with fear. Who can believe the words of a German (after the bitter experiences that we have been through)? All kinds of anxieties have been voiced in this connection. Some believe that this is all a trick on their part and that their real goal is to prepare that place of terror for another slaughter. Others argue that they plan to lock up at the *Umschlagplatz* all those who are registered with the *Werterfassung* and who do not report for work. There are many apprehensions and great is the fear and great is the burden that weighs on our hearts and minds.

Isolated refugees who arrive here literally by miracle from Treblinka bring reports that freeze the blood in the veins. The killing-machine there never rests. In the past few days Jews from Radomsko were brought there and murdered.[431] News of this kind causes us hellish torments. Has anyone every described the suffering of someone who has been condemned to death and who is to go to the gallows? Even the Russian artists, of whom the greatest is Dostoyevsky, have not succeeded in giving a true description of what transpires in the depths of the soul of an innocent person who has been sentenced to death. When I hear these accounts of Treblinka, something begins to twist and turn in my heart. The fear of 'that' which must come is, perhaps, stronger than the torment a person feels when he gives up his soul. Will these terrible agonies of the spirit call up a literary response? Will there emerge a new Bialik able to write a new Book of Lamentations, a new 'In the Town of Slaughter'?[432]

In recent days there were killings once again in the streets of the ghetto. Yesterday there was talk of a number of victims. One report of a murder on Muranowska Street was confirmed. A relative of the baker at 64 Mylna Street, Goldberg (the name of the baker), was walking at one in the afternoon to take his shoes to the shoemaker for repair. A car drove by. The driver stopped the Jew and asked him why he wasn't working. The Jew replied that he was ill. The German struck him murderous blows. The Jew fell to the ground and the driver was about to go back to his car. At the last moment he changed his mind, took out his revolver and killed the Jew.

I heard confirmation from various sources of the report about the Polish children who were brought to Warsaw from the districts of Lublin and Zamość. They are being distributed among various families. Their parents were taken away to work and the children were brought here.

Monday, 11 January

On Friday in the afternoon there was uproar in several streets of the ghetto. The Jewish police were frightening people into not wandering around in the streets. At that time – half past four – I happened to be on Koża Street (formerly Kupiecka Street, and later named after Rabbi Meisels). The police were shouting: 'Don't bring disaster on yourselves and on us!' People have been saying that Himmler is in Warsaw.[433] The Jews began to run and to hide in the entrance-ways. After a few minutes I continued on my way along Muranowska Street (to my sister and daughter) and three elegant cars [limousines] drove past me. It may be that the head-butcher actually drove by, in order to see with his own eyes the fruits of his 'work', the destruction of the greatest Jewish community in Europe. He was no doubt happy with the results.

Someone who knows many people, including those at present at the head of the *Judenrat*, told me that there really was a very grave danger hanging over our heads these past days. There was a proposal, or a plan, for a new expulsion of the Jews of the ghetto or of the survivors. It was to have been carried out at night, when everyone is asleep in bed and it is impossible for them to take refuge anywhere. This time we escaped disaster because of the opposition of the military authorities, of the *Wehrmacht*. One of the generals opposed the planned expulsion on the grounds that the Jews were working and that their output was necessary at the moment. The opponents of a new slaughter came from the supply authorities, from the *Rüstungs-kommando* and not from the *Wehrmacht*, as I wrote above. But it is necessary that we recognize the bitter and terrible truth: *over our heads hangs the perpetual threat of total annihilation.* It seems they have decided to exterminate the whole of European Jewry.

Appalling reports are arriving from the provinces: towns that were designated as locations for Jewish ghettos have become *judenrein*. Among them: Siedlce and Sobolew. This means that as far as the Jews are concerned, no promise is binding, no order. There are in fact no human standards in the treatment of us, every trick, every lie, every falsification is legitimate, if it can serve in the destruction of further numbers of Jews.

There are rumours that in Brudno, near Warsaw, barracks are being built which are intended for us . . . if only it was just barracks that they were preparing for us.

A report taken from the Italian newspaper *Corriere della Sera* of 22 December made a strong impression on me. The newspaper carries the contents of the declaration (note) of the German government to the statements of Russia, England and America on the Jewish question, that is, on the extermination of the Jews by Hitler.[434] The German note states that the Jews were well aware of the Nazis' programme with regard to them ten years before they came to power. The Jews knew full well that according to this programme there was no place for them on German soil. The Jews had enough time to leave the Reich and also . . . the other European countries. If they didn't do this – they have only harmed themselves (in Polish: *to tym gorzej dla nich*). Even after the war had broken out they could have left certain countries and even today they can leave several countries. At the end the note mentions the *Führer*'s proclamation at the outbreak of the war to the effect that if the Jews cause a new world war they will be the first to suffer the consequences.[435]

It is hardly worth discussing the insanity of this reply: nine million people, men, women and children, were supposed to leave Europe entirely (where, for instance, were they supposed to go?), that is, even those countries where no Germans have ever trod, such as Yugoslavia, Greece, the Russian interior, etc. And if they failed to do this, then they all must die a nameless death, together with their women, children and old people. Words that cut like sharp sword-blades, and we can see from them that the murderers have no intention of halting their terrible crimes. This is their answer to the protests of the nations.

Our mood is one of deep despair and depression. The reports that reach us from various locations show that this time they are intent on the total destruction of the Jews. They are not leaving even a single Jew behind. This is the fate of Radomsko and other towns. These reports plunge us into black despair. We are terrified of a new 'action' here, which will mean the end for us all, that is, for everyone who is left in the ghetto. A few individuals will be saved who have hidden on the other side among the Poles. But the fate of these Jews is also not at all sure, apart from the fact that they live in continual fear, and are liable at any moment to fall into the net of the Germans and of Polish agents. There is also the fear of a special 'action' directed against them.

I heard yesterday that Germans were looking through material in the records of the General Government. It is not known what kind of plan they have in mind: are they going to inspect the new registration of the inhabitants, that is, the Jews, in order to catch them, or do they want to get to know the Polish situation, in order to plan something evil against them – the Poles?

In the town, outside the ghetto, proclamations have been posted about 200 hostages who have been taken from the Poles because of various acts of sabotage and attacks on German soldiers. Great tension and agitation can be felt in the air. The feeling one gets is that the Germans want to drown the disaster that must come to them in a sea of innocent blood. They began with us and will finish with other peoples: Poles, Czechs, Serbs and many others.

My daughter, who is working for the *Werterfassung*, told me the following story: a few days ago three Polish boys and two Polish girls stole into the former ghetto on Leszno and Ogrodowa Streets in order to fill their pockets with Jewish property that is left there that the Germans are collecting. A German soldier, 19 years old, who was guarding the Jewish workers, shot at the Polish children and wounded them all mortally. They all died that day. This soldier is a terrible sadist. One day – perhaps the same day – he beat the Jews savagely, including the women and the young girls. This soldier was removed from his post at the *Werterfassung* in connection with the shooting of the Polish children. But it is interesting to see the reason for his dismissal: not because he shot and killed five human beings, but because he didn't shoot properly, that is, he didn't kill them on the spot, since the five children lived for almost a whole day afterwards and died in the evening. This is the reality in which we live and this is the new order that the Nazis want to erect in the world.

Friday, 15 January

The Jews have been living in dread of this day. Many Jews did not go to sleep until very late last night. The fear of a new 'action' set them on edge and robbed them of sleep. In the past few days, rumour after rumour has been circulating among us, good and bad. As I have already mentioned, an 'action' had been predicted for the 15th of this month. Later it was said that the Germans denied these rumours and the community leaders reassured the Jews. Do we not recall that on Sunday, three days before the beginning of the 'expulsion' – the slaughter, the commissar of the ghetto, Auerswald, reassured the leader of the Jewish community, Czerniaków, that no 'action' would be carried out in Warsaw and just three days later the action began? We cannot believe the Germans, the servants of savage killers. We can be content that the night passed peacefully, and that today there is no news of incidents or tragic events. But one cannot but be afraid none the less, since we will be unable to help ourselves and to rescue the few remaining survivors when the day of destruction comes.

I have also heard that a report or a telegram has come from Berlin that the Todt organization intends to employ Jews in Warsaw. This will lead to increased demand for manpower of Jewish workers, and thus will strengthen the security of the ghetto. It is also said that the working conditions in the Todt units are better than in the work-places run by the SS or others. It is hard to know if these are just false or fabricated rumours, or if they have any substance to them.

I have been told that yesterday eight Jews were killed at the Marki Station, seven men and one woman from the work-camp at the Eastern Station. They were sitting in the canteen when suddenly the SS came in and killed everyone they found there. I couldn't find out if they were caught there during working hours or if the unfortunates were doing business with the Poles at that moment (the selling of *ciuchy* and the buying of all kinds of groceries for the ghetto). Be that as it may, eight Jews of the few who remain have perished. Our blood is being spilled like water, it flows without respite. Someone who has arrived from Lwów said that during the new 'action' that was carried out there a few weeks ago 1,000 Jews were rounded up and killed, mainly children and old people. This was a sort of new 'verification'.

I heard that in the small town of Opoczno all the Jews were called into the town hall with the promise that they were to be registered in order to be exchanged for Palestinian Germans, that is, the Opoczno Jews were to go to Palestine. The Jews believed this lie and arrived at the appointed hour. Then they were rounded up and herded into train-wagons, which means they were taken away to their death to Treblinka or Oświęcim.[436]

There is talk that there were arrests among the Poles during the night. There is also word of an 'action' taking place today among the Poles: they are being rounded up to be sent away to work. This 'action' took place in various sections of the city: Żelazne Bramy, Grochów, Żoliborz and in general throughout the town. They informed us over the telephone that the trams are running empty and that the streets are deserted. They – just like us – are hiding from the enemy.

Saturday, 16 January

The day before yesterday 20 Jews were removed from the building at 3 Dzika Street where the returnees from the work-camps (*obozowicze*) were living. They were taken to Rembertów to work. Rembertów has already devoured many Jewish victims.

The number of Poles rounded up yesterday is estimated at 7,000–8,000; among them were 16 Jews. We have as yet no idea what will be done with them: if they will be killed or held in prison. There is a further 'action' in the Polish streets today. It is said that the *gubernia* must supply 300,000 workers for Germany. Warsaw alone – 30,000. Yesterday and today the arrestees were taken into the Pawiak.

Appendix

Eulogy Read at a Commemorative Evening in Honour of
Yitshak Meir Weissenberg, 13 September 1941

We live in a prison. We have been degraded to the level of homeless and uncared-for animals. When we look at the swollen, half-naked bodies of Jews lying in the streets, we feel as if we find ourselves at some subhuman level. The half-dead, skeletal faces of Jews, especially those of dying little children, frighten us and recall pictures of India, or of the isolation-colonies for lepers which we used to see in films. Reality surpasses any fantasy; and possibly one thing only could still surprise us. This would be mass-murder in the place of systematic extermination. Hard as it is to utter words such as these, one has to say that for all those who perish of starvation, a swift and violent death would certainly be a release from the protracted terrible suffering of their dying agony.

The proportions of life and death have radically changed. Times were, when life occupied the primary place, when it was the main and central concern, while death was a side phenomenon, secondary to life, its termination. Nowadays, death rules in all its majesty; while life hardly glows under a thick layer of ashes. Even this faint glow of life is feeble, miserable and weak, poor, devoid of any free breath, deprived of any spark of spiritual content. The very soul, both in the individual and in the community, seems to have starved and perished, to have dulled and atrophied. There remain only the needs of the body; and it leads merely an organic-physiological existence.

Such is our situation in the Jewish Wailing-Quarters in Warsaw as well as in other places. However, we do not forget that we are human beings and not primitive, lowly creatures. And, in spite of it all, we remember that only two years ago we used to be free men. We constituted a live and organic community which had and preserved a human image in spite of the negative and dark sides. We used to seek education; we used to strive and to create in every province of life; we used to enrich life. We used to yearn for art as the highest expression of human existence and we used to cultivate art in all its forms as much as our powers and potential permitted. And we used to have both a feeling and an inclination for science.

To sum up – we were human and whatever was human attracted and excited us. How is it nowadays? – How suppressed, how disgraced and miserable are we now!

Yet, we wish to live on, to continue as free and creative men. This will be our test. If, under the thick layer of ashes our life is not extinguished, this will prove a triumph of the human over the inhuman and that our will to live is mightier than the will to destruction; that we are capable of overcoming all evil forces which attempt to engulf us.

The cultural assemblies, the first of which we attend this evening, are meant to be one of the proofs of our vigorous instinct for life. They are supposed to remind us of our past and to stimulate us for a better future. They should recall to us that we used to occupy a place higher than the Gypsies or any of the wild tribes of Africa. And they must arouse in us a renewed intellectual effort and creativity. They must not let us slide into the eternal sleep. I believe in Jewish youth. I believe that they, on whom the war has had such a tragic impact (for they did not yet enjoy the fruits of life, having been deprived of any benefit of school, of science, of literature, of theatre or other human achievements in spiritual or material fields) – to say nothing of physical miseries, of starvation and death – I believe that this youth will enthusiastically accept our initiative and will find in these assemblies a new strength to invigorate themselves and preserve their human image.

We have consecrated this first evening to the late writer, Weissenberg. This may have been just an accident but it is, nevertheless, somewhat symbolic. Weissenberg is one of those creative artists who come to us as though born by themselves, who grow like a flower in an untilled field. In this respect, he reminds us of the Russian author Gorky, who also grew out of an environment devoid of understanding for culture or literature. Artists such as these are evidence of the life-forces of man, of his eternal drive towards light and progress, of his inner creative thrust. These forces sprout unexpectedly, spring up like a hidden source from under the earth.

May the memory of Weissenberg be a symbol of our vital forces which shall, in defiance of any restrictions and stone walls, flow forth unseen until they burst out of hiding in a free world and spread in joy and jubilation all over the field of our life.

Hear, O Jewish Youth! Maybe among you, here in this hall, there is, there are potential Weissenbergs. Do not lose courage! Keep strong and gather power, pick up strength to withstand until the sun shines for all children of the earth without distinction. Then, at that hour, Weissenbergs will appear anew among us, along with other creators. At that hour, we shall honour and celebrate not only the memory of deceased writers, but also the fame and excellence of the living, creating young Jewish artists in every field of culture and of civilization.

Notes

Introduction

1 Quoted in T. Berenstein, A. Eisenbach, Adam Rutkowski (eds), *Eksterminacja Żydów na ziemiach polskch: zbiór dokumentów* (*The Extermination of Jews on Polish Lands: Collection of Documents*) (Warsaw, 1957), p. 107.

2 E. Ringelblum, *Ksovim fun geto* (*Ghetto Writings*) vol. I 1939–42, vol. II 1942–3, ed. A. Eisenbach, T. Berenstein, B. Mark, A. Rutkowski (Warsaw, 1961, 1963; henceforth: Ringelblum, *Ksovim*), I. p. 239.

3 L. Hirszfeld, *Historia jednego życia* (*The Story of One Life*) (Warsaw, 1946), p. 197.

4 *Akten zur Deutschen Auswärtigen Politik 1918-1945*, series D, vol. 4 (Baden-Baden, 1951), p. 291.

5 H. Buchheim et al., *Anatomie des SS-Staates*, vol. II (Munich, 1967), p. 28.

6 Quoted in N. Baynes (ed.), *The Speeches of Adolf Hitler*, vol. I, *April 1922-August 1939* (London, 1942), p. 741.

7 On this, see M. Gilbert, *The Holocaust: The Jewish Tragedy* (London, 1986), pp. 84–98.

8 There is a vast literature on Nazi policies in occupied Poland. Among the most useful accounts are: M. Broszat, *Nationalsozialistische Polenpolitik 1939-1945*, rev. edn (Munich, 1963); C. Madajczyk, *Polityka III Rzeszy w okupowanej Polsce* (*The Policies of the Third Reich in Occupied Poland*) (Warsaw, 1970; 2 vols); J. T. Gross, *Polish Society under German Occupation: The Generalgouvernement, 1939-1944* (Princeton, NJ, 1979). Also interesting are: Polish Ministry of Information, *The New German Order in Poland* (London, 1942); J. Buhler (ed.), *Das Generalgouvernement - seine Verwaltung und seine Wirtschaft* (Krakow, 1943); H. Streng, *Die Landwirtschaft im Generalgouvernement* (Göttingen, 1955).

9 For this, see Broszat, *Nationalsozialistische Polenpolitik*, pp. 20–2.

10 E. Duraczynski, *Wojna i Okupacja* (*War and Occupation*) (Warsaw, 1974), p. 69.

11 Diary entry for 19 Dec. 1939, S. Piotrowski (ed.), *Hans Frank's Diary* (Warsaw, 1961).

12 On forced labour see Y. Gutman, *The Jews of Warsaw, 1939-1943. Ghetto, Underground, Revolt* (Brighton, 1982), pp. 21–4; T. Berenstein, 'Praca przymusowa Żydów w Warszawie' ('Forced labour of Jews in Warsaw'), *Biuletyn Żydowskiego Instytutu Historycznego* (henceforth *BŻIH*), 45–6.

13 On Piotrków, see Gilbert, *The Holocaust*, pp. 96, 103. On Łódź, L. Dobroszycki (ed.), *The Chronicle of the Lodz Ghetto 1941-44* (London, 1984).

14 On the establishment of the ghetto, see Gutman, *The Jews of Warsaw*, pp. 48–61 and Berenstein, Eisenbach and Rutkowski, *Eksterminacja Żydów*, pp. 99–108.

15 *The Warsaw Diary of Chaim A. Kaplan*, Trans. and ed. Abraham Katsch (New York, 1973), pp. 213–14. This is the English version of *Megillat Yisurin. Yoman Geto Varshe (A Scroll of Agony. A Diary from the Warsaw Ghetto)* (Tel Aviv, 1966). Henceforth cited as Kaplan, *Warsaw Diary*.

16 T. Bialer, 'Recollections', *Colliers*, New York, 20 Feb. 1943, p. 17, quoted in Gilbert, *The Holocaust*, pp. 129–30.

17 These and subsequent details about Lewin's life have been taken from the Introduction to the Hebrew edition of the diary of Tsvi Shner. This was published by Beit Lohamei Hagetaot and Kibbutz Hameuchad in 1969, under the title *Mipinkaso shel hamoreh mi-Yehudia: Geto Varshe, April 1942-Januar 1943 (From the Notebooks of the Teacher from Yehudia School: Warsaw Ghetto, April 1942-January 1943).* Henceforth cited as *Mipinkaso shel hamoreh*.

18 According to the account of Zofia Marminska, first headmistress of the school. Introduction, *Mipinkaso shel hamoreh*, p. 6.

19 Ibid., p. 5.

20 According to the account of Nina Danzig-Weltser, a former pupil of the school, who joined the staff in 1932. It was she who, together with Nehama (Hella) Herzberg (neé Zucker), collected the documentary material for the Introduction to the Hebrew edition. Introduction, *Mipinkaso shel hamoreh*, p. 7.

21 Ibid.

22 David Pearlman of Warsaw. Quoted in Introduction, *Mipinkaso shel hamoreh*, p. 10.

23 Letter to Nehama Herzberg written on 3 Jan. 1933 while Lewin was on holiday in the Tatra mountains. Introduction, *Mipinkaso shel hamoreh*, p. 9. There is a copy of this letter in the *Beit Lohamei Hagetaot* archives.

24 Account of Ida Hochberg-Menuz. Introduction, *Mipinkaso shel hamoreh*, p. 11.

25 Account of Nehama Herzberg. Introduction, *Mipinkaso shel hamoreh*, p. 11.

26 Introduction, *Mipinkaso shel hamoreh*, pp. 10–11.

27 Account of Iska Feibikh Ben-Daat. Introduction, *Mipinkaso shel hamoreh*, p. 11.

28 Introduction, *Mipinkaso shel hamoreh*, pp. 11–12.

29 *Kantanisten: vegn der Yidisher rekrutshina in Rusland in di tsaytn fun Tsar Nikolai der ershtn, 1825-1856 (Cantonists: On Jewish Recruitment in Russia in the Reign of Nicholas I, 1825-1856* (Warsaw, 1934).

30 Introduction, *Mipinkaso shel hamoreh*, pp. 12–13.

31 On the Jewish Self-help Organization, see Gutman, *The Jews of Warsaw*, pp. 40–5, 102–6. Michael Weichert, who headed the organization in Kraków, has written his memoirs, *Milkhama zikhronot (War Memoirs)* (Tel Aviv, 1963), as well as an account of the Self-help Organization: *Yidishe alaynhilf (Jewish Self-help)* (Tel Aviv, 1962). Ringelblum discusses the dilemmas facing the organization in *Ksovim*, I, p. 360. See also the selection of documents from the Ringelblum archive published in Israel by *Yad Vashem*: J. Kermish (ed.), *To Live with Honor*

and Die with Honor: Selected Documents from the Warsaw Ghetto Underground Archives (OS) (Oneg Shabbath) (Jerusalem, 1986). (Henceforth cited as *To Live with Honor and Die with Honor*.) Section on the Self-help Organization, pp. 332–69.

32 Ringelblum, *Ksovim*, II, p. 102. An English version of Ringelblum's account of *Oneg Shabbes* can be found in Kermish, *To Live with Honor and Die with Honor*, pp. 2–21. It is dated correctly as late December, while the Warsaw published version in Yiddish is dated as late January.

33 *To Live with Honor and Die with Honor*, p. 20.

34 On the population of the ghetto, see 'Materialn tsu demografishn forshung vegn der Yidisher befelkerung in Varshe beys di hitlerishe okupatsie' ('Materials for demographic research into the Jewish population of Warsaw during the Hitlerite occupation'), *Bleter far Geshikhte*, VIII, nos 3–4 (1955); T. Berenstein and A. Rutkowski, 'Liczba ludności żydowskiej i obszar przez nią zamieszkany w Warszawie w latach okupacji hitlerowskiej' ('The size of the Jewish population and the area it occupied in the years of the Hitlerite occupation'), *BŻIH*, 26 (1958); and Gutman, *The Jews of Warsaw*, pp. 62–5.

35 K. Dunin-Wąsowicz et al. (eds), *Raporty Ludwiga Fischera, gubernatora distryktu warszawskiego 1939-1944* (*The Reports of Ludwig Fischer, Governor of the Warsaw District, 1939-1944*) (Warsaw, 1987), pp. 115, 140–1.

36 On the *Judenrat*, see the article by N. Blumenthal, 'Geto Varshe vehurbano' ('The Warsaw ghetto and its destruction') in Y. Grünbaum (ed.), *Entsiklopedia shel galuyot* (*Encyclopedia of the Diasporas*) vol. II (Jerusalem, Tel Aviv, 1959); I. Trunk, *Judenrat: The Jewish Council in Eastern Europe under Nazi Occupation* (New York, 1971); Gutman, *The Jews of Warsaw*, especially pp. 36–8, 78–85; Kermish, *To Live with Honor and Die with Honor*, pp. 289–331. On Czerniaków, *The Warsaw Diary of Adam Czerniakow: Prelude to Doom*, ed. Raul Hilberg, Stanislaw Staron and Josef Kermish (New York, 1979) and Y. Gutman, 'Czerniakow – Haish ve-hayoman' ('Czerniaków, the Man and the Diary') in *Yalkut Moreshet*, 10, pp. 115–44.

37 This passage was not included in the published diary and is in the *Moreshet* archive. Quoted in Gutman, *The Jews of Warsaw*, p. 38.

38 *Yad Vashem* archives, JM – 1112.

39 Czerniaków, *Warsaw Diary*, p. 172.

40 On the postal service, see R. Sakowska, 'Łączność pocztowa warszawskiego getta', *BŻIH*, 45–6, pp. 94–109 and Gutman, *The Jews of Warsaw*, p. 111.

41 On Nossig, see Gutman, *The Jews of Warsaw*, pp. 341–2 and Y. Zuckerman, M. Basuk (eds), *Sefer milkhamot hagetaot: Beyn hahomot, hemakhanot, beya'arot* (*The Book of the Ghetto Wars: Between the Walls, in the Camps, in the Forests*) (Tel Aviv, 1947), pp. 737–8.

42 On the Jewish police, see Gutman, *The Jews of Warsaw*, pp. 86–90; Ringelblum, *Ksovim*, II, pp. 34–7. On the gaol on Gęsia Street, see Kermish, *To Live with Honor and Die with Honor*, pp. 155–7.

43 On the 'Thirteen', see Zuckerman and Basum, *Sefer milkhamot*, pp. 714–15; A. Rosenberg, 'Dos "Dreitsentl"' ('The Thirteen'), *Beit Lohamei Hagetaot* archives,

V, 1–2; A. Weiss, '*Dreitsentl*' ('The Thirteen') in *Yalkut Moreshet*, 21 (1976) and Gutman, *The Jews of Warsaw*, pp. 90–4.

44 M. Berg, *Warsaw Ghetto: A Diary by Mary Berg*, ed. S. L. Schneiderman (New York, 1945), entry for 22 Dec. 1940.

45 Kaplan, *Warsaw Diary*, p. 234.

46 Ringelblum, *Ksovim*, I, pp. 197, 216.

47 Ibid., II, p. 31.

48 Ibid., I, pp. 251ff. See also Kermish, *To Live with Honor and Die with Honor*, pp. 249–88.

49 Quoted in *Okupacja i ruch oporu w dzienniku Hansa Franka, 1939-1945* (*Opposition and Resistance in Hans Frank's Diary, 1939-1945*), vol. I (Warsaw, 1972), p. 249.

50 Ringelblum, *Ksovim*, I, p. 348. On the economic situation in the ghetto see Gutman, *The Jews of Warsaw*, pp. 72–7, and Kermish, *To Live with Honor and Die with Honor*, pp. 533–84.

51 That of Stanislaw Adler, quoted in Gutman, *The Jews of Warsaw*, p. 76.

52 Gutman, *The Jews of Warsaw*, p. 77.

53 Stefan Ernest, 'Diary', pp. 74–5. In *Yad Vashem* archives, 0-6/103.

54 Dunin-Wąsowicz et al., *Raporty Ludwiga Fischera*, pp. 120, 323.

55 Berenstein and Rutkowski, 'Liczba ludności żydowskiej i obszar przez nią zamieszkany w Warszawie w latach okupacji hitlerowskiej', *BŻIH*, 26 (1958), p. 117.

56 Diary of S. Szymkowicz, p. 90, in *Yad Vashem* archive. Quoted in Gutman, *The Jews of Warsaw*, p. 67. Diary of Henryk Brysker, p. 43, in the possession of Y. Gutman and quoted by him in *The Jews of Warsaw*, p. 67. On smuggling generally, see the study written in the ghetto for the *Oneg Shabbes* archive by M. Passenstein, 'Šmugiel w getcie warszawskim' ('Smuggling in the Warsaw ghetto'), *BŻIH*, 26, pp. 42–72. Also P. Opoczynski, *Reportazhn fun varshever geto* (*Reportages about the Warsaw Ghetto*) (Warsaw, 1954), and Gutman, *The Jews of Warsaw*, pp. 66–70.

57 Dunin-Wąsowicz et al., *Raporty Ludwiga Fischera*, p. 120.

58 Passenstein, 'Šmugiel w getcie warszawskim', p. 69.

59 Diary of S. Symkowicz, p. 103. Quoted in Gutman, *The Jews of Warsaw*, p. 69.

60 Passenstein, 'Šmugiel w getcie warszawskim', p. 71.

61 Ringelblum, *Ksovim*, II, p. 196.

62 Henryka Lazowert, the author of 'A History of a Jewish Family during the War', for which she was awarded a prize by *Oneg Shabbes*, died in Treblinka during the great deportation. For the full text of the poem see Zuckerman and Basuk, *Sefer milkhamot*, p. 90.

63 R. Auerbach, *Be-Huzot Varshe* (*In the Ruins of Warsaw*) (Tel Aviv, 1954), II, p. 658.

64 Ringelblum, *Ksovim*, II, p. 232.

65 Ibid., I, p. 350.

66 On these episodes, see Kaplan, *Warsaw Diary*, pp. 80, 82, 106–7; Ringelblum, *Ksovim*, I, pp. 232, 234; and Gutman, *The Jews of Warsaw*, pp. 32–3.

67 H. Berlinski, 'Zikhronot' ('Memoirs'), *Yalkut Moreshet*, I (1964), pp. 24–5.

68 Ringelblum, *Ksovim*, I, p. 327.

69 Ibid., II, p. 109.

70 On this incident see Gutman, *The Jews of Warsaw*, pp. 176–80.

71 These two poems were written in response to the pogrom in Kishinev, Tsarist Russia, in 1903. They are reprinted in H. N. Bialik, *Shirim* (*Poems*) (Odessa, 1905), pp. 233–46. For English versions see I. Efros (ed.), *Selected Poems of Hayyim Nahman Bialik* (rev. edn; New York, 1965), pp. 112–29.

72 In Warsaw, as elsewhere, the Germans put Gypsies into the ghetto. They wore white armbands bearing the letter Z (for *Zigeuner*). They quickly disappeared from the ghetto, apparently having managed to escape. See N. Eck, *Hatoim bedarkhey hamavet: Havey rehagut beyamey hakhilayon* (*Wanderers on the Paths of Death: Reflections on Life in Times of Annihilation*) (Jerusalem, 1970), p. 17.

73 For some of the views expressed, see Ringelblum's study, *Polish-Jewish Relations during the Second World War*, ed. J. Kermish and S. Krakowski (Jerusalem, 1974) and Kermish, *To Live with Honor and Die with Honor*, pp. 607–44.

74 For these developments, see Gilbert, *The Holocaust*, *passim*, and Kermish, *To Live with Honor and Die with Honor*, pp. 170–213.

75 Czerniaków, *Warsaw Diary*, p. 385. On the great deportation, see Gutman, *The Jews of Warsaw*, pp. 197–233; S. Piotrowski, *Misja Odyla Globocnika* (*The Mission of Odylo Globocnik*) (Warsaw, 1949); Kermish, *To Live with Honor and Die with Honor*, pp. 691–716; Y. Arad, *Operation Reinhard* (Indianapolis, 1987).

76 Lewin uses the word הבל, which Alkalay's Hebrew–English dictionary defines as: steam, vapour, breath.

77 *Likwidacja żydowskiej Warszawy: Wedlug oficjalnych dokumentów otrzymanych przez Reprezentacje Żydostwa Polskiego, Pázdziernik 1943, Tel Aviv* (*The Liquidation of Warsaw Jewry According to Official Documents Obtained in October 1943 by the Representative Body of Polish Jewry in Tel Aviv*) (Tel Aviv, 1943), p. 25.

78 Ringelblum, *Ksovim*, II, p. 31.

79 Y. Katznelson, *Katavim aharonim* (*Last Writings*) (*Beit Lohamei Hagetaot*, 1956), p. 197.

80 For accounts of the 'small ghetto', see Gutman, *The Jews of Warsaw*, pp. 268–80; and the reports of Fischer, governor of the Warsaw district, on the ghetto following the mass deportation: *Raporty Ludwiga Fischera*, pp. 540–50.

81 For the German attempt to liquidate the ghetto in January and the development of resistance culminating in the uprising of April–May 1943, see Gutman, *The Jews of Warsaw*, pp. 268–430. A contemporary account of the January action by Yehiel Gorny is reprinted in Kermish, *To Live with Honor and Die with Honor*, pp. 591–4. There is a vast literature on the actual uprising, which is fully discussed in Gutman.

82 Kermish, *To Live with Honor and Die with Honor*, p. 20.

A Cup of Tears

Part I   From the Notebooks

1 In Feb. 1942, the number of Jews in Wąwolnica was approximately 1,250. After the slaughter of Mar. 1942 they were deported to Opole and from there they were taken to Bełżec and exterminated.

2 *Volksdeutsch* – the population of German origin ('ethnic Germans') in the occupied territories who had declared their allegiance (voluntarily or otherwise) to the German people and thereby enjoyed extra rights; an important source of support for the German authorities.

3 In Nov. 1941, 10,000 Jews were murdered in Słonim, most of them women and children. They were shot next to a mass grave prepared beforehand at some distance from the town.

4 The reference is to the murder of 5,000 Jews on the outskirts of the town on 5–6 Dec. 1941. Those considered fit for work were herded into the ghetto. News of the mass-murders on Poland's former eastern borders caused tremendous unrest in the ghetto and aroused fears that a similar fate awaited the Jews of Warsaw.

5 The 10 Jews were arrested on the basis of a list drawn up by the Germans. The ghetto police were ordered to do the hanging themselves, and some 3,000 Jews were forced to watch the execution. Gallows were also erected at other places in the region on that day. This atrocity was repeated by the Germans on the festival of Shavuot 1942. Zduńska Wola – some 40 km west of Łódź.

6 The author seems to have written Biezuń (a township in the Warsaw district) instead of Będzin (a township near Łódź).

7 In March 1942, the Jews in Izbica Lubelska (some 2,000 or more) were sent to Bełżec to be exterminated. At that time transports of Jews were reaching Izbica from Germany, Vienna, and even Theresienstadt in occupied Czechoslovakia. On this see T. Bernstein, 'Martyrologia, opór i walka ludności żydowskiej w lubelskiem' ('The martyrology, resistance and struggle of the Jewish population in the Lublin area'), *Biuletyn Żydowskiego Instytutu Historycznego* (henceforth *BŻIH*), 21.

8 The approaches to the ghetto were controlled from the outside (the Aryan side) by Polish policemen, the *Polnische Hilfspolizei*, generally known as the 'Navy Blue Police' (*Policja granatowa*) from the colour of their uniforms.

9 In Polish the word *meta* means target or finishing-post; in ghetto slang it meant a place that could be used for smuggling. On the system for smuggling and on the dangers facing the smuggler, see the article written by M. Passenstein for the Ringelblum archive 'Śmugiel w getcie warszawskim' ('Smuggling in the Warsaw ghetto'), reprinted in *BŻIH*, 26, pp 42–72; Perets Opoczynski, *Reportazhen fun várshever geto* (*Reportages about the Warsaw Ghetto*) (Warsaw, 1954) and Y. Gutman, *The Jews of Warsaw, 1939-1943: Ghetto, Underground, Revolt* (London, 1982), pp. 66–70.

10 On the same strange gendarme, nicknamed 'the gentleman' because of his exceptional behaviour towards the Jewish smugglers; see also E. Ringelblum, *Ksovim fun getto (Ghetto Writings)*, vol. I: 1939–42, vol. II: 1942–3, ed. A. Eisenbach, T. Berenstein, B. Mark, A. Rutkowski (Warsaw, 1961, 1963; henceforth: Ringelblum, *Ksovim*), I, p. 350. The cruel ruses of the gendarmes controlling the approaches to the ghetto and their occasional demonstrations of 'softheartedness' towards the young smugglers are described at length in the diary of Rachel Auerbach, *Be-Huzot Varshe (In the Ruins of Warsaw)* (Tel Aviv, 1954).

11 Pomerania – a district of northern Poland; Poznań – a district capital in the west of Poland; Warthegau; the Warta region, an area in the west of Poland. These areas were annexed to the Reich administratively by an order of 8 Oct. 1939. Under the Occupation, the Jews from these areas were deported to central Poland. On this see D. Dąbrowska, 'Zagłada skupisk żydowskich w kraju Warty' ('The destruction of the Jewish settlements in the Warta area'), *BŻIH*, 13–14.

12 In his entry of 8 May 1942, Ringelblum also included Ostrowiec-Kieleckie in the list of cities where mass-murders had taken place such as that which occurred in the streets of Warsaw at dawn on 18 Apr. (see n. 29 below). He explains the wave of fear that overwhelmed the ghetto by the Germans' desire to spread terror among the population because of the spring offensive on the eastern front (see *Ksovim*, I, pp. 347–8).

13 Dr Zofia Syrkin-Biernstein, a very active member of the community; in charge of the health services of the *Judenrat* (Jewish Council; officially, Council of Jewish Elders); committed suicide in Jan. 1943 in the railway-car taking her to Treblinka.

14 Here and below the diarist uses this term ('the community' – *Kehilla*) for the *Judenrat* and its institutions. Until the massive deportation of the summer of 1942, Warsaw's *Judenrat* operated from the building formerly used by the community organization (*Kehilla*). On the *Judenrat* in the Warsaw ghetto, see the article by N. Blumenthal, 'Geto varshe vehurbano' ('The Warsaw ghetto and its destruction') in Y. Grünbaum (ed.), *Entsiklopedia shel galuyot (Encyclopedia of the Diasporas)*, vol. II (Jerusalem, Tel Aviv, 1959), pp. 553, 557 and Gutman, *The Jews of Warsaw*, especially pp. 36–8, 78–85.

15 Since before the war Danilowiczowska Street had been the site of Warsaw's main police prison. The *Judenrat* set up a prison inside the ghetto in Gęsia Street; the prison yard was used for the execution of 'criminals' (people who were caught leaving the ghetto, or smuggling food). The prisoners – as many as 2,000 – were the first to be deported to Treblinka.

16 Before the war the head of the State Teacher Training College for Jewish religion teachers in Warsaw. His daughter was at Yehudia, the secondary school at which the diarist taught. He was killed in the main deportation (Ringelblum, *Ksovim*, II, pp. 225–6).

17 Lesh Street was the name by which Leszno Street was generally known. Katznelson, the poet of the Warsaw ghetto, also uses this name in his works. It was one of the main streets in the ghetto in that period; it was via Tłomackie Street,

Leszno Street, and Karmelicka Street that the Germans used to make their way to the Pawiak.

18 Dr Hans Frank, a German lawyer who belonged to Hitler's inner circle; minister of justice; among those responsible for formulating the Nuremberg Laws. A decree dated 12 Oct. 1939 and signed by Hitler created him head of the General-Government, an administrative unit which covered central districts of occupied Poland and which was referred to by Lewin as the *gubernia*. He lived in Kraków, and was one of the chief figures accused at the international military tribunal at Nuremberg.

19 Before the war the Nieszawa area had had a Jewish population of some 3,300; between Apr. and June 1942 most were sent to the death camp in Chelmno. Some of those who were fit for work were sent to the Łódź ghetto. The rural population were also deported to different parts of the General-Government in order to make room for German settlers brought in from the newly occupied areas in the east. Nieszawa was a district capital before the war and at the beginning of the Occupation; later the district was incorporated into the Warta region and Ciechocinek became the capital. On this see Dąbrowska 'Zagłada skupisk żydowskich w kraju Warty' (see n. 11).

20 Gestapo agents used to spread false rumours among the Jewish population about information supposedly deriving from people deported to the various distant regions. The Germans used this ruse frequently in order to facilitate the deportations. Ringelblum describes the Jews' tendency to cling to the false reports rather than to believe in the killing of the deportees in his article 'The Ten Tribes', *Ksovim*, II, pp. 42–4.

21 It is not clear what meeting the author is referring to; the erroneous belief that increasing productivity would guarantee the continued survival of the ghetto was held in many circles. Thus, Ringelblum notes at this time, 'Within the community there are those who claim that the danger of deportation which hangs over us has passed, thanks to the workshops in the ghetto that are producing for the German army' (*Ksovim*, I, p. 348).

22 Marszałkowska Street and Aleje Jerozolimskie (Jerusalem Avenue) were two of the main streets in Warsaw. The 'pregnant German women' were brought to Warsaw because the main cities of Germany were being bombed.

23 The *Jüdischer Ordnungsdienst* (Jewish Service to Maintain Order), set up by the Germans as the executive arm of the *Judenrat*. It was popularly known as the 'Jewish police' or the 'Ghetto police'. For a sensitive account of its activities see Gutman, *The Jews of Warsaw*, pp. 86–90.

24 Nowy Dwór – a district centre in the Warsaw region; Modlin – a castle located at the confluence of the Bug and the Vistula that controlled the approach to Warsaw. The reference is probably to Estonia, which was included in the Reichskommissariat Ostland – an administrative unit that included Estonia, Lithuania, Latvia and Byelorussia, all of which were occupied by the Germans. In the Baltic regions there were numerous landowners of German origin.

25 The Gestapo prison in Warsaw, used for political prisoners, Jewish and Gentile, many of whom were executed there. Named after nearby Pawia Street.

26 There was a curfew in the ghetto: between 9.00 p.m. and 5.00 a.m. Jews were forbidden to be in the streets. On the eve of the main deportation in July 1942, the curfew was delayed till 10.00 p.m. – one of the German ruses to inspire false confidence.

27 Galeazzo Ciano, Mussolini's son-in-law and foreign minister (1936–43): Victor Emmanuel III – king of Italy from 1900, who was forced to renounce the throne in 1946 as a result of a referendum.

28 Ze'ev von Wiesel, a doctor and publicist; formerly one of the leaders of the Revisionist Party. Settled in Israel.

29 On Saturday night, just before the dawn of 18 Apr. 1942, the Gestapo carried out a terror operation against the Jewish underground in Warsaw. They arrested 60 activists according to a list drawn up in advance and executed 48 of them on the spot. At the same time they also executed Gestapo agents that they wanted to get rid of. Following this the underground cut back on the publication of its newspaper and stopped its open political activity almost entirely. On this, see Gutman, *The Jews of Warsaw*, pp. 176–80.

30 Moshe Sklar, a member of the socialist Bund and actively involved in the Printers' Union; arrested at dawn on 18 Apr., shot only on 12 May; tortured but revealed nothing of what he knew. A portrait of Moshe Sklar – 'a gifted administrator and responsible worker', the scrupulous director of the communal kitchen in the ghetto – is to be found in the diary of S. Sheinkinder, who had known him since before the war when they had both worked on the same newspaper (*Der Moment*). For this, *Yad Vashem, Kovets mekhkarim beparshiot hashoa ve hagvura* (*'Yad Vashem', A Compendium of Research on the Holocaust and Valour*) (Jerusalem, 1958; henceforth *Yad Vashem*), V, pp. 203–5. On the circumstances of Sklar's tragic death, see also Auerbach's diary, *Be-Huzot Varshe*, II, pp. 655–6.

31 At the beginning of 1941, the *Judenrat* undertook to organize the postal service in the ghetto. According to contract with the Post Office administration in Warsaw, the workers of the 'Jewish post' were to receive all the post addressed to the Jewish population in bulk. The Jewish post office was situated at 19 Zamenhof Street. On the postal service in the Warsaw ghetto see R. Sakowska, 'Łączność pocztowa warszawskiego getta', *BŻIH*, 45–6, pp. 94–109 and Gutman, *The Jews of Warsaw*, p. 111.

32 The name of the tram driver shot on 12 May 1942 was in fact Roman (Abraham) Patt. Sheinkinder recorded in his diary: 'It is said that he was active in the PPS (the Polish Socialist Party), and that he did business with "the other side", thanks to his connections with the tram workers' (Sheinkinder, *Yad Vashem*, V, pp. 205, 207). He was the only Jew to work as a tram driver in Warsaw before the war.

33 Ringelblum lists the people killed on 12 May by name: 'Sklar, Fast, Sachs (a sportsman), and Tennenbaum' (*Ksovim*, I, p. 351).

34 On 5 May 1942, 2,500 Jews were deported from Dęblin. The 1,200 who remained were herded into a labour camp at the nearby airfield; the following day the Jews of Ryki were also deported to Sobibor; only 40 Jews remained. Both towns were in the Lublin district. On this, see M. Gilbert, *The Holocaust: The Jewish Tragedy* (London, 1986), pp. 336–7.

35 Record of this atrocity survives in another diary: 'Bearded Jews and smart young women were rounded up off the streets and taken to the baths in Dzielna Street, ordered to strip naked, paired up in all sorts of ridiculous ways, and told to dance; anyone who did not want to died a martyr's death. That's the story being told' (Sheinkinder, *Yad Vashem*, V, p. 208).

36 Kercelak Square – Warsaw's flea market, near the walls of the ghetto. The raid hit the Jews hard because much of what was confiscated were goods they had consigned for sale.

37 *Placówka* – in Polish, 'stop' or 'station'; here – places of work outside the ghetto. People working in *placówkarze* went out to work each day and returned to the ghetto in the evening, under guard. In mid-July 1942 there were 75 such places of work, including institutions of the *Wehrmacht*, the SS, and railway workshops, together employing more than 6,000 Jewish workers.

This outside work was considered among the most difficult and dangerous, jobs that offered the possibility of smuggling food and establishing contact with the outside world. On the forced labour of the Jews of Warsaw see T. Berenstein, 'Praca przymusowa Żydów w Warszawie' ('Forced labour of Jews in Warsaw'), *BŻIH*, 45–6.

38 Apparently Rabbi Shimon Huberband from Piotrków; he was in the Warsaw ghetto during the war. He was active in the Orthodox section of the Jewish Self-help Organization and one of the chief workers of Ringelblum's underground archive. On Huberband, see J. Kermish's Introduction in *To Live with Honor and Die with Honor* (Jerusalem, 1986), pp. xxviii–xxx.

39 On 22 Nov. 1939, 53 Jews, all of 9 Nalewki Street, were killed. This mass-execution was said to be a reprisal for the murder of one Polish policeman and the wounding of another. The Germans announced this publicly (in Warsaw and Kraków, but not in the newspapers of the Reich), in order to spread fear among the Jewish population. See *The Warsaw Diary of Chaim I. Kaplan*, trans. and ed. Abraham Katsch (New York, 1973), pp. 80, 82. This is the English version of *Megillat yisurin. Yoman Geto Varshe. (A Scroll of Agony: A Diary from the Warsaw Ghetto)* (Tel Aviv, 1966). Henceforth cited as Kaplan, *Warsaw Diary*. Gutman, *The Jews of Warsaw*, pp. 32–3.

40 In mid-Jan. 1940 some 100 Jewish intellectuals in Warsaw – doctors, lawyers, and teachers – were arrested and executed. The pretext for this was the activities of a man called Andrzej Kott in one of the Polish underground organizations. Rumour had it that Kott, a Christian by birth, had Jewish blood. The Germans were unable to arrest him, despite the price on his head; the *Judenrat* was thus ordered to hand him over, something which they had no power to do. (Ringelblum, *Ksovim*, I, pp. 232, 234). This atrocity is also reported at length by Kaplan, in *Warsaw Diary* (pp. 106–7), who estimates that the number killed reached several hundred.

41 Austria was annexed to the Reich in March 1938.

42 The fall of Kerch on 16 May 1942 completed the German conquest of the Crimean peninsula.

43 25 Aleja Sucha – the Gestapo headquarters in Warsaw. Like other German institutions, it employed Jewish slave-labour – in May 1942, 141 people.

44 Franz von Papen, a German politician, one of the leaders of the Catholic 'Centre Party', prime minister in 1932. Paved the way for Hitler's rise to power by assuring him of the support of leading economic figures. Hitler's deputy as prime minister. Often mentioned in connection with plans to establish a German government without Hitler.

45 From the beginning of 1942, certain employers stopped the practice of daily trips from the ghetto: henceforth the workers were held in labour camps near the factories and returned to the ghetto only on Saturdays.

46 After Maurycy Majzel, the chairman of the Jewish community council (*Kehilla*), left Warsaw (together with the heads of the Central Government in the capital), the Polish mayor, who had retained his position, appointed an engineer, Adam Czerniaków, as acting head of the Jewish community. After the occupation of Warsaw the Germans appointed Czerniaków head of the *Judenrat* (*Obmann des Judenrates*). The circumstances of the appointment are related in the memoirs of A. M. Hartglass in *Yediot Yad Vashem* (*Yad Vashem News*), 32. On Czerniaków's suicide see n. 156 below. Czerniaków left a diary: *The Warsaw Diary of Adam Czerniaków: Prelude to Doom* ed. Raul Hilberg, Stanislaw Staron and Josef Kermish (New York, 1979).

47 Just before the main deportation, the Germans took many photographs in the ghetto. It was said that they intended to produce a propaganda film which was to be called *Asia in the Heart of Europe*. On this see Yonas Turkau, *Azoy iz es geven - Hurban Varshe* (*This is How it Was - The Holocaust in Warsaw*) (Buenos Aires, 1948), p. 130. It was mostly a compendium of staged scenes set in the streets of the ghetto, in restaurants, and in places of entertainment, and shots of circumcision ceremonies, weddings, funerals, and so on. Its objective was to emphasize the Jews' utter baseness: the rich gorging themselves and having a good time while turning their backs on their brethren weak from hunger and totally ignoring their fate. Many of the cameramen were in the uniforms of the German airforce. The film-making is also recorded and commented on by other diarists.

The film in fact survived and was discovered in the state film archive in East Berlin. A copy is to be found in the archive of *Beit Lohamei Hagetaot*. See also n. 53 below.

48 Between 17 Mar. and 20 Apr. 1942, 30,000 Jews from Lublin were deported to Bełżec or taken to the outskirts of the city and shot; only a few thousand skilled workers remained, now herded into two labour camps in the city.

49 The streets mentioned here (Bagatela, Długa, Ujazdowskie) were in the fashionable part of Warsaw where there were many public gardens and avenues. The school at which Lewin taught was in the Jewish quarter, which did not have much in the way of public open space. In addition to teaching at the school, Lewin also served as its secretary.

50 Junaks – young people in uniform, mostly *Volksdeutsch*, Ukrainians and others who had been recruited by the Germans and served as a kind of auxiliary police. The name (meaning 'young warrior') was common in the para-military labour service in pre-war Poland.

51 A resort near Radom with a large Jewish population. They belonged to the Gnieszów community.

52 Dr Natan Eck, a well-known figure in the fields of education and self-help in the Warsaw ghetto, records: 'I myself saw the filming of a staged funeral, and the same day my friend Schnerson told me how he had been snatched off the street, taken into a restaurant and forced, together with others, to eat and drink till they vomited while living skeletons dying of starvation were made to stand opposite and watch their gluttony, and the bodies of dying people were placed by the door' (*Yad Vashem*, VI, p. 30).

53 A description of the filming is also given by Kaplan, who concludes his entry: 'This is the way of deceit, lies and falsehoods of Nazism. Nazis distort the truths of life, and the unfortunate Jews are forced to help them . . . All of these are segments of some anti-Semitic movie, which upon being spliced together will emerge as a gross falsification of the life of the Jews in the Warsaw ghetto' (*Warsaw Diary*, p. 336).

Even before the 'film craze' in the Warsaw ghetto, the German propaganda machine used films in order to 'justify' the policy of oppression and isolation towards the Jewish population; for example, a film was made in Lublin in the first months of the occupation showing Jews taunting German soldiers (Ringelblum, *Ksovim*, II, p. 259), while in Łódź the Germans filmed the deportation of the Jewish population to the ghetto and described it as an 'act of humanity' (ibid., I, p. 129).

54 Pinhas Szerman, second cantor in the Great Synagogue of Tłomackie Street, originally from Staszow, a pupil of A. B. Birnbaum. A similar incident is described in another testimony: 'Once the Germans came to the cemetery to film a funeral. They demanded a "ceremonial" funeral: a decorated wagon, horses in black livery, a cantor, a choir, and so on. If I am not mistaken, they chose old Serota as the cantor. The Germans filmed and filmed – and then left' (A. A. Carmi, *Yediot Yad Vashem*, 33, p. 33).

55 People holding such passports were ordered to present themselves in the Pawiak 'in order to undergo quarantine before their departure'. Only a few of them ever left the ghetto; most fell into the trap set for them by the Gestapo. Before the mass deportation all those holding such passports who had obeyed the authorities and presented themselves at the Pawiak were executed. They included public figures such as L. Neustadt, the director of the 'Joint' (the American Jewish Joint Distribution Committee) in Warsaw, and his wife, the actress Clara Segalowitz. Turkau, *Azoy iz es geven* pp. 140–50.

56 East Galicia (Western Ukraine, formerly the south-eastern part of Poland) was occupied by the Germans in July 1941 and annexed to the General-Government as a fifth district. As a result, its population rose to 16.8 million and its area was extended by 54,585 square miles.

57 Apparently a reference to Menahem-Mendel Kon, a friend of the diarist and a colleague in his work in the underground archive. On Kon, see J. Kermish's Introduction to the Israeli edition of material from this archive, *To Live with Honor and Die with Honor*, pp. xxix–xxx.

58 On 27-8 Apr. some 100 people were executed, mostly people active in the workers' movement. On 6 May members of the *Judenrat* were murdered in Tomaszów Mazowiecki together with intellectuals and community figures. Here too the number of victims reached about 100.

59 From 19 to 21 Apr. 1941 a major operation was conducted in the ghetto and thousands were sent to labour camps. Members of the community complained to the *Judenrat* that the people sent to the labour camps were those too poor to buy themselves out (Ringelblum, *Ksovim*, I, pp. 251ff). Even before 1940, according to Ringelblum, only the poor were sent to labour camps (ibid., p. 137).

The deportations to labour camps, with their terrible work regimes and living conditions, were one of the ways of destroying the fabric of Jewish life. Thousands of youths and young men were killed or crippled in these camps. Yitshak Zuckerman, who was arrested together with a group of pioneers in the manhunt of Passover 1941, published an account in the underground newspaper *Dror* (no. 13, Iyar-Sivan 1941) on such a labour camp in the Kampinos forest. The article, which appeared under the pen-name of A. Viltash, was reproduced in an anthology entitled *Tsvishen leben un tot (Between Life and Death)* (Warsaw, 1955).

60 This complaint is also voiced by Ringelblum (*Ksovim*, I, p. 370). He notes that to make themselves look better young girls would even steal from their parents.

61 In the spring of 1942, 3,872 Jews were brought to the ghetto from the territory of the Reich. The German Jews stood out in that they had to wear a yellow Star of David bearing the word *Jude* on their chests and backs, whereas the other Jewish inhabitants of the General-Government had to wear a white armband with a blue Star of David.

62 Abe Kahan – a writer and publicist in Yiddish and English, one of the architects of the Jewish labour movement in the United States. From 1903 on, for some 50 years or more, he was the editor of the Yiddish daily *Forverts*. His memoirs contain valuable historical material on the history of the Jewish community in the United States.

63 The Jewish Russian author Josef (Osip) Rabinowicz (1817–69) describes in one of his stories the ruses adopted by community leaders who did not fulfil their quota for recruitment to the Tsar's army. He concludes: 'What is a community leader like? A murderer or a saint: there is nothing in between.' Lewin quotes this story in his book *Kantanisten: vegn der Yidisher rekrutshina in Rusland in di tsaytn fun Tsar Nikolai der ershtn 1825-1856 (Cantonists: On Jewish recruitment in Russia in the reign of Nicholas I, 1825-1856)* (Warsaw, 1934), pp. 103ff.

64 Pierre Laval, French politician, served several times as minister and prime minister, including as prime minister of the Vichy regime. Collaborated with the Germans and after the war was sentenced to death as a traitor.

65 Alfred Hugenberg, a German politician and industrialist. Leader of the right-wing German National People's Party, close to Hitler, served as minister of the economy in 1933.

66 Rudolf Hess. From 1933, Hitler's deputy as party leader. Went to England on

10 May 1941 to hold political talks. Imprisoned for the rest of the war; sentenced to life imprisonment at the Nuremberg trials.

67 Ramon Serrano Suner, Franco's brother-in-law, minister of the interior, foreign minister from 1940 to 1942.

68 Erich Ludendorff (1865–1937), Field Marshal Hindenburg's chief of staff in World War I. From 1916 till the surrender he effectively directed Germany's military campaign: an extreme nationalist, one of Hitler's most enthusiastic supporters.

69 Prince Max of Baden, a liberal politician appointed in Oct. 1918 to head the government that was henceforth to be responsible not to the Kaiser but to Parliament, but this change was not sufficient to rescue the defeated Germans from absolute surrender to the Allies.

70 Similar opinions on the expected collapse of the German Reich were probably common in the diarist's circle. Ringelblum comments (*Ksovim*, I, p. 346): 'The opinion is seriously voiced that the situation in Germany indeed resembles that of 1918', and he cites much evidence in support of this view. Similarly, a manifesto calling for 'immediate struggle forthwith' published in *Dror*, a journal of the Zionist movement in the Warsaw ghetto underground, explained the intensification of German terrorism as evidence of the regime's awareness of the 'impending revolutionary torrent' that would wipe it off the face of the earth (*Yediot*, 25 May 1942), cited in Yitshak Zuckerman and Moshe Basuk (eds), *Sefer milkhamot hagetaot: Beyn hahomot, bemakhanot, beya'arot (The Book of the Ghetto: Between the Walls, in the Camps, in the Forests)* 3rd edn (Tel Aviv, 1957; henceforth *Sefer milkhamot*), p. 67.

71 Haim Henig, member of the Central Committee of the Po'alei Tsion-Left party and a regular contributor to its journals. One of the delegates to the 21st Zionist Congress in Geneva (16–25 Aug. 1939) who returned to Poland. Left Warsaw in May 1940. Settled in Israel.

72 Hirsch Wasser, one of the two secretaries of the secret archive in the ghetto, an active member of the Po'alei Tsion-Left in the underground and one of the organizers of the *Landsmannschaft* groups. He survived the war, and with his guidance the hiding place of the archive in Nowolipie Street was revealed. Settled in Israel.

73 Hanka Tauber, daughter of Dr M. Tauber. Her activities and those of her friend Rubinsztajn were discussed on 9 Apr.

74 *Morg* – a common unit of land measurement in Poland, equivalent to approximately 0.6 hectares.

75 Head of an administrative unit under the Germans. Responsible for the district.

76 Thanks to the assistance of Julek Brand, one of the most experienced commanders of Betar in Silesia and secretary of the *Judenrat* in Hrubieszów, in the summer and autumn of 1941 some 600 members of Betar left the Warsaw ghetto for Hrubieszów. Work was found for them, in small groups, on farms, which were then experiencing a severe shortage of labour, especially on the farm of Max Glazerman. The Betar groups kept working until the start of deportations in the region. Some of them took to the forests and set up partisan bands, but in

the end they too lost their lives. C. Lazar, *Metsada shel Varshe; Ha-Irgun hatsvay hayehudi bemered geto Varshe* (*The Masada of Warsaw: The Jewish National Movement in the Revolt of the Warsaw Ghetto*) (Tel Aviv, 1966), pp. 73–9.

77 The prison warders' unit was headed by Mrs Horowitz, a lawyer from Łódź. On the women warders in the Warsaw ghetto prison see Turkau, *Azoy iz es geven*, pp. 130, 180–94.

78 In Dec. 1941 an order was issued throughout the Reich to collect furs for the soldiers on the eastern front. The Jews in the area of the General-Government had to hand over all the fur garments in their possession. Czerniaków offered the governor of the Warsaw district a large quantity of new furs (which would not require disinfection and could therefore be dispatched to their destination immediately) in return for the release of Jews being held in prison. He purchased furs on the open market at a high price, and the 'furs for prisoners' deal got under way. The money was raised through a general fund-raising drive among the population of the ghetto.

Henryk Rosen, a member of the *Judenrat* in the ghetto; head of the Labour Department, his responsibilities included supplying slave-labour to meet the demands of German authorities and institutions. Shot by the Germans during the main 'selection' in the Miła Street area on 6 Sept. 1942.

79 From 1940 to the middle of 1944, Treblinka was also the location of the Treblinka 1 work-camp. This camp was used primarily for Poles but there were also some Jews. The inmates of this camp were employed in factories and in work in the fields. Most were murdered once they lost the strength to work.

80 The head of the Refugees Department in the *Judenrat*. Responsible for theatre-related activities. Later organizer of the police in the ghetto.

81 The Rubinsztajn family mentioned on 9 Apr.

82 The name used for the Gestapo unit set up in the ghetto in Nov. 1940 ostensibly as the Office to Combat Usury and Profiteering. Its offices were at 13 Leszno Street, and hence its name. Its director was Abraham Gancwajch. Associated with it there was a special police force with 300–400 Jewish policemen. The commander of this police force was David Szternfeld, Gancwajch's right-hand man. The 'Thirteen' supplied the Germans with information on the underground in the ghetto, on cultural activities, on the state of the economy there, and so on. For accounts of the 'Thirteen', see A. Rosenberg, 'Dos Dreitsentl' ('The Thirteen') *Beit Lohamei Hagetaot*, V, v. 1–2, Gutman, *The Jews of Warsaw*, pp. 90–4, and W. Weiss, 'Dreitsentl' ('The Thirteen'), *Yalkut Moreshet*, 21 (1976).

Of Gancwajch, Rachel Auerbach wrote in her diary, 'He is very concerned about finding alibis for the Jewish public bodies; he imposes his authority in particular on journalists, artists, and writers, and gave voice to his opinions in public at every opportunity' (*Warsaw*, II, p. 54).

83 In May 1942 groups of sick and retarded children were taken away from the Łódź ghetto to be killed. The main round-up of children took place only in Sept. of that year.

84 The hope that a second front would open in Europe was of course not to be fulfilled for more than another two years (June 1944), when the destruction of

European Jewry was almost completed. Typical of the mood at the time in the ghetto in this regard was the bitter joke recorded by Ringelblum (*Ksovim*, I, p. 35), to the effect that a German capitulation would be brought about in one of two ways: either a million seraphs would land on the territory of the Reich with flaming swords in their hands – that was the natural way; or a million Englishmen would invade conquered Europe – but that would be a miracle.

85 The new court-building at 56 Leszno Street, on the border of the ghetto. Access was permitted to anyone seeking the services of the court, and for some time it served as a meeting place between Jews and Poles. The entrance from the ghetto side was from Leszno Street, while the entrance for Poles was from Bielańska Street on the Aryan side.

86 The German tax office, whose staff were especially expert at stripping the Jews of their property through the tax system and special currency laws.

87 The accepted means of transport in occupied Warsaw and in the ghetto: a pedal tricycle with a seat for a passenger or a case for goods.

88 Jakub Tombeck, a doctor; married to Frume, Lewin's sister.

89 Dr Heinz Auerswald – originally, responsible for Jewish affairs in the Warsaw district administration; from 15 May 1941 to the eve of the main deportation he was Commissar of the Warsaw ghetto and responsible to the administrative authorities of the General-Government. One of the Nazi war criminals who was not brought to justice. On his activities, see Gutman, *The Jews of Warsaw*, pp. 98–101, 201–3.

90 The official name of the Jewish ghetto police (see n. 23). In the summer of 1942, the eve of the deportation, it numbered some 2,000 men.

91 A reference to *Nowy Kurier Warszawski*, a Polish-language newspaper licensed by the Occupation authorities and published in Warsaw. It was boycotted by the Polish patriots, who referred to it as *szmatławica* ('the rag') or *gadzinówka* ('the reptile press').

92 In Warsaw as elsewhere, the Germans also put Gypsies into the ghetto. They wore white armbands bearing the letter Z (for *Zigeuner*). They quickly disappeared from the ghetto, apparently having managed to escape. N. Eck, *Hatoim bedarkhey hamavet: Havey rehagut beyamey hakhilayon* (*Wanderers on the Paths of Death: Reflections on Life in Times of Annihilation*) (Jerusalem, 1970), p. 17.

In one entry Ringelblum relates that 240 Gypsies were placed in the ghetto, led by Kawik, who had been crowned king of the Gypsies a few years before the war. On the settling of several thousand Gypsies in the ghetto in June 1942, see Kaplan, *Warsaw Diary*, pp. 354–5.

93 Hitler's country residence was at Berchtesgaden. These two verses are also quoted verbatim in the underground newspaper *Yediot* of 25 May 1942.

94 Ringelblum's view of these rumours of Hitler's failures and of the disturbances in Germany was rather more sober. He ascribes them to 'unemployed journalists' who had to sell such wares in order to make a living. However, he also notes the increasing wave of optimism in the ghetto and the Jews' belief that the war would come to a speedy end (Ringelblum, *Ksovim*, I, p. 346).

95 A reference to the organized escape of two Polish reserve officers, Gomuliński and Szymański, in Mar. 1942. Both their admission to the hospital (ostensibly as typhoid patients) and their escape were executed with the assistance of the doctors. On this see B. Mark (ed.), *Tsum tsenten yartog fun oyfshtand in varshever getto. Dokumenten un materialen gezamelt un mit a forvort fun B. Mark (On the Tenth Anniversary of the Warsaw Ghetto Revolt: Documents and Materials Collected, with an Introduction by B. Mark)* (Warsaw, 1953), pp. 70–1.

96 Regina Judt had interests in a dance club in the ghetto and other entertainment outlets. Thanks to her contacts with the Germans she obtained a licence to operate a Yiddish theatre in the ghetto. Among its patrons were Warsaw's military commander, whom she had known since World War I. Turkau, *Azoy iz es geven*, pp. 206–8; Ringelblum, *Ksovim*, I, pp. 357–69.

97 This first deportation from Lwów lasted for more than two weeks (14 Mar.– 1 Apr. 1942) and encompassed some 15,000 Jews, mostly those without work permits. Those who were fit to work were sent to the Janowska camp; the others were sent to the death-camp at Bełżec. In May of the same year 9,000 of the Jews from Lwów in the Janowska camp were executed.

98 Once the Germans had taken eastern Galicia in July 1941 it was annexed to the General-Government as a fifth district (*Distrikt Galizien*). The deportation of the Jews of this region to Bełżec started in mid-Mar. 1942 and encompassed the communities of Lwów, Żółkiew, Drohobycz, Sambor, Tarnopol, Rawa Ruska, and Stanisławów. In the summer the responsibility for the Jews was transferred from the administrative authorities to the Gestapo, and by the end of July the systematic deportation to the death camps, district by district, was already under way. On this, see Gilbert, *The Holocaust*, pp. 302–20.

99 Eliyahu Gutkowski, a history teacher from Łódź. During the war he taught history in the Dror secondary school run by the Warsaw ghetto underground. He was among the organizers of the secret archive of the ghetto, one of its most important contributors and a member of its executive. Murdered in Apr. 1943.

100 A unit of the 'Organization Todt', which exploited the labour of millions of Germans and slave-labourers of the conquered races. Its chief activities were constructing fortifications, airfields, etc. Called after Fritz Todt, munitions minister in the Reich until 1942. The Jewish slave-labourers were executed in their thousands when the projects they were working on were completed.

101 The horse-drawn tramway company of the ghetto belonged to two partners, Moritz Kohn and Zelig Heller. Both were Gestapo agents. They were executed by the Germans in August 1942. On Kohn and Heller, see Gutman, *The Jews of Warsaw*, pp. 92–3 and Ringelblum, *Ksovim*, II, p. 14.

102 The Jewish Self-help Organization (Żydowska Samopomoc Społeczna) was set up during the siege of Warsaw in Sept. 1939 and reorganized in Jan. 1940. It covered the whole area of the General-Government and divided the ghetto into five action districts. The diarist was active in the second district. The Jewish Self-help Organization, which until the entry of the US into the war received funds from the Joint Distribution Committee, was the only Jewish organization to operate over the whole of the General-Government. In Oct. 1940, its name

was changed to Jewish Organization for Social Care (Żydowskie Towarzystwo Opieki Spolecznej – ŻTOS). On its activities, see Gutman, *The Jews of Warsaw*, pp. 40–5, 102–6. Michael Weichert, who headed the organization in Kraków, has written his memoirs, *Milkhama zikhronot* (*War Memoirs*) (Tel Aviv, 1963), as well as an account of the Self-help Organization: *Yidishe Alaynhilf (Jewish Self-help)* (Tel-Aviv, 1962). A sensitive account of the dilemmas of the organization is provided by Ringelblum, *Ksovim*, I, p. 365.

103 Abraham Gancwajch, a Gestapo agent, who headed the 'Thirteen' (see n. 82) was in Warsaw at the time. After the main 'action' he approached the Jewish Fighting Organization and offered to supply weapons for self-defence. Despite the attempts of the organization to find him, he succeeded in eluding them. He was active for some time on the Aryan side against the Polish underground, and then disappeared without trace. *Sefer milkhamot*, pp. 714–15.

104 At 84 Leszno Street, in the building formerly occupied by the Kolegium Secondary School, there was a branch of the German labour recruitment office. The work department of the *Judenrat* was next door.

105 The postcard bore the following message:

Liber Joysef.

Deine Karte hob ikh erhalten und mit bedoyrn gelesen dos krank varst. Vos mayne Perzon [anbelangt] bin ikh gezund und file mikh zer wohl. Ikh leide nikht mer an dos vos ikh mikh shtets beklagt [habe], aber bin one mittel un makhtloz dir tsu helfen. Trotsdem bin ikh im besten humor, do di zakhe mit der Pepi und Leah, vi oykh Rivke zer interesant virt . . . der herr Khazen hot zayne sheyne tenor-shtime ferlirt un zingt iberhoypt nikht mer. Zonst vays ikh nikht mer dir tsu zagen.

106 The last advance by the German–Italian forces in North Africa began on 26 May 1942. It was as a result of this that General Rommel reached El-Alamein (30 June).

Cologne was bombed on the last night of May. The town suffered heavy losses. More than 1,000 heavy bombers participated in the attack.

107 Reinhard Heydrich, head of the SD (the Reich's Intelligence Service). From September, Protector of Czechoslovakia and Moravia. On 27 May 1942 he was shot by the underground and died of his wounds a few days later. To commemorate him; the Germans called the operation to exterminate the Jews of Poland 'Einsatz Reinhard'.

108 Dr Michael Weichert, theatre producer and writer, president of the Jewish Self-help Organization; its director was Bakrakov. See n. 102.

The Jewish Fighting Organization accused Weichert of collaboration with the Germans on the grounds that his organization bolstered the illusion that the Jews were not being exterminated but simply held in camps. They sentenced him to death. The sentence was never carried out. Weichert's activities in this period are described in the report of the Jewish National Committee of 24 May 1944 in M. Niestat (ed.), *Hurban vemered shel yehudey Varshe: Sefer eduyot veazkarot (The Destruction and Revolt of the Jews of Warsaw: A Book of Testimonies and Memorials)*, 2nd edn (Tel Aviv, 1947), pp. 141–2 (henceforth Niestat, *Hurban vemered*) and in *Yediot Beit Lohamei Hagetaot*, 20: 2 (1954), p. 34. Dr Weichert died in Israel in 1967.

109 In the beginning of June the Jewish settlements in the Hrubieszów area suffered a wave of mass deportations. Some 10,000 Jews were herded into a transit camp near Hrubieszów, whence they were sent to the death-camp in Sobibor, a short distance away.

110 Łódź lay within the Warthegau area annexed to the Reich by an order signed by Hitler on 8 Oct. 1939. Warsaw came under the General-Government, the administrative unit that included the central parts of Poland – hence the 'border' between Łódź and Warsaw.

The Kohn–Heller Co. (see n. 101) used to smuggle Jews, for a high fee, from the Łódź ghetto, which was totally sealed off, to the Warsaw ghetto. Eck, *Hatoim bedarkhey hamavet*, p. 14.

111 The last Jews from Germany transported to Warsaw were settled in the Great Synagogue in Tłomackie Street, which was then outside the ghetto.

112 On the concerts of the Philharmonic Orchestra, which took place on Saturdays and Sundays at the Femina Theatre, on the ban on its performances for a period of two months, and on cultural activities in general in the ghetto, see Turkau, *Azoy iz es geven*, pp. 236–7.

113 The followers of Andrzej Towiański (1799–1878), the founder of a religious sect among the Polish emigrés in France. They believed that the oppressed Polish people would by their suffering save the world, seeing Poland as the 'Christ of Peoples'.

114 At the time that the diarist was recording these fears, Jews were in fact no longer to be found in these places.

The deportation from Gostynin to Chelmno took place in Apr. 1942. The deportation from Włocławek took place between 30 Apr. and 2 May.

115 In fact, the honey substitute produced in the ghetto.

116 A reference to the weekly meetings of the workers of the secret archive established by the historian Dr Emanuel Ringelblum, which were held on Saturdays and referred to as the *Oneg Shabbes* group. *Oneg Shabbes* was directed by a scientific-organizational advisory board and had many active supporters – public figures, teachers, writers, rabbis and ordinary people. Lewin was a member of the *Oneg Shabbes* directorate. For a detailed description of the activities, contributors and operation of the archive written by Ringelblum himself see Ringelblum, *Ksovim*, II, pp. 76–102. The activity of the *Oneg Shabbes* is described in detail in J. Kermish's Introduction to the Israeli edition of selected documents from its archive, *To Live with Honor and Die with Honor* (Jerusalem, 1986).

117 Dr Aharon Solovietchik, a public figure and well-known doctor who headed the surgical department in the Jewish hospital in Warsaw, spent a number of months in Lida at the house of Dr Maisnik, his student and assistant before the war. He continued his work as a doctor even in the conditions of the ghetto. Died in the Warsaw ghetto at the end of Oct. 1942.

118 Another testimony on the 'action' in Pabianice was recorded by Rachel

Auerbach: 'The under-10s and the over 60s were shot; all the others had to submit to the "selection" process ... the able-bodied were sent to work, while those who were unable to work or weak were taken out of the town and machine-gunned by open pits' (*Be-Huzot Varshe*, II, p. 650). A survivor describes this incident in the liquidation of the ghetto in the following words: 'On Saturday 16 May 1942 at 4.00 p.m. Hitler's jackbooted soldiers came and dragged us out of our houses. They lined us up in fours and took us off to the square by the Krushe–Andar works. There they split us up – healthy men and women together, and the old, the sick, and the children together. The healthy were sent to the Łódź ghetto, the old, the sick, and the children – to be exterminated at Chelmno.' *Sefer Pabianits* (*The Book of Pabianice*) (Tel Aviv, 1956), pp. 323–4.

119　At the end of 1941, 1,200 Jews from Ciechanów were sent to the nearby village of Nowe Miasto, where they were put into a sealed ghetto. The conditions and regime there were much more rigorous than in Chiechanów itself, where the Jews were less isolated from the general population. The ghetto in Ciechanów was finally liquidated in Nov. 1942.

120　Number 6 of *Yediot*, the underground newspaper of the Dror movement in the Warsaw ghetto (9 June 1942), carried the following description of the hanging of the 10 people in Zduńska Wola: 'After the German hangmen hanged 10 Jews on Purim 1942, they repeated the atrocious performance on the eve of Shavuot. They erected gallows, chose their 10 victims, and terrified the entire population of Zduńska Wola into watching the performance. Among those sentenced to death was a *Hasid*, an ordinary Jew, Shlomo Zhelokhovski, who raised the spirits of all the Jews unwillingly gathered there by forbidding them to mourn and permeating his words with confidence. He saw it as an honour to sacrifice himself on the altar of his people. He went the whole tortured route singing, never letting his spirit flag.' This account inspired Yitshak Katznelson to write his poem 'Dos Lid vegn Shlomo Zhelokhovski' ('A Poem about Shlomo Zhelokhovski'), published in a Hebrew translation by M. Z. Wolpowski in *Katavim aharonim, 1940-1944* (*Last Writings*) (Kibbutz Hameuchad – *Beit Lohamei Hagetaot*, 1956), pp. 52–8. See also the version in the later edition by Y. Szteintuch: Y. Katznelson, *Yidishe geto-ksovim: Varshe 1940-43* (*Yiddish Ghetto Writings: Warsaw 1940-43*) (Kibbutz Lohamei Hagetaot and Kibbutz Hemeuchad, 1984). According to survivors from Pabianice, Shlomo Zhelokhovski came from that town.

121　On 1 June almost 2,000 Jews were deported from Kraków to the death-camp at Bełżec. Among those deported then were Dr Artur Rosenzweig, head of the *Judenrat*, and his family.

122　The story of the life and death of the Radzyner rebbe (Hasidic rabbi), Shlomo Layner, was the inspiration for Yitshak Katznelson's poem 'Dos lid vegn Radziner ('The Song of the Radzyner Rebbe'), which was written in the Warsaw ghetto between Nov. 1942 and Jan. 1943 and published in the original and in a Hebrew translation by M. Z. Wolpowski in *Katavim aharonim*; according to *Yediot*, 5 (2 June 1942), 'In the second half of May 1942 the Gestapo instigated a massacre in Włodawa. More than a hundred Jews were murdered, among them the Radzyner rabbi and the local rabbi. A story of martyrdom has emerged: a young Jew was asked by the murderers where the rabbi was to be found; in order to save the rabbi's life, he indicated that it was he they were looking for. He was shot on the spot.' See also *Katavim aharonim*, pp. 450, 451, and also N. Blumenthal in *Yediot Beit Lohamei Hagetaot*, 8 (1955).

123 The day of the mass departure from the Polish capital following an announcement broadcast on Radio Warsaw calling to all men of military age to leave the city and make their way east. Some hold that this was a work of treachery inspired by the Germans.

124 This opinion was shared by Yitshak Katznelson: 'In this they [the Germans] succeeded ... they managed to deceive the majority of the Polish people through hate, murder, deeds of abomination, and scheming plots that persuaded them to believe what every Pole ... knew were bare-faced lies' (*Katavim aharonim*, p. 185).

125 Ringelblum also reaches the conclusion that 'co-operation between smugglers on both sides of the wall is one of the finest of all stories in the history of the relations between Poles and Jews during the Second World War' (Ringelblum, *Ksovim*, II, p. 274).

126 A reference to the pogrom against the underground (see n. 29).

127 The communal kitchens were one of the most important forms of mutual aid in the Warsaw ghetto. The 80 such kitchens that operated in the ghetto supplied more than 100,000 portions of soup (*zupkes*) a day for the starving population.

128 The Second Jewish Anti-Fascist Congress in the Soviet Union took place on 24 May 1942. The congress issued an emotional call to the Jews of the world to 'intensify the war against the hangmen and pogromists who have drenched thousands of cities and villages with the blood of our people'. Among those who spoke at the Congress were S. Michoels, Shakhna Epstein, D. Bergelson, A. Kushnirov, and Colonel Faivel Michlin. See 'Tsweyter, anti-fashistisher miting fun di forstekher funm yidishen folk', *Emes* (1942), quoted in *Yad Vashem Studies*, VI, pp. 324–5.

129 Aharon Kushnirov (1890–1949), a Soviet Jewish poet and raconteur. Joined the army on the outbreak of war; earned military decorations. A member of the editorial board of *Eynikhkeit*, the organ of the Jewish anti-Fascist committee in Moscow.

130 The Jews' name for a German gendarme renowned for his cruelty and thirst for Jewish blood. Descriptions of him are to be found in many memoirs.

131 In its economic activity the ghetto tried to accommodate itself to the abnormal conditions of the cruel regime of deprivation and starvation. In addition to smuggling provisions into the ghetto, the Jews set up workshops to manufacture food products, including illicit flour mills.

132 SA: *Sturm-Abteilungen*, the storm troops of the Nazi Party. SS: *Schutz-Staffeln*, the crack defence troops of the Nazi Party, groomed as a racially and ideologically elite corps.

133 A workers' district in Berlin.

134 The author of an extensive survey of smuggling in the ghetto (drawn up secretly in Warsaw in 1943) comes to the conclusion that 'the role of the smugglers in the struggle against the evil plan of the Occupation authorities to starve the Jewish population was so great that they deserve to be placed in the first rank of those who fought the tyrant' (M. Passenstein, 'Szmugiel w getcie warszaw-skim', *BŻIH*, 26, pp. 42–72). Henryka Lazowert's poem in Polish, 'The Little Smuggler' was widely read at gatherings in the ghetto. It was described by Ringelblum as 'a song in praise of the thousands of children who endangered themselves countless numbers of times in order to sustain their families and the community as a whole' (*Ksovim*, II, p. 196). Its last verse reads:

> I shall not return to you again
> No more than a voice from afar,
> The dust in the street is my grave
> An infant's fate is sealed
> And on my lips alone
> A single care is frozen
> Who, my soul's delight,
> Will bring you a crust tomorrow?

Rachel Auerbach also accords 'a place of honour to Jewish and Polish smug-glers alike ... for their persistence and bravery in the on-going battle between unequal parties ... honour to the unknown smuggler, the grey soldier on the walls of the besieged city' (*Be-Huzot Varshe*, II, p. 658).

135 The deportation from Tłuszcz to Warsaw (a distance of some 60 miles) took place on 26 May 1942, as mentioned in the diary for 3 June. On the terrible journey that the deportees underwent and the brutality that accompanied it see Auerbach, *Be-Huzot Varshe*, II, p. 667; Kaplan, *Warsaw Diary*, p. 507.

Part II Diary of the Great Deportation

136 One of the main streets of Warsaw. These notes, made by Lewin on 20 July just before the start of the great deportation, were never fully written up and testify to his anguish of spirit in the face of the great catastrophe confronting Warsaw Jewry. It is at this stage that he switches from Yiddish to Hebrew.

137 The porter of this house was put to death because he would not reveal the supposed hiding place of a young man being pursued by a German gendarme. Kaplan, *Warsaw Diary*, p. 379.

138 21 July.

139 A Jewish policeman who was killed on the same day. The murder is recorded in Kaplan, *Warsaw Diary*, pp. 378–9. According to the memoirs of an anonymous police officer, between 20 and 30 members of the Jewish police were murdered or deported for refusing to participate in the round-up. Gutman, *The Jews of Warsaw*, p. 447.

140 Apparently Dr Zygmunt Steinkalk, a well-known Warsaw paediatrician;

murdered by the Germans on 21 July 1942 at the entrance to 26 Karmelicka Street, Kaplan, *Warsaw Diary*, p. 378. Yitshak Katznelson was also an eyewitness to the murder (*Katavim aharonim*, p. 194).

141 Zaklad Zaopatrzenia (Supply Office), the supply institution of the ghetto, under the supervision of the *Judenrat*. Set up on 1 Aug. 1941, its functions were the acquisition and distribution of food as well as the importation of other essential goods. In spite of its sensitive function it enjoyed more confidence among the ghetto population than any other institution of the *Judenrat*. This was mainly because of the effectiveness and impartiality of its head, the veteran businessman Abraham Gepner. On this see Gutman, *The Jews of Warsaw*, pp. 85–6.

142 The same day some 60 members of the *Judenrat* and the intellectuals of the ghetto were arrested as hostages. The arrests were accompanied by murders in the streets.

143 Perhaps Shmuel Breslaw, a member of the Anti-Fascist Bloc and Hashomer Hatsair activist. Murdered by the Gestapo in the Pawiak.

144 The first day of the massive deportation. The orders for the deportation had been dictated in the morning at a meeting of the *Judenrat* by the SS officer who headed the deportation staff. Czerniaków has described this in his *Diary*, p. 385. For the full text of the announcement see *BŻIH*, 1, pp. 65–6.

145 A shelter for refugees, deportees from elsewhere who were resettled in the Warsaw ghetto: 'points', a literal translation of the Polish *punkty*, here meaning depot, assembly point. For the most part these were miserable refugees, with great numbers of sick and starving people concentrated at terrible density. The mortality in such places was extremely high, in some cases as much as 30 per cent. J. Kermish, 'Class Distinctions in the Warsaw Ghetto', in Grunbaum (ed.), *Entsiklopedia shel galuyot*, vol. II, entry under Warsaw.

146 With the establishment of the ghetto, the hospital – one of the most impressive institutions of the Warsaw Jewish community – was transferred from its premises in the suburb of Czyste to Czysta Street near the *Umschlagplatz*. With the beginning of the deportation the hospitals were used as assembly points and the patients, 761 in number, were transferred to improvised hospitals. In the final stage of the deportation, on 12 Sept. 1942, the hospital was completely destroyed and the patients and the medical team, some 1,000 people in all, were deported to Treblinka.

147 Even for those with exemptions from the deportation order, the exemption only covered wives and children and did not extend to aged parents. The problem facing the diarist and his family preoccupied many others. A similar situation is described in M. Shereshevska, *Haperek ha-aharon: Zikhronot migeto Varshe* (*The Final Chapter: Memoirs from the Warsaw Ghetto*) (Tel Aviv, 1968), p. 17. Under the heading 'Tragedy of Parents', Ringelblum records that 'children poisoned their parents; children went together with their parents to the *Umschlagplatz*; children sacrificed themselves in order to save their parents' (*Ksovim*, II, p. 23).

148 Ora – the diarist's daughter – who was fourteen. The sentence is unclear.

Literally it reads 'Ora – shotzia, fabricated stories'. 'Shotzia' is perhaps a reference to the false information coming from Sweden (*Szwecja* in Polish) to the effect that the end of the war was approaching, as related above.

149 The 'Aryan' Chłodna Street cut the ghetto into two parts, a northern sector (the 'main ghetto') and a southern sector (the 'small ghetto'), which occupied approximately 23 per cent of the area of the ghetto. Between the two ghettos there is an alleyway, at the corner of Żelazna and Chłodna Streets. Eventually a wooden bridge was constructed over Chłodna Street. The small ghetto was liquidated completely during the deportation of Aug. 1942.

150 Uri Tombeck, the diarist's nephew.

151 Even in the darkest days of the deportation the diarist continued to record the information reaching him on deportations and murders in other places. Garbatko – a resort near Radom.

152 The main 'action' in Warsaw was carried out in the form of a siege or 'blockade', first on individual houses and later on streets and entire neighbourhoods. In the initial stage, the deportation was carried out entirely by the ghetto police. The historians of the Warsaw ghetto have left us many descriptions of atrocities committed at the time of the blockades. On this see Gutman, *The Jews of Warsaw*, pp. 203–18.

153 A tram still traversed the ghetto but the route was short: from Żelazna Street via Leszno and Karmelicka Street to Dzika Street. It stopped running on 15 Aug., when the deportation intensified.

154 A reference to the bombing at the time of the German siege in Sept. 1939. The Jewish neighbourhoods in Warsaw were shelled heavily during the Jewish New Year.

155 The Staff of the *Judenrat* and its associated bodies were ordered to assist the Jewish police in carrying out the deportation order. They were supplied with special armbands bearing the symbol of the *Judenrat*, a serial number and an appropriate caption in German. In contravention of this order, the community institutions forbade their staff to assist in the deportation.

156 On the second day of the deportation, 23 July, at 8.30 p.m., the chairman of the *Judenrat* killed himself by taking poison. He did this after the Germans had informed him that the daily deportation quota was to be increased. For a detailed account of how this action was assessed by various groups in the ghetto, see the appendices to Y. Gutman, 'Czerniaków – Haish ve-hayoman' ('Czerniaków, the man and the diary'), *Yalkut Moreshet*, 10, pp. 115–44.

The *Report* of the Jewish underground (15 Nov. 1942), which was sent to London, was very critical of Czerniaków for not warning the public and not making them aware of the Germans' plan to completely destroy the ghetto (p. 7). Perla writes in a similar vein: 'He [Czerniaków] had neither the strength nor the courage to say before he died: "Defend yourselves, don't let yourselves be slaughtered" – [and thus it happened] that 300,000 Jews went to the slaughter like a flock of sheep.' Y. Perla, 'Hurban Varshe' ('The destruction of Warsaw') in B. Mark (ed.) *Tsvishn lebn un tot: Literarishe shafungen in di getos un lagern* (*Between Life and Death: Literary Creativity in the Ghettos and Camps*) (Warsaw,

1955), p. 140. However, Professor Arie Tartakower considers this accusation unrealistic and an injustice to the man 'who made a supreme effort to achieve even a slight lessening of the tribulations of his people'. He concludes his article by saying: 'If a pantheon of the nation should ever be established, Czerniaków's picture deserves to take its place alongside those of the freedom fighters of the ghetto' (*Yad Vashem*, 35).

Mention should also be made of Kaplan's opinion that Czerniaków 'may not have lived his life with honour but he did die with honour. Some merit paradise by the deeds of an hour but President Adam Czerniaków earned his right to paradise in a single moment' (Kaplan, *Diary*, p. 385). (I have not followed the English translation here, since it does not give the true sense of what Kaplan wrote. See the Hebrew text, p. 548.) The writer mentions that Czerniaków refused to sign the deportation order, which was therefore signed, irregularly, merely 'The Jewish Council' (ibid., p. 384). The Pole who signed himself M. B. (Antoni Szymonowski), author of the report on 'The Destruction of the Warsaw Ghetto', wrote: 'I feel a great sense of honour towards this death. They intended to make him the instrument of destruction of his own people; in his powerlessness he saw this as the only alternative, as an honourable and proud act' (*Sefer milkhamot*, p. 72).

157 This is apparently a reference to a party held in the community-building in 26 Grzybowska Street some 10 days before the deportation to mark the birthday of Abraham Gepner, a man who had long been a leading figure in the community and was head of the supply institution of the ghetto. (See n. 141.)

A slightly different version, equally typical of the mood of the chairman at that time, was recorded by Perets Opoczynski. 'Last week Czerniaków stalked around his office, clearly in a rage. A woman approached him and advised him to put a scarf round his neck because he had a cold. Czerniaków responded, "What are you afraid of, madam, I'll die anyway."' Unpublished diary in *Yad Vashem* archives. Entry for 12 July.

158 Guta, the diarist's young sister. Fictitious marriages between brothers and sisters were not unknown; see Shereshevska, *Haperek ha-aharon*, p. 150 (see n. 147). Ringelblum also records the wave of fictitious weddings; he notes that the rabbis permitted themselves to give out the *ketubot* (marriage contracts) without seeing the couple face to face (Ringelblum, *Ksovim*, II, p. 30).

159 On this topic Ringelblum notes: 'The Jewish police were known for their terrible corruption, but they reached the apogee of depravity at the time of the deportation' (*Ksovim*, II, p. 31). Among those complaining most strongly about the ghetto police and the moral decline was Yitshak Katznelson: 'Our police [force] is an ugly creature which oppresses us like the Tsar or cruellest enemy' (*Katavim aharonim*, p. 197). See Gutman, *The Jews of Warsaw*, pp. 207–11.

160 Fritz Schultz, a German industrialist, owner of one of the largest workshops in the Warsaw ghetto. The workshop owners made a great deal of money from the plight of the Jews. They stole their possessions, exploited their labour, sold jobs in their factories at extortionate prices, and co-operated with the Gestapo in deporting them from the ghetto.

161 Żydowskie Towarzystwo Opieki Społecznej, the official name of the Jewish Self-help Organization, see nn. 102 and 108. Of all the institutions in the ghetto, it had most successfully maintained its independence, operated many social welfare programmes and served as a cover for many underground operations. In accordance with the deportation order of 22 July, its workers were exempt from deportation, and in fact in the first days of the deportation possession of work-papers from this institution did constitute some immunity.

162 That is, is there no danger of being ambushed here? Is the street blockaded?

163 *Umschlagplatz*: a square on the outskirts of the ghetto, on Stawki Street, by the railway sidings. In this square, which had previously been used for the handling of merchandise, and the adjacent buildings the Jews were assembled before being shipped off to Treblinka. Only a few of those brought to the *Umschlagplatz* ever succeeded, by trickery or bribery, in returning to the ghetto.

164 Even in the first days of the deportation, exemptions extended only to the wives and children of those who held them (including people in the Jewish police), not to parents. See n. 147.

165 The chairman of the *Judenrat* was required to deliver 7,000 Jews for deportation on 22 July, and on the following day 10,000. This was the reason for Czerniaków's suicide.

   Yitshak Katznelson dedicates the fifth section of his elegy 'A Song for the Murdered Jewish People' to 'A Meeting in the Community with respect to the Ten'. The poet rails against the chairman of the *Judenrat*: 'Is it the ten that is important to you? To six you would agree?' (*Katavim aharonim*, pp. 399–400).

166 Among those who killed themselves were many members of the intelligentsia. At the time of the deportation, 'hundreds of cases of suicide were recorded, particularly among professional people. The intellectuals used to walk around with a phial of a drug such as potassium cyanide or Luminal on them' (Ringelblum, *Ksovim*, II, p. 54).

167 This number is consistent with the German figures, which state that in the first four days of the campaign 29,078 people were 'deported'.

168 The report of the Jewish underground mentions another factor: there were cases of people volunteering for deportation in order to be reunited with members of their family who had been deported earlier: 'Every day one can see children aged 8, 10 or 12 walking in the direction of the *Umschlag* in order to travel with their parents.' Quoted in *Likwidacja żydowskiej Warszawy: Według oficjalnych dokumentów otrzymanych przez Reprezentacja Żydostwa Polskiego, Październik 1943, Tel Aviv* (*The Liquidation of Warsaw Jewry According to Official Documents Obtained in October 1943 by the Representative Body of Polish Jewry in Tel Aviv*) (Tel Aviv, 1943), p. 10. (Henceforth, *Likwidacja żydowskiej Warszawy.*)

   In his review of the establishment of the Jewish Fighting Organization, Yitshak Zuckerman writes: 'Moreover, they would present themselves of their own free will for a "voyage of migration". Where to? Letters used to arrive from the towns of Bessarabia, Smolensk and Minsk saying that the migrants had arrived safely and were satisfied. Of course, this was a German ruse. And thus the Jews would travel to foreign parts – to "agricultural work"' (Niestat, *Hurban vemered*, p. 96).

Ringelblum assumes that the number of those arriving at the *Umschlagplatz* of their own free will was as many as 20,000. (*Ksovim*, II, p. 13).

169 After Czerniaków's death the *Judenrat* issued a proclamation (on the basis of promises by Gestapo officers) refuting the rumours circulating in the ghetto and appealing to the population not to hide but to present themselves for deportation. The proclamation stressed that the evacuation was aimed only at those who were not productive, and that the evacuees were indeed being sent to the borderlands of the east. A Hebrew translation of the proclamation is to be found in Niestat, *Hurban vemered*, p. 54.

In order to strengthen the belief in this promise, at the start of the deportation the policeman used to make a point of releasing those who were employed in workshops and institutions.

170 *Gazeta Żydowska*, a Polish-language 'Jewish' newspaper published in Kraków two or three times a week with the permission of the German authorities.

171 The diarist renders the German *Aktion* into Hebrew as 'מִפְעָל' literally the 'undertaking' or 'project'. In reality it meant deportation to a death-camp.

172 Israel Winnik, active in the Bund after the war, one of the young writers of the ghetto, organizer of the underground archive of the Bund in the ghetto; prepared a survey of the *punktim*, the assembly points for refugees in the ghetto. Killed during the deportation.

173 Through a rumour originated by the Gestapo, word spread in the ghetto that letters were arriving from people from Warsaw deported to the east (Brześć, Białystok, Pinsk) with news of good conditions in the areas in which they had been resettled.

174 As of 23 July 1942, all postal links between the ghetto and the outside world ceased; the post office at 19 Zamenhof Street was closed the next day. On 29 July, however, the delivery of post addressed to the ghetto was renewed (as noted in the entry for 30 July), but the ban on sending letters from the ghetto continued. 'All outgoing post and all post for inhabitants of the ghetto who had been deported were handed over to the authorities' (*Likwidacja żydowskiej Warszawy*, app. 10, p. 36).

175 Aharon Libuszycki, Jewish writer and teacher, came to Warsaw from Łódź; M. Lejzerowicz, one of the editors of the Yiddish-language daily *Haynt*. Both lost their lives in the deportation.

176 Other diarists voiced similar condemnations of the ghetto police, 'filling their pockets with gold', who released some of those arrested in return for money (see Kaplan, *Warsaw Diary*, pp. 386, 389; Ringelblum *Ksovim*, II, pp. 10, 12, 13). Katznelson terms them the 'shame of creation, the decomposing rat floating on the surface of the swamp' (*Katavim aharonim*, p. 81).

177 Yakir Warszawski, writer and Hebrew teacher, a friend of the diarist. Died in the ghetto. The author writes of him again, at length, on 30 Nov.

178 At the beginning of the deportation the Germans let it be known that the intention was to deport non-productive people, while those employed in a German *shop* (workshop) would be allowed to stay in the ghetto. Hence *shopomania* – the blind race for employment in a workshop as security against deportation; *shopovatzim* – people employed in workshops.

179 After Czerniaków's death, an engineer by the name of Marc Lichtenbaum was appointed head of the *Judenrat*. His deputies were Dr Gustaw Wielikowski and Alfred Sztolcman. Collaborators with the Germans and staunch opponents of the underground, all three were murdered by the Germans when the uprising broke out in Apr. 1943. Orliański was probably Mścisław Orliański, one of the senior *Judenrat* officials and head of the Industrial Department.

180 Throughout 1941 and in the first months of 1942, food parcels continued to reach the ghetto from provincial towns in the General-Government as well as from abroad. These parcels were an important source of sustenance for many families in the ghetto. In the summer of 1942 the German authorities frequently confiscated them, on the pretext of a war against smuggling, although before they did so they would make the clerks in the Jewish post office sign that they had received the parcel. On the eve of the massive deportation some 2,000 parcels were reaching the ghetto daily. It is known that the postal workers 'not infrequently worked overtime in order to deliver parcels immediately they arrived so as to pre-empt the greedy Germans' (Eck, *Hatoim bedarkhey hamavet*). The archive of *Beit Lohamei Hagetaot* has several receipts for parcels delivered to the ghetto.

181 In the first stage of the deportation the Germans used to kill the old and the sick to reinforce the impression that the other deportees really were being taken to work in the east. The execution took place on the spot, in the *Umschlagplatz* or the Jewish cemetery. (Testimony of Yitshak Zuckerman at the Eichmann trial.)

182 A reference to Odilo Globocnik, head of the SS and the police in the Lublin district; directed the operation to destroy the Jews in the General-Government.

183 According to one witness, who wrote under the name of Tsvia: 'They came with "reliable" information from the community or from the Germans that the "action" would be stopping on such and such a date. They would take out only 50,000, then they brought it up to 70,000, and finally 100,000, and the "action" would stop . . .' in D. Gutsfrukht, H. Hadari, and A. Raykhman (eds), *Biyamey khilayon vemered. Sefer 'Dror' (Annihilation and Revolt. The Book of the Zionist group 'Dror')* (Kibbutz Hameuchad, 1952), p. 473.

Grochów, Pelcowizna – small towns near Warsaw on the east bank of the Vistula.

184 With the start of the deportation command over the ghetto passed to the SS. Auerswald, the Ghetto Commissar, retained nominal control and up to the last minute assured Czerniaków that rumours of an impending deportation were false. This, of course, was merely a ruse to facilitate the Nazis' murderous plans.

See Czerniaków, *Diary*, p. 384 and Gutman, *The Jews of Warsaw*, pp. 201–4.

185 Leon Neustadt, one of the directors of the 'Joint' in Warsaw: as the holder of a South American passport he presented himself at the Pawiak at the beginning of the deportation and was shot. See also n. 425.

186 With the growing wave of rumours about the approaching deportation, some of the wealthier families left the ghetto for places in the vicinity of the city, mainly Otwock; within a short time the deportation orders reached these places too.

187 Apparently the family of Rozencwajg, a poet and Hebrew teacher. Yitshak Katznelson writes: 'Here lived Yehiel Rozencwajg, his wife and son, his aged father-in-law, his two brothers-in-law, his sisters-in-law and their children. They were all sent to Treblinka' (*Katavim aharonim*, p. 199).

188 The mother of Leib Gruzalc, a member of the Bund youth movement, Tsukunft, and a commander of one of the fighting groups during the uprising.

189 Walter Caspar Többens, a German industrialist, owner of the largest work-shops in the Warsaw ghetto. Made a great deal of money from exploiting the cheap labour of his Jewish employees. After the revolt of Jan. 1943 he was made responsible for the evacuation of the ghetto and the transfer of the factories, together with their equipment and workers, to the Poniatowo and Trawniki labour camps. He was prevented from fulfilling this task by the Jewish Fighting Organization.

190 Here and below the reference is apparently to Menahem-Mendel Kon, a public figure, one of the moving spirits behind the Jewish underground. A colleague of the diarist in the secret archive. See also n. 57.

191 Ringelblum blames the leaders of the *Judenrat* and the commanders of the Jewish police for the attempt to close down the Self-help Organization at the time of the deportation because of its opposition to 'the deception of the community'. Even though in theory those working for the organization were exempt from deportation, the Jewish police were secretly instructed to ignore their papers (Ringelblum, *Ksovim*, II, p. 63).

192 Józef Szeryński, commander of the ghetto police. A convert to Catholicism. Before the war, a colonel in the Polish police. On Szeryński, see Gutman, *The Jews of Warsaw*, pp. 88–90.

193 The Jewish police in the ghetto included a women's unit which was headed by Mrs Horowitz, a lawyer from Łódź. The policewomen were posted, together with their male colleagues, by the gates of the ghetto, and their job was to search the women coming through. Sometimes they also used to direct the traffic in the streets of the ghetto. The female warders in the Jewish prison in the ghetto belonged to the same unit.

194 Owners of sewing-machines tried to get themselves into the existing work-shops or those that were set up at the time of the deportation.

195 Bełżec – a death-camp in the Lublin district. Operated from Mar. 1942 to June 1943. Piaseczno, Pustelnik – settlements in the Warsaw district, close to the capital.

196 See n. 116.

197 Yidishe Visenshaftlikher Organizatsie, the Jewish Scientific Institute,

established in Vilno in 1925; after the outbreak of war its offices were transferred to New York.

198 Apparently a reference to two colleagues of the diarist at *Oneg Shabbes*. Eliyahu
Gutkowski and Menahem-Mendel Kon. On Kon, see nn. 57 and 190.

199 The commander of the ghetto police announced that people presenting themselves at the *Umschlagplatz* of their own free will on the 29, 30 and 31 July would
receive 3 kg of bread and 1 kg of jam – a strong temptation to the starving inhabitants of the ghetto. The proclamation was issued again on 1 Aug. and the
offer extended for a further three days. See also the entry for 2 Aug. For the text
of the announcement see *Likwidacja żdowskiej Warszawy*, p. 25.

200 Lewin uses the word 'Shopomania'; –שפמניה– to refer to the panic to obtain
work in one of the German workshops. The illusion that people employed in
the workshops were immune from deportation was carefully maintained by the
Germans. Katznelson regarded these workshops as 'mined booby-traps for
Jews' and as 'explicit addresses for the murderers of the SS – here they could
just stretch out a hand and pluck Jews off the shelves' (*Katavim aharonim*,
p. 215).

201 Megaphones were installed in the streets of Warsaw to broadcast German
propaganda. The inhabitants ridiculed these broadcasts and regarded the
official pronouncements with great scepticism.

202 Apparently a reference to an event that occurred at a place of work outside the
ghetto. The name 'Warsaw-Praga' refers to the railway station in Praga, to the
east of Warsaw, across the Vistula; at that time the railway workshops were
employing many Jewish slave-labourers.

203 That is, the victims murdered there were 1 per cent of all those deported in the
'action'.

204 Apparently Obersturmführer Witossek, responsible for Jewish Affairs in the
Ministry of Defence.

205 On receiving this false promise the *Judenrat* issued a comforting pronounce-
ment: see n. 169. We likewise read in Hirsch Berlinski's diary: 'Two SS officers
gave their word as officers that not one of the deportees was sent to their death.'
Reprinted in *Drei: Andenkbukh* (*Three: A Memorial Book*) (Tel Aviv, 1966),
p. 161.

206 Michael Brandstetter, an experienced teacher and educationist, son of the
writer M. D. Brandstetter; before the war, headmaster of the Jewish secondary
school for girls in Łódź. In the Warsaw ghetto worked in the social assistance
organization and as a teacher at the underground Jewish secondary school. Shot
in the first uprising (Jan. 1943).

207 Klima (real name Bluma) Fusverg, teacher, director of the puppet theatre in the
ghetto; later served as the contact of the Jewish National Committee on the
Aryan side; among the survivors.

208 Untersturmführer Karl Georg Brandt, SS officer, among those responsible
(together with Witossek) in the Jewish Department IV-B-4 in the Warsaw
Gestapo. Took an active part in the destruction of the Jews.
    Katznelson describes how he met Brandt coming out of the community-

building: 'This Brandt – I saw him and didn't see him. A waiter, they say. Serves beer to drunk Germans. Ugly face, fat and pale' (*Katavim aharonim* 1, p. 213).

209 A reference to Herman Höfle, Globocnik's chief of staff. Commander of the deportation operation in Warsaw. Never brought to trial, as he committed suicide in a Vienna prison in 1964.

210 This deportation of the children of the Pnimia orphanage on Ogrodowa Street marked the beginning of a systematic campaign to destroy all the children's institutions in the ghetto. On the efforts to save the children from deportation see A. Berman, *BŻIH*, 28, pp. 65–78.

211 This word has two meanings in Polish: 'Get out' and 'departure'.

212 A few of those fit for work were taken from the *Umschlagplatz* and sent to a transit camp (*Dulag - Durchgangslager*) and from there to places of work.

213 A reference to the headquarters of the Self-help Organization. The diarist worked in one of the branch offices.

214 The wife of Rabbi Yitshak Nisenbaum, one of the spiritual mentors of the Zionist movement and a leader of the religious-zionist party Mizrachi; the rabbi lost his life.

215 An organization very active before the war in looking after abandoned children and orphans, which continued to operate in the ghetto.

216 That is, volunteers for deportation, who came to the *Umschlagplatz* of their own free will.

217 The mobile murder squads who carried out the deportations throughout the General-Government under 'Operation Reinhard'.

218 *Bona*; in the ghetto slang, a food coupon. The number of coupons, on the basis of which supply was allocated, exceeded the number of people living in the ghetto. The difference ('the dead people') was not, however, as large as the diarist claims.

219 Shakhne Sagan, one of the leaders of Po'alei Tsion-Left and one of the most active figures in the field of self-help in the ghetto. Among the founders of the anti-Fascist groups. Ringelblum provides a character sketch in the context of his public activity in the ghetto in his article, 'Shakhne Sagan, der Yidisher arbeter-tuer beshas der tsvayte velt-milkhome' ('Shakhne Sagan, a Jewish labour activist in World War II'), Ringelblum, *Ksovim*, II, pp. 102–22. On the circumstances of Sagan's arrest and on the efforts to free him see the diary of Hirsch Berlinski, *Drei: Andenkbukh*, pp. 164–5.

220 Ben-Tsion Chilinowicz, journalist, a contributor to the main Yiddish newspaper *Der Moment*. In the ghetto he was active on the Journalists' and Authors' Aid Committee.

221 Dr Edmond (Menachem) Sztajn, historian, lecturer in the Jewish Pedagogical Institute in Warsaw. Organizer of an illegal high school in the Warsaw ghetto. Among those deported to Trawniki, he was murdered at the beginning of Jan. 1943 when the camps near Lublin were evacuated.

222 Zołotow, Karcewicz, Prync – teachers at the Yehudia Secondary School.

223 Perets Opoczynski, journalist and writer. Active in Zionist-Socialist Po'alei Tsion in the Warsaw ghetto underground; one of the close assistants of

Ringelblum in *Oneg Shabbes*; wrote many reports and articles about life in the ghetto. Some were published in Warsaw in 1954: *Reportazhn fun varshever geto*. His unpublished diary is in the *Yad Vashem* archives. On his activity, see J. Kermish's Introduction to *To Live with Honor and Die with Honor*, pp. xviii–xx.

224 That is, 50 among those who were eating.

225 The ghetto police had been promised that their parents and other relatives (in addition to wives and children) would also have protection (Ringelblum, *Ksovim*, II, p. 29). This privilege was now revoked.

226 The proclamation was issued on 1 Aug. and called on people to present themselves voluntarily at the *Umschlagplatz*. *Likwidacja żydowskiej Warszawy*, pp. 4, 26.

227 The original deportation order gave exemption to its staff. Branches of the organization existed in every district capital.

228 The carpentry works of the Landau brothers (who lived in the United States) was expropriated by the Germans. Renamed the Ostdeutsche Bautischlerei Werkstätte (OBW), it was managed by the youngest brother, Alexander Landau. During the 'action' it gave shelter to many of the people active in the parties and the youth movements, among them the diarist. According to Hirsch Berlinski, this workshop became 'the most important centre of public life. It gave refuge to the whole of Hashomer Hatsair, the entire leadership of Po'alei Tsion-Left and the Polish Workers' Party (PPR). *Oneg Shabbes* was also there' (Berlinski, *Drei: Andenkbukh*, p. 166). On this workshop, see also Gutman, *The Jews of Warsaw*, who describes it as 'the most important centre of the ghetto underground during the deportation' (p. 222).

229 Towarzystwo Ochrony Zdrowia (Society for the Protection of Health), a very active association for medical aid and preventive medicine among the Jewish masses in Poland; in the ghetto, one of the affiliates of the general organization for mutual assistance.

230 Apparently Attorney Kahanowicz, an established community figure who worked in the Self-help Organization together with the diarist.

231 The diarist's relatives on his wife's side. Luba Lewin was the granddaughter of the chief rabbi of Warsaw, Yehuda Segal. Niestat, *Hurban vemered*, p. 346.

232 Inmates of the ghetto prison who had been sentenced to death (mainly for escaping from the ghetto or smuggling) were executed in the Jewish cemetery. For a description of this execution, see the testimony of Carmi, in *Yediot Yad Vashem*, 33.

233 A former pupil of Yehudia.

234 On the letters that ostensibly arrived from the eastern borders see n. 173. A proclamation of the Jewish Fighting Organization of Dec. 1942 that warned the inhabitants of the ghetto not to believe the false rumours and promises of the Germans said, *inter alia*: 'We mention the reliable "letters" from Brześć, Mińsk, Białystok, which were the handiwork of the Germans.' Quoted in B. Mark (ed.), *Tsum tsenten yartog fun oyfshtand in varshever geto*, pp. 121–3.

235 Hillel Cajtlin (1872–1942), writer and publicist, one of the outstanding figures of Polish Jewry. Perla describes him thus: 'Hillel Cajtlin hauled himself on to the

deportation cart, completely covered in his *tallit* [prayer shawl] . . . he wanted
to be buried in his *tallit* in the Jewish way. It was a shocking sight – a cart full of
women and children, all being taken to their death, and among them a tall, lone
old man, with a long, snow-white beard, shrouded in his *tallit'* (*Hurban Varshe*,
pp. 129–30). On this occasion the old writer came back from the *Umschlagplatz*.
Sick and very weak, he spent some time in the Jewish hospital. With the evacuation of the hospital during the deportation, Hillel Cajtlin was among those sent
to Treblinka. He wrote a great deal, even during the war – among other things
he translated the Book of Psalms into Yiddish – but his literary legacy was lost.
Ringelblum, *Ksovim*, II, p. 69.

236 Professor Majer Balaban, a historian and teacher who was active in many fields
and the author of many works on the history of Polish Jewry. In the ghetto he
worked as director of the community archive. This time he was spared deportation. He died in the Warsaw ghetto in Dec. 1942.

237 Dr Alfred Bornsztajn, economist and journalist. In the ghetto he associated
himself with underground circles. He lost his life on the Aryan side when he
was working in the Jewish Department of the Polish Government Delegation in
the underground.

238 Gestapo agents in the ghetto (see n. 101). The Germans killed their informers if
they no longer needed them. Many of them knew too much and could have
endangered their masters. Ringelblum comments that the two were killed for
trying to warn the public of the approaching disaster and influence the deportation operations (Ringelblum, *Ksovim*, II, p. 14). In the ghetto their murder was
seen as 'a portent of doom for the entire community' (Eck, *Hatoim bedarkhey
hamavet*, p. 51).

239 The Admor (*Adonenu veMorenu*, our Master and Teacher) of Radomsko, Rabbi
Shlomo Hanoh Rabinowitz, his wife Esther, their daughter and son-in-law
were killed in their flat at 30 Nowolipki Street. M. Unger, *Sefer kedoshim* (*The
Book of Martyrs*) (New York, 1967), pp. 389–90.

240 Apparently a reference to Popower, the chief accountant of the Jewish council,
who maintained contact with the underground.

241 Janusz Korczak (the pen-name of Dr Henryk Goldszmid), doctor, writer,
renowned educator. He was an innovator in the field of education, particularly
in the care of orphans and street urchins. In the ghetto he continued to head an
orphanage. During the deportation he refused to stay in the ghetto and abandon
his pupils. Ringelblum described his character in an article entitled 'Janusz
Korczak, the Children's Great Friend' (*Ksovim*, II, pp. 210–14). There he also
gives an eyewitness's account of the last journey of Korczak and his children: 'It
wasn't "going to the wagons" but a silent, organized protest against the regime
of murder.' Perla concludes his description (*Hurban Varshe*, pp. 118–20) with
these words: 'The very paving stones wept at the sight of this procession. But
the Nazi murderers hit out with their whips and fired shots every few moments.
Janusz Korczak, holding a child by the hand, led the way. With him were the
women childminders in white aprons and behind them 200 children, clean and
tidy, their hair combed, going to their slaughter.'

242 Bat-Sheva (Stefania) Hertzberg-Schweiger, the headmistress of the Yehudia Secondary School. See Introduction, pp. 7–8.

243 Bluma Kirschenfeld-Wasser, active in *Oneg Shabbes*, the wife of Hirsch Wasser. A survivor.

244 The wife of the teacher Natan Smolar; see below, n. 255. The circumstances of her arrest are related in the memoirs of Natan Eck, *Hatoim bedarkhey hamavet*, p. 48. Eck was himself a witness to these events.

245 The long-time skilled employees of the sawmill, who lost their wives and children, stormed against the 'new workers' (intellectuals who had found refuge in the plant), whom they considered to be endangering them by their presence. Natan Eck, who himself found refuge in Landau's factory, wrote: 'They [the workers] threatened to tell them [the Germans] that the Landau brothers had filled the factory with lazy good-for-nothings, sycophants, petty politicians, associates and friends, while they, the real workers, were now paying the price, for if all this motley crowd had not been there, the Germans would not have entered the factory at all' (*Hatoim bedarkhey hamavet*, p. 49).

246 Rabbi Mendel Alter, the president of the Association of Rabbis in Poland, the brother of the Admor of Gur; lived before the war in Panevezys (Lithuania) and Kalisz.

247 Yehiel Górny – one of the participants in *Oneg Shabbes*, later a member of the Jewish Fighting Organization. His account of the second deportation, in Jan. 1943, has survived.

248 Saul Stupnicki, journalist and publicist; before the war edited *Lubliner Tagblat*, later a member of the editorial board of *Der Moment*. Committed suicide by taking poison at the *Umschlagplatz*, at the threshold of the deportation wagon.

249 A reference to the death-camp at Treblinka, in the vicinity of these two locations.

250 A reference to Josef Erlich ('Yosele Kapote'), an underworld figure who, thanks to his links with the SD (Sicherheitsdienst, the German Intelligence Service) reached a position of dominance in the ghetto, holding the office of Inspector in the ghetto police. Erlich dealt with the holders of foreign passports, who used to present themselves at the Pawiak Prison in order to be exchanged for Germans in Allied countries. As the 'action' intensified he too presented himself, together with all his family, at the prison, foreign passports in hand. He was shot by the SD men whom he had served for so long. For a lengthy description of him, see Turkau, *Azoy iz es geven*, pp. 146–52.

251 Shmuel Hirszhorn, journalist, an editor of the Polish-language Jewish newspaper *Nasz Przegląd*. A contributor to the Yiddish newspaper *Der Moment*.

252 The house at 14 Wolność Street was the largest of the children's homes in the ghetto; some thousand children lived there after it had taken in children from other institutions during the deportation. Most of the workers of the home went to be deported together with the children.

253 Nathan (Aharon) Koniński, educator, head of a children's home in the ghetto. Did not abandon his pupils in the deportation but went with them to the *Umschlagplatz* and then to Treblinka (Ringelblum, *Ksovim*, II, pp. 23, 61).

254 Landau's carpentry shop, in which the author worked, was at 30 Gęsia Street.

255 Natan Smolar, a teacher in schools founded by Tsysho (the Bundist educational organization), headmaster of the Borokhov School; worked in the carpentry shop together with Lewin. Died in Apr. 1943.

256 We have not found a satisfactory explanation for this sentence nor identified the farm referred to.

257 Luba Lewin, née Hotner, the diarist's wife: Ora was their only daughter.

258 67 Dzielna Street was an orphanage for young children; the entire staff, led by the headmistress, Sarah Janowska, went to the *Umschlagplatz* together with the children.

259 A report of the liquidation of the ghetto written on the initiative of the Polish underground soon after the deportation mentions an instance of 'brave and poignant self-defence. When the gendarmes came to seize Seweryn M(ajda), formerly director of the theatre, he threw a heavy ashtray at one of them and was shot on the spot (*Sefer milkhamot*, p. 86).

260 In Radom the first stage of the deportation took place in Aug. 1942. The result was 10,000 people deported to Treblinka. Some 20,000 Jews from Radom were deported on 16 and 17 Aug. All that now remained of the Jewish community was some 4,000 Jewish slave-labourers employed in German factories. On this, see Gilbert, *The Holocaust*, pp. 405, 417.

261 On 10 Aug., some three weeks after the start of the deportation, a decree was issued giving the inhabitants of the small ghetto (see n. 149) a few hours to leave their homes and move to the large ghetto. After the evacuation the southern area ceased to be part of the ghetto. Only the workers of Többens' workshop remained there, in Prosta Street.

262 The wife, son, and daughter of Daniel David Guzik, a director of the 'Joint' in Poland. At the time of the ghetto Guzik was one of the important figures in the Jewish Self-help Organization, was connected with underground circles and supported the efforts of the pioneering movement. Died in a plane crash in Mar. 1946.

263 That is, the *Judenrat*.

264 Shmuel Wolkowicz, journalist, an editor of the Polish-language Jewish newspaper *Nasz Przegląd*. Settled in Israel.

265 A talented and popular singer, the daughter of Dawid Ajzensztat, the conductor of the choir of the Great Synagogue in Warsaw. Finished her studies at the Yehudia Secondary School in 1939. Frequently appeared at ghetto theatre evenings and concerts. Known as 'the nightingale of the ghetto'. Also appeared at performances organized by the youth movements and the underground. Mentioned in the Ringelblum–Berman report on cultural activity in the ghetto; Ringelblum also dedicated a special article to her (*Ksovim*, II, p. 206), Shot at the *Umschlagplatz* for resisting the SS.

266 Dr Jakub Tombeck, the diarist's brother-in-law.

267 The liquidation of the small ghetto forced the *Judenrat* to leave its offices in the former community-building, at 26–8 Grzybowska Street. It now operated from 19 Zamenhof Street, the premises of the Jewish post office in the ghetto.

268 The quotation marks around 'death' (לְמִיתָה) suggest that communication of the terrible news was based on the similarity in sound between the word for 'death' (*mot*) and the word for 'bed' in Hebrew (*mita*).

269 Decrees took effect in mid-Aug. limiting the area of the ghetto and evacuating entire streets. These internal 'transfers' were designed to confuse the Jews, to distract their attention from the deportations and to facilitate the plunder of their property.

270 The workshops of Többens, Schultz and Zimmerman – among the largest in the ghetto – were considered to be safe and employed thousands of Jewish labourers in conditions of severe exploitation. Karl Heinz Müller's workshop in Mylna Street employed many painters and artists – the shop was liquidated during the deportation and all its workers died. Ringelblum frequently mentions this workshop, in the end a trap for many of the artists in the ghetto. Ringelblum, *Ksovim*, II, pp. 60, 228–30.

271 Elhonon Cajtlin, writer and well-known journalist, a contributor to the Yiddish daily *Unzer Express*; worked for the Self-help Organization of the ghetto; saved from the *Umschlagplatz* and died in the ghetto in Dec. 1942.
  David Cajtlin, his son, was taken to Treblinka in Jan. 1943. He jumped off the train and returned to the ghetto; died a short time after the liberation, in one of the camps in Germany, at the age of 18. Ringelblum devoted an entire article to Elhonon and David Cajtlin, in which he mentions the great talents of the young David and sees him as 'the rising star in Yiddish literature' (Ringelblum, *Ksovim*, II, pp. 182–3).

272 Among the deportees on that day was Yitshak Katznelson's wife Hanna (née Rosenberg) and their two young sons, Ben-Tsion and Binyomin.

273 A few of those assembled in the *Umschlagplatz* would be sent to a transit camp (*Durchgangslager, Dulag*) in Leszno Street, and thence to labour camps; according to German statistics, in July, 1,612, in Aug., 7,403, and in Sept., 2,565; in total during the deportation, 11,580.

274 Czerniaków was a suburb of Warsaw where a Dror kibbutz training farm (*hakhshara*) still operated.
  The Jewish cemetery on the edge of the ghetto served as a transit point in the smuggling of goods and people.
  Gutkowski was secretary of *Oneg Shabbes* (see n. 99).

275 During the deportation the relative immunity of the children's institutions was rescinded: in all, some 30 institutions of different sorts were destroyed, and some 4,000 children were deported to Treblinka.

276 Mordecai Haim Rumkowski, the Jewish elder (*Judenälteste*), the sole ruler of the Jews in the ghetto of Łódź.

277 Members of Hashomer Hatsair in the Warsaw ghetto who were employed in the OBW (Ostdeutsche Bautischlerei Werkstätte) factory (formerly Landau's sawmill). They cultivated a plot of land in the cemetery. The firm provided cover for this, and hence the involvement of Commissar Hensel, the German supervisor of the workshop. For an account of this, see Y. Gutman, *Mered hanotsrim. Mordekhai Anieliewicz umilkhemet geto Varsha* (*The Revolt of the*

Besieged. Mordecai Anieliewicz and the Revolt of Warsaw Ghetto) (Merkhavia, 1963), p. 240.

278 This proclamation was published on 16 Aug. 1942. It stated that the only Jews permitted south of Leszno Street were those working in factories in this part of the city. The second paragraph stated that henceforth the families of people with permanent places of work would also be subject to deportation.

279 The broom factory (*brushter-shop*) on Franciszkańska Street was one of the largest manufacturing establishments in the ghetto. It produced brooms for the German army. Many community figures and members of the pioneering youth movement were employed there.

280 Shulamit Mokarska, an active member of women's organizations in Łódź; in the Warsaw ghetto she was active in the Łódź refugee *Landsmannschaften*; head of the women's self-help organization. Praised by Ringelblum in his article on the loss of the Jewish intellectuals (*Ksovim*, II, pp. 69–70).

281 Rabbi Shimon Huberband, one of the permanent workers of the secret archive; his writings from this period were discovered in the archive's milk churn (see n. 38). He was 33 years old when he was murdered.

282 Rav Yitshak Nisenbaum was one of the leaders of the religious-zionists in Poland (see n. 214). Leib Szczeranski was an important figure in Mizrachi in Poland.

283 Before the war, Dr Rokhl Sztajn had headed the women's organization of the Bund and been a member of the Warsaw city council; an active member of Centos, the organization for Jewish children.

284 Bat-Sheva (Stefania) Herzberg-Schweiger. See above, n. 242.

285 During the 'action' in Otwock, near Warsaw, some 10,000 people were deported to Treblinka. Many days after the deportation the Germans were still hunting down people who had gone into hiding. Anyone caught was shot on the spot. Their number reached some 2,000, among them not a few who had escaped from the Warsaw ghetto.

286 According to a report by the governor of the Warsaw district (12 Oct. 1942) the number of suicides in August was 155, and in Sept. 60. Niestat, *Hurban vemered*, p. 55.

287 There were two Jewish medical institutions in Otwock: Briuś, for people with tuberculosis; and Sofjówka, for mental patients. A report drawn up close to the deportation by Adolph and Batya Berman stated that many of the doctors and staff of the two institutions committed suicide. Reprinted in *BŻIH*, 45–6, p. 150.

288 The Soviet bombardment was a source of encouragement to the population of the ghetto, allowing them to believe – if only for a short while – that this was a response to the terrors of the *Umschlagplatz*. As one of them recalls, 'That night, not one Jew went down to the shelter' (Shereshevska, *Haperek ha-aharon*, p. 58). She relates that one shell hit Schulz's workshop, killing some and wounding others.

289 An attempt was made on the life of the commander of the ghetto police not by the Polish underground but by Yisrael Kanal, a commander in the Jewish Fighting Organization (ZOB) and a member of the religious-zionist youth

movement Akiva. At the time of the incident, Kanal was wearing the uniform of a policeman. The attack is described in Gutman, *The Jews of Warsaw*, pp. 237–40. Yitshak Zuckerman writes: 'That day the Jewish Fighting Organization fired its first salvo. With two shots, Yisrael Kanal severely wounded Józef Szeryński (Niestat, *Hurban vemered*, p. 99).

Another report, submitted after the war, states: 'we decided to kill the commander of the Jewish police, Szeryński, who was also director of the evacuation . . . [we wanted] the Jews to feel that there was a force and authority in the ghetto other than that of the community and the Jewish police' (Tsvia in Gutsfrukht et al., *Biyame khilayon vemered*, p. 476). The same report also contains Yisrael Kanal's description of the incident. According to Dr Adolph Berman's account of the resistance movement in the ghetto written in 1943, 'the attack was generally regarded with satisfaction and admiration as the police were detested; the *Judenrat* and the police let it be known that the attack was carried out by a Polish socialist' (*BŻIH*, 29, p. 52). On Szeryński, see n. 192.

It is interesting to note that although Lewin was a member of the *Oneg Shabbes* and thus had links with the underground, and although he was working in the OBW factory, where many of the Jewish Fighting Organization's leaders were sheltering, he never suspected that they were involved in the attempted assassination of Szeryński. Note also Lewin's diary entries for 21 and 25 Aug.

290 The proclamation censuring the Jewish *Ordnungsdienst* for the role they played in the deportation was also issued by the Jewish Fighting Organization. For the text of the verdict against Szeryński see n. 307. On the hostile reaction of many Jews, who considered the posters (and the fires started by the Jewish Fighting Organization) a dangerous provocation of the Germans, Tsvia writes: 'Our boys and girls . . . were seized by Jews and badly beaten. While they were indeed pleased by the attack on Szeryński, they attributed the incident to the PPS [Polish Socialist Party]. They did not believe that Jews could have done it . . . how it hurt that these posters, which we had worked so hard to print and had endangered our lives to put up, were now being torn off the walls by Jews themselves' (*Biyamey khilayon vemered*, p. 477). Ringelblum likewise writes, 'The posters were seen as provocation' (*Ksovim*, II, p. 11).

291 A town in the Warsaw district. The deportation there took place on 21 Aug.; about a thousand people were murdered on the spot; the members of the *Judenrat* were shot the following day; two work-groups remained. 'The gang' – the mobile extermination squad of 'Operation Reinhard'.

292 The diarist's sister and brother-in-law.

293 In the week of 14–21 Oct., more than 20,000 Jews were deported from Piotrków. Some 2,000 were allowed to remain in factories, and 2,000 managed to hide. On this, see Gilbert, *The Holocaust*, pp. 481–2.

294 This too is a reference to Treblinka, which was close to Kosow.

295 A resort between Warsaw and Otwock, which was very popular with the inhabitants of Warsaw; the 7,000 Jews of Falenica were deported to Treblinka on 20 Aug. 1942; only the 100 working in the sawmill remained.

296 A reference to the brother-in-law of Dr Natan Asch, the secretary of the

General Zionist Party in Poland, Al Hamishmar. A secretary of the Self-help Organization.

297 *Oneg Shabbes*, the secret archive; see n. 116. Beit Hashomrim, the premises of the youth movement Hashomer Hatsair, nearby at 61 Miła Street. In attendance at the meeting were the directorate of *Oneg Shabbes* at the time:

> Emanuel Ringelblum, founder and initiator of the secret archive.
>
> Yitshak Guterman, a leader of the 'Joint' in the Warsaw ghetto, a very active public figure, trusted in the underground.
>
> David Daniel Guzik, one of the directors of the 'Joint' during the Occupation (see n. 262).
>
> Lippe-Leib Bloch, a leading figure in the General Zionist Party Al Hamishmar, a director of the main office of the Jewish National Fund (Keren Kayemet Le-Yisrael), active in the Jewish self-help, lecturer in seminars of the pioneering movement in the ghetto.
>
> Abraham Lewin, the diarist.
>
> Eliyahu Gutkowski, the secretary of *Oneg Shabbes* and editor of its information bulletin (see n. 99 and J. Kermish's Introduction to *To Live with Honor and Die with Honor*, p. xxi).
>
> Hirsch Wasser, a secretary of *Oneg Shabbes*; among the survivors (see n. 72).
>
> Shmuel Breslaw, one of the leaders of Hashomer Hatsair in the Warsaw ghetto and a founder of the Jewish Fighting Organization; see also n. 330.
>
> Josef Kaplan, a founder of the Jewish Fighting Organization and one of its first commanders; a member of the executive of Hashomer Hatsair in Poland; see also n. 329.
>
> Alexander Blau, an engineer, a sympathizer of the pioneering movement and the underground.

298 Aharon Einhorn, an editor of *Haynt*, the largest of the Yiddish newspapers in pre-war Poland; translated works of French literature into Yiddish. In the ghetto – took an active part in the Self-help Organization. Shot in his room in Otwock (Ringelblum, *Ksovim*, II, p. 59).

299 Towarzystwo Popierania Rolnictwa (Association for the Advancement of Agriculture); in the ghetto, one of the areas of activity of the Self-help Organization; encouraged the utilization of every inch of land for growing vegetables.

300 The rumour was incorrect; Szeryński was wounded by a bullet fired by Yisrael Kanal (see n. 289) and from then on went into hiding from fear of the Jewish Fighting Organization. Committed suicide in Jan. 1943.

301 A reference to Jakub (Tombeck), the diarist's brother-in-law, who was a doctor.

302 The young man Shmuel – possibly a reference to Shmuel Breslaw (see n. 297), a member of Hashomer Hatsair and a director of *Oneg Shabbes*. The German headquarters – the *Befehlstelle* at 101 Żelazna Street where the extermination squad was stationed.

303 Brazil joined the war against Germany on 28 Aug. 1942 – the first of the Latin American countries to do so. It was followed by Colombia, in Nov. 1943. Others delayed doing so until Feb. 1945, while Argentina declared war on Germany only on 27 Mar. 1945.

304 In fact Roosevelt made a declaration on 21 Aug. in response to the conference of governments in exile which took place in St James's Palace in London in Jan. 1942. Both the conference resolutions and Roosevelt's response spoke of ways of punishment for war crimes in general, and crimes against the civilian population of the occupied areas in particular. They contained nothing in the way of concrete assistance to the threatened Jews. On this see W. Laqueur, *The Terrible Secret* (London, 1980) and D. Engel, 'The Western Allies and the Holocaust' in *POLIN: A Journal of Polish-Jewish Studies*, 1 (1986).

305 In the first half of 1942 many reports started to reach other countries about the fate of the Jewish population on the continent of Europe and caused a tremendous stir among the public. Neither the British nor the US governments apparently wanted to give much publicity to these reports, since they felt that they were in no position to take any real steps to save the Jews. Publication of the reports was delayed on the grounds that they had not yet been sufficiently checked. S. Korbonski, *W imieniu Rzeczypospolitej* (*In the Name of the Republic*) (Paris, 1954), pp. 252–3 and Laqueur, *The Terrible Secret*.

306 Isaac Ber Ekerman, journalist and public figure in the Orthodox community of Warsaw; Bernard Zundelewicz, lawyer, chairman of the Traders' and Retailers' Association. Both were members of the community council before the war and served on the *Judenrat* during the Occupation – 'the Jewish advisers', in the words of the diarist. Arrested at the beginning of the 'action' and held as hostages.

307 This announcement was published in the ghetto by the Jewish Fighting Organization (ŻOB) and read: 'Komendant policji, oficerowie i szeregowi policjanci zostali postawieni w stan oskarzenia i w związku z tym dokonano zamachu na Jakuba Szerynskiego. Tego rodzaju dalsze represje będą nadal stosowane z całą bezwględnością.' Quoted in *BŻIH*, 22, p. 93.
  The first name of the commander of the ghetto police was cited erroneously in this announcement as 'Jakub' and should have been Józef. An earlier announcement condemning the commanders of the Jewish police and all who served in its ranks was published by the Jewish Fighting Organization on 17 Aug. 1942.

308 See *Likwidacja żydowskiej Warszawy* docs. 11 and 13, pp. 28, 29.

309 For an account of the 'selection' in the *Judenrat* offices, see Shereshevska, *Haperek ha-aharon* 42; also the report by Adolph and Batya Berman in *BŻIH*, 45–6, pp. 147–84.

310 Jüdisches Hilfskommittee, the official name of the Self-help Organization; see n. 161. By this time the committee was already subordinated to the *Judenrat*.

311 *Likwidacja żydowskiej Warszawy* (doc. 14, p. 29) gives details for mid-Aug. of all the workshops entitled to employ Jewish labourers, and reaches a total of 23,818 Jews, excluding those employed by communal institutions. Another 4,127 Jews were employed in 21 factories outside the ghetto.

312 Szymon Heller, an active member of Hashomer Hatsair in the Warsaw ghetto. Haim Zelmanowski, biologist, head of the illegal Dror Secondary School in the Warsaw ghetto. Among the survivors who reached Israel.

313 The wife of David Pulman, a Jewish scholar, director of the Great Synagogue in Tłomackie Street from 1927 and of the Hebrew Library associated with the Institute of Jewish Studies in Warsaw. The links between the Lewin and Pulman families were very close in the ghetto; Abraham Lewin taught Mrs Pulman Hebrew in order to help her prepare for *Aliya* (emigration to Palestine). The matriarch of the family, Sarah Pulman (née Friedman) came from a large Hasidic family. All three of the Pulmans' daughters went to the Yehudia Secondary School. The eldest, Lily, managed to get out of occupied Warsaw (in May 1940), while the younger girls – Henja (16) and Ada (14) – lost their lives. In the ghetto Ada used to see Ora Lewin frequently. (Based on the account of Mrs Lily Pulman-Goldenberg in the *Beit Lohamei Hagetaot* archives.)

314 Yehiel Cytrynowski, teacher of Hebrew language and literature; according to *Likwidacja żydowskiej Warszawy* one of the educators who had lost their lives. Participated in an educational seminar on the Gordonia youth movement that took place in the Warsaw ghetto at the end of Dec. 1940. (Zuckerman and Basuk (eds), *Sefer milkhamot hagetaot*, p. 21.) (Lewin also participated in the seminar, as a lecturer in Jewish history.) Head of the Tarbut School in the Warsaw ghetto. (Eck, *Hatoim bedarkhey hamavet*, p. 172.)

315 See n. 313.

316 One of the adult members of Hashomer Hatsair in Warsaw, among the organizers of the movement in the ghetto; later company commander in the Jewish Fighting Organization. On the testimony of Nowodworski, the 'newsbearing refugee' from Treblinka, see Gutman, *Mered hanotsrim*, p. 239 and Gutman, *The Jews of Warsaw*, p. 222.

317 During the operation to annihilate Polish Jewry the following settlements were destroyed: Radom (5 Aug., 16–17 Aug.), Siedlce (22 Aug.), Rembertów (20 Aug.).

318 Meaning, of course, only those murdered in Warsaw. According to the German report, the number of Jews shot in the streets of Warsaw or the *Umschlagplatz* during the entire deportation operation was 5,451 (Niestat, *Hurban vemered*, p. 55).

319 Apparently Brzezinski, an officer in the ghetto police, responsible for loading at the *Umschlagplatz*. A 'warning' issued by the Jewish Fighting Organization on 3 Mar. 1943 to informers and Gestapo agents stated that he was 'killed on 26 Feb.' (*BŻIH*, 36). The list of people shot compiled by Ringelblum states that 'this monster boasted that with his own hands he had herded a quarter of a million of Warsaw's Jews on to the wagons of death.' Quoted in N. Blumenthal and J. Kermish, *Ha-meri vehamered begeto Varshe: Sefer mismakhim* (*The Resistance and Uprising in the Warsaw Ghetto. A Book of Documents*) (Jerusalem, 1965), p. 147.

320 Ekerman, a religious Jew, came back from prison without a beard. His only son, Hilary, was a communal worker. See also n. 306.

321 The diarist mentions here people with whom he was connected through his work in *Oneg Shabbes* and in the Self-help Organization:

Rabbi Shimon Huberband, historian, one of the main figures in *Oneg Shabbes* (see n. 38).

Celina (Luba) Słapak, publicist; translated Dubnow into Polish. Her essay on the Jewish woman in wartime survived in the underground archive.

Celina Lewin, a contributor to *Oneg Shabbes*. See Kermish, Introduction, *To Live with Honor and Die with Honor*, p. xx.

Henryka Lazowert, a well-known Jewish poet writing in Polish; continued to write in the ghetto; active in the field of self-help. For her poem on a child smuggler, see n. 134.

Israel Winnik, involved in self-help, a writer, one of the organizers of the Bund archive in the ghetto (see n. 172).

322 Pinhas Czerski, one of the directors of the 'Joint' in Warsaw. L. Rakowski, a teacher, involved in self-help and Jewish education in the ghetto.

323 Gina Popower, killed in France in the anti-Nazi underground (from a letter by her mother, Miriam Popower, to Ora Perlman, in 1954). Her husband was a Christian Pole. Of France's 300,000 Jews, approximately 90,000 were deported to death-camps. The execution of the 'final solution' in France ran into difficulties both for technical reasons (shortage of rolling stock) and because the local population were not supportive of the anti-Jewish decrees.

324 The mobile extermination squad that came from Lublin under 'Operation Reinhard'.

325 Rabbi Yitshak Meir Kandal, the oldest of Warsaw's rabbis, deputy-chairman of the Association of Rabbis in Poland; aged 82 when he died. He is said to have tried to grab a rifle from the hands of a German gendarme at the *Umschlagplatz*, thereby ensuring that he would be killed on the spot and would be buried in the traditional Jewish way.

326 On 25 and 26 Aug. some 11,000 people were deported from Międzyrzec Podlaski to Treblinka.

327 Leon Ringelblum, brother of the historian; see also n. 346.

328 This attack was by Soviet bombers; the first bombardment was recorded in the entry for 21 Aug.

329 Josef Kaplan, member of the leadership of Hashomer Hatsair in Poland and one of the leaders of the movement in the ghetto; a founder of the Jewish Fighting Organization (ŻOB) in the ghetto and one of its first commanders. Together with a large group of his comrades from Hashomer Hatsair he worked in the same workshop (OBW) as that in which the diarist found refuge.

His arrest, the result of information derived from an arrested member of the ŻOB, was a serious blow to the underground, particularly since, in the subsequent attempt to hide traces of the ŻOB, a large cache of revolvers and grenades was lost. See Gutman, *Mered hanotsrim*, pp. 251–3, 267–80, and Gutman, *The Jews of Warsaw*, pp. 243–7.

330 Shmuel Breslaw, one of the leaders of Hashomer Hatsair in the Warsaw ghetto; a founder of the Jewish Fighting Organization and a member of its first high command; involved in *Oneg Shabbes*. He too worked in Landau's workshop.

331 A workers' suburb in west Warsaw.

332 The workshops of A. Ha-Ge Zimmermann & Co., manufacturers of paper goods, toys, haberdashery, etc. The workshop was set up at the beginning of the summer of 1942 and initially employed 2,500 people. During the 'action', it was completely destroyed. In the middle of August 1942 it employed some 1,000 workers (see *Likwidacja żydowskiej Warszawy*).

333 Natan Asch, one of the self-help activists. Eliyahu Gutowski of *Oneg Shabbes*. Zilberberg, of Hitahdut, the general Zionist organization. Albert Mazur, involved in the provision of medical assistance in the ghetto.

334 Shmuel Breslaw was laid to rest by his friends in the Sacra sports ground in Okopowa Street, near the Jewish cemetery. On the funeral, see Gutman, *Mered hanotsrim*, p. 254.

335 Frank–Schultz – meaning the workshops of Fritz Schultz in Nowolipie Street.

336 Gutkowski, Zilberberg, and Asch jumped off the deportation train. Asch found temporary shelter in one of the towns in the area (Wołomin), and there apparently fell victim to the deportations and murders of the beginning of Oct. Gutkowski and Zilberberg returned to the ghetto. With them in the wagon was Joseph Lewertowski-Finkelstein, one of the leaders of the Polish Workers' Party (PPR) in the ghetto. It is said that he encouraged them to escape; lame himself, he stayed in the wagon.

337 For five days the diarist did not open his notebook. This was the terrible week known as 'the cauldron days'. It was marked by the comprehensive *Selektion* which lasted from 6 to 10 Sept. and is described in Lewin's entry for 11 Sept. (falsely noted in the diary as 11 Aug.). During this period all Jews left in the ghetto were compelled to leave their homes and assemble in the streets adjacent to the *Umschlagplatz*. All those who were not part of the quota allocated to recognized workplaces were deported to Treblinka. This selection was called the 'cauldron' (Yiddish *kesl*, Polish *kocioł*) because it was carried out in so confined an area. The German plan was for 35,000 Jews to remain in the ghetto as slave-labourers. In addition, about 20,000–25,000 people remained illegally in the ghetto. The final stage of this selection took place on the Day of Atonement, 21 Sept. 1942, when the Jewish policemen and their families were deported. The *Ordnungsdienst* was now reduced to 380. On these developments see Gutman, *The Jews of Warsaw*, pp. 210–11.

338 The compulsory registration was announced on 5 Sept.; the proclamation concluded with the threat that 'Anyone remaining in the ghetto [beyond the area covered by the registration] after 10.00 a.m. on 6 Sept. will be executed. That night, on the eve of 6 Sept., Jews are permitted to be on the streets' (*Likwidacja żydowskiej Warszawy*, pp. 27–8).

339 A reference to 61 Miła Street, where the workers of Landau's factory lived.

340 Groups guarding German industrial plants. In the German factories in the Warsaw ghetto there was a Jewish *Werksschutz*; for the most part these were former members of the ghetto police. The Jewish Fighting Organization condemned the *Werksschutz* along with the other collaborators.

341 Isaiah Rabinowicz, active in Yivo (The Jewish Scientific Organization) in Warsaw before the war; involved in *Oneg Shabbes* in the ghetto.

342 Those who went through the 'selection' at the time of the cauldron and were employed in workshops received metal tags with the name and number of the workshop to wear round their necks.

343 *Likwidacja żydowskiej Warszawy* concludes the account of the liquidation of the hospitals in the Warsaw ghetto thus: 'And finally, on 12 Sept., at eleven o'clock, the order came through to evacuate the hospital. Representatives of the authorities and the ghetto police entered the hospital premises. All the patients – some 900 – together with the hospital staff were deported, and the hospital was closed. The ghetto now remained without a hospital. But the sick and wounded continued to arrive from workshops or from places of work outside the ghetto. On 17 Sept. temporary sickrooms were set up (12 beds and a room for auxiliary surgery) at 6 Pawia Street' (pp. 34–6).

344 The number of Jews who remained in hiding in deserted houses within the ghetto at the end of the deportation was slightly larger. In all, those who remained apparently numbered some 60,000–65,000.

345 A. Gorilow, an active figure in the Self-help Organization. Before the war he had been the secretary of the Actors' Union.

346 On the Ringelblum family of Dzika Street we have the testimony of Dr Raphael Mahler: 'Leon Ringelblum is most certainly Emanuel's brother. Among his friends he was known as Lusiek, from his Hebrew name which was Elazar (or perhaps Eliezer). Some two years younger than his brother Emanuel, like him he was tall and handsome. He studied social science at Warsaw University but it seems he did not finish his studies: he lacked Emanuel's ability to concentrate and persevere. Emotional and impulsive, full of enthusiasm, good-hearted, he was more "one of the people" than his brother; a faithful member of Po'alei Tsion-Left, in the students' circle. Thanks to his brother he worked for years at the economics and statistics bureau of Cekabe, an organization for constructive assistance that was established by the "Joint" in Poland. His wife Sala (Sarah), née Schiffer (the daughter of my mother's brother) returned to Poland after living with her father in Vienna, where she had received a doctorate in philosophy.' (From his letter in the *Beit Lohamei Hagetaot* archive.)

347 Dr Maurice (Marcus) Plonsker, a pathologist before the war, the head of the laboratory in the Jewish Hospital in Warsaw. Published many works of research. In the ghetto he continued his work in the hospital; participated in the research on starvation that was carried out in the ghetto in 1942 with support from the 'Joint'. This work was published immediately after the war under the title *Choroba glodowa; Badania kliniczne nad gloden wykonane w getcie warszawskim* (*Starvation: Clinical Studies on Famine Carried out in the Warsaw Ghetto*).

348 In fact the main deportation from the Częstochowa ghetto took place between 22 Sept. and 5 Oct. 1942. Some 40,000 Jews were sent to Treblinka.

349 The deportation from Kielce took place between 20 and 24 Aug. 1942 and encompassed some 21,000 people. We have not been able to authenticate the statements here about the stand the *Judenrat* took against the Germans. After the deportation only about 2,000 Jews remained in the city. On this, see Gilbert, *The Holocaust*, p. 417.

350 Josef Kaplan was held in the Pawiak until 11 Sept. That day he was in a group
     of prisoners being taken to the *Umschlagplatz* but he was shot by his guards in
     Dzielna Street, apparently by special order. The plans of his friends to see him
     when he was brought to the *Umschlagplatz* were thus frustrated. Joseph and
     Shmuel: Joseph Kaplan and Shmuel Breslaw.

351 Rabbi Yehiel Meir Blumenfeld, responsible for religious studies in the Takhe-
     moni rabbinical seminary in Warsaw.

352 Ida Hochberg, one of the first graduates of Yehudia; later a doctor in Israel.
     Adina, the daughter of Bat-Sheva Schweiger, the headmistress of the school.
     For Ida Hochberg's recollection of Lewin as a teacher, see Introduction, p. 9.

353 Rachel Brotmacher (a teacher of German), Gustava Złotowska (a teacher of
     Polish), and Dr Cecilia Weinberger (likewise) – teachers at the Yehudia
     Secondary School and colleagues of the diarist. 'Her mother' – Bat-Sheva
     Schweiger (see nn. 242 and 284).

354 'On 21 Sept. . . . the Nazis appeared in the street where the police lived; they
     surrounded the houses of the "privileged ones" . . . those who only yesterday
     had diligently performed the Nazis' orders were now forced along the same
     route [as all the other Jews]. No one shed a tear for them' (Gutman, *Mered
     hanotsrim*, p. 259).

355 Jakub Rabinowicz, a young man of 25, son of the Admor of Parczew; worked in
     the same workshop as Lewin (Hillel Zeidman, *Togbukh fun varshever geto* (*Diary
     of the Warsaw Ghetto*) (New York, 1957), p. 57). According to Hirsch Wasser,
     Rabinowicz's testimony served as the basis for an account of Treblinka
     prepared by *Oneg Shabbes* and added as App. 17 to the report presented in
     Likwidacja żydowskiej Warszawy, pp. 30–4.

356 At the entrance to the camp at Treblinka was a board headed: 'Attention,
     emigrants from Warsaw!' Its seven paragraphs stated that the arrivals need not
     worry about what was to happen to them. They would be transported east to
     work, but before that they must bathe and hand over their clothes for disinfec-
     tion. After the disinfection all their valuables would be returned to them,
     including their documents.

357 A reference to Alexander Landau, who was held in high regard by members of
     the underground. They testify that Landau was 'dedicated heart and soul to the
     Jewish Fighting Organization', and 'put his life and property to the service of
     the common good, to the preparation of the defence of the ghetto.' Y. Zucker-
     man, 'Mered ha-Yehudim' ('The revolt of the Jews'), *Mibnifim*, 12–13, 1947–8,
     pp. 403–4. See also n. 228.

358 A reference to Hirsch Wasser (see n. 72). and to his wife Bluma (see n. 243).

359 In Treblinka the Jews were of course murdered by introducing the gas from
     engine exhausts from the outside into the gas chambers. Lewin uses the word
     הבל, which Alkalay's Hebrew–English dictionary defines as 'steam, vapour,
     breath'.

360 On the German gendarme known as Frankenstein, see n. 130.

361 This order was dated 28 Sept. and bears the signature of the head of the *Judenrat*.
     It forbade the presence of Jews south of a line from Franciszkańska to Gęsia

Streets unless they were on their way to work and accompanied by police. North of this line, in the now-diminished ghetto, Jews were forbidden to be in the streets during work hours. Peddling, gathering and aimless wandering were also prohibited. For the text, see *Likwidacja żydowskiej Warszawy*, pp. 28–9.

362 A reference to Yitshak Giterman, director of the 'Joint'. Zuckerman in 'Mered ha-Yehudim' writes of him (p. 407): 'Giterman had our confidence. He was diligent and sober. He had an excellent sense of what was positive and was able to assess the vital strength hidden in the ghetto ... He had a clear, analytical brain. He was not a Zionist but supported the pioneering movement with all his strength. In the worst days ... he spared neither effort nor money to support the secret archive, the Yidishe Kultur Organizatsia, the pioneering seminars ... one of the first among the few to grasp what lay in store for us, he promised his assistance in establishing a Jewish fighting force.'

363 'Hallmannowa' – the German workshop for wood products at 57 Nowolipki Street belonging to B. Hallman, where Emanuel Ringelblum was employed.

364 In Wołomin the deportation took place on 4 Oct. and encompassed 3,000 Jews. Two days later more than 600 more were shot there.

365 The number of Jews deported to Treblinka in Oct. 1942 from Skarżysko-Kamienna reached 2,500.

366 The Białystok area of the former Polish province was not included in the General-Government with the Occupation in 1941 and a special administrative unit, Bezirk Białystok, was set up. From the last months of 1941 till Nov. 1942, the region as a whole, and the Białystok ghetto in particular, absorbed many refugees from the General-Government.

367 *Kennkarten*, identity cards distributed to the Poles within the General-Government.

368 This estimate does not seem exaggerated; according to the German statistics the number of deaths from 22 July to the end of Sept. reached 10,361, more than half of which (5,961) represented people murdered during deportation. In Oct. there were 423 deaths, including 58 people shot dead. *Likwidacja żydowskiej Warszawy*, pp. 14, 15, 20.

369 SS General Friedrich Krieger, the supreme commander of the SS and the police in the General-Government, the deputy of General-Governor Hans Frank for security; one of the worst of the Nazi criminals in Poland.

370 In the list of workshops in perpetual danger of closure, Ringelblum mentions the OBW, where Lewin worked, which he considers 'the best socially'. In the event its life was prolonged 30 days, but, he says, 'We shall not try to put ourselves in the place of those whose entire fate hangs on the fate of the workshop. With its closure they lose their right to life, for then they remain without their work tags, without a roof and without food coupons' (*Ksovim*, II, p. 20).

371 In his report on the stages by which the Warsaw ghetto was liquidated, SS Brigadier-General Jürgen Stroop writes that, 'The first large removal occurred during the period from 22 July to 3 Oct. 1942, when 310,322 Jews were removed.' *The Stroop Report: The Jewish Quarter of Warsaw Is No More!* (New York, 1979), p. 2.

372 This was a reprisal for the intensification of the sabotage attempts by fighters of the Polish underground. Trains had been blown up in several stations of the railway crossroads of Warsaw, and bombs had been placed in a café and restaurant frequented by German officers. As related below, the victims were buried in the Jewish cemetery.

373 Hillel Cajtlin (see n. 235) was sent together with the patients in the hospital.
   Aharon Gawze, journalist and contributor to *Haynt*. In the ghetto, involved in Self-help.

374 People active in *Oneg Shabbes* (see above, nn. 116, 321) and those employed by the local Self-help Committee (see above, n. 227).

375 *Werterfassung*, a German collection unit set up by the SS to carry out the organized theft of Jewish property. Its members also involved themselves in the deportation.
   Umsiedlungstab, the resettlement headquarters, that is the staff of 'Operation Reinhard'.

376 Jakub Lejkin, the deputy of Józef Szeryński, the commander of the *Ordnungsdienst*, the ghetto police. Condemned by the Jewish Fighting Organization as a traitor and a German lackey: 'We decided to cleanse the air of the ghetto by ridding ourselves of the most corrupt of criminals sold to the Germans . . . the death of the commander of the *Ordnungsdienst*, Jakub Lejkin . . . served as a warning to his colleagues in the police' (Yitshak Zuckerman in Niestat, *Hurban vemered*, pp. 103–4). See also Gutman, *The Jews of Warsaw*, pp. 208, 302, 305.
   The sentence was carried out on 29 Oct. by Eliyah Rozanski, Mordekhai Grobos and Margalit Landau (daughter of Alexander Landau, see n. 228).

377 The convert Marcelli Czapliński 'excelled' in the deportation; he personally commanded blockades and had the confidence of SS officers Brandt and Witossek. His brother Michael was Szeryński's adjutant. Turkau, *Azoy iz es geven*, pp. 139–40.

378 In a manifesto published on 30 Oct. the Jewish Fighting Organization announced the execution of Jakub Lejkin. The Organization also announced that it would take punitive action not only against the officers of the ghetto police but also against members of the *Judenrat* (for collaborating with the forces of the Occupation and signing the deportation orders), the managers of the workshops (for exploiting and oppressing employees) and against group leaders and officials of the *Werksschutz* (for persecuting Jewish employees and 'illegal' Jews). Blumenthal and Kermish, *Ha-meri vehamered begeto Varshe*, p. 110.

379 On the evening of 27 Oct., the SS surrounded the Kraków ghetto; that night the *Ordnungsdienst* began to enter apartments and pull people out, according to a pre-prepared list; the Ministry of Labour in the ghetto had made their 'selection' of all the workers. The deportation was accompanied by murders and bloodshed. In all, 6,000 people were deported to Bełżec. Residents of the old people's home and the orphanage were murdered. See D. Agatstein-Dormontow, 'Zydzi w Krakowie w okresie okupacji niemieckiej' ('Jews in Krakow under the German occupation'), *Rocznik Krakowski*, 31 (1949). On

29 Oct. more than 3,000 people were deported from Sandomierz and taken to the death-camp at Bełżec. See also A. Biberstein, *Zagłada Żydów w Krakowie* (*The Destruction of the Jews of Kraków*) (Kraków, 1985).

380 The diarist was apparently referring to SS Sturmbahnführer (Major) Herman Höfle, head of 'Operation Reinhard' in the General-Government and commander of the main deportation. By that time there were very few children still alive in the ghetto, after the systematic liquidation of the orphanages.

381 The death-camp in Treblinka operated until the revolt of the *Sonderkommando* there on 3 Aug. 1943. The erroneous information apparently had its origins in the fact that not far from the death-camp (Treblinka 2) there was a labour camp (Treblinka 1) used primarily for Polish prisoners.

382 In the spring of 1940 his movement renewed its operation in the underground in the Warsaw ghetto. Organizer of the kibbutz at 23 Nalewki Street. During the massive deportation he escaped, together with a group from Dror, and made for Werbkowice, the partisan base in the vicinity of Hrubieszów. On the way they were captured, and the entire group was murdered but for Zeltser, who somehow managed to stay alive and was brought to Warsaw and taken to the Pawiak. This failure brought with it other losses of life and weapons and led to the imprisonment and death of Josef Kaplan. Zeltser was executed on 11 Sept. 1943 in one of the courtyards in Dzielna Street. He was 29 years old. He was buried in the Sacra sportsground near the Jewish cemetery on Gęsia Street. See Zuckerman and Basuk, *Sefer milkhamot hagetaot*, p. 127 and Gutman, *The Jews of Warsaw*, pp. 243–6. On Zeltser and his activities in Gordonia, see also Eck, *Hatoim bedarkhey hamavet*, pp. 176ff.

383 The deportation operation began in many places in the Białystok region on 21 Nov. and encompassed more than 120,000 people.

384 A reference to a Polish-language newspaper *Nowy Kurier Warszawski*, which appeared in Warsaw with the permission of the Gestapo and was boycotted by the Polish patriots. A decree of 1 Nov. 1942 announced the establishment of Jewish ghettos in the Warsaw district (6 ghettos) and in the Lublin district (8 ghettos). *Likwidacja żydowskiej Warszawy*, p. 23, lists them individually. A second decree covering settlements in the districts of Radom, Kraków, and Galicia, in which Jews seem also to have been permitted to live, was published on 10 Nov. of the same year.

385 What the diarist feared came true: in the first part of Jan. 1943 the Jews from these places were deported to death camps.

Likwidacja żydowskiej Warszawy adds (p. 23) that the immediate political aim of the decrees establishing new ghettos for the Jews was to mislead the world as to the fate of the Jews of Europe being resettled in the east.

A proclamation of the Jewish Fighting Organization of Dec. 1942, attacked the German promises: 'We do not believe even for a moment in the "new" instruction about the establishment of ghettos for the Jews. This is a trap whose door could spring at any minute.' B. Mark (ed.) *Tsum tsenten yartog fun oyfshtand in varshever geto*, pp. 121–3.

386 The work of the *Judenrat*'s Department of Labour was renewed early in Nov. under Bernard Zundelewicz (see n. 306).

387 The camp in Lublin, at 7 Lipowa Street – originally a camp for Jewish prisoners of war of the Polish army (dating from the campaign in Sept. 1939); later it became a camp for slave-labourers. At the end of 1941 and the beginning of 1942 Jewish prisoners of war from the Russian army were also brought there. From the spring of 1942 it became a camp for craftsmen and skilled labourers, under the jurisdiction of the economic plants of the SS. Many of the slave-labourers engaged in constructing the camp at Majdanek. On this, see M. Gilbert, *The Holocaust*, p. 95.

388 Undoubtedly a reference to the Bełżec camp in the Lublin province (between Lublin and Lwów), which came into operation in Mar. 1942. According to an estimate prepared by the main committee investigating Nazi crimes in Poland, more than 600,000 Jews were exterminated at Bełżec from the various settlements of the districts of Lublin, Kraków and Galicia. Among the victims were transports from the Reich.

389 The railway station Warsaw East, in the suburb of Praga on the right bank of the Vistula; many Jewish slave-labourers were employed there.

390 On 8 Nov. the Nazis celebrated the anniversary of their attempted rebellion at Munich (1923), not the establishment of the party. Hitler addressed veterans of the National-Socialist Party, as he did each year.

391 11 Nov. was a national holiday in Poland to mark the re-establishment of an independent Poland after the defeat by the Germans in World War I.

392 In the last week of Oct. and the beginning of Nov. the British forces under Montgomery defeated the Axis forces near El-Alamein. 8 Nov. marked the beginning of the American–British landing on the coast of North Africa. This landing was to have little effect on the war in Europe.

393 On 1 Oct. 1942 Hitler said 'The Jews of Germany also scoffed once at my words of prophecy; and I don't know, maybe they are laughing today too, or perhaps they have already lost the desire to laugh. Now again I can promise you that wherever they are they will lose the desire to laugh, and this time too my prophecy will come true.' His words were published the following day in the newspaper *Völkischer Beobachter*.

394 In the aftermath of this round-up, the Jewish Fighting Organization (ŻOB) published the following proclamation: '. . . Remember the last "action", the round-up for "work" in Lublin. They needed "tailors" and rounded up old men, children. They rounded up people for "work" and sent them off as they were, naked and exposed . . . we would point out that near Lublin there is a place called Bełżec where tens of thousands of Jews were murdered as in Treblinka.' B. Mark (ed.), *Tsum tsenten yartog fun oyfshtand in varshever geto*, pp. 121–3.

395 *Nebenstelle*, a reference to the branch of the German labour exchange for the ghetto.

396 Auerswald, the official of the German administration reponsible for the ghetto, summoned the chairman of the *Judenrat* (who brought with him two members of the council) and informed him that in the coming days the population of the ghetto was to be increased by at least 5,000. He promised that food rations would be given to both workers and non-workers. He also asked to be given the

work programme for the ghetto population to May 1943. The conversation took place in the presence of the commander of the police and the SS in the Warsaw district. The Jewish representatives stood throughout the meetings.

On the 'legalization' of the remaining Jewish population, see nn. 384, 385.

397 The ghetto in Grodno was liquidated in Jan. 1943. In Białystok, the first 'action' took place between 5 and 12 Feb. 1943. The reference here is to the deportations and mass-murders that took place in the various settlements in the Białystok region.

398 See n. 396.

399 The daughter of Hirsch Yonah Silber, a public figure in the Orthodox community of Lublin, a member of the city council and chairman of the community council. Mr Water – Hirsch Wasser of *Oneg Shabbes*.

400 The deportation from the Lublin ghetto took place in Mar. and Apr. 1942. The great majority of the Jews of Lublin were deported to the death camp at Bełżec, and a few to the suburb of Majdan Tatarski. In Nov. 1942 the latter were deported to the camp of Majdanek which had been set up outside the city, on the road to the town of Piaski. The execution of the deportation in Lublin served as a model for the massive deportation of the Jews of the Warsaw ghetto.

401 Many of those who remained in the Warsaw ghetto considered the ghetto in Łódź an example of a Jewish settlement that survived thanks to the benefits it brought to the German economy. From Sept. 1942, after a bloody deportation operation focusing on old people, children and the sick, the Łódź ghetto was organized as a large concentration camp aimed primarily at exploiting the work-force of the ghetto. On the Łódź ghetto, see L. Dobroszycki (ed.), *The Chronicle of the Lodz Ghetto 1941-1944* (London, 1984).

402 The deportation from Częstochowa (Sept. and early Oct. 1942) encompassed some 40,000 people. About 6,000 people remained in the ghetto. In Częstochowa there were kibbutz training farms of Dror, Hashomer Hatsair and Gordonia. At the end of Dec. 1942, with the return of Rivka Glanc from Warsaw, a Jewish Fighting Organization was established in Częstochowa. It was supported by members of Erets Yisrael Ha-ovedet, the communists, and Po'alei Tsion-Left. See Zuckerman and Basuk, *Sefer milkhamot hagetaot*, p. 383.

403 The systematic liquidation of the Mława ghetto began on 10 Nov. 1942. That day 2,000 people 'unfit for work' were sent to Treblinka. A second transport, this time of young people, went to Auschwitz on 13 Nov. The final stage of the deportation was completed on 10 Dec. 1943.

404 Following the invasion of the British and American troops and the liberation of North Africa, the racist laws in Algeria and Morocco were repealed and the Jews' civil rights were restored.

405 *Report*, app. 15, presents the following figures: killed during the blockades, 5,961; sent to a *Dulag* (transit camp), 11,580; deported, 254,374. The report further notes that these statistics are from a German source and are not to be trusted. Niestat, *Hurban vemered*, pp. 55-7, gives similar figures.

406 The proclamation was published on 20 Nov. It promised people registering for work, food and somewhere to live, and threatened that people who were not employed by the 23rd of the month would be punished.

407 Kohn, Heller; see n. 101. Josef Erlich, see n. 250.

408 The Jewish Fighting Organization passed a death sentence on Yisrael First; it was executed by David Shulman, Berl Braudo and Sarah Greenstein (Zuckerman and Basuk, *Sefer milkhamot hagetaot*, p. 744 and Gutman, *The Jews of Warsaw*, p. 303). In his 'List of People Shot by Order of the Jewish Fighting Organization', Ringelblum says of First, 'Deputy director of the Economic Department of the Jewish Council. Aided the conqueror in the deportation "actions", maintained close ties with the Germans, acted with cruelty towards the employees of the Jewish Council.' Quoted in Blumenthal and Kermish, *Hameri vehamered begeto Varshe*, p. 146.

409 A reference to a collection of stories about Jewish life in the *shtetlach* of Poland *De letste; Fun mayn hasidishe heym* (*The Last Ones: From my Hasidic House*) (Warsaw, 1929).

410 Untersturmführer Mende was among those responsible for Jewish affairs in the Warsaw Gestapo. He spoke both Yiddish and Hebrew. Turkau, *Azoy iz es geven*, p. 49.

411 In Nov. 1942 Jews from the labour camps at Tarkomin, Wilanów, Kalbil, Częstochowa, Krwow, and Slomstyn were brought into the Warsaw ghetto. The liquidation of the labour camps near Warsaw continued in Dec., with prisoners in the camps at Karczew, Koplow and Klimontów also being transferred to the Warsaw ghetto (Ringelblum, *Ksovim*, II, p. 38, n. 63). The diarist calls these people by the Polish name *obozowicze*, meaning 'campers' or 'camp people'.

412 There was a basis of truth to the rumour that the diarist heard and recorded. On 22–24 Sept. 1942, the Nazi leadership did indeed meet in Berlin to discuss the efficient exploitation of labour in the German war economy. The opinions of the ministers for labour force utilization and armaments prevailed, and it was decided that the skilled workers among the Jewish population of Poland would for the time being be allowed to live and would not be integrated in war-time production in labour camps. This decision did not cause a significant change in the policy of total extermination of the Jews.

413 The response of the British press to the information regarding the destruction of the Jewish population of Poland was described in an article by Andrei Sharf (*Yad Vashem*, 5). His conclusion was that 'in each and every stage of the tragedy the fullest information was obtained and exploited by the British press. There can also be no doubt of the fact that the great majority were prepared to accept these testimonies as the absolute truth.' Such stories were particularly numerous in the British press in the second half of 1942. See also Laqueur, *The Terrible Secret*.

414 In May 1940, 70 members of Hehaluts, led by Leah Perlstein of Dror, went out to work in a Polish-owned estate in Czerniaków, not far from Warsaw. This continued until the end of the year, when all the labour camps near Warsaw were liquidated. The kibbutz at Czerniaków was an important base for underground operations outside the ghetto: 'The importance of this farm cannot be overestimated. At night, after a day of activity ... they would return and slip off

to the Aryan streets . . .' (Zuckerman, 'Mered ha-Yehudim', p. 404). During the massive deportation many members of the kibbutz at 34 Dzielna Street were transferred to Czerniaków. A visit by a Polish woman to the kibbutz in the Czerniaków estate is described in Halina Balicka-Kozłowska, *Mur miał dwie strony* (*The War Had Two Sides*) (Warsaw, 1958), pp. 19–24.

415 Towards the end of 1942, an energetic public campaign was conducted in London, the seat of the Polish government in exile and the Polish National Council, with the aim of stirring the Allies into real action to save the Jewish population of Poland. On 27 Nov. the Polish National Council made an appeal to the peoples of the world to try to save the Jews from the peril of imminent destruction. The only result of this public pressure was a joint declaration issued by the three Great Powers and the governments in exile, published on 17 Dec. 1942, condemning the Germans' policy of exterminating the Jews and pledging that the criminals would receive their due punishment. On this see D. Engel, *In the Shadow of Auschwitz. The Polish Government-in-Exile and the Jews, 1939-42* (Chapel Hill, N. Carolina, 1982).

416 Ringelblum's entry for 14 Dec., under the heading 'Will We Survive or Not?' reads: 'The liquidation of the ghettos of Kałuszyn and Siedlce made a strong impression. These towns were of the type where – according to the November decree – ghettos should have continued to exist, and now even they had been liquidated.' The author considered this a bad omen for the future of the Warsaw ghetto (Ringelblum, *Ksovim*, II, p. 38). See also n. 385.

417 At that time there were still 24,000 Jews in Lwów. At a roll-call conducted in the ghetto on 18 Nov. 1942 some 5,000 Jews were sent to their deaths; 12,000 were classed as armament workers. They put on armbands with the letter R (*Rüstungindustrie*) or W (*Wehrmacht*). The Jewish settlement in Lwów was liquidated in Feb. 1943.

In Kraków, the commander of the SS and the police issued an order (on 14 Dec.) to transfer the Jewish workers to a labour camp at Plaszów. The order to wear armbands with the Star of David was not rescinded, but in addition they now also had to wear the letter R, W, or Z (*Zivil*, for civilian factories important to the war economy) and their identification number.

418 One of the historic palaces of Warsaw; during the Occupation it was used by the governor who headed the district.

419 Transit camps were set up in the Białystok region to hold Jews deported from the towns before transporting them to Treblinka. These camps were later closed down and the deportees were sent to their deaths directly.

420 At the end of November an extensive act of reprisal was initiated against the Polish population in the Zamość area of the Lublin district which continued until the beginning of Aug. 1943. About 300 villages were burnt and some 11,000 people were murdered or sent to concentration camps. This operation was to have been the first stage of the plan to resettle the lands in the east with Germans.

421 Prof. Majer Balaban, the doyen of the Jewish historians in Poland; see n. 236. For a description of his funeral, see Turkau, *Azoy iz es geven*, pp. 499–500; Shereshevsky, *Haperek ha-aharon*, pp. 151–2.

422 *Choinka*, the fir tree used for Christmas trees, which was decorated with lighted candles.

423 David Cholodenko, a communal figure involved in the Bund, member of the directorate of *Oneg Shabbes*, active in the Self-help Organization.

424 During the deportation the horse-drawn carts of the Kohn–Heller Company were used to carry people to the *Umschlagplatz*; see n. 101. On the killing of the old and the sick in the cemetery a witness relates: 'Every day, towards evening, they would bring one or two groups and kill them. The Germans claimed that these people could not be transferred east. Some considered this a good sign, i.e. if they were killing the sick people in the ghetto, it was a sign that the healthy people taken east remained alive' (A. M. Carmi in *Yediot Yad Vashem*, 33, p. 34).

425 A reference to Alexander Margolis, a lawyer with a Honduran passport. One of the most prominent lawyers in Warsaw; known particularly for his defence of the Jewish defendants in the Przytyk case (Ringelblum, *Ksovim*, II, p. 230). On Przytyk, see also J. Rothenberg, 'The Przytyk pogrom', *Soviet Jewish Affairs*, 16: 2 (1986). Leon Neustadt, a director of the 'Joint', who was also cited in connection with this incident, held an Argentinian passport.

426 According to Mrs Nehama Eckheizer-Fahn, a former pupil of Yehudia, now living in Jerusalem: 'Fela Eckheizer was my older sister. She married Grisha Herma, who had been a Palestinian national for eight years. In 1939 he came to visit his parents in Warsaw. They married in October 1939, as soon as the Germans entered Warsaw ... with the start of the deportation, following a proclamation issued by the Germans, my brother-in-law and sister presented themselves to the authorities. After a week we got a letter from them from the Pawiak, and that was the only news we ever got from them ...' In the archive of Kibbutz Lohamei Hagetaot.

427 Ringelblum devoted a comprehensive survey to the question of how Warsaw's Jewish intellectual class was destroyed (Ringelblum, *Ksovim*, II, pp. 53–74).

428 See above, p. 182, and Introduction.

429 On the fate of the Jews of Słonim see n. 3.

430 Ringelblum also writes on 1 Jan. 1943: 'Lies in an article in *Das Schwarze Korps* about how the transfer of Polish Jewry failed – it seems that Jews are not suitable human material for resettlement, so 120,000 children, women and old people died. So that was the end of the deportation. The forced removal was imposed only on the non-productive elements of the Jewish population.' (*Ksovim*, II, p. 75).

431 More than 3,000 Jews were deported from Radomsko to Treblinka at the beginning of Jan.

432 Haim Nahman Bialik (1873–1934), one of the leading poets of the Hebrew revival. See also n. 71 to Introduction.

433 Himmler indeed visited the Warsaw ghetto at this time and even visited a few workshops. Following the visit he sent a letter to the head of the SS and the police in the General-Government (15 Jan.) with instructions with regard to property left by the Jews. The letter was published in a collection of documents

edited by A. Eisenbach, *Eksterminacja Żydów na ziemiach polskich* (*The Extermination of Jews on Polish Lands*) (Warsaw, 1957), pp. 181–3.

434 The German announcement came as a response to the proclamation issued simultaneously in London, New York and Moscow on 17 Dec. 1942 announcing the decision of the Great Powers and the governments in exile that those responsible for the murder of the Jewish population of Europe should be brought to justice (see n. 415).

435 In the festive session of the Reichstag on 30 Jan. 1939, Hitler had prophesied: 'If the international Jewish money power in Europe and beyond again succeeds in enmeshing the peoples in a world war, the result will not be the bolshevization of the world, and a victory for Jewry, but the annihilation of the Jewish race in Europe.' N. Baynes (ed.), *The Speeches of Adolf Hitler*, vol. I, *April 1922-August 1939* (London, 1942), p. 741.

436 On this cruel deception, see the description by Abraham Carmi in A. Carmi and C. Truminer, *Min ha-daleka ha-hi* (*From that Conflagration*) (Tel Aviv, 1961), pp. 43–50.

Index

Ackerman *see* Ekerman
Africa 114, 203
Agatstein-Dormontow, D. 292 n379
Ajnhorn 169
Ajzensztajn 135
Ajzensztat, David 280 n265
Ajzensztat, Marisia 152, 280 n265
Alberg 164
Aleksandrów-Kujawski 34, 67, 118
Algeria 203, 215, 295 n404
Alter, Abraham Mordekai 7
Alter, R. Mendel 149, 279 n246
America *see* Latin America; United States
Ankara 74
Apfel, Tosza 147, 148
Arad, Y. 250 n75
Argentina 165, 284 n303
Artur, a courier 125
Asch, Dr Nathan 164, 175, 176, 288 n333
Auerbach, Rachel 23, 260 n82, 265 n118, 267 n134
Auerswald, Heinz 14, 15, 18, 23, 52, 101, 107, 140, 208, 220, 240, 261 n89, 294 n396
Auschwitz *see* Oświęcim
Austria 73, 115, 255 n41

Bac *see* Patt, Roman
Baden, Prince Max von 89, 259 n69
Balaban, Dr Majer 148, 228, 278 n236, 297 n421
Balicka-Kozłowska, Helena (Halina) 297 n414

Baranowicze 38, 147
Bas *see* Patt, Roman
Będzin 251 n6
Beethoven, Ludwig van 117
Belgium 40, 184, 234
Belz 92
Bełżec 141, 251 n7, 256 n48, 274 n195, 294 n388
Ben-Daat, Iska *see* Feibikh Ben-Daat, Iska
Berchtesgaden 103
Berensohn, Leon 23
Berenstein, T. 246 n1, 248 n34
Berg, Mary 18
Bergelson, David 266 n128
Berger, Rishak 223
Bergson 79
Berkman, Yitshak 11
Berlin 26, 67, 85, 118, 130, 222, 240, 296 n412
Berlinski, Hirsh 24–5
Berman, Adolf 282 n287
Berman, Batya 282 n287
Bessarabia 67, 272 n168
Biała-Podlaska 156
Bialer, Toshia 6, 140
Bialik, Chaim Nachman 9, 31, 96, 121
Białystok 38, 46, 143, 156, 190, 200, 209, 214
Białystok, region of 188, 291 n366, 295 n397
Biberstajn 229, 230
Biernstein, Dr Zofia *see* Syrkin-Biernstein
Biezún 62

Birnbaum, A. B. 257 n54
Blau, Alexander 284 n297
Bloch, Lippe-Leib 284 n297
Blumenfeld, Rabbi Jechiel Meir 181
Bobruisk 27, 106, 108
Bornsztajn, Dr Alfred (and his wife)
148, 155
Borowski 201
Brand, Julek 259 n76
Brandl, of the family of bakers 188
Brandstetter, Michael 142, 275 n206
Brandt, Karl (SS Commandant) 49,
143, 158, 188, 193, 197, 236, 275 n208
Braudo, Berl 296 n408
Brauer, German 'shop' owner 155, 172,
205
Brazil 165, 284 n303
Bremen 120
Brenner 230
Breslaw, Shmuel 135, 165, 175, 268
n143, 287 n330
Britain 23, 35, 70, 88–9, 99, 114, 115,
119, 221–2, 223–4
Brotmacher, Rachel 11, 12, 182
Brudno, suburb of Warsaw 238
Brustman 139
Brześć (Brest) 138
Brzeziński, policeman 171
Byelorussia 253 n24

Cajtlin see Zeitlyn
Carmi, Abraham 299 n436
Chełm 69
Chelmno 264 n114
Chile 165
Chilinowicz, Ben-Tsion 145, 276 n220
Chmielewski 150
Cholodenko, David 229
Churchill, Winston 76, 88
Chvalkovsky, Frantisek 3
Ciano, Galeazzo 70
Ciechanów 34, 121
Ciechocinek 253 n19
Cologne 114, 120, 263 n106
Colombia 284 n303

Cracow see Kraków
Crimea 255 n42
Croatia 221
Cytryn family 140
Cytrynowski, Yehiel 168, 286 n314
Czapliński, Marcelli 50, 195, 292 n377
Czapliński, Michael 292 n377
Czechoslovakia 115, 119, 234, 251 n7
Czerniaków, Adam 14, 15, 21, 35, 52,
75, 94, 117, 137, 138, 158, 220, 240,
269 n156
Czerniaków, the place 156, 223, 296
n414
Czerski, Pinhas 172, 287 n322
Czerwińsk 224
Czerwinski, Herman 94
Częstochowa 46, 105, 167, 173, 180,
212, 214, 295 n402
Czudner, Meir 139
Czyste, suburb of Warsaw 268 n146

Danzig, Nina see Weltser-Danzig, Nina
Dawidowicz, Lucy 3
Dęblin 71, 78, 254 n34
Denmark 234
Diehl factory 186
Dluźniów 92
Dobrzyń 109
Dostoyevsky, Fyodor 205, 236
Drohobycz 262 n98
Dubnow, Simon 287 n321
Duisberg 120
Dziedzic 66, 75

Eck, Dr Nathan 245, 257 n52, 279 n244
Eckheizer, Fela 231, 298 n426
Eckheizer-Fahn, Nehama 11, 298 n426
Edjus family 159
Egypt 203
Ehrenburg, Ilya 86
Einhorn, Aharon I. 164–5, 284 n298
Eisenbach, Artur 246 n1, 299 n433
Eisenstadt see Ajzensztat
Ekerman, Hilary 286 n320
Ekerman, Isaac Ber 166, 171, 285 n306

El-Alamein 263 n106, 294 n392
England *see* Britain
Epstein, Shachna 266 n128
Erenberg family 110–11
Erlich, Josef 149, 158, 218, 279 n250
Ernest, Stefan 21
Essen 120
Estland *see* Estonia
Estonia 68, 234

Fahn-Eckheizer, Nehama *see*
  Eckheizer-Fahn, Nehama
Fajnkind 145
Falenica 27, 67, 163
Feibikh Ben Daat, Iska 247 n27
Fejga, Dora 152
First, Israel 50, 218
Fischer, Ludwig 13–14, 21, 22
France 40, 151, 162, 172, 184, 234
Frank, Anne 37
Frank, Hans, General-Governor 4, 14,
  19, 66, 253 n18
Frankenstein 129, 187
Frydland 144
Fuswerg, Dr 142
Fuswerg, Klima 142, 275 n207

Galicia 4, 11, 82, 107–8
Galilee 133
Gancwajch, Abraham 18, 95, 105, 111,
  123, 152, 158, 160, 167, 260 n82
Garbatko-Letnisko 78, 136, 269 n151
Garbitsky-Schechter, Yehudit 10
Gawze, Aron 191
General-Government (of German-
  occupied central and southern
  Poland) 4, 197, 221, 253 n18
Gepner, Abraham 15, 16, 268 n141, 270
  n157
Germany 11, 68, 73, 76, 84, 85, 86,
  88–9, 103, 115, 119–20, 125, 128, 234
Giterman, Yitshak 51, 188, 189, 191–2,
  195, 214, 215, 216
Glanc, Rivka 295 n402

Glazerman, Max 92–3, 259 n76
Globocnik, Odilo 139, 273 n182
Goering, H. W. 88
Goldberg, the baker 237
Goldenberg, Lily *see* Pulman-
  Goldenberg, Lily
Goldman 126
Goldschmid, Dr Henryk *see* Korczak,
  Janusz
Golub 34
Gomuliński 107
Góra Kalwarja 7, 10, 279 n246
Gorilow, A. 180, 289 n345
Gorky, Maxim 244
Górny, Yehiel 42, 149, 150, 279 n247
Gostynin 34, 118
Grajak, Szymon (or Syzmszon) 218
Greece 221, 234
Greenstein, Sarah 296 n408
Grobos, Mordechai 292 n376
Grochów 139, 241
Grodno 46, 209, 214, 227, 295 n397
Grodzisk 107
Grosberg 184
Grun, Mrs 148
Gruzalc, Leib 140
Gryca 32, 85
gubernia see General-Government
Gur *see* Gora Kalwarja
Gutgold 140
Gutkowski, Eliyahu 12, 108, 141, 156,
  175, 176, 262 n99, 275 n198, 281 n274,
  288 n333
Guzik, Daniel David 280 n262
Guzik family 152

Halevi, Rabbi Yehuda 62, 117
Hallman, Bernard, 'shop' owner 173,
  176
Hanover 85
Hanusel 95
Hartglass, M. 256 n46
Heller, Shimon 168
Heller, Zelik 109, 148, 218, 262 n101
Henig, Chaim 90, 259 n71

Hensel, Commissar 42, 158, 169, 177, 178, 230
Herman, Grisha 298 n426
Hertz, Alexander 8
Hertzberg-Schweiger, Stefania (Bat-Sheva) 7, 11, 12, 149, 161, 182, 279 n242
Herzberg, Nechama *see* Zucker-Herzberg, Nechama
Hess, Rudolf 89, 258 n66
Heydrich, Reinhard 4, 115, 119, 263 n107
Himmler, Heinrich 88, 189, 237, 298 n433
Hindenburg, Paul 259 n68
Hirszfeld, Ludwik 2
Hirszhorn, Samuel (Shmuel) 149, 279 n251
Hitler, Adolf 3, 25, 26, 37, 74, 84, 87, 88, 99, 103, 197, 203, 205, 210, 221, 226, 234, 238, 294 n393, 299 n435
Hochberg-Menuz, Dr Ida 182, 290 n352
Hoffmann, German 'shop' owner 203–4, 205, 206
Höfle, Herman 35–6, 143, 276 n209
Holland 40, 162, 184, 234
Holtzheimer 209
Horowitz, Mrs, an advocate 94, 260 n77, 274 n193
Hotner, Bat-Sheva 8
Hotner, Luba (Ahava) *see* Hotner-Lewin, Luba
Hotner, Rabbi Yehuda Leib 8
Hotner-Lewin, Luba 8, 45–6, 53, 150, 153–5, 159, 179, 194
Hrubieszów 11, 65, 92, 115
Huberband, Rabbi Shimon 12, 72, 160, 172, 255 n38, 282 n281
Hugenberg, Alfred 88, 258 n65
Hungary 234
Hurwicz, active in '13' 95
Hurwicz, a flour-dealer 90
Hurwicz, member of *Judenrat* 188

Ides family *see* Edjus

Igla, Ilenman 141
Italy 66, 70, 89, 99, 238
Izbica 62, 201

Jabłonna 46, 188
Jadów(a) 132
Janowska 262 n97
Janowski, Sarah 280 n258
Japan 165
Jaremcze 108
Jaszuński, Józef 15
Jerusalem 133
Josefowicz 228
Josephus, Flavius 133
Judt, Regina 107, 262 n96

Kadiszewicz 230
Kahan, Abe 86
Kahanowicz, an advocate 146, 277 n230
Kahn, Maurice *see* Kohn
Kalbil 296 n411
Kalisz 149
Kalman 140
Kałuszyn 46, 49, 201, 224, 297 n416
Kampinos 258 n59
Kanal, Rabbi Yitzhak Meir 44, 173
Kanal, Yisrael 282 n289
Kantonowicz *see* Lewin, mother of Abraham
Kapelusz, Lola 139
Kaplan, Chaim vii, 6, 15, 18, 36
Kaplan, Joseph 175, 181, 199, 287 n329, 290 n350
Kapota *see* Erlich, Joseph
Karcewicz 145, 146
Karczew 296 n411
Karmi *see* Carmi, Abraham
Karwow 296 n411
Kassel family 183
Katznelson, Ben-Tsion 156, 281 n272
Katznelson, Benjamin 156, 281 n272
Katznelson, Hannah 155, 156, 281 n272
Katznelson, Yitshak 37, 41, 155, 156, 159, 265 n120, 266 n124
Katzparek company 47, 191

Kawik, leader of Gypsies 261 n92
Kerch 74, 76, 98, 255 n42
Kermish, Dr Joseph 57
Kharkov 98, 99
Kielce 34, 46, 180–1, 289 n349
Kielce, region of 5, 65, 190
Kirschenbaum, Mordechai 184
Kirschenfeld-Wasser, Bluma 279 n243
Kirz(h)ner 139, 155
Kishinev 250 n71
Klimontów 296 n411
Kohn, Moritz (Maurice) 148, 152, 262
  n101
Kohn-Heller, tramway owners 109,
  116, 229, 262 n101, 264 n110
Kon, Menahem-Mendel vii, 12, 83, 140,
  141, 150, 257 n57
Koniński, Natan (Aron) 149, 279 n253
Końskowola 201
Korczak, Janusz 148, 156, 278 n241
Kosow 49, 163, 172, 201
Kott, Andrzej 24, 73, 255 n40
Kowno 34, 35, 73
Kraków 4, 24, 34, 35, 46, 115, 121, 195,
  197, 199, 200, 225
Kraków, district of 5
Krieger, Friedrich (SS General) 189
Krushe–Andar firm 265 n118
Kujawski 34
Kushnirov, Aharon 127, 266 n128

Landau, Aleksander 186, 230
Landau, Josef 156, 198
Landau, Margalit 292 n376
Landau brothers, sawmill owners 42,
  146, 148, 149, 169, 218
Landau family 47, 186, 191
Latin America (South America) 81, 82
Latvia 234
Laval, Pierre 88
Layner, Rabbi Shlomo of Radzyn 265
  n122
Lazar 140
Lazowert, Henryka 23, 172, 267 n134
Łęczyca 62

Lejkin, Jakub, lawyer 50, 195, 218
Lejzerowicz, M. 138, 272 n175
Leman family 126, 129
Lemberg *see* Lwów
Levite, Moshe 172
Lewertowski-Finkelstein, Joseph 288
  n336
Lewin, active in the '13' 95
Lewin, Celina 172, 287 n321
Lewin, Fruma *see* Tombeck, Fruma
Lewin, Guca 137, 154, 156, 160, 161;
  her daughter Hela 160, 161
Lewin, Guta 137, 270 n158
Lewin, Luba *see* Hotner-Lewin, Luba
Lewin, mother of Abraham 45, 162,
  165, 176
Lewin, Nacia 155, 156, 162, 165, 166,
  176, 183, 186
Lewin, Ora 8, 9, 45, 48, 53, 136, 150,
  154, 156, 158, 162, 165, 166–7, 175,
  178, 207, 209, 213
Lewin, Shabtai 6, 7
Lewinski 78
Libuszycki, Aharon 138, 272 n175
Lichtenbaum, Marc 139, 160, 217, 219,
  273 n179
Lida 120
Lifschitz 38, 157
Liman family *see* Leman family
Lithuania 35, 73, 120, 234
Łódź 4, 5, 67, 83, 96, 116, 212, 295
  n401, 297 n417
London 74, 88, 143, 222, 297 n415, 299
  n434
Łowicz 95
Lübeck 114
Lublin 35, 73, 76, 79, 111, 197, 201, 204,
  207, 208, 211
Lublin, region of 5, 61, 62, 65, 91, 116,
  122, 125, 201, 237
Ludendorff, Erich 89, 259 n68
Ludina 226
Łuków 201
Luzatto, Haim 11
Lwów 34, 35, 73, 81, 107–8, 225, 235, 241

Magidson 146
Mahler, Dr Rafal 289 n346
Majda, Seweryn 280 n259
Majdan Tatarski 211, 295 n400
Majdanek 294 n387, 295 n400
Majzel, Maurycy 15, 256 n46
Malkinia 39, 149
Mandel 95
Mandzicki, Norbert 185
Manel 68
Margolis, Alexander 231
Margolis family 188
Mark, Berl 55
Marminska, Sofia 7, 247 n18
Mazur, Albert 175, 288 n333
Mecklenburg 128
Mende, Gerhardt 219, 228
Mendrowski family 139
Merenlender 137
Michaels, Solomon 266 n128
Michlin, Faivel 266 n128
Międzyrzec (Misrich) Podlaski 173, 201
Mikanowska 94
Minc, Mrs 142
Mińsk Mazowiecki 84, 162, 202
Mława 46, 212, 214, 295 n403
Mławer, Mrs 144
Moabit, suburb of Berlin 130
Modlin 68
Mokarska, Shulamit 160, 282 n280
Montgomery, Field Marshal 294 n392
Moravia 234, 263 n107
Morocco 203, 215, 295 n404
Moronowitch, Leonora 11
Moscow 74, 128, 212, 299 n434
Mozart, Wolfgang 117
Müller, Karl Heinz 281 n270
Müller firm 155, 168, 169
Munich 294 n390
Mussolini, Benito 66
Mydlarska, Mrs 144

Nadel 83
Neufeld, Mrs 143
Neumann-Neurode, General von 5

Neustadt, Leon 140, 231, 257 n55, 274
    n185, 298 n425
New York 275 n197, 299 n434
Nicholas I, Tsar of Russia 11, 87
Niestadt *see* Nowe Miasto
Nieszawa district 67, 253 n19
Nisenbaum, Rabbi Yitshak 144, 160,
    276 n214
Nisenbaum, wife of Rabbi 144
Norway 234
Nossig, Dr Alfred 16
Nowe Miasto 121
Nowogródek (Novaredok) 34, 62
Nowowordski, David 39, 170
Nowy Dwór 46, 68, 69, 224
Nuremberg 253 n18

Opatowska 126
Opfel *see* Apfel, Tosza
Opoczno 46, 241
Opoczynski, Perets 145, 276 n223
Opole 251 n1
Oppenhajm 187
Orliański 139, 273 n179
Oschman factory 170, 205
Osnus 230
Ostrowicz 199
Ostrowiec girls 163
Ostrowiec Kielieckie 34, 65
Oświęcim (Auschwitz) 94, 224, 225,
    241, 295 n403
Otwock 27, 67, 79, 105, 149, 161, 163,
    165

Pabianice 34, 120, 264 n118
Palestine 8, 85, 241
Papen, Franz von 74, 88, 256 n44
Paraguay 81
Parczew 116, 201
Paris 88, 113
Passenstein, Mojzesz 22–3
Patt, Roman 71, 254 n32
Pawiak Prison 69, 71, 79, 80, 82–3,
    97–8, 103–4, 111, 123, 145, 156, 165,
    181, 199, 213, 230, 242

Pearlman, David 247 n22
Pelcowizna, suburb of Warsaw 139
Perla, Y. 269 n156, 277 n235
Perlman, Ora 287 n323
Perlrot 198
Perlstein, Leah 296 n414
Piaseczno 32, 85, 141
Piaski 201, 295 n400
Pigowski family 143
Pińsk 272 n173
Piotrków 5, 163, 283 n293
Pirow, Oswald 3
Plaszów 297 n417
Płońsk 46, 110, 212, 214, 224
Plonsker, Dr Maurice (Marcus) 180,
  289 n347
Pola family 139
Pomerania 65, 128
Poniatowo 274 n189
Pope 88-9, 226
Popower, accountant 148, 278 n240
Popower, Gina 172-3, 287 n323
Popower (Popowska), Miriam 287 n323
Poznán 65
Praga, suburb of Warsaw 203, 235
Prives, Mirke 156
Prync 145
Przytyk 298 n425
Pulman, Ada 286 n313
Pulman, David 169, 286 n313
Pulman, Henja 169, 286 n313
Pulman, Sarah 168, 286 n313
Pulman-Goldenberg, Lily 286 n313
Pustelnik 141

Rabinowicz, Esther 278 n239
Rabinowicz, Isaiah 178, 288 n341
Rabinowicz, Jakub 40, 185, 196, 290
  n355
Rabinowicz, Josef (Osip) 87
Rabinowicz, Shlomo Hanoch, the
  Admor of Radomsk 148, 278 n239
Racimor (Recymer) 49, 178, 196
Radom 39, 78, 144, 148, 151, 170, 280
  n260

Radomsko 46, 105, 167, 236, 239
Raduszyńska, Mrs 116
Raduszynski brothers 132
Radzymin 133
Radzyń 34, 121
Rajchner family 142
Rakowski, L. 172
Rawa Ruska 262 n98
Reichner family 142
Rembertów 49, 170, 200, 201, 242
Ringelblum, Emanuel vii, viii, 2, 8, 11,
  12–13, 18–19, 20, 23, 25, 41, 53, 55,
  188, 266 n125
Ringelblum, Leon 174, 180, 289 n346
Ringelblum, Sarah (Sala), 180, 289 n346
Roda *see* Ruda
Romania 67, 234
Rommel, Erwin 263 n106
Roosevelt, Franklin D. 56, 76, 88, 166,
  223, 285 n304
Rosen, Henryk 94, 260 n78
Rosenberg, Alfred 221
Rosenowicz 177
Rosenstrauch 129
Rosenzweig, Dr Artur 265 n121
Rosenzweig, Yechiel 274 n187
Rosenzweig family 140, 141, 149
Rostock 114, 128
Rozanski, Eliyahu 292 n376
Rozen (shot in June) 123
Rozen (shot in July) 135
Rozen family (taken away) 144
Rozencwajgs *see* Rosenzweig
Różycki 106
Rubinstajn, friend of Hanka Tauber 65
Rubinstein family 95
Ruda, Joseph-Chaim 109–10
Ruda, Rivka (Rywa) 109–10
Ruda family 56
Rudski factory 84
Rumkowski, Mordechai Chaim 158,
  281 n276
Rusak 146
Russia *see* Soviet Union
Rutkowski, Adam 248 n34

Ryba 177
Ryki 71, 254 n34
Rzeszów 5

Sagan, Shakhne 17, 145
Samaria 133
Sambor 262 n98
Sandomierz (Suzmir) 195, 198, 293 n379
Sch *see also under* Sh
Schilling, German 'shop' owner 173
Schipper, Ignacy 17
Schmidt factory 168
Schön, von, factory 185
Schön, Waldemar 5
Schultz, Fritz 137, 270 n160
Schultz factory 47, 155, 174, 176, 201,
     207, 208, 229
Schweiger, Adina 12, 182
Schweiger, Stefania (Bat-Sheva) *see*
     Hertzberg-Schweiger, Stefania
Segal, Jehoszua 146
Segal, R. Yehuda 8, 277 n231
Segal family 146, 147
Segalowitz, Clara 257 n55
Senenski 207
Serbia 221
Serota, Cantor 257 n54
Serrano Suner, Ramon 89, 259 n67
Sh *see also under* Sch
Shachnarowicz-Hochberg, Ida *see*
     Hochberg-Meruz, Ida
Shapiro, Henryk *see* Szaro
Sharf, Dr Andrei 296 n413
Shatsky, Yakov 8
Shcharanski, Leib *see* Szczeranski
Sheinkinder, S. 254 n30; n32
Sherman *see* Szerman
Shner, Tsvi 57, 247 n17
Shulman, David 296 n408
Shultz *see* Schultz
Shweiger, Stefania *see* Hertzberg-
     Schweiger, Stefania
Siedlce 38, 39, 46, 49, 157, 170, 200, 201,
     224, 238, 297 n416
Silber, Hirsch Yonah 211, 295 n399

Silberberg *see* Zylberberg, Mrs
Simchoni, Dr Jacob Naftali Hertz 133
Skarżysko-Kamienna 46, 188, 291 n365
Sklar, Moshe 70, 254 n30
Słapak, Celina 172
Slawa 39, 153
Słomczyń 296 n411
Słonim 34, 35, 61, 73, 233, 251 n3
Slovakia 234
Smocza 150
Smolar, Natan 39, 42, 150, 153, 279
     n244
Smolar, wife of Natan 149
Smolensk 181
Sobibor 254 n34, 264 n109
Sobolew 46, 49, 201, 238
Sokal 92
Sokołów 39, 149, 153, 200, 201
Solovietchik, Dr Aharon 120, 264 n117
Sonszajn 156
Sosnowica 116
South America 81, 82
Soviet Union 11, 16, 26, 35, 70, 73, 89,
     90, 106, 115, 119, 128, 234
Spain 85, 89
St *see also under* Szt
Stanisławów 262 n98
Starzynski, Stefan 15
Staszów 257 n54
Stein, Dr Rachel *see* Sztajn
Steinkalk, Dr Zygmunt 135, 267 n140
Steinweiss, Renya *see* Sztajnwajs
Stolypin, Piotr 176
Stroop, Jürgen 291 n371
Stupnicki, Saul 149, 279 n248
Suchecki brothers 216, 217
Sucholowska 164
Suner, Ramon Serrano 89, 259 n67
Sweden 89, 136
Świeca family 46, 179, 180
Switzerland 81, 82, 111
Syria 133
Syrkin-Biernstein, Dr Zofia 65
Szaro (Szapiro), Henryk 126
Szczeranski, Leib 160, 282 n282

Szereszewski, a banker 110
Szerman, Pinhas 80
Szeryński, Józef 17, 42, 140, 162, 165, 167, 195, 274 n192
Szparag, Mrs 104
Sztajn, Dr Edmond 145, 276 n221
Sztajn, Dr Rókhl 160, 282 n283
Sztajnk, Dr *see* Steinkalk
Sztajnwajs, Renja 155
Szternberg 168
Szternfeld, David 95, 105, 123, 260 n82
Sztolcman, Alfred 139, 148, 208, 273 n179
Szulc's restaurant 80
Szymański 262 n95
Szymkowicz, Symkhon 21, 22
Szymonowicz 95
Szymonowski, Antoni 270 n156

Tarkomin 296 n411
Tarnopol 262 n98
Tartakower, Dr Arie 270 n156
Tatarów, 108
Tauber, Dr Meir 65
Tauber, Hanka 27, 65, 91–3
Tauber family 159
Tchernihowsky, Shaul 9
Tenenbaum, Lea (Lejke) 213
Theresienstadt 251 n7
Tintpulwer 42, 149, 150
Tłuszcz 26, 34, 116, 132–3, 267 n135
Többens, Walter Caspar 274 n189
Többens factory 47, 140, 143, 153, 154, 155, 156, 170, 174, 176, 183, 187, 201, 204, 205, 207, 229
Todt, Fritz 262 n100
Tolstoy, Lev 136
Tomaszów Mazowiecki 83, 258 n58
Tombeck, Dr Jacub 100, 152, 158, 165, 176, 182, 261 n88
Tombeck, Fruma 156, 158, 159, 162, 176, 183, 261 n88
Tombeck, Uri 136, 158, 159, 269 n150
Tombeck family 162
Towiański, Andrzej 117, 264 n113

Trans-Jordan 133
Trawniki 274 n189, 276 n221
Treblinka vii, 12, 17, 36–40, 49, 94, 148, 149, 153, 163, 170, 183, 184, 185, 186, 190, 194, 198, 199, 214, 221, 223, 225, 227, 230, 236, 237, 241
Troki 10
Tsvia (pen-name) 273 n183, 283 n290
Turkau, Y. 256 n47, 262 n95
Tyszowce 115

Ukraine, the 257 n56
United States 35, 67, 74, 99, 115, 119, 221–2, 258 n62
Upper Silesia 4
Uruguay 81

Vichy 258 n64
Victor Emmanuel III, King of Italy 70
Vienna 73
Vilna *see* Wilno

Wajcblum family 138
Wajngot family 81–2
Walfisz brothers 140
Warsawski, Aaron 219
Warsawski, Amram 219
Warsawski, Yakir 139, 219, 272 n177
Warthegau 4, 65
Wasser, Hirsch 12, 92, 187, 211, 259 n72
Wasser family 40, 186
Waser-Kirschenfeld, Bluma 149
Wąwolnica 34, 61, 251 n1
Weichert, Dr Michael 115, 263 n108
Weinberger, Dr Cecilia 11, 12, 182
Weingot family *see* Wajngot
Weissenberg, Yitshak Meir 12, 29, 32, 54, 243–5
Weltser-Danzig, Nina 10
Werbkowice 293 n382
Wermus 116
Wielkowski, Dr Gustaw 139, 273 n179
Wiesel, Dr Ze'ev von 70, 254 n28
Wilanów 296 n411

Wilner family 56, 106–7, 111–12
Wilno 10, 15, 34, 35, 73, 126
Wilson, Woodrow 89
Winnik, Israel 138, 172
Winokur 74
Winter, Shmuel 12, 15
Wislicki, Dr 180
Witossek (SS Obersturmführer) 142, 207, 275 n204
Włocławek 34, 118
Włodawa 121, 201
Wola 34, 175, 208, 209
Wolcher-Danzig, Nina *see* Weltser-Danzig, Nina
Wolkowicz, Shmuel 280 n264
Wolkowicz, wife of Shmuel 152
Wołomin 46, 176, 188
Wolynia 126

York, Archbishop of 223
Yugoslavia 234

Zachariasz brothers 105, 123
Zagen, Shachne *see* Sagan, Shakhne
Zakhajm 137
Zaklików 201
Zamość 122, 227, 233, 237, 297 n420

Zduńska Wola 34, 62, 121
Zegal *see* Segal
Zeitlyn, David 281 n271
Zeitlyn, Elhonen 155, 281 n271
Zeitlyn, Hillel 148, 160, 191, 277 n235
Zeitlyn, wife of Hillel 160
Żelazna Bramy 241
Zelman 123
Zelmanowski, Chaim 168
Zeltser, Yisrael 199, 293 n382
Zhelokhovski, Shlomo 265 n120
Zimmerman, Mrs, meat vendor 133
Zimmerman firm 155, 175, 182, 288 n332
Zitrinowski, Yechiel *see* Cytrynowski, Yechiel
Złotowska, Gustava 11, 12, 182
Żoliborz 241
Żółkiew 262 n98
Zołotov, Gustava 145, 276 n222
Zucker-Herzberg, Nechama (Hella) 247 n20
Zuckerman, Yitzhak 258 n59, 271 n168
Zundelewicz, Bernard 17, 166, 285 n306
Zürich 131
Zylberberg 148, 175, 176, 198
Zylberberg, Mrs 198